# Mastering Networks

# Macmillan Master Series

| | |
|---|---|
| Accounting | Italian |
| Advanced English Language | Global Information Systems |
| Advanced Pure Mathematics | Internet |
| Arabic | Italian 2 |
| Banking | Java |
| Basic Management | Marketing |
| Biology | Mathematics |
| British Politics | Mathematics for Electrical and |
| Business Administration | Electronic Engineering |
| Business Communication | Microsoft Office |
| C Programming | Microsoft Windows, Novell |
| C++ Programming | NetWare and UNIX |
| Chemistry | Modern British History |
| COBOL Programming | Modern European History |
| Communication | Modern World History |
| Counselling Skills | Networks |
| Database Design | Pascal and Delphi Programming |
| Desktop Publishing | Philosophy |
| Economic and Social History | Photography |
| Economics | Physics |
| Electrical Engineering | Psychology |
| Electronic and Electrical Calculations | Shakespeare |
| Electronics | Social Welfare |
| English Grammar | Sociology |
| English Language | Spanish |
| English Literature | Spanish 2 |
| Fashion Styling | Statistics |
| French | Systems Analysis and Design |
| French 2 | Visual Basic |
| Geography | World Religions |
| German | |

**Macmillan Master Series**
**Series Standing Order ISBN 0–333–69343–4**
*(outside North America only)*

You can receive future titles in this series as they are published by placing a standing order. Please contact your bookseller or, in case of difficulty, write to us at the address below with your name and address, the title of the series and the ISBN quoted above.

Customer Services Department, Macmillan Distribution Ltd
Houndmills, Basingstoke, Hampshire RG21 6XS, England

Mastering

# Networks

William J. Buchanan, BSc (Hons.), CEng, PhD
*Senior Lecturer*
*School of Computing*
*Napier University*
*Edinburgh*

Series Editor
William Buchanan, BSc (Hons.), CEng, PhD

MACMILLAN

This book is dedicated to the music of Neil Young, REM and Runrig, which has kept me going through the long nights of book writing.

First published in 1999 by
MACMILLAN PRESS LTD
Houndmills, Basingstoke, Hampshire RG21 6XS
and London
Companies and representatives throughout the world

ISBN 0–333–74804–2

A catalogue record for this book is available from the British Library.

This book is printed on paper suitable for recycling and made from fully managed and sustained forest sources.

10   9   8   7   6   5   4   3   2   1
08   07   06   05   04   03   02   01   00   99

Typeset by W.Buchanan and J.Buchanan in Great Britain

Printed by Biddles Ltd, Guildford and King's Lynn

# Contents

# Preface

Computer networks are a crucial part of many organisations and many users now even have a network connection in their own home. Without networks there would be no Electronic Mail, no Internet access and no Networked Applications. It is one of the fastest moving technologies areas and brings benefits to virtually every country in the world. With the interconnection of networks to the Internet, the world has truly become a Global Village. For many people, especially children, the first place to search for a given topic is the World Wide Web (WWW).

Who would believe the pace of technology over ten short years, such as:

- From networks of tens of computers operating at speeds of a thousands of bits per second to networks with thousands of computers operating at billions of bits per second.
- From organisations which passed paper documents back and forward, to totally paperless organisations.
- From people who sent one letter each month to people who send tens of electronic mails every day?
- From sending letters around the world which would take days or weeks to be arrive to the transmission of information around the world within a second.
- From businesses who relied on central operations to ones that can be distributed around the world, but can communicate as if they were next door.
- From the transmission of message which could be viewed by people and organisation which were not meant to the read the message, to the transmission of messages can only be read by the intended destination (and maybe, space aliens).
- From written signatures that can be easily forged, to digital signatures which are almost impossible to forge, and not only authenticate the sender but also all of the contents of a message.

The number of applications of networks increases by the day, they include:

- Electronic Mail.
- Video Conferencing.
- Downloading Hardware Drivers.
- Distributing Information.
- Multimedia Education.
- Remote Access.
- Application Software Downloads.
- Client/server Processing.
- News Groups.
- Product Information.
- Remote Control/Transmission of Data.
- Chat Programs.
- Daily News Events.
- Information Archives.
- On-line Libraries.
- Electronic Commerce.
- Search Facilities.
- WWW Surfing.
- Sampling Material.

- Centralised Configuration.
- Centralised Software Licence Control.
- Distributed/Centralised Printer/File Facilities.
- Networked Peripherals.
- Source Code Download.
- Direct Access to Experts.
- Special Interest Groups.

- On-line Help.
- Software Registration.
- Distributed Databases.
- Bulletin Boards.
- Internet Telephone.
- Archived/Off-line Conferencing.
- Distributed Databases.
- Digital TV/Hi-fi.

The amount of transmitted information over networks increases by a large factor every year (over the Internet, traffic doubles every 100 days), and the demand for bandwidth seems unlimited. Unfortunately there are many different types of networks, from low-speed single computer connections, to high-speed multiple computer networks. There are also many different types of computer systems, there are different protocols, and so on. It is an exciting area, but also a difficult area to keep up-to-date with. Thus, the main aim of this book is to cover many of the important networking areas, from networking technologies to data encryption. It splits into ten main areas, these are:

1. **Networking Technologies**. Network Topologies, Ethernet (including Fast and Gigabit Ethernet), Token Ring, FDDI, ATM, ISDN and Example MANs.
2. **Networking Protocols**. TCP/IP, ICMP, DNS, ARP, Bootp, IP multicasting, UDP, WinSock, IP Version 6, SPX/IPX and HTTP.
3. **Sockets**. C++/Java/Visual Basic implementation.
4. **World Wide Web**. HTTP, Client/server architecture, Web browsers, Internet resources, URLs, URI, Web browser design, SSL, S-HTTP, Content advisor, Security zones, Microsoft Wallet and Profile assistant.
5. **Network Security/Intranets**. Proxy servers, Firewalls, Filtering routers, Passwords, Extranets, Hacking methods, Hacker problems and Hardware security.
6. **Data Encryption Principles**. Cryptography, Legal issues, Cracking the code, Message hash, Private-Key Encryption, Public-key Encryption, RSA, PGP, Sample PGP encryption.
7. **Authentication**. Shared secret-key authentication, Diffie-Hellman key exchange, Key distribution centre, Digital signatures and PGP authentication.
8. **Electronic Mail**. Architecture, Email addresses, SMTP, X.400 and MIME.
9. **Viruses**. Virus types, Anti-virus programs, Trojan horses, Polymorphic viruses, Stealth viruses, Slow viruses, Retro viruses, Worms and Macro viruses.
10. **Appendices**. Extensive Glossary and Abbreviations, HDLC and RFC listings.

The Macmillan Mastering IT and Computing series is expanding rapidly and this book is another key foundation book in the whole series. Others include:

- Mastering Microsoft Windows, Novell NetWare and UNIX.
- Mastering Java.
- Mastering Pascal and Delphi.
- Mastering Visual Basic.

- Mastering C++.
- Mastering Microsoft Office.
- Mastering Database Design.
- Mastering Structured Analysis and Design.
- Mastering the Internet.
- Mastering Global Information Systems.

Further information can be found on one of the following WWW pages:

```
http://www.dcs.napier.ac.uk/~bill/books.html
http://www.eece.napier.ac.uk/~bill_b/books.html
```

Help from myself can be sought using on of the following email addresses:

```
w.buchanan@napier.ac.uk
bill@dcs.napier.ac.uk
```

Finally, I would personally like to thank Suzannah Tipple, Isobel Munday and Christopher Glennie at Macmillan for their hard work and their continued support for the Mastering IT and Computing series. Also, I would like to thank my family, Julie, Billy, Jamie and David for their love and understanding.

**Dr. William Buchanan**

Series Editor,
IT and Computing, Macmillan.

Senior Lecturer,
School of Computing, Napier University.

# 1 Introduction

## 1.1 Introduction

These days virtually every computer in a company is networked and networks are key to the effective working of an organisation. Without them, few people could work effectively. It provides us with:

- Electronic mail.
- Networked application software.
- Remote connections.
- Shared printers.

- Networked video conferencing.
- Remote control of remote equipment.
- Remote data acquisition.
- Shared disk resources.

Generally networking is moving towards standardisation in terms of hardware and software. Figure 1.1 shows the main standards used for the hardware and software. The most common network operating systems are:

- **Novell NetWare.** This is the network created using Novell NetWare, typically NetWare 3 or NetWare 4. NetWare 4 has many great advantages over NetWare 3. NetWare 4 uses NetWare Directory Services (NDS) to create global networks.
- **Windows NT/95/98/2000.** Windows 95/98 and Windows 2000 (Workstation) create peer-to-peer networks where computers share resources, such as disk drives and printers. Windows NT/2000 (Server) can create a network with a network server, which allows the creation of network logins, file sharing, and so on.
- **UNIX.** A well-proven operating system which is typically used with high-powered workstations. It has always supported networking and is robust and extremely reliable.

The main technologies used in making a network are:

- **Ethernet.** The most widely used networking technology where computers either connect to a network hub or a common bus.
- **FDDI.** A ring-based network, where computers connect either to a network hub or onto a fibre ring.
- **ISDN.** Used to connect computers over a telephone connection.

A network protocol is the set of rules which two network operating systems use to communicate with each other. Typical network protocols are:

1

- **TCP/IP**. This is the standard protocol which computers use to connect to the Internet and over UNIX-based networks. Each node on the network is granted an IP address which it uses for the time of its connection, or it can have a permanently assigned address.
- **SPX/IPX**. This protocol is used by computers over a NetWare-based network.
- **NetBEUI**. This protocol is used in a Microsoft Windows network.

A particular problem in networking is the interface between the software and the network adapter. In the past this was achieved by the manufacturer supplying a driver file which contains the required information to interface to the adapter. Typically, now, standard interfaces, such as NDIS2 and ODI are used to provide this interface.

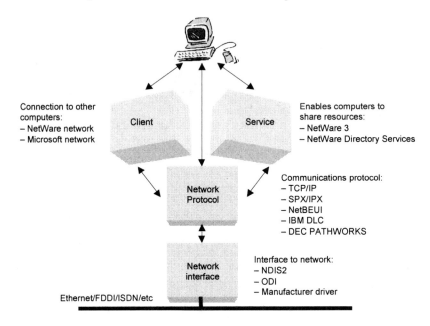

**Figure 1.1**   Common protocols

## 1.2    TCP/IP - The world's most important protocol

As the PC and other computers became more powerful, there was a demand for increased remote access of information and interconnection. This required a common communication language (network protocol). Many protocols were developed, but the most important was developed by the US Defense Advanced Research Projects Agency (DARPA). This protocol was named TCP/IP and has since allowed computers around the world to intercommunicate, no matter their operating system, their type or their network connection. DARPA's initial aim was simply to connect a number of universities and other research establishments to its own network. The resultant interconnected network (internet) is now known as the Internet. It has since outgrown this original application and many commercial organisations and home users now connect to the Internet. The Internet uses TCP/IP as a standard to transfer data and each node on the Internet is assigned a unique network address, called an IP address.

The IP part of the TCP/IP protocol provides for the routing of the data around the Internet and also a standardised addressing structure, where each node on the Internet is assigned a unique IP address. This address is a 32-bit address and takes the form of WWW.XXX.YYY.ZZZ (where WWW, XXX, YYY and ZZZ range from 0 to 255). IP addresses identify the location of the sender and also of the receiver. They can either be permanently assigned to a node or can be dynamically assigned when the node accesses the Internet. Organisations who want to limit access to the Internet can thus only assign IP addresses to nodes which are allowed access to the Internet (with dynamic allocation).

IP addresses are difficult to remember, thus Domain Name Services (DNS) are used to allow users to use symbolic names rather than IP addresses. DNS computers on the Internet determine the IP address of the named destination resource or application program. This dynamic mapping has the advantage that users and application programs can move around the Internet and are not fixed to an IP address. An analogy relates to the public telephone service. A telephone directory contains a list of subscribers and their associated telephone number. If someone looks for a telephone number, first the user name is looked up and their associated telephone number found. The telephone directory listing thus maps a user name (symbolic name) to an actual telephone number (the actual address). When a user enters a domain name (such as `www.fred.co.uk`) into the WWW browser then the local DNS server must try and resolve the domain name to an IP address, which can then be used to send the data to it. If it cannot resolve the IP address then the DNS server interrogates other servers to see if they know the required IP address. If it cannot be resolved then the WWW browser displays an error message.

The Internet naming structure uses labels separated by periods (full stops); an example is `eece.napier.ac.uk`. It uses a hierarchical structure where organisations are grouped into primary domain names. These include `com` (for commercial organisations), `edu` (for educational organisations), `gov` (for government organisations), `mil` (for military organisations), `net` (Internet network support centres) and `org` (other organisations). The primary domain name may also define the country in which the host is located, such as `uk` (United Kingdom), `fr` (France), and so on. All hosts on the Internet must be registered to one of these primary domain names.

Domain name labels after the primary field describe the subnetworks (subnets) within the network. For example, in the address `eece.napier.ac.uk`, the `ac` label relates to an academic institution within the `uk`, `napier` to the name of the institution and `eece` the subnet within that organisation.

TCP/IP has been unbelievably successful and has outgrown its original application. The addressing structure only allows for up to 4 billion addresses (many of these will be unused). As the number of devices which connect to the Internet increases by the day (not only computers, but printers, fax machines, mobile phones, and so on, can be allocated IP addresses), there is thus a need for a new addressing structure which provides many more addresses. For this, the IP Version 6 protocol is being developed. This, in the future, will replace the existing IP Version 4 protocol and provide for 128-bit addresses.

IP, itself, allows for the routing and addressing of the transmitted data, whereas, TCP supports the communication between application programs, using a stream of data. The main function of TCP is to provide a robust and reliable transport protocol. With TCP, a connection is initially established and is then maintained for the length of the transmission. It contains simple acknowledgement messages and a set of sequential numbers. It also supports multiple simultaneous connections using destination and source port numbers, and manages them for both transmission and reception. A port number relates to the type of data being transmitted, for example port 23 allows for remote connection (telnet), and the socket number relates to the transmitted stream. With sockets, a node can have multiple connections, each with its own unique socket number.

## 1.3  Java, The WWW and Intranets

Along with the growth of the Internet came the World Wide Web (WWW). It was initially conceived in 1989 by CERN, the European particle physics research laboratory in Geneva, Switzerland. Its main objective was to allow various different types of information, such as text, graphics and video, to be integrated together in an easy-to-use manner. It also supports the interlinking of information. One of the main characteristics of the WWW is that stored information tends to be distributed over a geographically wide area.

The result of the CERN project has been the world-wide acceptance of the protocols and specifications used. A major part of its success was due to the full support of the National Center for Supercomputing Applications (NCSA), which developed a family of user interface systems known collectively as Mosaic. Netscape and Microsoft have both developed excellent WWW browsers which have an easy-to-use interface to the WWW. Typical modern enhancements are:

- Search facilities. Browsers now support many search engine connections.
- Favourites list. This allows users to add WWW pages to a favourites list or folder. See Figure 1.3 for an example of a favourites folder using Internet Explorer.
- History of recently visited WWW pages. See Figure 1.3 for an example of a history folder using Internet Explorer.
- Increased security. This allows Internet sites to be zoned into security levels, such as High (most secure), Medium and Low (least secure). In the most secure level, the browser will exclude any material (called content) that could do damage to the computer.
- Content advisors. Microsoft Internet Explorer uses a rating system which was developed by the Recreational Software Advisory Council (RSAC). This is based on the work of Dr. Donald F. Roberts of Stanford University, who has studied the effects of media for nearly 20 years. In this the content of the material is graded into 4 main levels, which is rated for:

  - Language (from inoffensive slang to explicit or crude language).

- Nudity (from no nudity and provocative frontal nudity).
- Sex (from no sex to explicit sexual activity).
- Violence (from no violence to wanton and gratuitous violence).

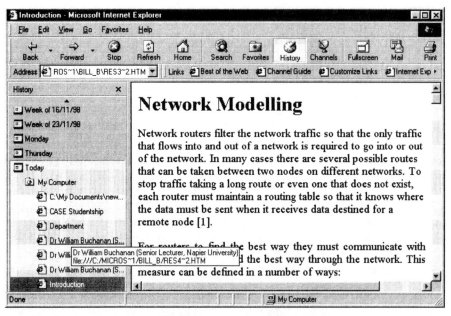

**Figure 1.2**  History folder

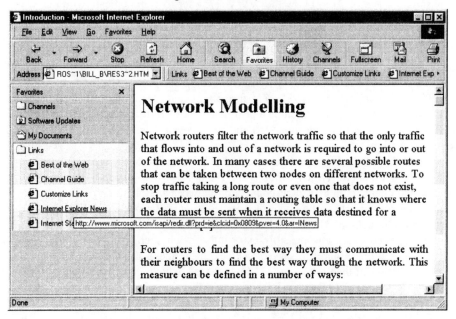

**Figure 1.3**  Favourites folder

- Usage of site certificates. These allow sites to positively identify themselves. Certificate granting authorities include ATT Certificate Services, Microsoft Root Authority and Verisign.
- Support for secure transmissions. This includes support for SSL2 (Secured Sockets Layer, Level 2), the standard protocol for secure transmissions. Secure WWW sites support this protocol and some also support PCT (Personal Communications Technology) which is more secure than SSL2.
- Support for cookies. This is a file which is sent by the Internet site and is stored locally on the user's computer. It stores information about the user's identity and preferences when revisiting that site.

The WWW, or Web, is basically an infrastructure of information. This information is stored on the WWW on by Web servers and it uses the Internet to transmit data around the world. These servers run special programs that allow information to be transmitted to remote computers which are running a Web browser.

The standard language developed was HTML (HyperText Markup Language), which is a text-based language that contains certain formatting tags. These tags are identified within a less than (<) and a greater than (>) symbol. Most have an opening and closing version; for example, to highlight bold text, the bold opening tag is <B> and the closing tag is </B>. When a greater than or a less than symbol is required then a special character sequence can be used. HTML is acceptable for low quality and medium print quality documents, but it is difficult to produce any high quality printed material. It is likely that new versions of HTML will support enhanced presentation.

The WWW uses TCP/IP for the transmission of the data, and HTTP (Hyper Text Transmission Protocol) to allow the WWW browser to communicate with the WWW server. HTTP is a stateless protocol where each transaction is independent of any previous transactions. The advantage of being stateless is that it allows the rapid access of WWW pages over several widely distributed servers. It uses the TCP protocol to establish the connection between the client and the server for each transaction then terminates the connection once the transaction completes.

HTTP also support many different formats of data. Initially, a client issues a request to a server which may include a prioritised list of formats that it can handle. This allows new formats to be easily added and also prevents the transmission of unnecessary information.

A client's WWW browser (the user agent) initially establishes a direct connection with destination server which contains the required WWW page. To make this connection the client initiates a TCP connection between the client and the server. After this has been established, the client then issues an HTTP request, such as, the specific command (the method), the URL (Universal Resource Locator, which is the full name of the requested data), and possibly extra information such as request parameters or client information. When the server receives the request, it attempts to perform the requested action. It then returns an HTTP response, which includes status information, a success/error code, and extra information. After the client receives this, the TCP connection is closed.

HTML is a rather limited language. This includes limited user interaction and it lacks much of the functionality of a programming language, such as having expressions, loops or decisions. A short-term fix is the JavaScript language which integrates into an HTML page. JavaScript allows some of the functionality of a high-level language for developing client and server Internet applications. It can be used to respond to user events, such as mouse clicks, form input and page navigation. A major advantage of JavaScript over HTML is that it supports the use of functions without any special declarative requirements.

Since the growth in the Internet there has been great investment in local area networks (LANs), wide area networks (WANs) and metropolitan area networks (MANs). The demand for bandwidth and faster applications increases as the applications of networks, the Internet and the WWW increase by the day. Along with this growth has come the introduction of many different types of networks, such as ISDN, Modems, Ethernet, Token Ring, ATM, FDDI, Frame relay and X.25. The great achievement, though, has been the world-wide acceptance of TCP/IP which has allowed nodes on these networks to intercommunicate.

The increased power of computers allowed the development of the Java programming language. It was first released in 1995 and was quickly adopted as it integrates well with Internet-based programming. Java 1.0 introduced the concept of an applet, which is a machine-independent program which runs within a WWW browser. It was quickly followed by Java 1.1 which gave faster interpretation of Java applets and included many new features (and now by Java 1.2). Java is a general-purpose, concurrent, class-based, object-oriented language and has been designed to be relatively simple to built complex applications. Java evolved from C and C++, but some parts of C++ (mainly the most difficult parts, such as pointers and parameter passing) have been dropped and others added.

Java has the great advantage over conventional software languages in that it produces code which is computer hardware independent. This is because the compiled code (called bytecode) is interpreted by the WWW browser. Unfortunately, this leads to slower execution, but, as much of the time in a graphical user interface program is spent updating the graphics display, then the overhead is, as far as the user is concerned, not a great one.

Another advantage that Java has over conventional software languages is that it directly supports the Internet and networking, especially for the transmission of compressed image, audio and video formats. The small 'black-box' networked computer is one of the founding principles of Java, and it is hoped that in the future small Java-based computers could replace the complex PC/workstation for general-purpose applications, like accessing the Internet or playing network games.

Many organisations are wary of the Internet as it allows external users to 'hack' into their network and possibly steal secrets or damage their computer systems. Thus many companies have set-up a special internet, known as an intranet. These are in-house, tailor-made internets for use within the organisation and provide limited access (if any) to outside services and also limit the external traffic into the intranet (if any). An intranet might have access to the Internet, but there will be no access from the Internet to the organisation's intranet.

Intranets normally have a firewall, which filters incoming and outgoing network traffic. This can be set-up to limit access from external and internal users, block access to certain external systems, or block certain types of network traffic (such as video conferencing or remote file transfer).

## 1.4 Data encryption

The best way to stop external parties from reading transmitted or stored data is to encrypt it. Encryption techniques can use either public keys or secret keys. Secret-key encryption uses a secret key which is only known to the two communicating parities. This key can be fixed or can be passed between the two parties over a secure communications link (for example, over the postal network or a leased line). The two most popular private-key techniques are DES (Data Encryption Standard) and IDEA (International Data Encryption Algorithm) and popular public-key technique are RSA (named after its inventors, Rivest, Shamir and Adleman) and PGP (Pretty Good Privacy).

In 1977, the National Bureau of Standards (now the National Institute of Standards and Technology) published the DES technique for commercial and unclassified US government applications. DES is a block cipher scheme which operates on 64-bit block sizes. The private key has only 56 useful bits as eight of its bits are used for parity. This gives $2^{56}$ or $10^{17}$ possible keys. DES uses a complex series of permutations and substitutions; the result of these operations is XOR'ed with the input. This is then repeated 16 times using a different order of the key bits each time. DES is a very strong code and has never been broken, although several high-powered computers are now available which, using brute force, can crack the code. A possible solution is 3DES (or triple DES) which uses DES three times in a row. First to encrypt, next to decrypt and finally to encrypt. This system allows a key-length of more than 128 bits.

IDEA operates over 17 rounds with a complicated mangler function. During decryption this function does not have to be reversed and can simply be applied in the same way as during encryption (this also occurs with DES). IDEA uses a different key expansion for encryption and decryption, but every other part of the process is identical. The same keys are used in DES decryption but in the reverse order.

Public-key algorithms use a secret element and a public element to their key. One of the main algorithms is RSA. Compared with DES it is relatively slow but it has the advantage that users can choose their own key whenever they need one.

RSA stands for Rivest, Shamir and Adelman, and is one of the most commonly used public-key cryptosystems. It is patented only in the USA and is secure for key-length of over 728 bits. RSA uses two encryption keys. One is a public key, which is used by someone sending the user the encrypted message, and the other is a private key, which is used to decrypt the message. The amazing thing about using the RSA algorithm is that once the sender encrypts the message with the recipient's public key, only the recipient can decrypt it with their own private key (not even the sender can decrypt it). The algorithm relies of the fact that it is difficult to factorise large numbers. Unfortunately, it is particularly vulnerable to chosen plaintext attacks and a new timing attack (spying on keystroke time) was announced on the 7 December 1995. This attack would be able to break many existing implementations of RSA.

## 1.5 LANs, WANs and MANs

Computer systems operate on digital data and can communicate with other digital equipment over a network or through an independent connection. Networks are normally defined as either:

- Wide area networks (WANs), which normally connect networks over a large physical area, such as between different buildings, towns or even countries.
- Local area networks (LANs), which connect computers within a single office or building. They typically connect to a common electronic connection – commonly known as a network backbone. LANs can connect to other networks either directly or through a WAN.
- Metropolitan area networks (MANs), which normally connect networks around a town or city. An example of a MAN is the EaStMAN network that connects universities and colleges in Edinburgh and Stirling, UK.

The four main methods of connecting to a network (or an independently connected computer) to another network are:

- Through a modem connection. A modem converts digital data into an analogue form that can be transmitted over a standard telephone line.
- Through an ISDN connection. An ISDN (integrated services digital network) connection uses the public telephone service. It differs from a modem connection in it sends data in a digital form.
- Through a gateway. A gateway connects one type of network to another type.
- Through a bridge or router. Bridges and routers normally connect one type of network to one of the same type.

Modems are used to connect a network (or independently attached computer) over the public switched telecommunications network (PSTN). Normally, telephone-type connections are unsuitable for digital data as they have a limited bandwidth of between 400 to 3 400 Hz. A modem must then be used to convert the digital information into an analogue form that is transmittable over the telephone lines. Figure 1.4 illustrates the connection of computers to a network. These computers can connect to a WAN through a service provider (such as CompuServe) or through another network which is connected a modem. The service provider has the required hardware to connect to the WAN.

ISDN allows the transmission of many types of digital data into a truly global digital network. Transmittable data types include digitised video, digitised speech and computer data. Since the switching and transmission are digital, fast access times and relatively high bit-rates are possible. Typical base bit-rates include 64 kbps. All connections to the ISDN require network termination equipment (NTE).

Figure 1.4 also shows a network server connected to a LAN. This server can be used for the following:

- Allowing users to login and set-up their computer.
- Store user profiles.
- Allow access to networked resources, such as tape backup, networked CD-ROMs, and so on.
- Provides general file and print services.

- Sets up group access rights.

Peer-to-peer connections involve computers connecting without the need for a network server.

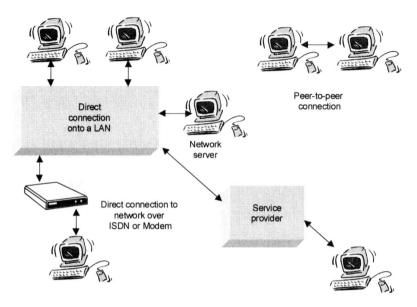

**Figure 1.4** Connection of nodes to a network

## 1.6 OSI model

A major problem in the electronics industry is the interconnection of equipment and software compatibility. Other problems can occur in the connection of electronic equipment in one part of the world to another, in another part. For these reasons, the International Standards Organisation (ISO) developed a model known as the OSI (open systems interconnection) model. Its main objects were to:

- Allow manufacturers of different systems to interconnect their equipment through standard interfaces.
- Allow software and hardware to integrate well and be portable on differing systems.
- Create a model which all the countries of the world use.

Figure 1.5 shows the OSI model. Data passes from the top layer of the sender to the bottom and then up from the bottom layer to the top on the recipient. Each layer on the sender, though, communicates directly the recipient's corresponding layer. This creates a virtual data flow between layers.

The top layer (the application layer) initially gets data from an application and appends it with data that the recipients application layer reads. This appended data passes to the next layer (the presentation layer). Again, it appends it with its own data, and so on, down to the physical layer. The physical layer is then responsible for transmitting the data to the recipient. The data sent can be termed as a data frame, whereas data send by the network or transport layer is typically referred to as a data packet.

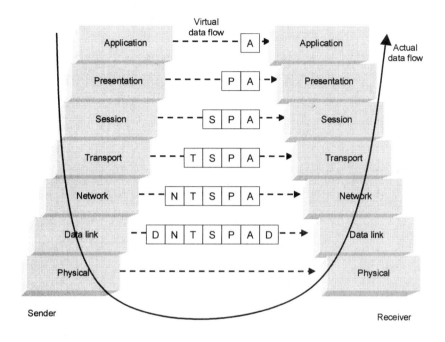

**Figure 1.5**   Seven-layer OSI model

The basic function of each of the layers are:

1. **Physical**. Defines the electrical characteristics of the communications channel and the transmitted signals, such as voltage levels, connector types, cabling, and so on.
2. **Data link**. Ensures that the transmitted bits are received in a reliable way, such as adding extra bits to define the start and end of a data frame, adding extra error detection/correction bits and ensuring that multiple nodes do not try to access a common communication channel at the same time.
3. **Network**. Routes data frames through a network. If data packets require to go out of a network then the transport layer routes them through interconnected networks. Its task may involve, for example, splitting data for transmission and re-assembling it upon reception. The IP part of TCP/IP is involved with the network layer.
4. **Transport**. Network transparent data transfer and transmission protocol. It supports the transmission of multiple streams from a single computer. The TCP part of TCP/IP is involved with the transport layer.
5. **Session**. Provides an open communications path with the other system. It involves the setting up, maintaining and closing down of a session. The communication

channel and the internetworking of the data should be transparent to the session layer. A typical session protocol is telnet, which allows for the remote login over a network.

6. **Presentation**. Uses a set of translations that allows the data to be interpreted properly. It may have to translate between two systems if they use different presentation standards, such as different character sets or differing character codes. The presentation layer can also add data encryption for security purposes.

7. **Application**. Provides network services to application programs, such as file transfer and electronic mail.

Figure 1.6 shows how typical networking systems fit into the OSI model. The data link and physical layers are covered by networking technologies such as Ethernet, Token Ring and FDDI. The networking layer is covered by IP (internet protocol) and transport by TCP (transport control protocol).

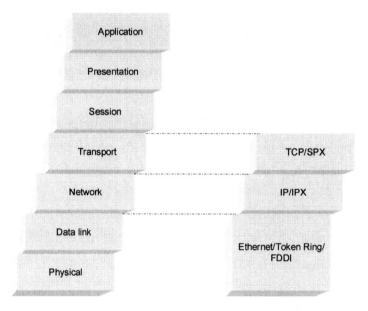

**Figure 1.6**   Typical technologies used in network communications

## 1.7   Exercises

The following questions are multiple choice. Please select from a–d.

**1.7.1**   The standard networking protocol used on the Internet is:

    (a)    Ethernet        (b)    TCP/IP
    (c)    SPX/IPX      (d)    Token Ring

**1.7.2**     The default networking protocol used by Novell NetWare is:

(a)     Ethernet          (b)     TCP/IP
(c)     SPX/IPX          (d)     Token Ring

**1.7.3**     What address is used by computers connecting to the Internet:

(a)     IP address          (b)     Node address
(c)     Interrupt address     (d)     Router address

**1.7.4**     Which organisation originally developed the Internet:

(a)     DARPA          (b)     ISO
(c)     CERN           (d)     IEEE

**1.7.5**     Which organisation originally developed the initial specifications for the WWW:

(a)     DARPA          (b)     ISO
(c)     CERN           (d)     IEEE

**1.7.6**     Which organisation originally developed the OSI model:

(a)     DARPA          (b)     ISO
(c)     CERN           (d)     IEEE

**1.7.7**     A network which connects computers within a single building is normally defined as:

(a)     local area network          (b)     wide area network
(c)     metropolitan area network   (d)     enterprise area network

**1.7.8**     The function of DNS is:

(a)     To allow a login to a network
(b)     To map IP addresses to symbolic names
(c)     To locate networked resources
(d)     To allow connection onto the Internet

**1.7.9**     The three lower layers of the OSI model are:

(a)     Physical, data link and application
(b)     Physical, network and transport
(c)     Physical, data link and network
(d)     Physical, network and session

**1.7.10** Why will IP Version 4 be replaced in the coming years:
- (a)    It is not supported by most routers
- (b)    It is not supported by many networks
- (c)    It does not support enough IP addresses
- (d)    It does not allow the interconnection of computers over the Internet

**1.7.11** Which is the most popular networking technology for a LAN:

| | | | |
|---|---|---|---|
| (a) | FDDI | (b) | Token Ring |
| (c) | ISDN | (d) | Ethernet |

**1.7.12** What is the transport and networking protocol used by WWW servers:

| | | | |
|---|---|---|---|
| (a) | HTTP | (b) | SPX/IPX |
| (c) | TCP/IP | (d) | DNS |

**1.7.13** What is the protocol used to pass WWW pages between a WWW server and a WWW client:

| | | | |
|---|---|---|---|
| (a) | HTTP | (b) | SPX/IPX |
| (c) | TCP/IP | (d) | DNS |

**1.7.14** Which language is used to design pages on the WWW:

| | | | |
|---|---|---|---|
| (a) | C/C++ | (b) | FORTRAN |
| (c) | Microsoft Word | (d) | HTML |

**1.7.15** An extension to HTML which supports functions and user events is:

| | | | |
|---|---|---|---|
| (a) | JavaScript | (b) | Extended HTML |
| (c) | C++ | (d) | Java |

**1.7.16** One of the main advantages of Java is:

- (a)    It is modern and has a nice name
- (b)    It can produce machine-independent code which can be run within a browser
- (c)    It is the easiest programming language
- (d)    It can be developed using standard English statements

**1.7.17** Which of the following is **not** an advantage of the OSI model:

- (a)    Its allows manufacturers of different systems to interconnect their equipment through standard interfaces
- (b)    It allows computers to operate faster
- (c)    Its allows software and hardware to integrate well and be portable on differing systems

(d)     It creates a model which all the countries of the world use

**1.7.18**     The function of the data link layer in the OSI model is:

(a)     To ensure that the transmitted bits are received in a reliable
way
(b)     Routing, switching and flow control over a network
(c)     Network transparent data transfer and transmission control
(d)     Administrative and control of session between two nodes

**1.7.19**     In public key encryption, how many keys are required by a user:

(a)     One, which is shared by the sender and the recipient
(b)     Two, both are shared by the sender and the recipient
(c)     Two, one is secret and the other is public
(d)     Four, two are secret and two are private

**1.7.20**     A typical public key encryption technique is:

(a)     PGP        (b)     DES
(c)     IDEA       (d)     3DES

**1.7.21**     Investigate a known LAN and determine which network operating system it
uses, such as Microsoft Windows, Novell NetWare or UNIX.

---

## 1.8     Note from the author

*Many of the great inventions/developments of our time were things that were not
really predicted, such as CD-ROMs, RADAR, silicon transistors, fibre optic cables,
and, of course, the Internet. The Internet itself is basically an infrastructure of interconnected networks which run a common protocol. The nightmare of interfacing the
many computer systems around the world was solved because of two simple protocols:
TCP and IP. Without them the Internet would not have evolved so quickly and possibly
would not have occurred at all. TCP and IP are excellent protocols as they are simple
and can be run over any type of network, on any type of computer system.*

*The Internet is often confused with the World Wide Web (WWW), but the WWW is
only one application of the Internet. Others include electronic mail (the No.1 application), file transfer, remote login, and so on.*

*The amount of information transmitted over networks increases by a large factor
every year. This is due to local area networks, wide area networks, of course, traffic
over the Internet. It is currently estimated that traffic on the Internet doubles every
100 days and that three people join the Internet every second. This means an eight-
fold increase in traffic over a whole year. It is hard to imagine such growth in any
other technological area. Imagine if cars were eight times faster each year, or could
carry eight times the number of passengers each year (and of course roads and drive-
ways would have to be eight times larger each year).*

# 2 Networking Fundamentals

## 2.1 Introduction

Most computers in organisations connect to a network using a LAN. These networks normally consist of a backbone, which is the common link to all the networks within the organisation. This backbone allows users on different network segments to communicate and allows data into and out of the local network. Figure 2.1 shows a local area network which contains various segments: LAN A, LAN B, LAN C, LAN D, LAN E and LAN F. These are connected to the local network via the BACKBONE 1. Thus, if LAN A talks to LAN E then the data must travel out of LAN A, onto BACKBONE1, then into LAN C and through onto LAN E.

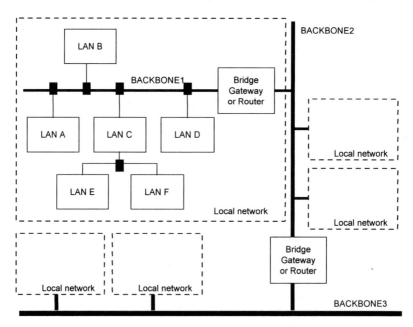

**Figure 2.1** Interconnection of local networks

Networks are partitioned from other networks with a bridge, a gateway or a router. A bridge links a network of one type to an identical type, such as Ethernet to Ethernet, or Token Ring to Token Ring. A gateway connects two dissimilar types of networks and routers operate in a similar way to gateways and can either connect to two similar or dissimilar networks. The essential operation of a gateway, bridge or router is that they only allow data traffic through, that is intended for another network, which is outside the connected network. This filters traffic and stops traffic, not indented for the network, from clogging-up the backbone. Most modern bridges, gateways and routers are intelligent and can automatically determine the topology of the network.

Spanning-tree bridges have built-in intelligence and can communicate with other bridges. They can then build up a picture of the interconnected networks. So, if more than one path exists between individual segments, the bridge automatically finds alternate routes. This is useful when a fault develops on a route or a route becomes too heavily loaded. Conventional bridges can cause frames to loop around forever.

### 2.1.1 Peer-to-peer and client/server

An important concept is the differentiation between a peer-to-peer connection and a client/server connection. A peer-to-peer connection allows users on a local network access to a local computer. Typically, this might be access to:

 **Local printers**. Printers, local to a computer, can be accessed by other users if the printer is shareable. This can be password protected, or not. Shareable printers on a Microsoft network have a small hand under the icon.

 **Local disk drives and folders**. The disk drives, such as the hard disk or CD-ROM drives can be accessed if they are shareable. Normally the drives must be shareable. On a Microsoft network a drive can be made shareable by selecting the drive and selecting the right-hand mouse button, then selecting the Sharing option. User names and passwords can be set-up locally or can be accessed from a network server. Typically, only the local computer grants access to certain folders, while others are not shared.

These shared resources can also be mounted as disk drives to the remote computer. Thus, the user of the remote computer can simply access resources on the other computers as if they were mounted locally. This option is often the best when there is a small local network, as it requires the minimum of set-up and does not need any complicated server set-ups.

A client/server network has a central server which is typically used to:

- Store usernames, group names and passwords.
- Run print queues for networked printers.
- Allocate IP addresses for Internet access.
- Provide centralised file services, such as hard disks or networked CD-ROM drives.
- Provide system back-up facilities, such as CD-R disk drives and DAT tape drive.
- Centralise computer settings.
- Provide access to other centralised peripherals, such as networked faxes, dial-in network connections, and so on.
- Provide WWW and TCP/IP services, such as remote login, file transfer, and so on.

If in doubt, a peer-to-peer network is normally the best for a small office environment. Care must be taken, though, when setting up the attributes of the shared resources. Figure 2.2 shows example of the sharing setting for a disk drive. It can be seen that the main attributes are:

- Read-only. This should be used when the remote user only requires to copy or execute files. The remote user cannot modify any of the files.
- Full. This option should only be used when the remote user has full access to the files and can copy, erase or modify the files.
- Depends on Password. In this mode the remote user must provide a password for either read-only access or full access.

If the peer-to-peer network has a local server, such as Novell NetWare or Windows NT/2000 then access can be provided for certain users and/or groups, if they provide the correct password.

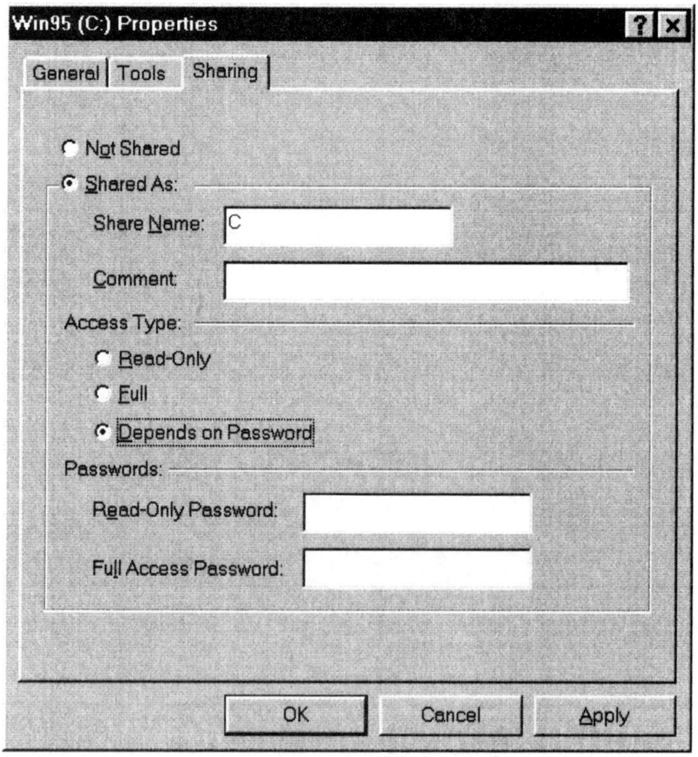

**Win95 (C:) Properties** ? ✕

General | Tools | Sharing |

○ Not Shared

● Shared As:

Share Name: C

Comment:

Access Type:

○ Read-Only

○ Full

● Depends on Password

Passwords:

Read-Only Password:

Full Access Password:

OK | Cancel | Apply

**Figure 2.2** File access rights

## 2.2 Network topologies

There are three basic topologies for LANs, which are shown in Figure 2.3. These are:

- A star network.
- A ring network.
- A bus network.

There are other topologies which are either a combination of two or more topologies or are derivatives of the main types. A typical topology is a tree topology, that is essentially a combined star and a bus network, as illustrated in Figure 2.4. A concentrator (or hub) is used to connect the nodes to the network.

### 2.2.1 Star network

In a star topology, a central server switches data around the network. Data traffic between nodes and the server will thus be relatively low. Its main advantages are:

- Since the data rate is relatively low between central server and the node, a low-specification twisted-pair cable can be used connect the nodes to the server.
- A fault on one of the nodes will not affect the rest of the network. Typically, mainframe computers use a central server with terminals connected to it.

The main disadvantage of this type of topology is that the network is highly dependent upon the operation of the central server. If it were to slow significantly then the network becomes slow. In addition, if it were to become un-operational then the complete network would shut down.

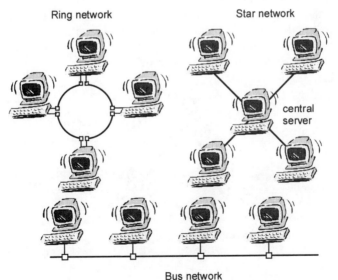

**Figure 2.3** Network topologies

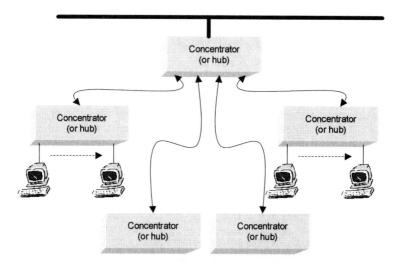

**Figure 2.4** Tree topology

### 2.2.2 Ring network

In a ring network, computers link together to form a ring. To allow an orderly access to the ring, a single electronic token passes from one computer to the next around the ring, as illustrated in Figure 2.5. A computer can only transmit data when it captures the token. In a manner similar to the star network, each link between nodes is a point-to-point link and allows the usage of almost any type of transmission medium. Typically twisted-pair cables allow a bit rate of up to 16Mbps, but coaxial and fibre optic cables are normally used for extra reliability and higher data rates.

A typical ring network is IBM Token Ring. The main advantage of token ring networks is that all nodes on the network have an equal chance of transmitting data. Unfortunately it suffers from several problems; the most severe is that if one of the nodes goes down then the whole network may go down.

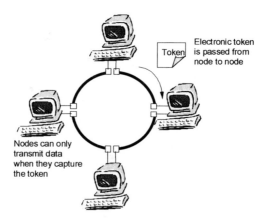

**Figure 2.5** Token passing ring network

### 2.2.3 Bus network

A bus network uses a multi-drop transmission medium, as shown in Figure 2.6. All nodes on the network share a common bus and all share communications. This allows only one device to communicate at a time. A distributed medium access protocol determines which station is to transmit. As with the ring network, data frames contain source and destination addresses, where each station monitors the bus and copies frames addressed to itself.

Twisted-pair cables give data rates up to 100 Mbps, whereas, coaxial and fibre optic cables give higher bit rates and longer transmission distances. A bus network is a good compromise over the other two topologies as it allows relatively high data rates. Also, if a node goes down, it does not affect the rest of the network. The main disadvantage of this topology is that it requires a network protocol to detect when two nodes are transmitting at the same time. It also does not cope well with heavy traffic rates. A typical bus network is Ethernet 2.0.

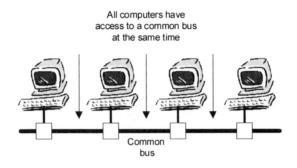

**Figure 2.6** Bus topology

## 2.3 Routers, bridges and repeaters

Networks connect to other networks through repeaters, bridges or routers. A repeater corresponds to the physical layer of the OSI model and routes data from one network segment to another. Bridges, on the other hand, route data using the data link layer (with the MAC address), and routers route data using the network layer (that is, using a network address, such as an IP address). Normally, at the data link layer, the transmitted data is known as a data frame, while at the network layer it is referred to as a data packet. Figure 2.7 illustrates the three interconnection types.

### 2.3.1 Repeaters

All network connections suffer from a reduction in signal strength (attenuation) and digital pulse distortion. Thus, for a given cable specification and bit rate, each connection will have a maximum length of cable that can be used to transmit the data reliably. Repeaters can be used to increase the maximum interconnection length, and may do the following:

- Clean signal pulses.
- Pass all signals between attached segments.
- Boost signal power.
- Possibly translate between two different media types (such as fibre to twisted-pair cable).

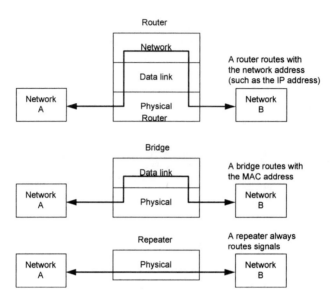

**Figure 2.7**  Repeaters, bridges and routers

### 2.3.2  Bridges

Bridges filter input and output traffic so that only data frames distended for a network are actually routed into that network and only data frames destined for the outside are allowed out of the network.

The performance of a bridge is governed by two main factors:

- **The filtering rate**. A bridge reads the MAC address of the Ethernet/ Token ring/ FDDI node and then decides if it should forward the frames into the network. Filter rates for bridges range from around 5000 to 70 000 pps (packets per second).
- **The forward rate**. Once the bridge has decided to route the frame into the internetwork, the bridge must forward the frame onto the destination network. Forwarding rates range from 500 to 140 000 pps and a typical forwarding rate is 90 000 pps.

A typical Ethernet bridge has the following specifications:

Bit rate:          10 Mbps
Filtering rate:    17 500 pps
Forwarding rate:   11 000 pps

| Connectors: | Two DB15 AUI (female), one DB9 male console port, two BNC (for 10BASE2) or two RJ-45 (for 10BASE-T). |
|---|---|
| Algorithm: | Spanning tree protocol. This automatically learns the addresses of all devices on both interconnected networks and builds a separate table for each network. |

### 2.3.3 Spanning tree architecture (STA) bridges

The IEEE 802.1 standard has defined the spanning tree algorithm. It is normally implemented as software on STA-compliant bridges. On power-up they automatically learn the addresses of all the nodes on both interconnected networks and build up a separate table for each network.

They can also support two connections between two LANs so that when the primary path becomes disabled, the spanning tree algorithm re-enables the previously disabled redundant link, as illustrated in Figure 2.8.

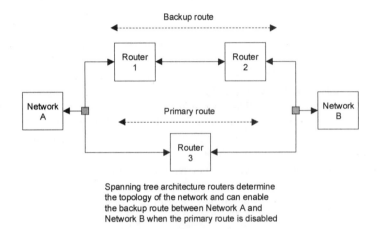

Spanning tree architecture routers determine
the topology of the network and can enable
the backup route between Network A and
Network B when the primary route is disabled

**Figure 2.8**   Spanning tree routers

### 2.3.4 Source route bridging

With source route bridging a source device, not the bridge, is used to send special explorer packets, these are then used to determine the best path to the destination. Explorer packets are sent out from the source routing bridges until they reach their destination workstation. Each source routing bridge along the route enters its address in the routing information field (RIF) of the explorer packet. The destination node then sends back the completed RIF field to the source node. When the source device has determined the best path to the destination, it sends the data message along with the path instructions to the local bridge. It then forwards the data message according to the received path instructions.

### 2.3.5 Routers

Routers examine the network address field and determine the best route for the packet. They have the great advantage in that they normally support several different types of network layer protocols.

Routers need to communicate with other routers so that they can exchange routing information. Most network operating systems have associated routing protocols which support the transfer of routing information. Typical routing protocols using Internet communications are:

- BGP (border gateway protocol).
- EGP (exterior gateway protocol).
- OSPF (open shortest path first).
- RIP (routing information protocol).

Most routers support RIP and EGP. In the past, RIP was the most popular router protocol standard. Its widespread use is due, in no small part, to the fact that it was distributed along with the Berkeley Software Distribution (BSD) of UNIX (from which most commercial versions of UNIX are derived). It suffers from several disadvantages and has been largely replaced by OSFP and EGB. These newer protocols have the advantage over RIP in that they can handle large internetworks, as well as reducing routing table update traffic.

RIP uses a distance vector algorithm which measures the number of network jumps (known as hops), up to a maximum of 16, to the destination router. This has the disadvantage that the smallest number of hops may not be the best route from source to destination. The OSPF and EGB protocol uses a link state algorithm that can decide between multiple paths to the destination router. These are based, not only on hops, but on other parameters such as delay capacity, reliability and throughput.

With distance vector routing each router maintains table by communicating with neighbouring routers. The number of hops in its own table are then computed as it knows the number of hops to local routers, as illustrated in Figure 2.9. Unfortunately, the routing table can take some time to be updated when changes occur, because it takes time for all the routers to communicate with each other (known as slow convergence).

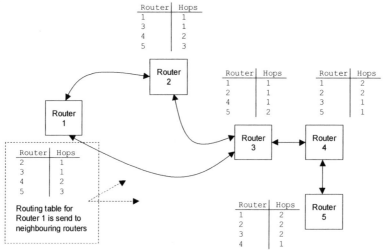

**Figure 2.9** Routing tables with number of hops

## 2.4 Network cable types

The cable type used on a network depends on several parameters, including:

- The data bit rate.
- The reliability of the cable.
- The maximum length between nodes.
- The possibility of electrical hazards and tolerance to harsh conditions.
- Power loss in the cables.
- Expense and general availability of the cable.
- Ease of connection, maintenance and ease of running cables.

The main types of cables used in networks are twisted-pair, coaxial and fibre optic; these are illustrated in Figure 2.10. Twisted-pair and coaxial cables transmit electrical signals, whereas fibre optic cables transmit light pulses.

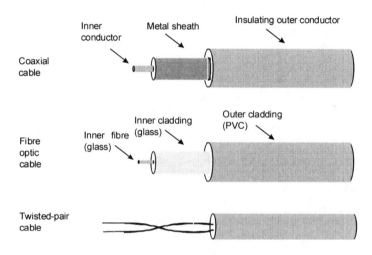

**Figure 2.10**   Typical network cable types

The basic specification for the cable types are:

- Twisted-pair cables. Unshielded twisted-pair (UTP) cables are not shielded and thus interfere with nearby cables, whereas, shielded twisted-pair (STP) cables have a less effect on nearby cables. Public telephone lines generally use UTP cables. In LANs, they are generally used up to bit rates of 100Mbps and with maximum lengths of 100 m.
- Coaxial cables. These have a grounded metal sheath around the signal conductor. This limits the amount of interference between cables and thus allows higher data rates. Typically, they are used at bit rates of 100 Mbps for maximum lengths of 1 km.

- Fibre optic. The highest specifications of the three types. They allow extremely high bit rates over long distances. Fibre optic cables do not interfere with nearby cables and give greater security, give more protection from electrical damage from by external equipment, are more resistance to harsh environments and are safer in hazardous environments. A typical bit rate for a LAN using fibre optic cables is 100 Mbps, in other applications this can reach several gigabits/sec. The maximum length of the fibre optic cable depends on the transmitter and receiver electronics, but a single length of 20 km is possible.

## 2.5 Exercises

The following questions are multiple choice. Please select from a-d.

**2.5.1** The cable type which offers the highest bit rate is:

    (a)   Fibre optic cable    (b)   Twisted pair cable
    (c)   Coaxial cable    (d)   Untwisted pair cable

**2.5.2** Which of the following is the main disadvantage of a star network:

    (a)   That the data transmitted between the central server and the node is relatively high compared to other network topologies
    (b)   That the network is reliant on a central server
    (c)   All nodes compete for the network
    (d)   Nodes can only transmit data once they have a token

**2.5.3** Which of the following is the main disadvantage of a ring network:

    (a)   That the data transmitted between the central server and the node is relatively high compared to other network topologies
    (b)   That the network is reliant on a central server
    (c)   All nodes compete for the network
    (d)   A break in the ring stops data from being transmitted

**2.5.4** Which of the following is the main disadvantage of a bus network:

    (a)   Nodes can only transmit data once they have a token
    (b)   That the network is reliant on a central server
    (c)   All nodes compete for the network
    (d)   A break in the ring stops data from being transmitted

**2.5.5** On a network which address does a bridge route with:

    (a)   IP address
    (b)   Interrupt address
    (c)   MAC address

(d)     Source address

**2.5.6**     On a network which address does a router route with:

(a)     IP address
(b)     Interrupt address
(c)     MAC address
(d)     Source address

**2.5.7**     Which of the following best describes a peer-to-peer network:

(a)     Resources are centralised on a server
(b)     Local resources, such as memory and processor, are shared between users over the network
(c)     Local resources, such as disk-drives and printers, are shared between users over the network
(d)     Internet connections are allocated centrally

**2.5.8**     Which of the following best describes a client/server network:

(a)     Resources are centralised on a server
(b)     Local resources, such as memory and processor, are shared between user
(c)     Local resources, such as disk-drives and printers, are shared between users
(d)     Internet connections are allocated centrally

**2.5.9**     Explain how peer-to-peer networks differ from server-based networks. When might peer-to-peer networks be used and how must they be carefully set-up.

**2.5.10**     If possible, set-up a peer-to-peer connection between two computers and share some folders.

**2.5.11**     Locate a LAN within an organisation, such as a college or university network, and determine the cables that are used.

---

## 2.6   Note from the author

*Networks have grown vastly over the past twenty years, and most companies now have some form of network. At the beginning of the 1980s, PCs were relatively complex machines to use, and required application programs to be installed locally to their disk drives. Many modern computers now run their application programs over a network, which makes the administration of the application software must simpler, and also allows users to share their resources.*

*The topology of a network is all-important, as it can severely effect the perform-ance of the network, and can also be used to find network faults. I have run a network for many years and know the problems that can occur if a network grows without any long-term strategy. Many users (especially managers) perceive that a network can be expanded to an infinite degree. Many also think that new users can simply be added to the network without a thought on the amount of traffic that they are likely to generate, and its effect on other users. It is thus important for Network Managers to have a short-term, a medium-term and a long-term plan for the network.*

*So, what are the basic elements of a network. I would say:*

- *IP addresses/Domain names (but only if the network connects to the Internet or uses TCP/IP).*

- *A network operating system (such as Microsoft Windows, Novell NetWare, UNIX and Linux). Many companies run more than one type of network operating system, which causes many problems, but has the advantage of being able to migrate from one network operating system to another. One type of network operating system can also have advantages over other types. For example, UNIX is a very robust networking operating system which has good network security and directly sup-ports TCP/IP for all network traffic.*

- *The cables (twisted-pair/fibre optic or coaxial cables). These directly affect the bit rate of the network, its reliability and the ease of upgrade of the network.*

- *Network servers, client/server connections and peer-to-peer connections.*

- *Bridges, routers and repeaters. These help to isolate traffic from one network seg-ment to another. Routers and bridges are always a good long-term investment and help to isolate network traffic and can also isolate segment faults.*

*The networking topology of the future is likely to evolve around a client/server archi-tecture. With this, server machines run special programs which wait for connections from client machines. These server programs typically respond to networked applica-tions, such as electronic mail, WWW, file transfer, remote login, date/time servers, and so on.*

*Many application programs are currently run over local area networks, but in the future many could be run over wide area networks, or even over the Internet. This means that computers would require the minimum amount of configuration and allows the standardisation of programs at a single point (this also helps with bug fixes and updates). There may also be a time when software licensing is charged by the amount of time that a user actually uses the package. This requires applications to be run from a central source (the server).*

# 3 Ethernet

## 3.1 Introduction

Most of the computers in business now connect through a LAN and the most commonly used LAN is Ethernet. DEC, Intel and the Xerox Corporation initially developed Ethernet and the IEEE 802 committee has since defined standards for it, the most common of which are Ethernet 2.0 and IEEE 802.3. This chapter discusses Ethernet technology and the different types of Ethernet.

In itself Ethernet cannot make a network and needs some other protocol such as TCP/IP to allow nodes to communicate. Unfortunately, Ethernet in its standard form does not cope well with heavy traffic, but this is offset by the following:

- Ethernet networks are easy to plan and cheap to install.
- Ethernet network components, such as network cards and connectors, are cheap and well supported.
- It is a well-proven technology, which is fairly robust and reliable.
- It is simple to add and delete computers on the network.
- It is supported by most software and hardware systems.

A major problem with Ethernet is that, because computers must contend to get access to the network, there is no guarantee that they will get access within a given time. This contention also causes problems when two computers try to communicate at the same time, they must both back off and no data can be transmitted. In its standard form Ethernet allows a bit rate of 10 Mbps, but new standards for fast Ethernet systems minimise the problems of contention and also increase the bit rate to 100 Mbps (and even 1Gbps). Ethernet uses coaxial, fibre optic or twisted-pair cable.

Ethernet uses a shared-media, bus-type network topology where all nodes share a common bus. These nodes must then contend for access to the network as only one node can communicate at a time. Data is then transmitted in frames which contain the MAC (media access control) source and destination addresses of the sending and receiving node, respectively. The local shared media is known as a segment. Each node on the network monitors the segment and copies any frames addressed to it.

Ethernet uses carrier sense, multiple access with collision detection (CSMA/CD). On a CSMA/CD network, nodes monitor the bus (or Ether) to determine if it is busy. A node wishing to send data waits for an idle condition then transmits its message. Unfortunately, collisions can occur when two nodes transmit at the same time, thus nodes must monitor the cable when they transmit. When a collision occurs, both nodes stop transmitting frames and transmit a jamming signal. This informs all nodes on the network that a collision has occurred. Each of the nodes involved in the collision then waits a random period of time before attempting a re-transmission. As each node has a random delay time then there can be a prioritisation of the nodes on the network.

Each node on the network must be able to detect collisions and be capable of transmitting and receiving simultaneously. These nodes either connect onto a common Ethernet connection or can connect to an Ethernet hub, as illustrated in Figure 3.1. Nodes thus contend for the network and are not guaranteed access to it. Collisions generally slow the network.

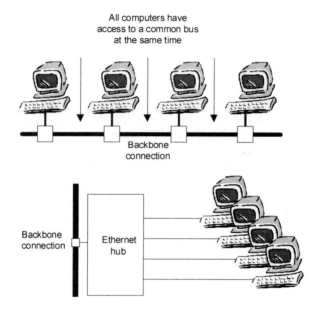

**Figure 3.1**    Connections to an Ethernet network

## 3.2    IEEE standards

The IEEE are the main standards organisation for LANs and they refer to the standard for Ethernet as CSMA/CD. Figure 3.2 shows how the IEEE standards for CSMA/CD fit into the OSI model. The two layers of the IEEE standards correspond to the physical and data link layers of the OSI model. On Ethernet networks, most hardware complies with IEEE 802.3 standard. The MAC layer allows many nodes to share a single communication channel. It also adds the start and end frame delimiters, error detection bits, access control information, and source and destination addresses. Each frame also has an error detection scheme known as cyclic redundancy check (CRC).

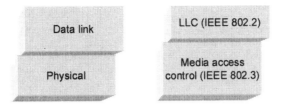

**Figure 3.2** Standards for IEEE 802 LANs

## 3.3 Ethernet - media access control (MAC) layer

When sending data the MAC layer takes the information from the LLC link layer. Figure 3.3 shows the IEEE 802.3 frame format. It contains 2 or 6 bytes for the source and destination addresses (16 or 48 bits each), 4 bytes for the CRC (32 bits) and 2 bytes for the LLC length (16 bits). The LLC part may be up to 1500 bytes long. The preamble and delay components define the start and end of the frame. The initial preamble and start delimiter are, in total, 8 bytes long and the delay component is a minimum of 96 bytes long.

A 7-byte preamble precedes the Ethernet 802.3 frame. Each byte of the preamble has a fixed binary pattern of 10101010 and each node on the network uses it to synchronise their clock and transmission timings. It also informs nodes that a frame is to be sent and for them to check the destination address in the frame.

The end of the frame there is a 96-bit delay period, which provides the minimum delay between two frames. This slot time delay allows for the worst-case network propagation delay.

The start delimiter field (SDF) is a single byte (or octet) of 10101011. It follows the preamble and identifies that there is a valid frame being transmitted. Most Ethernet systems use a 48-bit MAC address for the sending and receiving node. Each Ethernet node has a unique MAC address, which is normally defined as hexadecimal digits, such as:

```
        4C - 31 - 22 - 10  - F1 - 32
or      4C31 : 2210: F132.
```

A 48-bit address field allows $2^{48}$ different addresses (or approximately 281 474 976 710 000 different addresses).

The LLC length field defines whether the frame contains information or it can be used to define the number of bytes in the logical link field. The logical link field can contain up to 1500 bytes of information and has a minimum of 46 bytes; its format is given in Figure 3.3. If the information is greater than this upper limit then multiple frames are sent. Also, if the field is less than the lower limit then it is padded with extra redundant bits.

The 32-bit frame check sequence (or FCS) is an error detection scheme. It is used to determine transmission errors and is often referred to as a cyclic redundancy check (CRC) or simply as a checksum.

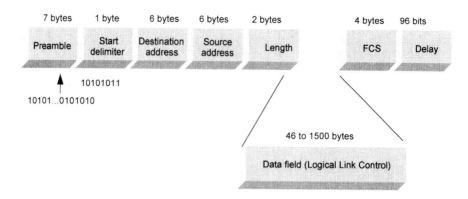

**Figure 3.3** IEEE 802.3 frame format

If the transmission rate is 10Mbps, the time for one bit to be transmitted will be:

$$T = \frac{1}{\text{bit rate}} = \frac{1}{10 \times 10^6} s = 100ns$$

Thus the maximum and minimum times to transmit a frame will be:

$$T_{\max} = (7+1+6+6+2+1500+4+12) \times 8 \times 100ns = 1.2ms$$
$$T_{\min} = (7+1+6+6+2+46+4+12) \times 8 \times 100ns = 0.067\mu s$$

It may be assumed that an electrical signal propagates at about half the speed of light ($c=3\times10^8$m/s). Thus, the time for a bit to propagate a distance of 500m is:

$$T_{500m} = \frac{dist}{speed} = \frac{500}{1.5 \times 10^8} = 3.33\mu s$$

by which time, the number of bits transmitted will be:

$$\text{Number of bits transmitted} = \frac{T_{500m}}{T_{bit}} = \frac{3.33\mu s}{100ns} = 33.33$$

Thus, if two nodes are separated by 500m then it will take more than 33 bits to be transmitted before a node can determine if there has been a collision of the line, as illustrated in Figure 3.4. If the propagation speed is less that this, it will take even longer. This shows the need for the preamble and the requirement for a maximum segment length.

### 3.3.1 Ethernet II

The first standard for Ethernet was Ethernet I. Most currently available systems implement either Ethernet II or IEEE 802.3 (although most networks are now defined as being IEEE 802.3 compliant). An Ethernet II frame is similar to the IEEE 802.3 frame;

it consists of 8 bytes of preamble, 6 bytes of destination address, 6 bytes of source address, 2 bytes of frame type, between 46 and 1500 bytes of data, and 4 bytes of the frame check sequence field.

When the protocol is IPX/SPX the frame type field contains the bit pattern 1000 0001 0011 0111, but when the protocol is TCP/IP the type field contains 0000 1000 0000 0000.

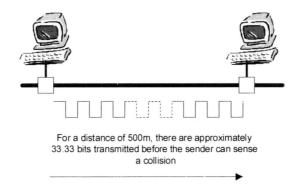

For a distance of 500m, there are approximately
33.33 bits transmitted before the sender can sense
a collision

**Figure 3.4**   Bits transmitted before a collision is detected

## 3.4   IEEE 802.2 and Ethernet SNAP

The LLC is embedded in the Ethernet frame and is defined by the IEEE 802.2 standard. Figure 3.5 illustrates how the LLC field is inserted into the IEEE 802.3 frame. The DSAP and SSAP fields define the types of network protocol used. A SAP code of 1110 0000 identifies the network operating system layer as NetWare, whereas 0000 0110 identifies the TCP/IP protocol. These SAP numbers are issued by the IEEE. The control field is, among other things, for the sequencing of frames.

In some cases, it was difficult to modify networks to be IEEE 802-compliant. Thus, an alternative method was to identify the network protocol, known as Ethernet SNAP (SubNetwork Access Protocol). This was defined to ease the transition to the IEEE 802.2 standard and is illustrated in Figure 3.6. It simply adds an extra two fields to the LLC field to define an organisation ID and a network layer identifier. NetWare allows for either Ethernet SNAP or Ethernet 802.2 (as Novell used Ethernet SNAP to translate to Ethernet 802.2).

Non-compliant protocols are identified with the DSAP and SSAP code of 1010 1010, and a control code of 0000 0011. After these fields:

- Organisation ID which indicates where the company that developed the embedded protocol belongs. If this field contains all zeros it indicates a non-company-specific generic Ethernet frame.
- EtherType field which defines the networking protocol. A TCP/IP protocol uses 0000 1000 0000 0000 for TCP/IP, while NetWare uses 1000 0001 0011 0111. NetWare frames adhering to this specification are known as NetWare 802.2 SNAP.

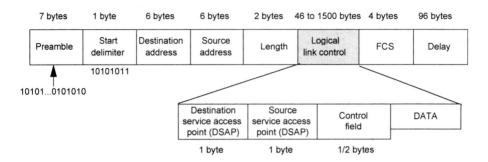

Figure 3.5   Ethernet IEEE 802.3 frame with LLC

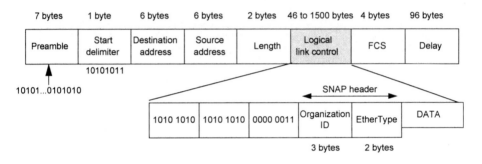

Figure 3.6   Ethernet IEEE 802.3 frame with LLC containing SNAP header

### 3.4.1  LLC protocol

The 802.3 frame provides some of the data link layer functions, such as node address-ing (source and destination MAC addresses), the addition of framing bits (the pream-ble) and error control (the FCS). The rest of the functions of the data link layer are performed with the control field of the LLC field; these functions are:

- Flow and error control. Each data frame sent has a frame number. A control frame is sent from the destination to a source node informing that it has or has not re-ceived the frames correctly.
- Sequencing of data. Large amounts of data are sliced and sent with frame numbers. The spliced data is then reassembled at the destination node.

Figure 3.7 shows the basic format of the LLC frame. There are three principal types of frame: information, supervisory and unnumbered. An information frame contains data, a supervisory frame is used for acknowledgement and flow control, and an unnum-bered frame is used for control purposes. The first two bits of the control field de-termine which type of frame it is. If they are 0X (where X is a don't care) then it is an information frame, 10 specifies a supervisory frame and 11 specifies an unnumbered frame.

An information frame contains a send sequence number in the control field which ranges from 0 to 127. Each information frame has a consecutive number, N(S) (note that there is a roll-over from frame 127 to frame 0). The destination node acknowledges that it has received the frames by sending a supervisory frame. The function of the supervisory frame is specified by the 2-bit S-bit field. This can either be set to Receiver Ready (RR), Receiver Not Ready (RNR) or Reject (REJ). If an RNR function is set then the destination node acknowledges that all frames up to the number stored in the receive sequence number N(R) field were received correctly. An RNR function also acknowledges the frames up to the number N(R), but informs the source node that the destination node wishes to stop communicating. The REJ function specifies that frame N(R) has been rejected and all other frames up to N(R) are acknowledged.

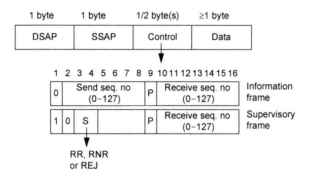

**Figure 3.7**  LLC frame format

---

## 3.5   OSI and the IEEE 802.3 standard

Ethernet fits into the data link and the physical layer of the OSI model. These two layers only deal with the hardware of the network. The data link layer splits into two parts: the LLC and the MAC layer.

The IEEE 802.3 standard splits into three sublayers:

- MAC (media access control).
- Physical signalling (PLS).
- Physical media attachment (PMA).

The interface between PLS and PMA is called the attachment unit interface (AUI) and the interface between PMA and the transmission media is called the media dependent interface (MDI). This grouping into modules allows Ethernet to be very flexible and to support a number of bit rates, signalling methods and media types. Figure 3.8 illustrates how the layers interconnect.

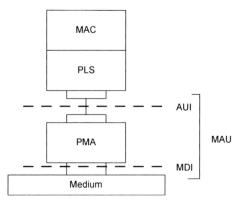

**Figure 3.8**   Organisation of the IEEE 802.3 standard

### 3.5.1  Media access control (MAC)

CSMA/CD is implemented in the MAC layer. The functions of the MAC layers are:

- When sending frames: receive frames from LLC; control whether the data fills the LLC data field, if not add redundant bits; make the number of bytes an integer, and calculate the FCS; add the preamble, SFD and address fields to the frame; send the frame to the PLS in a serial bit stream.
- When receiving frames: receive one frame at a time from the PLS in a serial bit stream; check whether the destination address is the same as the local node; ensure the frame contains an integer number of bytes and the FCS is correct; remove the preamble, SFD, address fields, FCS and remove redundant bits from the LLC data field; send the data to the LLC.
- Avoid collisions when transmitting frames and keep the right distance between frames by not sending when another node is sending; when the medium is free, wait a specified period before starting to transmit.
- Handle any collision that appears by sending a jam signal; generate a random number and back off from sending during that random time.

### 3.5.2  Physical signalling (PLS) and physical medium attachment (PMA)

PLS defines transmission rates, types of encoding/decoding and signalling methods. In PMA a further definition of the transmission media is accomplished, such as coaxial, fiber or twisted-pair. PMA and MDI together form the media attachment unit (MAU), often known as the transceiver.

## 3.6    Ethernet transceivers

Ethernet requires a minimal amount of hardware. The cables used to connect it are typically either unshielded twisted-pair cable (UTP) or coaxial cables. These cables must be terminated with their characteristic impedance, which is 50 Ω for coaxial cables and 100 Ω for UTP cables.

Each node has transmission and reception hardware to control access to the cable and also to monitor network traffic. The transmission/reception hardware is called a transceiver (short for *trans*mitter/re*ceiver*) and a controller builds up and strips down the frame. For 10Mbps Ethernet, the transceiver builds the transmitted bits at a rate of 10 Mbps – thus the time for one bit is $1/10 \times 10^6$, which is 0.1 μs (100 ns).

The Ethernet transceiver transmits onto a single ether. When there are no nodes transmitting, the voltage on the line is +0.7 V. This provides a carrier sense signal for all nodes on the network, it is also known as the heartbeat. If a node detects this voltage then it knows that the network is active and there are no nodes currently transmitting.

Thus, when a node wishes to transmit a message it listens for a quiet period. Then, if two or more transmitters transmit at the same time, a collision results. When they detect a collision, each node transmits a 'jam' signal. The nodes involved in the collision then wait for a random period of time (ranging from 10 to 90 ms) before attempting to transmit again. Each node on the network also awaits for a retransmission. Thus, collisions are inefficient in networks as they stop nodes from transmitting. Transceivers normally detect collisions by monitoring the DC (or average) voltage on the line.

When transmitting, a transceiver unit transmits the preamble of consecutive 1s and 0s. The coding used is a Manchester coding, which represents a 0 as a high to a low voltage transition and a 1 as a low to high voltage transition. A low voltage is –0.7 V and a high is +0.7 V. Thus, when the preamble is transmitted the voltage changes between +0.7 and –0.7 V; as illustrated in Figure 3.9. If after the transmission of the preamble no collisions are detected then the rest of the frame is sent.

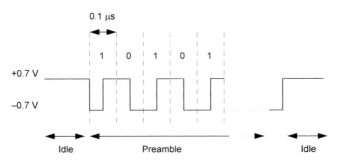

**Figure 3.9** Ethernet digital signal

## 3.7 Ethernet types

The six main types of standard Ethernet are:

- Standard, or thick-wire, Ethernet (10BASE5).
- Thinnet, or thin-wire Ethernet, or Cheapernet (10BASE2).
- Twisted-pair Ethernet (10BASE-T).

- Optical fibre Ethernet (10BASE-FL).
- Fast Ethernet (100BASE-TX and 100VG-Any LAN).
- Gigabit Ethernet (1000BASE-SX, 1000BASE-T, 1000BASE-LX and 1000BASE-CX).

The thin- and thick-wire types connect directly to an Ethernet segment; these are shown in Figure 3.10 and Figure 3.11. Standard Ethernet, 10BASE5, uses a high specification cable (RG-50) and N-type plugs to connect the transceiver to the Ethernet segment. A node connects to the transceiver using a 9-pin D-type connector and a vampire (or bee-sting) connector can be used to clamp the transceiver to the backbone cable.

Thin-wire, or Cheapernet, uses a lower specification cable (it has a lower inner conductor diameter). The cable connector required is also of a lower specification, that is, BNC rather than N-type connectors. In standard Ethernet the transceiver unit is connected directly onto the backbone tap. On a Cheapernet network the transceiver is integrated into the node.

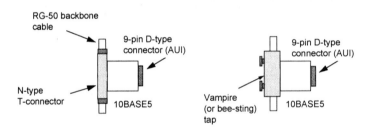

**Figure 3.10**   Ethernet connections for Thick Ethernet

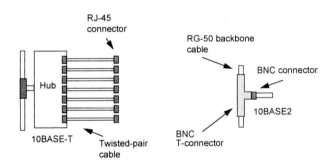

**Figure 3.11**   Ethernet connections for Thin Ethernet and 10BASE-T

Most modern Ethernet connections are to a 10BASE-T hub, which connects UTP cables to the Ethernet segment. An RJ-45 connector is used for 10BASE-T. The fibre optic type, 10BASE-FL, allows long lengths of interconnected lines, typically up to 2 km. They use either SMA connectors or ST connectors. SMA connectors are screw-on types while ST connectors are push-on. Table 3.1 shows the basic specifications for the different types.

Table 3.1   10BASE network parameters

| Parameter | 10BASE5 | 10BASE2 | 10BASE-T |
|---|---|---|---|
| Common name | Standard or thick-wire Ethernet | Thinnet or thin-wire Ethernet | Twisted-pair Ethernet |
| Data rate | 10 Mbps | 10 Mbps | 10 Mbps |
| Maximum segment length | 500 m | 200 m | 100 m |
| Maximum nodes on a segment | 100 | 30 | 3 |
| Maximum number of repeaters | 2 | 4 | 4 |
| Maximum nodes per network | 1024 | 1024 | |
| Minimum node spacing | 2.5 m | 0.5 m | No limit |
| Location of transceiver electronics | located at the cable connection | integrated within the node | in a hub |
| Typical cable type | RG-50 (0.5″ diameter) | RG-6 (0.25″ diameter) | UTP cables |
| Connectors | N-type | BNC | RJ-45/ Telco |
| Cable impedance | 50 Ω | 50 Ω | 100 Ω |

## 3.8   Twisted-pair hubs

Twisted-pair Ethernet (10BASE-T) nodes normally connect to the backbone using a hub, as illustrated in Figure 3.12. Connection to the twisted-pair cable is via an RJ-45 connector. The connection to the backbone can either be to thin- or thick-Ethernet. Hubs are also stackable, with one hub connected to another. This leads to concentrated area networks (CANs) and limits the amount of traffic on the backbone. Twisted-pair hubs normally improve network performance.

10BASE-T uses two twisted-pair cables, one for transmit and one for receive. A collision occurs when the node (or hub) detects that it is receiving data when it is currently transmitting data.

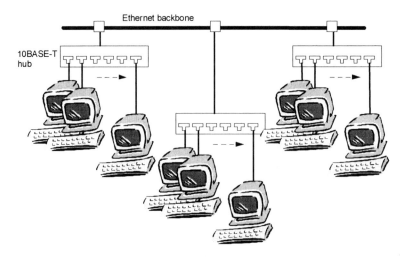

**Figure 3.12** 10BASE-T connection

## 3.9    100 Mbps Ethernet

Standard 10 Mbps Ethernet does not perform well when many users are running multimedia applications. Two improvements to the standard are Fast Ethernet and 100VG-AnyLAN. The IEEE has defined standards for both of them, IEEE 802.3u for Fast Ethernet and 802.12 for 100VG-AnyLAN. They are supported by many manufacturers and use bit rates of 100 Mbps. This gives at least 10 times the performance of standard Ethernet.

New standards relating to 100 Mbps Ethernet are now becoming popular:

- 100BASE-TX (twisted-pair) – which uses 100 Mbps over two pairs of Cat-5 UTP cable or two pairs of Type 1 STP cable.
- 100BASE-T4 (twisted-pair) – which is the physical layer standard for 100 Mbps over Cat-3, Cat-4 or Cat-5 UTP.
- 100VG-AnyLAN (twisted-pair) – which uses 100 Mbps over two pairs of Cat-5 UTP cable or two pairs of Type 1 STP cable.
- 100BASE-FX (fibre-optic cable) – which is the physical layer standard for 100 Mbps over fibre-optic cables.

Fast Ethernet, or 100BASE-T, is simply 10BASE-T running at 10 times the bit rate. It is a natural progression from standard Ethernet and thus allows existing Ethernet networks to be easily upgraded. Unfortunately, as with standard Ethernet, nodes contend for the network, reducing the network efficiency when there are high traffic rates. Also, as it uses collision detect, the maximum segment length is limited by the amount of time for the farthest nodes on a network to properly detect collisions. On a Fast Ethernet network with twisted-pair copper cables this distance is 100 m, and for a fibre-optic link, it is 400 m. Table 3.2 outlines the main network parameters for Fast Ethernet.

**Table 3.2**   Fast Ethernet network parameters

|  | 100BASE-TX | 100VG-AnyLAN |
|---|---|---|
| Standard | IEEE 802.3u | IEEE 802.12 |
| Bit rate | 100 Mbps | 100 Mbps |
| Actual throughput | Up to 50 Mbps | Up to 96 Mbps |
| Maximum distance (hub to node) | 100 m (twisted-pair, CAT-5) 400 m (fibre) | 100 m (twisted-pair, CAT-3) 200 m (twisted-pair, CAT-5) 2 km (fibre) |
| Scaleability | None | Up to 400 Mbps |
| Advantages | Easy migration from 10BASE-T | Greater throughput, greater distance |

Since 100BASE-TX standards are compatible with 10BASE-TX networks then the network allows both 10 Mbps and 100 Mbps bit rates on the line. This makes upgrading simple, as the only additions to the network are dual-speed interface adapters. Nodes with the 100 Mbps capabilities can communicate at 100 Mbps, but they can also communicate with slower nodes, at 10 Mbps.

The basic rules of a 100BASE-TX network are:

- The network topology is a star network and there must be no loops.
- Cat-5 cable is used.
- Up to two hubs can be cascaded in a network.
- Each hub is the equivalent of 5 metres in latency.
- Segment length is limited to 100 metres.
- Network diameter must not exceed 205 metres.

### 3.9.1   100BASE-T4

100BASE-T4 allows the use of standard Cat-3 cables. These contain eight wires made up of four twisted-pairs. 100BASE-4T uses all of the pairs to transmit at 100 Mbps. This differs from 10BASE-T in that 10BASE-T uses only two pairs, one to transmit and one to receive. 100BASE-T allows compatibility with 10BASE-T in that the first two pairs (Pair 1 and Pair 2) are used in the same way as 10BASE-T connections. 100BASE-T then uses the other two pairs (Pair 3 and Pair 4) with half-duplex links between the hub and the node. The connections are illustrated in Figure 3.13.

### 3.9.2   Line code

100BASE-4T uses four separate Cat-3 twisted-pair wires. The maximum clock rate that can be applied to Cat-3 cable is 30 Mbps. Thus, some mechanism must be devised which reduces the line bit rate to under 30 Mbps but give a symbol rate of 100 Mbps. This is achieved with a 3-level code (+, − and 0) and is known as **8B6T**. This code converts eight binary digits into six ternary symbols.

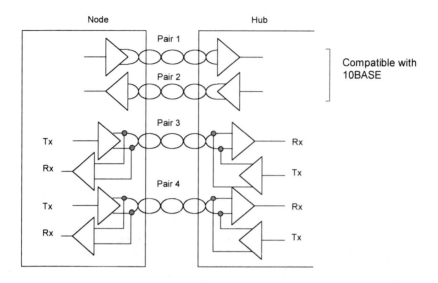

**Figure 3.13** 100BASE-4T connections

The first six codes are:

| Data byte | Code | Data byte | Code | Data byte | Code |
|-----------|------|-----------|------|-----------|------|
| 00000000 | −+0 0−+ | 00000001 | 0−+ −+0 | 00000010 | 0−+ 0−+ |
| 00000011 | 0−+ +0− | 00000100 | −+0 +0− | 00001001 | +0− −+0 |

Thus, the bit sequence 00000000 will be coded as a negative voltage, a positive voltage, a zero voltage, a zero voltage, a negative voltage and a positive voltage.

The maximum base frequency for a 100 Mbps signal will be produced when the input bitstream is 010101010 ...01010. As each bit lasts 10 ns then the period between consecutive levels is 20 ns. Thus, the minimum frequency contained will be 50 MHz. This is greater than the bandwidth of Cat-3 cable, so it would not pass through the cable.

Apart from reducing the frequencies with the digital signal, the 8B6T code has the advantage of reducing the DC content of the signal. Most of the codes contain the same number of positive and negative voltages. This is because only 256 of the possible 729 ($3^6$) codes are actually used. The codes are also chosen to have at least two transitions in every code word, thus the clock information is embedded into the signal.

Unfortunately, it is not possible to have all codes with the same number of negative voltages as positive voltages. Thus, there are some codes that have a different number of negatives and positives, these include:

0100 0001    + 0 − 0 0 +
0111 1001    + + + − 0 −

Most transceiver circuits use a transformer to isolate the external equipment from the computer equipment. These transformers do not allow the passage of DC current. Thus if the line code has a sequence which consecutively has more positives than negatives, the DC current will move away from its zero value. As this does not pass across the transformer, the receive bitstream on the output of the transformer can reduce the amplitude of the received signal (and may thus cause errors). This phenomenon is known as DC wander. A code that has one more positive level than the negative levels is defined as having a weighing of +1.

The technique used to overcome this is to invert consecutive codes that have a weighing of +1. For example, suppose the line code were:

$$+0++-- \quad ++0+-- \quad +++--0 \quad +++--0$$

it would actually be coded as:

$$+0++-- \quad --0-++ \quad +++--0 \quad ---++0$$

The receiver detects the −1 weighted codes as an inverted pattern.

### 3.9.3  100VG-AnyLAN

The 100VG-AnyLAN standard (IEEE 802.12) was developed mainly by Hewlett Packard and overcomes the contention problem by using a priority based round-robin arbitration method, known as demand priority access method (DPAM). Unlike Fast Ethernet, nodes always connect to a hub which regularly scans its input ports to determine whether any nodes have requests pending.

100VG-AnyLAN has the great advantage over 100BASE in that it supports both IEEE 802.3 (Ethernet) and IEEE 802.5 (Token Ring) frames and can thus integrate well with existing 10BASET and Token Ring networks.

100VG-AnyLAN has an in-built priority mechanism with two priority levels: a high priority request and a normal priority request. A normal priority request is used for non-real-time data, such as data files, and so on. High priority requests are used for real-time data, such as speech or video data. At present, there is limited usage of this feature and there is no support mechanism for this facility after the data has left the hub.

100VG-AnyLAN allows up to seven levels of hubs (i.e. one root and six cascaded hubs) with a maximum distance of 150 m between nodes. Unlike other forms of Ethernet, it allows any number of nodes to be connected to a segment.

### Connections

100BASE-TX, 100BASE-T4 and 100VG-AnyLAN use the RJ-45 connector, which has eight connections. 100BASE-TX uses pairs 2 and 3, whereas 100BASE-T4 and 100VG-AnyLAN use pairs 1, 2, 3 and 4. The connections for the cables are defined in Table 3.3. The white/orange colour identifies the cable which is white with an orange stripe, whereas orange/white identifies an orange cable with a white stripe.

**Table 3.3** Cable connections for 100BASE-TX

| Pin | Cable colour | Cable colour | Pair |
|-----|--------------|--------------|--------|
| 1 | white/orange | white/orange | Pair 4 |
| 2 | orange/white | orange/white | Pair 4 |
| 3 | white/green | white/green | Pair 3 |
| 4 | blue/white | blue/white | Pair 3 |
| 5 | white/blue | white/blue | Pair 1 |
| 6 | green/white | green/white | Pair 1 |
| 7 | white/brown | white/brown | Pair 2 |
| 8 | brown/white | brown/white | Pair 2 |

**Migration to Fast Ethernet**

If an existing network is based on standard Ethernet then, in most cases, the best network upgrade is either to Fast Ethernet or 100VG-AnyLAN. Since the protocols and access methods are the same, there is no need to change any of the network management software or application programs. The upgrade path for Fast Ethernet is simple and could be:

- Upgrade high data rate nodes, such as servers or high-powered workstations to Fast Ethernet.
- Gradually upgrade NICs (network interface cards) on Ethernet segments to cards which support both 10BASE-T and 100BASE-T. These cards automatically detect the transmission rate to give either 10 or 100 Mbps.

The upgrade path to 100VG-AnyLAN is less easy as it relies on hubs and, unlike Fast Ethernet, most NICs have different network connectors, one for 10BASE-T and the other for 100VG-AnyLAN (although it is likely that more NICs will have automatic detection). A possible path could be:

- Upgrade high data rate nodes, such as servers or high-powered workstations to 100VG-AnyLAN.
- Install 100VG-AnyLAN hubs.
- Connect nodes to 100VG-AnyLAN hubs and change over connectors.

It is difficult to assess the performance differences between Fast Ethernet and 100VG-AnyLAN. Fast Ethernet uses a well-proven technology, but suffers from network contention. 100VG-AnyLAN is a relatively new technology and the handshaking with the hub increases delay time. The maximum data throughput of a 100BASE-TX network is limited to around 50 Mbps, whereas 100VG-AnyLAN allows rates up to 96 Mbps. 100VG-AnyLAN allows possible upgrades to 400 Mbps.

## 3.10 Comparison of Fast Ethernet other technologies

Table 3.4 compares Fast Ethernet with other types of networking technologies.

**Table 3.4** Comparison of Fast Ethernet with other networking technologies

| | 100VG-AnyLAN (Cat 3, 4, or 5) | 100BASE-T (TX/FX/T4) | FDDI | ATM | Gigabit Ethernet (802.3z) |
|---|---|---|---|---|---|
| Maximum segment length | 100 m | 100 m (Cat-5) 412 m (Fibre) | 2000 m | 200 m (Cat-5) 2000 m (Fibre) | 100 m (Cat 5) 1000 m (Fibre) |
| Maximum network diameter with repeater(s) | 6000 m | 320 m | 100 km | N/A | To be determined by the standard |
| Bitrate | 100 Mbps | 100 Mbps | 100 Mbps | 155 Mbps | 1 Gbps |
| Media access method | Demand Priority | CSMA/CD | Token passing | PVC/SVC | CSMA/CD |
| Maximum nodes on each domain | 1024 | Limited by hub | 500 | N/A | To be determined |
| Frame type | Ethernet and Token Ring | Ethernet | 802.5 | 53-byte cell | Ethernet |
| Multimedia support | ✓ | ✗ | FDDI-I (✗) FDDI-II (✓) | ✓ | YES (with 802.1p) |
| Integration with 10BASE2 | YES with bridges, switches and routers | YES with switches | YES with routers and switches | YES with routers or switches | YES with 10/100 Mbps switching |
| Relative cost | Low | Low | Medium | High | Medium |
| Relative complexity | Low | Low | Medium | High | Low |

## 3.11 Switches and switching hubs

A switch is a very fast, low-latency, multiport bridge that is used to segment LANs. They are typically also used to increase communication rates between segments with multiple parallel conversations and also communication between technologies (such as between FDDI and 100BASE-TX).

A 4-port switching hub is a repeater that contains four distinct network segments (as if there were four hubs in one device). Through software, any of the ports on the hub can directly connect to any of the four segments at any time. This allows for a maximum capacity of 40 Mbps in a single hub.

Ethernet switches overcome the contention problem on normal CSMA/CD networks. They segment traffic by giving each connect a guaranteed bandwidth allocation. Figure 3.14 and Figure 3.15 show the two types of switches; their main features are:

- Desktop switch (or workgroup switch). These connect directly to nodes. They are economical with fixed configurations for end-node connections and are designed for standalone networks or distributed workgroups in a larger network.
- Segment switch. These connect both 10 Mbps workgroup switches and 100 Mbps interconnect (backbone) switches that are used to interconnect hubs and desktop switches. They are modular, high-performance switches for interconnecting workgroups in mid- to large-size networks.

### 3.11.1 Segment switch

A segment switch allows simultaneous communication between any client and any server. A segment switch can simply replace existing Ethernet hubs. Figure 3.15 shows a switch with five ports each transmitting at 10 Mbps; this allows up to five simultaneous connections giving a maximum aggregated bandwidth of 50 Mbps. If the nodes support 100 Mbps communication then the maximum aggregated bandwidth will be 500 Mbps. To optimise the network, nodes should be connected to the switch that connects to the server with which it most often communicates. This allows for a direct connection with that server.

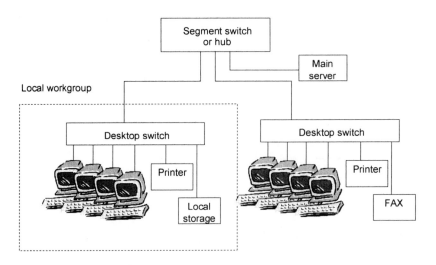

**Figure 3.14** Desktop switch

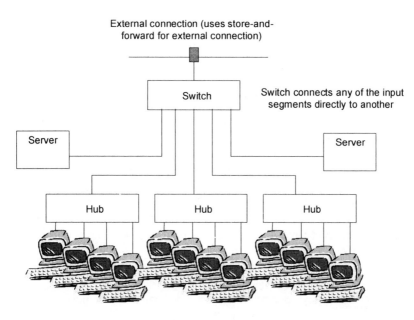

External connection (uses store-and-forward for external connection)

Switch

Switch connects any of the input segments directly to another

Server

Server

Hub

Hub

Hub

**Figure 3.15**   Segment switch

### 3.11.2 Desktop switch

A desktop switch can simply replace an existing 10BASET/100BASET hub. It has the advantage that any of the ports can connect directly to any other. In the network in Figure 3.14, any of the computers in the local workgroup can connect directly to any other, or to the printer, or the local disk drive. This type of switch works well if there is a lot of local traffic, typically between a local server and local peripherals.

### 3.11.3 Store-and-forward switching

Store-and-forwarding techniques have been used extensively in bridges and routers, and are now used with switches. It involves reading the entire Ethernet frame, before forwarding it, with the required protocol and at the correct speed, to the destination port. This has the advantages of:

- Improved error check. Bad frames are blocked from entering a network segment.
- Protocol filtering. Allows the switch to convert from one protocol to another.
- Speed matching. Typically, for Ethernet, reading at 10 Mbps or 100 Mbps and transmitting at 100 Mbps or 10 Mbps. Also, can be used for matching between ATM (155 Mbps), FDDI (100Mbps), Token Ring (4/16 Mbps) and Ethernet (10/100 Mbps).

The main disadvantage is:

- System delay. As the frame must be totally read before it is transmitted there is a delay in the transmission. The improvement in error checking normally overcomes this disadvantage.

### 3.11.4 Switching technology

A switch uses store-and-forward packets to switch between ports. The main technologies used are:

- Shared bus. This method uses a high-speed backplane to interconnect the switched ports. It is frequently used to build modular switches that give a large number of ports, and to interconnect multiple LAN technologies, such as FDDI, 100VG-AnyLAN, 100BASE-T, and ATM.
- Shared memory. These use a common memory area (several MBs) in which data is passed between the ports. It is very common in low-cost, small-scale switches and has the advantage that it can cope with different types of network, which are operating at different speeds. The main types of memory allocation are:

  - Pooled memory. Memory is allocated as it is needed by the ports from a common memory pool.
  - Dedicated shared memory. Memory is fixed and shared by a single pair of I/O ports.
  - Distributed memory. Memory is fixed and dedicated to each port.

## 3.12 NIC design

When receiving data, the NIC copies all data transmitted on the network, decodes it and transfers it to the computer. An Ethernet NIC (network interface card) contains three parts:

- Physical medium interface. The physical medium interface corresponds to the PLS and PMA in the standard and is responsible for the electrical transmission and reception of data. It consists of two parts: the transceiver, which receives and transmits data from or onto the transmission media; and a code converter that encodes/decodes the data. It also recognises a collision on the media.
- Data link controller. The controller corresponds to the MAC layer.
- Computer interface.

It can be split into four main functional blocks:

- Network interface.
- Manchester decoder.
- Memory buffer.
- Computer interface.

### 3.12.1 Network interface

The network interface must listen, recreate the waveform transmitted on the cable into a digital signal and transfer the digital signal to the Manchester decoder. The network interface consists of three parts:

- BNC/RJ-45 connector.
- Reception hardware. The reception hardware translates the waveforms transmitted on the cable to digital signals then copies them to the Manchester decoder.
- Isolator. The isolator is connects directly between the reception hardware and the rest of the Manchester decoder; it guarantees that no noise from the network affects the computer, and vice-versa (as it isolates ground levels).

The reception hardware is called a receiver and is the main component in the network interface. It acts as an earphone, listening and copying the traffic on the cable. Unfortunately, the Ether and transceiver electronics are not perfect. The transmission line contains resistance and capacitance which distort the shape of the bit stream transmitted onto the Ether. Distortion in the system causes pulse spreading, which leads to intersymbol interference. There is also a possibility of noise affecting the digital pulse as it propagates through the cable. Therefore, the receiver also needs to recreate the digital signal and filter noise.

Figure 3.16 shows a block diagram of an Ethernet receiver. The received signal goes through a buffer with high input impedance and low capacitance to reduce the effects of loading on the coaxial cable. An equaliser passes high frequencies and attenuates low frequencies from the network, flattening the network passband. A 4-pole Bessel low-pass filter provides the average dc level from the received signal. The squelch circuit activates the line driver only when it detects a true signal. This prevents noise activating the receiver.

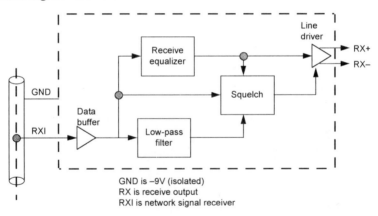

**Figure 3.16**  Ethernet receiver block diagram

### 3.12.2 Manchester decoder

Manchester coding has the advantage of embedding timing (clock) information within the transmitted bits. A positively edged pulse (low → high) represents a 1 and a negatively edged pulse (high → low) a 0, as shown in Figure 3.17. Another advantage of this coding method is that the average voltage is always zero when used with equal positive and negative voltage levels.

Figure 3.18 is an example of transmitted bits using Manchester encoding. The receiver passes the received Manchester-encoded bits through a low-pass filter. This extracts the lowest frequency in the received bit stream, i.e., the clock frequency. With this clock the receiver can then determine the transmitted bit pattern.

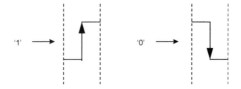

**Figure 3.17** Manchester encoding

For Manchester decoding, the Manchester-encoded signal is first synchronised to the receiver (called bit synchronisation). A transition in the middle of each bit cell is used by a clock recovery circuit to produce a clock pulse in the centre of the second half of the bit cell. In Ethernet the bit synchronisation is achieved by deriving the clock from the preamble field of the frame using a clock and data recovery circuit. Many Ethernet decoders use the SEEQ 8020 Manchester code converter, which uses a phase-locked loop (PLL) to recover the clock. The PLL is designed to lock onto the preamble of the incoming signal within 12-bit cells. Figure 3.19 shows a circuit schematic of bit synchronisation using Manchester decoding and a PLL.

The PLL is a feedback circuit which is commonly used for the synchronisation of digital signals. It consists of a phase detector (such as an EX-OR gate) and a voltage-controlled oscillator (VCO) which uses a crystal oscillator as a clock source.

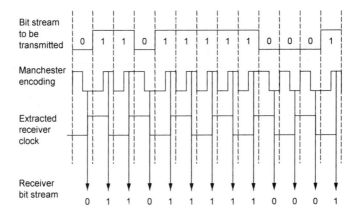

**Figure 3.18** Example of Manchester coding

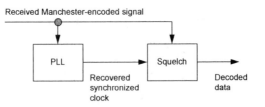

**Figure 3.19** Manchester decoding with bit synchronization

The frequency of the crystal is twice the frequency of the received signal. It is so constant that it only needs irregular and small adjustments to be synchronised to the received signal. The function of the phase detector is to find irregularities between the two signals and adjusts the VCO to minimise the error. This is accomplished by comparing the received signals and the output from the VCO. When the signals have the same frequency and phase the PLL is locked. Figure 3.20 shows the PLL components and the function of the EX-OR.

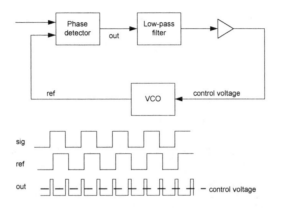

**Figure 3.20** PLL and example waveform for the phase detector

### 3.12.3 Memory buffer

The rate at which data is transmitted on the cable differs from the data rate used by the receiving computer, and the data appears in bursts. To compensate for the difference between the data rate, a first-in first-out (FIFO) memory buffer is used to produce a constant data rate. An important condition is that the average data input rate should not exceed the frequency of the output clock; if this is not the case the buffer will be filled up regardless of its size.

A FIFO is a RAM that uses a queuing technique where the output data appears in the same order that it went in. The input and output are controlled by separate clocks, and the FIFO keeps track of the data that has been written and the data that has been read and can thus be overwritten. This is achieved with a pointer. Figure 3.21 shows a block diagram of the FIFO configuration. The FIFO status is indicated by flags, the empty flag (EF) and the full flag (FF), which show whether the FIFO is either empty or full.

### 3.12.4 Ethernet implementation

The completed circuit for the Ethernet receiver is given in Section 3.16 and is outlined in Figure 3.22. It uses the SEEQ Technologies 82C93A Ethernet transceiver as the receiver and the SEEQ 8020 Manchester code converter which decodes the Manchester code. A transformer and a dc-to-dc converter isolate the SEEQ 82C92A and the network cable from the rest of the circuit (and the computer). The isolated dc-to-dc converter converts a 5 V supply to the −9 V needed by the transceiver.

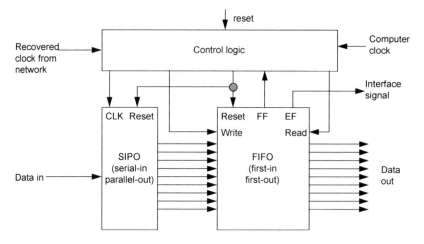

**Figure 3.21** Memory buffering

The memory buffer used is the AMD AM7204 FIFO which has 4096 data words with 9-bit words (but only eight bits are actually used). The output of the circuit is eight data lines, the control lines $\overline{FF}$, $\overline{EF}$, $\overline{RS}$, $\overline{R}$ and $\overline{W}$, and the +5 V and GND supply rails.

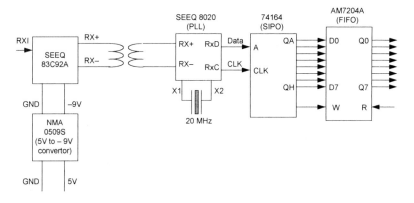

**Figure 3.22** Ethernet receiver

## 3.13 Gigabit Ethernet

The IEEE 802.3 working group initiated the 802.3z Gigabit Ethernet task force to create the Gigabit Ethernet standard (which was finally defined in 1998). The Gigabit Ethernet Alliance (GEA) was founded in May 1996 and promotes Gigabit Ethernet collaboration between organisations. Companies, which were initially involved in the GEA, include: 3Com, Bay Networks, Cisco Systems, Compaq, Intel, LSI Logic, Sun and VLSI.

The amount of available bandwidth for a single segment is massive. For example, almost 125 million characters (125MB) can be sent in a single second. A large reference book with over 1000 pages could be send over a network segment, ten times in a single second. Compare it also with a ×24, CD-ROM drive which transmits at a maximum rate of 3.6MB/s (24×150kB/sec). Gigabit Ethernet operates almost 35 times faster than this drive. With network switches, this bandwidth can be multiplied a given factor, as they allow multiple simultaneous connections.

Gigabit Ethernet is an excellent challenger for network backbones as it interconnects 10/100BASE-T switches, and also provides a high-bandwidth to high-performance servers. Initial aims were:

- Half/full-duplex operation at 1000Mbps.
- Standard 802.3 Ethernet frame format. Gigabit Ethernet uses the same variable-length frame (64- to 1514-byte packets), and thus allows for easy upgrades.
- Standard CSMA/CD access method.
- Compatibility with existing 10BASE-T and 100BASE-T technologies.
- Development of an optional Gigabit Media Independent Interface (GMII).

The compatibility with existing 10/100BASE standards make the upgrading to Gigabit Ethernet much easier, and considerably less risky than changing to other networking types, such as FDDI and ATM. It will happily interconnect with, and autosense, existing slower rated Ethernet devices. Figure 3.23 illustrates the functional elements of Gigabit Ethernet. Its main characteristics are:

- Full-duplex communication. As defined by the IEEE 802.3x specification, two nodes connected via a full-duplex, switched path can simultaneously send and receive frames. Gigabit Ethernet supports new full-duplex operating modes for switch-to-switch and switch-to-end-station connections, and half-duplex operating modes for shared connections using repeaters and the CSMA/CD access method.
- Standard flow control. Gigabit Ethernet uses standard Ethernet flow control to avoid congestion and overloading. When operating in half-duplex mode, Gigabit Ethernet adopts the same fundamental CSMA/CD access method to resolve contention for the shared media.
- Enhanced CSMA/CD method. This maintains a 200 m collision diameter at gigabit speeds. Without this, small Ethernet packets could complete their transmission before the transmitting node could sense a collision, thereby violating the CSMA/CD method. To resolve this issue, both the minimum CSMA/CD carrier time and the Ethernet slot time (the time, measured in bits, required for a node to detect a collision) have been extended from 64 bytes (which is 51.2µs for 10BASE and 5.12µs for 100BASE) to 512 bytes (which is 4.1µs for 1000BASE). The minimum frame length is still 64 bytes. Thus, frames smaller than 512 bytes have a new carrier extension field following the CRC field. Packets larger than 512 bytes are not extended.
- Packet bursting. The slot time changes effect the small-packet performance, but this has been offset by a new enhancement to the CSMA/CD algorithm, called packet bursting. This allows servers, switches and other devices to send bursts of small packets in order to fully utilise the bandwidth.

Devices operating in full-duplex mode (such as switches and buffered distributors) are not subject to the carrier extension, slot time extension or packet bursting changes. Full-duplex devices use the regular Ethernet 96-bit interframe gap (IFG) and 64-byte minimum frame size.

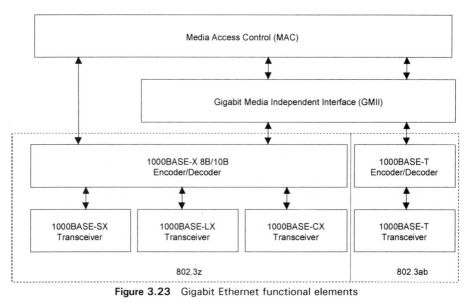

**Figure 3.23**  Gigabit Ethernet functional elements

### 3.13.1 Ethernet transceiver

The IEEE 802.3z task force spent much of their time defining the Gigabit Ethernet standard for the transceiver (physical layer), which is responsible for the mechanical, electrical and procedural characteristics for establishing, maintaining and deactivating the physical link between network devices. The physical layers are:

- 1000BASE-SX (Low cost, multi-mode fibre cables). These can be used for short interconnections and short backbone networks. The IEEE 802.3z task force have tried to integrate the new standard with existing cabling, whether it be twisted-pair cable, coaxial cable or fibre optic cable. These tests involved firing lasers in long lengths of multi-mode fibre cables. Through these test it was found that a jitter component results which is caused by a phenomenon known as differential mode delay (DMD). The 1000BASE-SX standard has resolved this by defining the launch of the laser signal, and enhanced conformance tests. Typical maximum lengths are: 62.5 μm, multi-mode fibre (up to 220 m) and 50 μm, multi-mode fibre (550 m).
- 1000BASE-LX (Multi-mode/single mode-mode fibre cables). These can be used for longer runs, such as on backbones and campus networks. Single-mode fibres are covered by the long-wavelength standard, and provide for greater distances. External patch cords are used to reduce DMD. Typical lengths are: 62.5 μm, multi-mode fibre (up to 550 m), 50 μm, multi-mode fibre (up to 550 m) and 50 μm, single-mode fibre (up to 5 km).

- 1000BASE-CX (Shielded Balanced Copper). This standard supports interconnection of equipment using a copper-based cable, typically up to 25 m. As with the 1000BASE-LX/SX standards, it uses the Fibre Channel-based 8B/10B coding to give a serial line rate of 1.25 Gbps. The 1000BASE-T is likely to supersede this standard, but it has been relatively easy to define, and to implement.
- 1000BASE-T (UTP). This is a useful standard for connecting directly to workstations. The 802.3ab Task Force has been assigned the task of defining the 1000BASE-T physical layer standard for Gigabit Ethernet over four pairs of Cat-5 UTP cable, for cable distances of up to 100 m, or networks with a diameter of 200 m. As it can be used with existing cabling, it allows easy upgrades. Unfortunately, it requires new technology and new coding schemes in order to meet the potentially difficult and demanding parameters set by the previous Ethernet and Fast Ethernet standards.

### 3.13.2 Fibre Channel components

The IEEE 802.3 committee based much of the physical layer technology on the ANSI-backed X3.230 Fibre Channel project. This allowed many manufacturers to re-use physical-layer Fibre Channel components for new Gigabit Ethernet designs, and has allowed a faster development time than is normal, and increased the volume production of the components. These include optical components and high-speed 8B/10B encoders.

The 1000BASE-T standard uses enhanced DSP (Digital Signal Processing) and enhanced silicon technology to enable Gigabit Ethernet over UTP cabling. As Figure 3.23 shows, it does not use the 8B/10B encoding.

### 3.13.3 Buffered distributors

Along with repeaters, bridges and switches, a new device called a buffered distributor (or full-duplex repeater) has been developed for Gigabit Ethernet. It is a full-duplex, multiport, hub-like device that connects two or more Gigabit Ethernet segments. Unlike a bridge, and like a repeater, it forwards all the Ethernet frames from one segment to the others, but unlike a standard repeater, a buffered distributor buffers one, or more, incoming frames on each link before forwarding them. This reduces collisions on connected segments. The maximum bandwidth for a buffered distributor will still only be 1 Gbps, as opposed to Gigabit switches which allow multi-Gigabit bandwidths.

### 3.13.4 Quality of Service

Many, real-time, networked applications require a given Quality of Server (QoS), which might relate to bandwidth requirements, latency (network delays) and jitter. Unfortunately, there is nothing built into Ethernet that allows for a QoS, thus new techniques have been developed to overcome this. These include:

- RSVP. Allows nodes to request and guarantee a QoS, and works at a higher-level to Ethernet. For this, each network component in the chain must support RSVP and communicate appropriately. Unfortunately, this may require an extensive investment to totally support RSVP, thus many vendors have responded in implementing proprietary schemes, which may make parts of the network vendor-specific.

- IEEE 802.1p and IEEE 802.1Q. Allows a QoS over Ethernet by 'tagging' packets with an indication of the priority or class of service desired for the frames. These tags allow applications to communicate the priority of frames to internetworking devices. RSVP support can be achieved by mapping RSVP sessions into 802.1p service classes.
- Routing. Implemented at a higher layer.

### 3.13.5 Gigabit Ethernet migration

The greatest advantage of Gigabit Ethernet is that it is easy to upgrade existing Ethernet-based networks to higher bit rates. Typical migration might be:

- Switch-to-switch links. Involves upgrading the connections between switches to 1Gbps. As 1000BASE switches support both 100BASE and 1000BASE then not all the switches require to be upgraded at the same time; this allows for gradual migration.
- Switch-to-Server links. Involves upgrading the connection between a switch and the server to 1Gbps. The server requires an upgraded Gigabit Ethernet interface card.
- Switched Fast Ethernet Backbone. Involves upgrading a Fast Ethernet backbone switch to a 100/1000BASE switch. It thus supports both 100BASE and 1000BASE switching, using existing cabling.
- Shared FDDI Backbone. Involves replacing FDDI attachments on the ring with Gigabit Ethernet switches or repeaters. Gigabit Ethernet uses the existing fibre-optic cable, and provides a greatly increased segment bandwidth.
- Upgrade NICs on nodes to 1Gbps. It is unlikely that users will require 1Gbps connections, but this facility is possible.

### 3.13.6 1000BASE-T

One of the greatest challenges of Gigabit Ethernet is to use existing Cat-5 cables, as this will allow fast upgrades. Two critical parameters, which are negligible at 10BASE speeds, are:

- Return loss. Defines the amount of signal energy that is reflected back towards the transmitter due to impedance mismatches in the link (typically from connector and cable bends).
- Far-End Crosstalk. Noise that is leaked from another cable pair.

The 1000BASE-T Task Force estimates that less than 10% of the existing Cat-5 cable were improperly installed (as defined in ANSI/TIA/EIA568-A in 1995) and might not support 1000BASE-T (or even, 100BASE-TX). 100BASE-T uses two pairs, one for transmit and one for receive, and transmits at a symbol rate of 125Mbaud with a 3-level code. 1000BASE-T uses:

- All four pairs with a symbol rate of 125 Mbaud (symbols/sec). One symbol contains two bits of information.
- Each transmitted pulse uses a 5-level PAM (Pulse Amplitude Modulation) line code, which allows two bits to be transmitted at a time.

- Simultaneous send and receive on each pair. Each connection uses a hybrid circuit to split the send and receive signals.
- Pulse shaping. Matches the characteristics of the transmitted signal to the channel so that the signal-to-noise ratio is minimised. It effectively reduces low frequency terms (which contain little data information, can cause distortion and cannot be passed over the transformer-coupled hybrid circuit), reduces high frequency terms (which increases crosstalk) and rejects any external high-frequency noise. It is thought that the transmitted signal spectrum for 1000BASE will be similar to 100BASE.
- Forward Error Correction (FEC). This provides a second level of coding that helps to recover the transmitted symbols in the presence of high noise and crosstalk. The FEC bit uses the fifth level of the 5-level PAM.

A 5-level code (–2, –1, 0, +1, +2) allows two bits to be sent at a time, if all four pairs are used then eight bits are sent at a time. If each pair transmits at a rate of 125Mbaud (symbols/sec), the resulting bit rate will be 1Gbps.

## 3.14 Exercises

**3.14.1**  The base bit rate of standard Ethernet is:

|     |         |     |          |
|-----|---------|-----|----------|
| (a) | 1 kbps  | (b) | 1 Mbps   |
| (c) | 10 Mbps | (d) | 100 Mbps |

**3.14.2**  The base bit rate of Fast Ethernet is:

|     |         |     |          |
|-----|---------|-----|----------|
| (a) | 1 kbps  | (b) | 1 Mbps   |
| (c) | 10 Mbps | (d) | 100 Mbps |

**3.14.3**  Standard Ethernet (Thick-wire Ethernet) is also known as:

|     |          |     |           |
|-----|----------|-----|-----------|
| (a) | 10BASE2  | (b) | 10BASE5   |
| (c) | 10BASE-T | (d) | 10BASE-FL |

**3.14.4**  Thin-wire Ethernet (Cheapernet) is also known as:

|     |          |     |           |
|-----|----------|-----|-----------|
| (a) | 10BASE2  | (b) | 10BASE5   |
| (c) | 10BASE-T | (d) | 10BASE-FL |

**3.14.5**  Standard Ethernet (Thick-wire Ethernet) uses which type of cable:

|     |                   |     |               |
|-----|-------------------|-----|---------------|
| (a) | Twisted-pair cable | (b) | Coaxial cable |
| (c) | Fibre optic cable | (d) | Radio link    |

**3.14.6**  Thin-wire Ethernet (Cheapernet) uses which type of cable:

(a)     Twisted-pair cable     (b)     Coaxial cable
(c)     Fibre optic cable      (d)     Radio link

**3.14.7**     The IEEE standard for Ethernet is:

(a)     IEEE 802.1     (b)     IEEE 802.2
(c)     IEEE 802.3     (d)     IEEE 802.4

**3.14.8**     The main disadvantage of Ethernet is that:

(a)     Computers must contend for the network.
(b)     It does not network well.
(c)     It is unreliable.
(d)     It is not secure.

**3.14.9**     A MAC address has how many bits:

(a)     8 bits     (b)     24 bits
(c)     32 bits    (d)     48 bits

**3.14.10**     Which bit pattern identifies the start of an Ethernet frame:

(a)     11001100...1100     (b)     00000000...0000
(c)     11111111...1111     (d)     10101010...1010

**3.14.11**     The main standards relating to Ethernet networks are:

(a)     IEEE 802.2 and IEEE 802.3
(b)     IEEE 802.3 and IEEE 802.4
(c)     ANSI X3T9.5 and IEEE 802.5
(d)     EIA RS-422 and IEEE 802.3

**3.14.12**     Which layer in the Ethernet standard communicates with the OSI network layer:

(a)     the MAC layer        (b)     the LLC layer
(c)     the Physical layer   (d)     the Protocol layer

**3.14.13**     Standard, or Thick-wire, Ethernet is also known as:

(a)     10BASE2     (b)     10BASE5
(c)     10BASE-T    (d)     10BASE-F

**3.14.14**     Twisted-pair Ethernet is also known as:

(a)     10BASE2     (b)     10BASE5
(c)     10BASE-T    (d)     10BASE-FL

**3.14.15**     Fibre optic Ethernet is also known as:

(a)     10BASE2    (b)     10BASE5

(c)     10BASE-T   (d)     10BASE-F

**3.14.16**    Which type of connector does twisted-pair Ethernet use when connecting to a network hub:

(a)     N-type    (b)     BNC

(c)     RJ-45     (d)     SMA

**3.14.17**    Which type of connector does Cheapernet, or thin-wire Ethernet, use when connecting to the network backbone:

(a)     N-type    (b)     BNC

(c)     RJ-45     (d)     SMA

**3.14.18**    What is the function of a repeater in an Ethernet network:

(a)     It increases the bit rate

(b)     It isolates network segments

(c)     It prevents collisions

(d)     It boosts the electrical signal

**3.14.19**    Discuss the limitations of 10BASE5 and 10BASE2 Ethernet.

**3.14.20**    Discuss the main reasons for the preamble in an Ethernet frame.

**3.14.21**    Discuss 100 Mbps Ethernet technologies with respect to how they operate and their typical parameters.

**3.14.22**    Explain the usage of Ethernet SNAP.

**3.14.23**    State the main advantage of Manchester coding and show the line code for the bit sequence:

0111101010110101010001011010

**3.14.24**    Explain the main functional differences between 100BASE-T, 100BASE-4T and 100VG-AnyLAN.

**3.14.25**    Prove that the maximum length of segment that can be used with 10 Mbps Ethernet is 840 metres. Assume that the propagation speed is $1.5\times10^8$ m/s and the length of the preamble is 56 bits. Note, a collision must be detected by the end of the transmission of the preamble. Also, why might the maximum length of the segment be less than this?

**3.14.26**    What problem might be encountered with Fast Ethernet, with respect to the maximum segment length?

## 3.15 Ethernet crossover connections

The standard connections for 10BASE and 100BASE is given below:

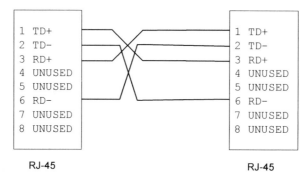

```
1 TD+                    1 TD+
2 TD-                    2 TD-
3 RD+                    3 RD+
4 UNUSED                 4 UNUSED
5 UNUSED                 5 UNUSED
6 RD-                    6 RD-
7 UNUSED                 7 UNUSED
8 UNUSED                 8 UNUSED
```

RJ-45                               RJ-45

where RD is the receive signals (this is known as RECEIVE in 100BASE) and TD the transmit signals (TRANSMIT). These cable connections are difficult to set-up and most connections use a straight through connection (as given in Table 3.3). Ports which have the cross-over connection internal in the port are marked with an "X".

The standard connections for 100BASE-T4 is given below:

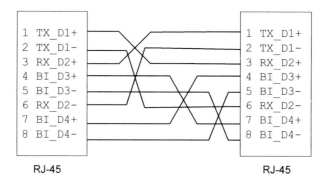

```
1 TX_D1+                 1 TX_D1+
2 TX_D1-                 2 TX_D1-
3 RX_D2+                 3 RX_D2+
4 BI_D3+                 4 BI_D3+
5 BI_D3-                 5 BI_D3-
6 RX_D2-                 6 RX_D2-
7 BI_D4+                 7 BI_D4+
8 BI_D4-                 8 BI_D4-
```

RJ-45                               RJ-45

where BI represents the bi-directional transmission signals, TX the transmit signals and RX the receive signals. These cable connections are difficult to set-up and most connections use a straight through connection (as given in Table 3.3). Ports which have the cross-over connection internal in the port are marked with an "X".

## 3.16 Ethernet monitoring system

The schematic below shows an Ethernet monitoring system. Its component values are:

R1 = 1 kΩ     R2 = 500 Ω     R3 = 10 MΩ     R4 = 39 Ω     R5 = 1.5 kΩ
R6 = 10 Ω     L1 = 1:1, 200 μH   C1 = 100 mF     C2 = 0.1 μF     C3 = 1.5 pF
XTAL = 20 MHz

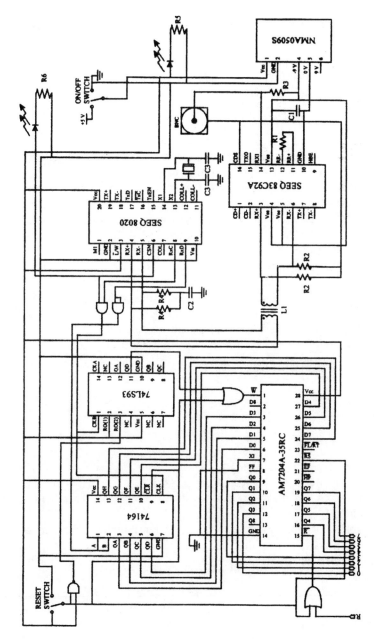

# 4 Token Ring

## 4.1 Introduction

Token Ring networks were developed by several manufacturers, the most prevalent being the IBM Token Ring. Unlike Ethernet, they cope well with high network traffic loadings, and were at one time extremely popular but their popularity has since been overtaken by Ethernet. Token Ring networks have, in the past, suffered from network management problems and poor network fault tolerance.

Token Ring networks are well suited to situations which have large amounts of traffic and also work well with most traffic loadings. They are not suited to large networks or networks with physically remote stations. The main advantage of Token Ring is that it copes better with high traffic rates than Ethernet, but requires a great deal of maintenance, especially when faults occur or when new equipment is added to or removed from the network. Many of these problems have now been overcome by MAUs (multistation access units), which are similar to the hubs using in Ethernet.

The IEEE 802.5 standard specifies the MAC layer for a Token Ring network with a bit rate of either 4 Mbps or 16 Mbps. There are two main types of Token Ring networks. Type 1 Token Ring uses Type 1 Token Ring cable (shielded twisted-pair) with IBM style universal connectors. Type 3 Token Ring networks use either Cat-3, Cat-4 or Cat-5 unshielded twisted-pair cables with modular connectors. Cat-3 has the advantage of being cheap to install and is typically used in telephone connections. Unfortunately, the interconnection distance is much less than for Cat-4 and Cat-5 cables.

## 4.2 Operation

A Token Ring network circulates an electronic token (named a control token) around a closed electronic loop. Each node on the network reads the token and repeats it to the next node. The control token circulates around the ring even when there is no data being transmitted.

Nodes on a Token Ring network wishing to transmit must await a token. When they get it, they fill a frame with data and add the source and destination addresses then send it to the next node. The data frame then circulates around the ring until it reaches the destination node. It then reads the data into its local memory area (or buffer) and marks an acknowledgement on the data frame. This then circulates back to the source (or originating) node. When it receives the frame, it tests it to determine whether it contains an acknowledgement. If it does then the source node knows that the data frame was received correctly, else the node is not responding. If the source node has finished transmitting data then it transmits a new token, which can be used by other nodes on the ring.

Figure 4.1(a)–(d) shows a typical interchange between node B and node A. Initially, in (a), the control token circulates between all the nodes. This token does not contain any data and is only three bytes long. When node B finally receives the control token it then transmits a data frame, as illustrated in (b). This data frame is passed to node C, then to node D and finally onto A. Node A then reads the data in the data frame and returns an acknowledgement to node B, as illustrated in (c). After node B receives the acknowledgement, it passes a control token onto node C and this then circulates until a node wishes to transmit a data frame. No nodes are allowed to transmit data unless they have received a valid control token. A distributed control protocol determines the sequence in which nodes transmit. This gives each node equal access to the ring.

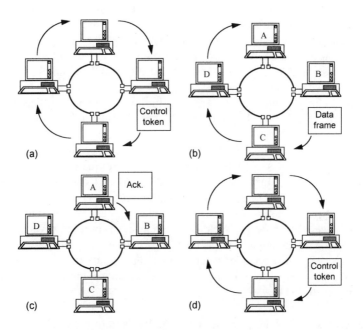

**Figure 4.1** Example data exchange

## 4.3    Token Ring - media access control (MAC)

Token passing allows nodes controlled access to the ring. Figure 4.2 shows the token format for the IEEE 802.5 specification. There are two main types of frame: a control token and a data frame. A control token contains only a start and end delimiter, and an access control (AC) field. A data frame has start and end delimiters (SD/ED), an access control field, a frame control field (CF), a destination address (DA), a source address (SA), frame check sequence (FCS), data and a frame status field (FS).

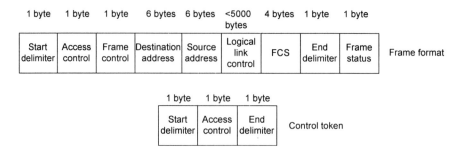

**Figure 4.2** IEEE 802.5 frame format

The access control and frame control fields contain information necessary for managing access to the ring. This includes priority reservation, priority information and information on whether the data is user data or control information. It also contains an express indicator which informs networked nodes that an individual node requires immediate action from the network management node.

The destination and source addresses are both 6 bytes long. Logical link control information has variable length and is shown in Figure 4.2. It can either contain user data or network control information.

The frame check sequence (FCS) is a 32-bit cyclic redundancy check (CRC) and the frame control field is used to indicate whether a destination node has read the data in the token.

The start and end delimiters are special bit sequences which define the start and end of the frame and thus cannot occur anywhere within the frame. As with Ethernet the bits are sent using Manchester coding. The start and end delimiters violate the standard coding scheme. The standard Manchester coding codes a 1 as a low-to-high transition and a 0 as a high-to-low transition. In the start and end delimiters, two of the bits within the delimiters are set to either a high level (H) or a low level (L). These bits disobey the standard coding as there is no change in level, i.e. from a high to a low or a low to a high. When the receiver detects this violation and the other standard coded bits in the received bit pattern, it knows that the accompanying bits are a valid frame. The coding is as follows:

- If the preceding bit is a 1 then the start delimiter is HL0HL000, else
- If the preceding bit is a 0 then the start delimiter is LH0LH000.

These are shown in Figure 4.3. The end delimiter is similar to the start delimiter, but 0's are replaced by 1's. An error detection bit (E) and a last packet indicator bit (I) are also added. If the bit preceding the end delimiter is a 1 then the end delimiter is HL1HL1IE. If it is a 0 then it is LH1LH1IE. The E bit is used for error detection and is initially set by the originator to a 0. If any of the nodes on the ring detects an error, the E bit is set to a 1. This indicates to the originator that the frame has developed an error as it was sent. The I bit determines whether the data being sent in a frame is the last in a series of data frames. If the I bit is a 0 then it is the last, else it is an intermediate frame.

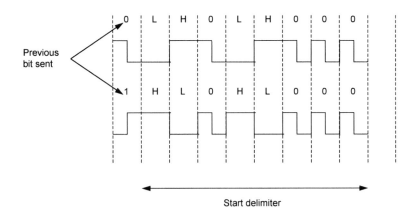

**Figure 4.3** Start delimiter

The access control field controls the access of nodes on the ring. It takes the form of PPPTMRRR, where:

PPP — indicates the priority of the token; this indicates which type of token the destination node can transmit.

T — is the token bit and is used to discriminate between a control token and a data token.

M — is the monitor bit and is used by an active ring monitor node to stop tokens from circulating around a network continuously.

RRR — are the reservation bits and allow nodes with a high priority to request the next token.

The frame control field contains control information for the MAC layer. It takes the form FFDDDDDD, where:

FF indicates whether the frame is a data frame; if it is not then the DDDDDD bits control the operation of the Token Ring MAC protocol.

DDDDDD controls the operation of the Token Ring MAC protocol.

The source and destination addresses can either be two or six bytes (that is, 16 or 48 bits) in length. This size must be the same for all nodes on a ring. The first bit specifies the type of address. If it is a 0 then the address is an individual node address, else it is a group address. An individual node address is used to transmit to a single node, whereas a group address transmits to all nodes with the same group address. The source address will always by an individual address as it indicates the node which originated the token. A special destination address of all 1's is used to transmit to all nodes on a ring (broadcast).

The frame status field contains information on how a frame has been operated upon as it circulates round the ring. It takes the form ACXXACXX, where:

A — indicates if the destination address has been recognised. It is initially set to a

0 by the source node and is set to a 1 when the destination reads the data. If the source node detects that this bit has not been set then it knows the destination is either not present on the network or is not responding.

c – indicates that a destination node has copied a frame into its memory. This bit is also initially set to a 0 by the source node. When the destination node reads the data from the frame it is set to a 1. By testing this bit and the A bit, the source node can determine whether the destination node is active but not reading data from the frame.

## 4.4 Token Ring maintenance

A Token Ring system requires considerable maintenance; it must perform the following functions:

- Ring initialisation – when the network is started, or after the ring has been broken, it must be reinitialised. A co-operative decentralised algorithm sorts out which nodes start a new token, which goes next, and so on.
- Adding to the ring – if a new node is to be physically connected to the ring then the network must be shut down and reinitialised.
- Deletion from the ring – a node can disconnect itself from the ring by joining together its predecessor and its successor. Again, the network may have to be shut down and reinitialised.
- Fault management – typical Token Ring errors occur when two nodes think it is their turn to transmit or when the ring is broken as no node thinks that it is their turn.

## 4.5 Token Ring multistation access units (MAUs)

The problems of connecting and deleting nodes to or from a ring network are significantly reduced with a multistation access unit (MAU). Figure 4.4 shows two 3-way MAUs connected to produce a 6-node network. Normally, a MAU allows nodes to be switched in and out of a network using a changeover switch or by automatic electronic switching (known as auto-loopback). This has the advantage of not shutting down the network when nodes are added and deleted or when they develop faults.

If the changeover switches in Figure 4.4 are in the down position then the node is bypassed; if they are in the up position then the node connects to the ring. A single coaxial (or twisted-pair) cable connects one MAU to another and two coaxial (or twisted-pair) cables connect a node to the MAU (for the in ports and the out ports). Most modern application use STP cables.

The IBM 8228 is a typical passive MAU. It can operate at 4 Mbps or 16 Mbps and has 10 connection ports, i.e. eight passive node ports along with ring in (RI) and ring out (RO) connections. The maximum distance between MAUs is typically 650 m (at 4 Mbps) and 325 m (at 16 Mbps).

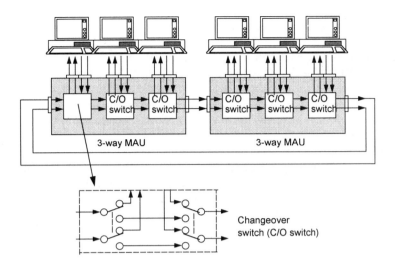

**Figure 4.4** Six-node Token Ring network with two MAUs

Most MAUs either have two, four or eight ports and can automatically detect the speed of the node (i.e. either 4 or 16 Mbps). Figure 4.5 shows a 32-node Token Ring network using four 8-port MAUs. Typical connectors are RJ-45 and IBM Type A connectors. The ring cable is normally either twisted-pair (Type 3), fibre-optic or coaxial cable (Type 1). MAU are intelligent devices and can detect faults on the cables supplying nodes then isolate them from the rest of the ring. Most MAUs are passive devices in that they do not require a power supply. If there are large distances between nodes then an active unit is normally used.

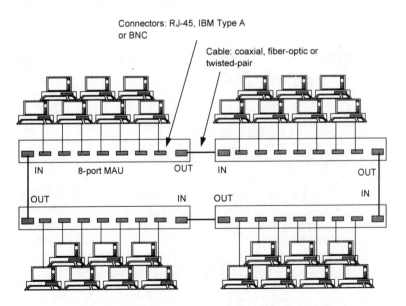

**Figure 4.5** A 32-node Token Ring network with 4 MAUs

## 4.6    Cabling and connectors

There are two main types of cabling used in Token Ring networks: Type 1 and Type 3. Type 1 uses STP (shielded twisted-pair) cables with IBM style male-female connectors. Type 3 networks uses Cat-3 or Cat-5 UTP (unshielded twisted-pair) cables with RJ-45 connectors. Unfortunately, Cat-3 cables are unshielded which reduces the maximum length of the connection. Type 1 networks can connect up to 260 nodes, whereas Type 3 networks can only connect up to 72 nodes.

A further source of confusion comes from the two different types of modern STP cables used in Token Ring networks. IBM type 1 cable has four cores with a screen tinned copper braid around them. Each twisted-pair is screened from each other with aluminised polyester tape. The characteristic impedance of the twisted-pairs is 150 $\Omega$. The IBM type 6 cable is a lightweight cable which is preferred in office environments. It has a similar construction but, because it has a thinner core, signal loss is higher.

## 4.7    Repeaters

A repeater is used to increase either main-ring or lobe lengths in a Token Ring LAN. The main-ring length is the distance between MAUs. The lobe length is the distance from an MAU to a node. Table 4.1 shows some typical maximum cable lengths for different bit rates and cable types. Fibre-optic cables provide the longest distances with a range of 1 km. The next best are STP cables, followed by Cat-5 and finally the lowest specification Cat-3 cables. Figure 4.6 shows the connection of two MAUs with repeaters. In this case, four repeaters are required as each repeater has only two ports (IN and OUT). The token will circulate clockwise around the network.

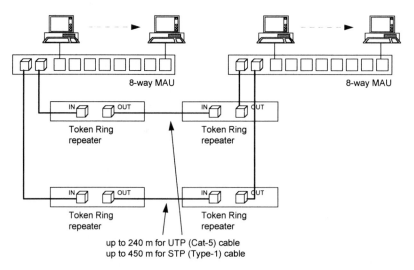

**Figure 4.6**    16-node Token Ring network with repeaters

**Table 4.1** Typical maximum cable lengths for different cables and bit rates

| Type | Bit rate | Cable type | Maximum distance |
|------|----------|------------|------------------|
| Type 1 | 4 Mbps | STP | 730 m |
| Type 3 | 4 Mbps | UTP (Cat-3 cable) | 275 m |
| Type 3 | 16 Mbps | UTP (Cat-5 cable) | 240 m |
| Type 1 | 16 Mbps | STP | 450 m |
| Type 1 | 16 Mbps | Fibre | 1000 m |

## 4.8  Jitter suppression

Jitter can be a major problem with Token Ring networks. It is caused when the nodes on the network operate with different clock rate and can lead to network slowdown, data corruption and station loss. Jitter is the reason that the number of nodes on a Token Ring is limited to 72 at 16 Mbps. With a jitter suppressor the number of nodes can be increased to 256 nodes. It also allows Cat-3 cable to be used at 16 Mbps. Normally a Token Ring Jitter Suppresser is connected to a group of MAUs. Thus, the network in Figure 4.6 could have one jitter suppresser unit connected to two of the MAUs (this would obviously limit to 7 the number of nodes connected to these MAUs).

## 4.9  Exercises

**4.9.1**    The main international specification for Token Ring is:

(a)    IEEE 802.2        (b)    IEEE 802.3
(c)    IEEE 802.4        (d)    IEEE 802.5

**4.9.2**    The main advantage that Token Ring has over Ethernet is:

(a)    It allows easier connection of computers
(b)    It allows for larger networks
(c)    It allows all computers an equal share of the network
(d)    It is more reliable

**4.9.3**    The main disadvantage of a Token Ring network is:

(a)    It is difficult to add and delete nodes from the network
(b)    It is limited in the number of computers that can connect to the network
(c)    It is difficult to interface to
(d)    It is expensive

**4.9.4**    The main function of a MAU is:

  (a)    To reduce contention on the network
  (b)    To reduce jitter problems
  (c)    To increase the bit rate
  (d)    To allow easy addition and deletion to the ring

**4.9.5**    How does a node acknowledge that it has received the data frame:

  (a)    It sends a special control token
  (b)    It sets an acknowledgement bit at the end of the data frame
  (c)    It deletes the data frame from the ring
  (d)    It sends a control token with its address in it

**4.9.6**    How are lost tokens dealt with:

  (a)    Computers wait a given time and then transmit a control token
  (b)    Computers wait a random time and then transmit a control token
  (c)    A ring management computer is responsible for generating new tokens, or deleting multiple tokens
  (d)    Computers generate a message for the system manager to initiate a new token

**4.9.7**    Outline the main advantages and disadvantages of a Token Ring network.

**4.9.8**    Discuss how Token Ring defines the start and end delimiters.

**4.9.9**    Discuss the main problems of a Token Ring network and describe some methods which can be used to overcome them.

**4.9.10**    Discuss how 4-core STP cables are screened to prevent crosstalk between the two pairs.

**4.9.11**    Discuss the main advantages of MAUs in a Token Ring network.

**4.9.12**    For twisted-pair cable the speed of propagation is 59% of the speed of light ($3\times10^8$ m.s$^{-1}$), determine the amount of time it takes a bit to go round a 1km ring.

## 4.10  Note from the author

*Ring-based networks have always out-performed contention-based networks (such as Ethernet), but they suffer from many problems, especially in adding and deleting stations to/from the ring, finding faults, and in start-up and shutting-down the ring. These have partly been overcome with MAUs, but the ring still needs a great deal of high-level management. Luckily, the FDDI standard has overcome the main problems.*

# 5 FDDI

## 5.1 Introduction

A token-passing mechanism allows orderly access to a network. Apart from Token Ring the most commonly used token-passing network is the Fibre Distributed Data Interchange (FDDI) standard. This operates at 100 Mbps and, to overcome the problems of line breaks, has two concentric Token Rings, as illustrated in Figure 5.1. Fibre optic cables have a much higher specification than copper cables and allow extremely long connections. The maximum circumference of the ring is 100 km (62 miles), with a maximum 2 km between stations (FDDI nodes are also known as stations). It is thus an excellent mechanism for connecting networks across a city or over a campus. Up to 500 stations can connect to each ring with a maximum of 1000 stations for the complete network. Each station connected to the FDDI highway can be a normal station or a bridge to a conventional local area network, such as Ethernet or Token Ring.

The two rings are useful for fault conditions but are also used for separate data streams. This effectively doubles the data-carrying capacity of FDDI (to 200 Mbps). However, if the normal traffic is more than the stated carrying capacity, or if one ring fails, then its performance degrades.

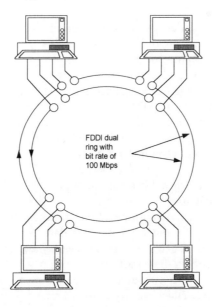

FDDI dual
ring with
bit rate of
100 Mbps

**Figure 5.1** FDDI network

The main features of FDDI are:

- Point-to-point Token Ring topology.
- A secondary ring for redundancy.
- Dual counter rotating ring topology.
- Distributed clock for the support of large numbers of stations on the ring.
- Distributed FDDI management – equal rights and duties for all stations.
- Data integrity ensured through sophisticated encoding techniques.

## 5.2   Operation

As with Token Ring, FDDI uses a token passing medium access method. FDDI uses a timed token-passing protocol to transmit data where a station can hold the token no longer than a specified amount of time. Therefore, there is a limit to the amount of data that a station can transmit on any given opportunity. The sending station must always generate a new token once it has transmitted its data frames, and the station directly downstream from a sending station has the next opportunity to capture the token. This feature and the timed token ensure that the capacity of the ring divides almost equally amongst the stations on the ring.

The time that a station holds a token is called the token holding time (THT). The token rotation time (TRT) defines the time that a token takes to transverse around the ring. It can be see that:

$$Nodes\_Transmitting \times THT + Ring\_Latency \geq TRT$$

where Nodes_Transmitting defines the number of nodes that require to transmit data and the Ring_Latency is amount of time it takes data to transverse round the ring when there are no stations transmitting data.

After initial negotiations, all stations on the ring agree to release the token within the target token rotation time (TTRT). Each station then measures the time between successive arrivals of the token (MTRT, or measured TRT). If the MTRT is greater than the agreed TTRT then the token is late, else it is early. With an early token, the station is allowed to use the token for difference between the TTRT and the MTRT. If the token is late, the station cannot transmit any data.

The problem with this method is that a station that receives an early token can hog it for the rest of the TTRT, thus the next node of the ring could not transmit any data. To overcome this, FDDI uses two transfer modes: asynchronous and synchronous. Synchronous transfer is used to transmit real-time traffic, such as video and audio, and asynchronous is used to transmit computer-type data. Synchronous transfers uses a continuous stream of frames and give a guaranteed bandwidth to transmitting stations (which is a requirement of real-time traffic).

Stations can send data in a synchronous mode, no matter on whether the token is early or late, but can only enter into asynchronous transfers when the token is early. The total time that can be used to transmit synchronous data is also bounded by the

TTRT. In the worst case, stations with asynchronous traffic first use up one TTRT's worth of time, next nodes with synchronous data use another TTRT's worth of time, thus it is possible that the MTRT at any given node could be as much as twice the TTRT. Note, that this would not happen when the synchronous traffic had used up one TTRT's worth of time, as there would be no time for asynchronous transfers.

The case can also occur when a station receives a token, and the MTRT is less than the TTRT, but the difference in time is not enough to transmit the whole data frame. In this case, the station is allowed to transmit it, thus the MTRT will actual have a maximum value of the TTRT plus the total time to transmit a full frame.

Other ways the FDDI differs from Token Ring are:

- Immediate token release. In FDDI, when a station has finished transmitting, it simply adds the token onto the end of the data frame. This allows for maximum usage of the bandwidth, as the station does not have to wait for the frame to be deleted before it initiates the token. Token Ring uses a delayed release mechanism.
- Token Generation. FDDI uses a token claim process for new tokens. A new token are generated when the ring is initiated, after an error has occurred or when a new station has been added or deleted. When this happens a station sends a special claim frame, which has the node's bid for the TTRT. When a node receives the claim frame, it checks its own TTRT bid against the value in the frame. If its value is higher then it sets its own TTRT to the value in the frame, and then passes the bid frame, unchanged, onto the next station. If its TTRT is less than the TTRT in the bid frame, it deletes the received claim frame and issues a new one with its bid for the TTRT. If the TTRT is the same then the highest address wins. Thus, the station that wins the bid process is the one that receives the claim frame which it originally sent. After this, it will transmit a new token.
- Token Regeneration. A major problem in Token Ring is the generation of new tokens. Normally Token Ring uses a monitor node a detect that tokens have been deleted. In FDDI, each station monitor the ring for tokens. If they do not receive one within a given time (typically, a maximum period of 2.5ms) the station will transmit a new bid frame. This allows for a distributed token generation method.

## 5.3 FDDI layers

The ANSI-defined FDDI standard defines four key layers:

- Media access control (MAC) layer.
- Physical layer (PHY).
- Physical media dependent (PMD).
- Station management (SMT) protocol.

FDDI covers the first two layers of the OSI model; Figure 5.2 shows how these layers fit into the model.

The MAC layer defines addressing, scheduling and data routing. Data is formed into data packets with a PHY layer. It encodes and decodes the packets into symbol streams for transmission. Each symbol has four bits and FDDI then uses the 4B/5B encoding to encode them into a group of five bits. The five bits have been chosen to contain, at most, two successive zeros. Table 5.1 shows the coding for the bits. This type of coding ensures that there will never be more than three consecutive zeros in a data bitstream. FDDI uses NRZI (non-return to zero with inversion) to transmit the bits. With NRZI, a 1 is coded with an alternative light (or voltage) level transition for each 1, and a zero does not change the light (or voltage) level. Figure 5.3 shows an example.

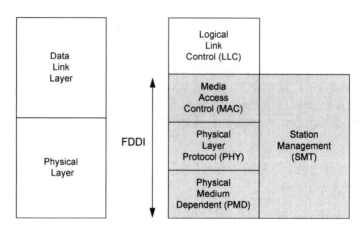

**Figure 5.2** FDDI network

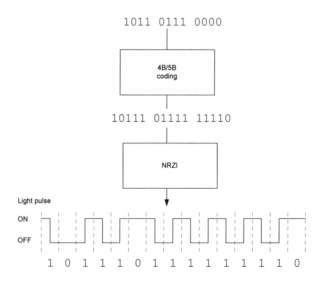

**Figure 5.3** Example of bit encoding

**Table 5.1** 4B/5B coding

| Symbol | Binary | Bitstream | Symbol | Binary | Bitstream |
|--------|--------|-----------|--------|--------|-----------|
| 0 | 0000 | 11110 | 8 | 1000 | 10010 |
| 1 | 0001 | 01001 | 9 | 1001 | 10011 |
| 2 | 0010 | 10100 | A | 1010 | 10110 |
| 3 | 0011 | 10101 | B | 1011 | 10111 |
| 4 | 0100 | 01010 | C | 1100 | 11010 |
| 5 | 0101 | 01011 | D | 1101 | 11011 |
| 6 | 0110 | 01110 | E | 1110 | 11100 |
| 7 | 0111 | 01111 | F | 1111 | 11101 |

**Table 5.2** 4B/5B coding

| Symbol | Bitstream | Symbol | Bitstream |
|--------|-----------|--------|-----------|
| QUIET | 00000 | K | 10001 |
| HALT | 00100 | T | 01101 |
| IDLE | 11111 | R | 00111 |
| J | 11000 | S | 11001 |

In this case the input bitstream is 1011, 0111 and 0000. This is encoded, as in Table 5.1, as 10111, 01111 and 11110. This is then transmitted in NRZI. The first bit sent is a 1 and is represented as a high-to-low transition. The next bit is a zero and thus has no transition. After this a 1 is encoded, this will be transmitted as a low-to-high transition, and so on. The main advantage of NRZI coding is that the timing information is inherent within the transmitted signal and can be easily filtered out.

Apart from the 16 encoded bit patterns given in Table 5.1 there are also eight control and eight violation patterns. Table 5.2 shows the eight other control symbols (QUIET, HALT, IDLE, J, K, T, R and S) and eight other violation symbols (the encoded bitstream binary values are 00001, 00010, 00011, 00101, 00110, 01000, 01100 and 10000).

The coding of the data symbols is chosen so that there are no more than three consecutive zeros in a row. This is necessary to ensure that all the stations on the ring have their clocks synchronised with all the others. Each station on an FDDI has its own independent clock. The control and violation symbols allow the reception of four or more zero bits in a row. Notice the IDLE condition has the most number of transitions.

## 5.4  SMT protocol

The SMT protocol handles the management of the FDDI ring, which includes:

- Adjacent neighbour indication.
- Fault detection and reconfiguration.
- Insertion and deletion from the ring.
- Traffic statistics monitoring.

## 5.5 Physical connection management

Within each FDDI station there are SMT entities called PCM (physical connection management). The number of PCM entities within a station is exactly equal to the number of ports the station has. This is because each PCM is responsible for one port. The PCM entities are the parts of the SMT which control the ports. In order to make a connection, two ports must be physically connected to each other by means of a fibre or copper cable.

## 5.6 Fault tolerance method

When a station on a ring malfunctions or there is a break in one of the rings then the rest of the stations can still use the other ring. When a station on the network malfunctions then both of the rings may become inoperative. FDDI allows other stations on the network to detect this and to implement a single rotating ring. Figure 5.4 shows an FDDI network with four connected stations. In this case, the link between the upper stations has developed a fault. These stations quickly determine that there is a fault in both cables and will inform the other stations on the network to implement a single rotating ring with the outer ring transmitting in the clockwise direction and the inner ring in the counterclockwise direction. This fault tolerance method also makes it easier to insert and delete stations from/to the ring.

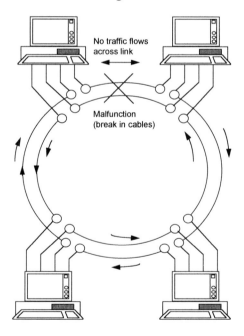

**Figure 5.4** Fault tolerant network

## 5.7 FDDI token format

A token circulates around the ring until a station captures it and then transmits its data in a data frame (see next section). Figure 5.5 shows the basic token format. The preamble (PA) field has four or more symbols of idle (bitstream of 11111). This is followed by the start delimiter (SD) which has a fixed pattern of 'J' (bitstream of 11000) and 'K' (bitstream of 10001). The end delimiter (ED) is two 'T' symbols (01101). The start and end delimiter bit patterns cannot occur anywhere else in the frame as they violate the standard 4B/5B coding for data coding (i.e. they may contain three or more consecutive zeros).

```
 2+ bytes      1 byte        1 byte        1 byte
┌───────────┬───────────┬───────────┬───────────┐
│           │           │           │           │
│    PA     │    SD     │    FC     │    ED     │
│           │           │           │           │
└───────────┴───────────┴───────────┴───────────┘
```

PA – preamble (4 or more symbols of idle)
SD – start delimiter ('J' and 'K')
FC – frame control (2 symbols)
ED – end delimiter (two 'T' symbols)

**Figure 5.5**   FDDI token format

## 5.8 FDDI frame format

Figure 5.6 shows the FDDI data frame format, which is similar to the IEEE 802.6 frame. The PA, SD and ED fields are identical to the token fields. The frame control field (FC) contains information on the type of frame that is to follow in the INFO field.
The fields are:

- Preamble. The preamble field contains 16 idle symbols which allow stations to synchronise their clocks.
- Start delimiter. This contains a fixed field of the 'J' and 'K' symbols.
- Control field. The format of the control field is SAFFxxxx where S indicates whether it is synchronous or asynchronous; A indicates whether it is a 16-bit or 48-bit address; FF indicates whether this is an LLC (01), MAC control (00) or reserved frame. For a control frame, the remaining 4 bits (xxxx) are reserved for control types. Typical (decoded) codes are:

0100 0000 – void frame      0101 0101 – station management frame
1100 0010 – MAC frame      0101 0000 – LLC frame

When the frame is a token the control field contains either 10000000 or 11000000.

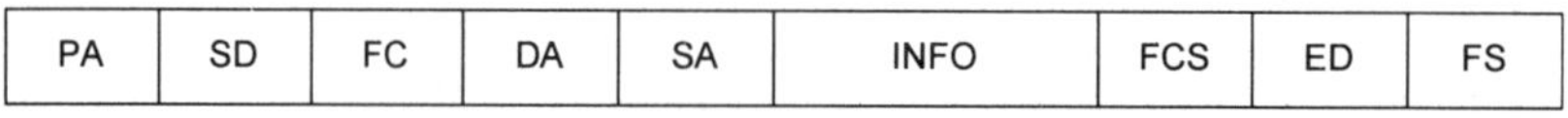

| PA | SD | FC | DA | SA | INFO | FCS | ED | FS |
|----|----|----|----|----|------|-----|----|----|

PA – preamble (2+ bytes)  
SD – starting delimiter (1 byte)  
FC – frame control (1 byte)  
DA – destination address (6 bytes)  
SA – source address (6 bytes)  

INFO – information (N bytes)  
FCS – frame check sequence (4 bytes)  
ED – end delimiter (1/2 symbols)  
FS – frame status (3 symbols)  

**Figure 5.6** FDDI data frame format

- The destination address (DA) and source address (SA) are 12-symbol (6-byte) codes which identify the address of the station from where the frame has come or to where the frame is heading. Each station has a unique address and each station on the ring compares it with its own address. If the frame is destined for a particular station, that station copies the frame's contents into its buffer.

  A frame may also be destined for a group of stations. Group addresses are identified by the start bit 1. If the start bit is 0 then the frame is destined for an individual station. A broadcast address of all 1's is used to send information to all the stations on the ring.

  Station addresses can either be locally or globally administered. For global addresses the first six symbols are the manufacturer's OUI; each manufacturer has a unique OUI for all its products. The last six symbols of the address differentiate between stations of the same manufacturer.

  The second bit in the address field identifies whether the address is local or global. If it is set (a 1) then it is a locally administered address, if it is unset then it is a globally administered address. In a locally administered network the system manager sets the addresses of all network stations.

- The information field (INFO) can contain from 0 to 4478 bytes of data. Thus the maximum frame size will be as follows:

| Field | Number of bytes |
|-------|-----------------|
| Start delimiter | 1 |
| Frame control | 1 |
| Destination address | 6 |
| Source address | 6 |
| DATA (maximum) | 4478 |
| Frame check sequence | 4 |
| End delimiter | 2 |
| End of frame sequence | 2 |
| TOTAL | 4500 |

- The frame check sequence contains a 32-bit CRC which is calculated from the FC, DA, SA and information fields.
- The ending delimiter contains two 'T' symbols.
- The frame status contains extra bits which identify the current status, such as frame copied indicators (F), errors detected (E) and address recognised (A).

## 5.9 Applications of FDDI networks

As was seen in Chapter 3, Ethernet is an excellent method of attaching stations to a network cheaply but is not a good transport mechanism for a backbone network or with high traffic levels. It also suffers, in its standard form, from a lack of speed. FDDI networks overcome these problems as they offer a much higher bit rate, higher reliability and longer interconnections. Thus typical applications of FDDI networks are:

- As a backbone network in an internetwork connection.
- Any applications which requires high security and/or a high degree of fault tolerance. Fibre-optic cables are generally more reliable and are difficult to tap into without it being detected.
- As a subnetwork connecting high-speed computers and their peripheral devices (such as storage units).
- As a network connecting stations where an application program requires high-speed transfers of large amounts of data (such as computer-aided design – CAD). Maximum data traffic for an FDDI network is at least 10 times greater than for standard Ethernet and Token Ring networks. As it is a token-passing network it is less susceptible to heavy traffic loads than Ethernet.

## 5.10 FDDI backbone network

The performance of the network backbone is extremely important as many users on the network depend on it. If the traffic is too heavy, or if it develops a fault, then it affects the performance of the whole network. An FDDI backbone helps with these problems because it has a high bit rate and normally increases the reliability of the backbone.

Figure 5.7 shows an FDDI backbone between four campuses. In this case, the FDDI backbone only carries traffic which is transmitted between campuses. This is because the router only routes traffic out of the campus network when it is intended for another campus. As tokens circulate round both rings, two data frames can be transmitted round the rings at the same time.

## 5.11 FDDI media

FDDI networks can use two types of fibre-optic cable, either single-mode or multi-mode. The mode refers to the angle at which light rays are reflected and propagated through the fibre core. Single-mode fibres have a narrow core, such as 10 μm for the core and 125 μm for the cladding (known as 10/125 micron cable). This type allows light to enter only at a single angle. Multi-mode fibres have a relatively thick core, such as 62.5 μm for the core and 125 μm for the cladding (known as 62.5/125 micron cable). Multi-mode cables reflect light rays at many angles. The disadvantage of these multiple propagation paths is that it can cause the light pulses to spread out and thus limit the rate at which data is accurately received. Thus, single-mode fibres have a higher bandwidth than multimode fibres and allow longer interconnection distances.

The fibres most commonly used in FDDI are 62.5/125, and this type of cable is defined in the ANSI X3T9.5 standard.

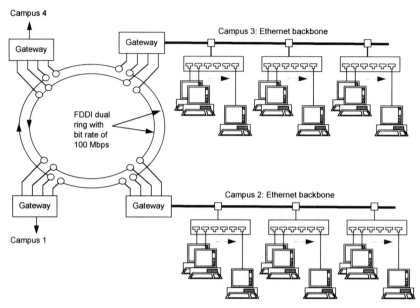

**Figure 5.7** FDDI backbone network

## 5.12 FDDI attachments

There are four types of station which can attach to an FDDI network:

- Dual attachment stations (DAS).
- Single attachment stations (SAS).
- Dual attachment concentrators (DAC).
- Single attachment concentrators (SAC).

Figure 5.8 shows an FDDI network configuration that includes all these station types. An SAS connects to the FDDI rings through a concentrator, so it is easy to add, delete or change its location. The concentrator automatically bypasses disconnected stations.

Each DAS and DAC requires four fibres to connect it to the network: Primary In, Primary Out, Secondary In and Secondary Out. The connection of an SAS only requires only two fibres. Normally Slave In and Slave Out on the SAS are connected to the Master Out and Master In on the concentrator unit, as shown in Figure 5.9.

FDDI stations attach to the ring using a media interface connector (MIC). An MIC receptacle connects to the stations and an MIC plug to the network end of the connection. A dual attachment station has two MIC receptacles. One provides Primary Ring In and Secondary Ring Out, the other has Primary Ring Out and Secondary Ring In, as illustrated in Figure 5.10.

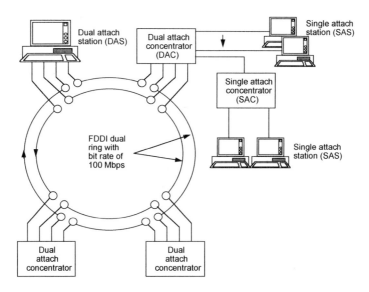

**Figure 5.8** FDDI network configuration

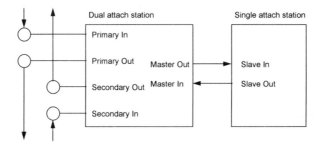

**Figure 5.9** Connection of a DAS and a SAS

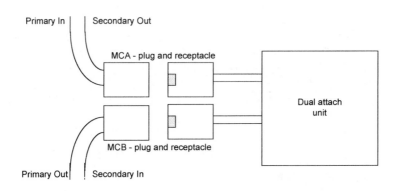

**Figure 5.10** Connection of dual attach units

## 5.13 FDDI specification

Table 5.3 describes the basic FDDI specification. Notice that the maximum interconnection distance for multi-mode cable is 2 km as compared with 20 km for single-mode cable.

**Table 5.3** Basic FDDI specification

| Parameter | Description |
|---|---|
| Topology | Token Ring |
| Access method | Time token passing |
| Transport media | Optical fibre, shield twisted pair, unshielded twisted pair |
| Maximum number of stations | 500 each ring (1000 total) |
| Data rate | 100 Mbps |
| Maximum data packet size | 4 500 bytes |
| Maximum total ring length | 100 km |
| Maximum distance between stations | 2 km (for multimode fibre cable), 20 km (for single-mode fibre cable) |
| Attenuation budget | 11 dB (between stations), 1.5 dB/km at 1300 nm for 62.5/125 fibre |
| Link budget | < 11 dB |

## 5.14 FDDI-II

FDDI-II is an upward-compatible extension to FDDI that adds the ability to support circuit-switched traffic in addition to the data frames supported by the original FDDI. With FDDI-II, it is possible to set up and maintain a constant data rate connection between two stations.

The circuit-switched connection consists of regularly repeating time slots in the frame, often called an isochronous frame. This type of data is common when real-time signals, such as speech and video, are sampled. For example, speech is sampled 8000 times per second, whereas high-quality audio is sampled at 44 000 times per second.

Figure 5.11 shows a layer diagram of an FDDI-II station. The physical layer and the station management are the same as the original FDDI. Two new layers have been added to the MAC layer; known as hybrid ring control. They consist of:

- Hybrid multiplexer (HMUX).
- Isochronous MAC (IMAC).

The IMAC module provides an interface between FDDI and the isochronous service, represented by the circuit-switched multiplexer (CS-MUX). The HMUX multiplexes the packet data from the MAC and the isochronous data from the IMAC.

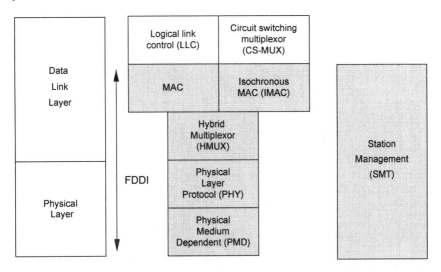

**Figure 5.11** FDDI-II layered model

An FDDI-II network operates in a basic mode or a hybrid mode. In the basic mode the FDDI ring operates as the original FDDI specification where tokens rotate around the network. In the hybrid mode a connection can either be circuit-switched or packet-switched. It uses a continuously repeating protocol data unit known as a cycle. A cycle is a data frame that is similar to synchronous transmission systems. The content of the cycle is visible to all stations as it circulates around the ring. A station called the cycle master generates a new cycle 8 000 times a second. At 100 Mbps, this gives a cycle size of 12 500 bits. As each cycle completes its circuit of the ring, it is stripped by the cycle master. Figure 5.12 shows the two different types of transmission.

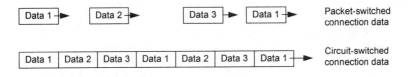

**Figure 5.12** Circuit-switched and packet-switched data

## 5.15 Standards

The FDDI standard was defined by the ANSI committee X3T9.5. This has since been adopted by the ISO as ISO 9314 which defines FDDI using five main layers:

- ISO 9314-1: Physical Layer Protocol (PHY).

- ISO 9314-2: Media Access Control (MAC).
- ISO 9314-3: Physical Media Dependent (PMD).
- ISO 9314-4: Station Management (SMT).
- ISO 9314-5: Hybrid Ring Control (HRC), FDDI-II.

## 5.16 Practical FDDI network – EaStMAN

The EaStMAN (Edinburgh and Stirling Metropolitan Area Network) consortium comprises seven institutions of Higher Education in the Edinburgh and Stirling area of Scotland. The main institutions are: the University of Edinburgh, the University of Stirling, Napier University, Heriot-Watt University, Edinburgh College of Art, Moray House Institute of Education and Queen Margaret College. FDDI and ATM networks have been installed around Edinburgh with an optical link to Stirling. It was funded jointly by the Scottish Higher Education Funding Council (SHEFC), the Joint Information Systems Committee (JISC) and the individual institutions.

Figure 5.13 shows the connections of Phase 1 of the project and Figure 5.14 shows the rings. The total circumference of the rings is 58 km (which is less than the maximum limit of 100 km).

The FDDI ring provides intercampus communications and also a link to the Super-JANET (Joint Academic NETwork) and the ATM ring is for future development. The ATM ring will be discussed in more detail in Chapter 6. Future plans for the network are to link it to the FDDI networks of FaTMAN (Fife and Tayside), ClydeNet (Glasgow network), and AbMAN (Aberdeen network).

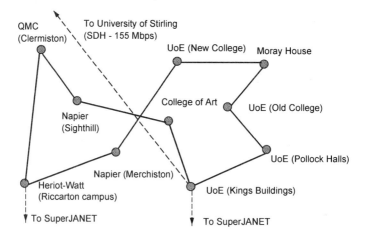

**Figure 5.13**   EaStMAN Phase 1 connections

### 5.16.1 Fibre optic cables

The new optical fibre network is leased from Scottish Telecom (a subsidiary of Scottish Power). The FDDI ring is 58 km and, for the purpose of FDDI standardisation across the MAN, the outer FDDI ring is driven anticlockwise and the inner ring clockwise. Figure 5.15 shows the attenuation rates and distance between each site (in dBs). Note that an extra 0.4 dB should be added onto each fibre connection to take into account the attenuation at the fibre termination. Thus, the total attenuation between the New College and Moray House will be approximately 2.4 dB.

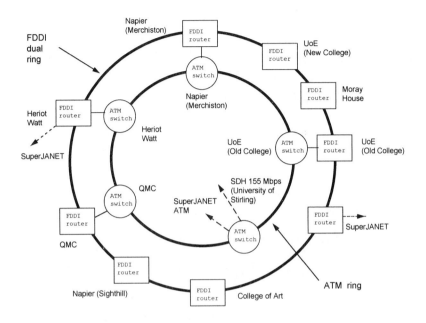

**Figure 5.14** EaStMAN ring connections

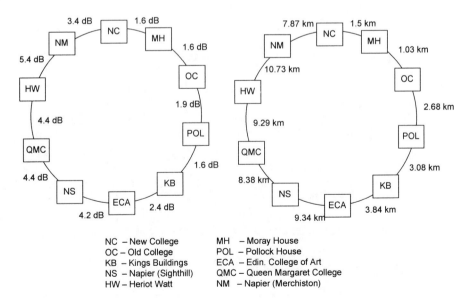

NC – New College     MH – Moray House
OC – Old College     POL – Pollock House
KB – Kings Buildings     ECA – Edin. College of Art
NS – Napier (Sighthill)     QMC – Queen Margaret College
HW – Heriot Watt     NM – Napier (Merchiston)

**Figure 5.15** Attenuation and distances of EaStMAN Phase I

## 5.17 Exercises

**5.17.1** The main international specification for Token Ring is:

    (a)    IEEE 802.2    (b)    IEEE 802.3
    (c)    IEEE 802.4    (d)    IEEE 802.5

**5.17.2** What is the maximum bit rate for an FDDI network:

    (a)    10 Mbps    (b)    100 Mbps
    (c)    200 Mbps    (d)    1000 Mbps

**5.17.3** Why would an FDDI network not be disabled by a break on the cables that connect two stations:

    (a)    They implement send collision signals
    (b)    They implement a bus type system
    (c)    The stations on either side of the break implement a loop back, and create a single loop from the two loops
    (d)    They reduce the bitrate, so that the data can pass over the breakage

**5.17.4** Why can the start and end delimiter not occur with the data frame:

    (a)    They have special optic pulses
    (b)    They violate the normal data coding (of no more that three consecutive zeros).
    (c)    They are inverted each time they are sent
    (d)    They will hardly ever occur in the data, so the odd error is acceptable

**5.17.5** What method does FDDI use to encode the bits on the fibre:

    (a)    Zero's are coded with alternate transitions, one's are coded with no transitions
    (b)    One's are coded with alternate transitions, zero's are coded with no transitions
    (c)    One's are coded with a high-to-low transition, zero's are coded with a low-to-high transition
    (d)    One's are coded with a low-to-high transition, zero's are coded with a high-to-low transition

**5.17.6** What is the maximum bit rate for an FDDI network:

    (a)    10 Mbps    (b)    100 Mbps
    (c)    200 Mbps    (d)    1000 Mbps

**5.17.7** Discuss the token-passing technique used in FDDI.

**5.17.8** Explain how FDDI allows robust networking after a cable break.

**5.17.9** For the input binary data given below determine the line code (after 4B/5B coding) on the line.

000010101111001100010011000111111111111111

**5.17.10** For the line coding (before 5B/4B decoding) given below determine the output data.

101010111011011111001110111101110010

**5.17.11** Identify the control characters and data from the following line code.

00000111111010001011100010110101111011011000

**5.17.12** Using the FDDI token format given in Figure 5.5, show the line code on the line from the preamble, start delimiter and end delimiter. Explain why the preamble, start delimiter and end delimiter cannot occur anywhere else in a token frame or data frame (apart from where they are intended to appear).

**5.17.13** How are new tokens generated on an FDDI network. What advantage does this method have when adding or deleting stations to/from the network, or when errors occurs.

**5.17.14** For the EaStMAN network prove that the maximum ring length is not violated.

**5.17.15** Define the following terms: token rotation time (TRT), token holding time (THT), TTRT (target token rotation time) and MTRT (measured TRT).

**5.17.16** For the EaStMAN network determine the approximate attenuation per kilometer. Also determine the input/output power ratio of each link by transposing the formula:

$$\text{Attenuation (dB)} = 10 \log_{10}\left(\frac{P_i}{P_o}\right)$$

# 6 ATM

## 6.1 Introduction

Most of the networking technologies discussed so far are good at carrying computer-type data and they provide a reliable connection between two nodes. Unfortunately, they are not as good at carrying real-time sampled data, such as digitised video or speech. Real-time data from speech and video requires constant sampling and these digitised samples must propagate through the network with the minimum of delay. Any significant delay in transmission can cause the recovered signal to be severely distorted or for the connection to be lost. Ethernet, Token Ring and FDDI simply send the data into the network without first determining whether there is a communication channel for the data to be transported.

Figure 6.1 shows some traffic profiles for sampled speech and computer-type data (a loading of 1 is the maximum loading). It can be seen that computer-type data tends to burst in periods of time. These bursts have a relatively heavy loading on the network. On the other hand, sampled speech has a relatively low loading on the network but requires a constant traffic throughput. It can be seen that if these traffic profiles were to be mixed onto the same network then the computer-type data would swamp the sampled speech data at various times.

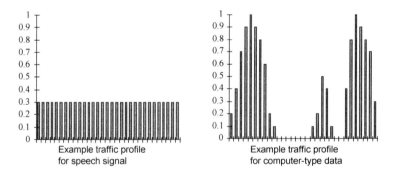

**Figure 6.1** Traffic profiles for sampled speech and computer-type data

Asynchronous transfer mode (ATM) overcomes the problems of transporting computer-type data and sampled real-time data by:

- Analysing the type of connection to be made. The type of data dictates the type of connection; for example, computer data requires a reliable connection, whereas real-time sampled data requires a connection with a low propagation time.

- Analysing the type of data to be transmitted and knowing its traffic profile. Computer data tends to create bursts of traffic whereas real-time data will be constant traffic.
- Reserving a virtual path for the data to allow the data profile to be transmitted within the required quality of service.
- Splitting the data into small packets which have the minimum overhead in the number of extra bits. These 'fast-packets' traverse the network using channels which have been reserved for them.

ATM has been developed mainly by the telecommunications companies. Unfortunately two standards currently exist. In the USA the ANSI T1S1 subcommittee have supported and investigated ATM and in Europe it has been investigated by ETSI. There are small differences between the two proposed standards, but they may converge into one common standard. The ITU-T has also dedicated study group XVIII to ATM-type systems with the objective of merging differences and creating one global standard for high-speed networks throughout the world.

## 6.2   Real-time sampling

Before introducing the theory of ATM, first consider the concept of how analogue signals (such as speech, audio or video) are converted into a digital form. The basic principle involves sampling theory and pulse code modulation.

### 6.2.1   Sampling theory

If a signal is to be reconstructed as the original signal then it must be sampled at a rate defined by the Nyquist criterion (Figure 6.2). This states:

*the sampling rate must be twice the highest frequency of the signal*

For telephone speech channels the maximum signal frequency is limited to 4 kHz and must therefore be sampled at least 8000 times per second (8 kHz). This gives one sample every 125 µs. Hi-fi quality audio has a maximum signal frequency of 20 kHz and must be sampled at least 40 000 times per second (many professional hi-fi sampling systems sample at 44.1 kHz). Video signals have a maximum frequency of 6 MHz, so a video signal must be sampled at 12 MHz (or once every 83.3 ns).

### 6.2.2   Pulse code modulation

Once analogue signals have been sampled for their amplitude they can be converted into a digital format using pulse code modulation (PCM). The digital form is then transmitted over the transmission media. At the receiver the digital code is converted back into an analogue form.

The accuracy of PCM depends on the number of bits used for each analogue sample. This gives a PCM-based system a dependable response over an equivalent analogue system because an analogue system's accuracy depends on component tolerance, producing a differing response for different systems.

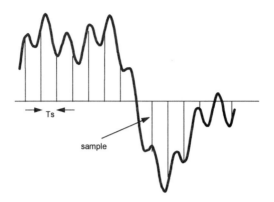

**Figure 6.2** The sampling process

## 6.3 PCM-TDM systems and ISDN

ATM tries to integrate real-time data and computer-type data. The main technology currently used in transmitting digitised speech over the public switched telephone network (PSTN) is PCM-TDM (PCM time division multiplexing). PCM-TDM involves multiplexing the digitised speech samples in time. Each sample is assigned a time slot which is reserved for the total time of the connection, as illustrated in Figure 6.3. This example shows the connection of Telephone 1–4 to Telephone A–D, respectively. The digitizer, in this case, consists of a sampler (at 8 kHz) and an analogue-to-digital converter (ADC). Four input channels are time-division multiplexed onto a signal line, the time between one sample from a certain channel and the next must be 125 µs.

The integrated services digital network (ISDN) is to be covered in Chapter 8. It uses a base bit rate of 64 kbps and can be used to transmit 8-bit samples at a rate of 8 kHz. ISDN is similar to a telephone connection but allows the direct connection of digital equipment. As with the PSTN the connection between the transmitter and the receiver is set up by means of a switched connection. On an ISDN network the type of data carried is transparent to the network. Higher bit rates are achieved by splitting the data into several channels and transmitting each channel at 64 kbps.

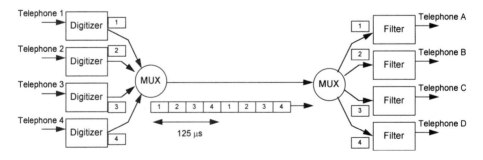

**Figure 6.3** PCM-TDM with four connections

## 6.4 Objectives of ATM

The major objective of ATM is to integrate real-time data (such as voice and video signals) and non-real-time data (such as computer data and file transfer). Computer-type data can typically be transferred in non-real-time but it is important that the connection is free of errors. In many application programs, a single bit error can cause serious damage. On the other hand, voice and video data require a constant sampling rate and low propagation delays, but are more tolerant to errors and any losses of small parts of the data.

An ATM network relies on user-supplied information to profile traffic flows so that the connection has the desired quality of service. Table 6.1 gives four basic data types. These are further complicated by differing data types either sending data in a continually repeating fashion (such as telephone data) or with a variable frequency (such as interactive video). For example a high-resolution video image may need to be sent as several megabytes of data in a short time burst, but then nothing for a few seconds. For speech the signal must be sampled constantly at 8 000 times per second.

Computer data will typically be sent in bursts. Sometimes a high transfer rate is required (perhaps when running a computer package remotely over a network) or a relatively slow transfer (such as when reading text information). Conventional circuit-switched technology (such as ISDN and PCM-TDM) are thus wasteful in their connection because they either allocate a switched circuit (ISDN) or reserve a fixed time slot (PCM-TDM), no matter whether there data is being transmitted at that time. And it may not be possible to service high burst rates by allocating either time slots or switched circuits when all of the other time slots are full, or because switched circuits are being used.

**Table 6.1** Four basic categories of data

| Data type | Error or loss sensitive | Delay sensitive |
|---|---|---|
| Real-time control system | yes | yes |
| Telephone/hi-fi music | no | yes |
| File transfer, application programs | yes | no |
| Teletex information | no | no |

## 6.5 ATM versus ISDN and PCM-TDM

ISDN and PCM-TDM use a synchronous transfer mode (STM) technique where a connection is made between two devices by circuit switching. The transmitting device is assigned a given time slot to transmit the data. This time slot is fixed for the period of the transmission. The main problems with this type of transmission are:

- Not all the time slots are filled by data when there is light data traffic; this is wasteful in data transfer.
- When a connection is made between two endpoints a fixed time slot is assigned and data from that connection is always carried in that time slot. This is also wasteful

because there may be no data being transmitted in certain time periods.

ATM overcomes these problems by splitting the data up into small fixed-length pack-ets, known as cells. Each data cell is sent with its a routing address and follows a fixed route through the network. The packets are small enough that, if they are lost, possibly due to congestion, they can either be requested (for high reliability) or cause little sig-nal degradation (typically in voice and video traffic).

The address of devices on an ATM network are identifier by a virtual circuit identi-fier (VCI), instead of by a time slot as in an STM network. The VCI is carried in the header portion of the fast packet.

## 6.6    ATM user network interfaces (UNIs)

A user network interface (UNI) allows users to gain access to an ATM network. The UNI transmits data into the network with a set of agreed specifications and the network must then try to ensure the connection stays within those requirements. These require-ments define the required quality of service for the entire duration of the connection.

It is likely that there will be several different types of ATM service provision. One type will provide an interface to one or more of the LAN standards (such as Ethernet or Token Ring) or FDDI. The conversion of the LAN frames to ATM cells will be done inside the UNI at the source and destination endpoints respectively. Typically it will be used as a bridge for two widely separated LANs. This provides a short-term solution to justifying the current investment in LAN technology and allows a gradual transition to a complete ISDN/ATM network.

The best long-term solution is to connect data communication equipment directly onto an ATM network. This allows computer equipment, telephones, video, and so on, to connect directly to a global network. The output from an ATM multiplexer inter-faces with the UNI of a larger ATM backbone network.

A third type of ATM interface connects existing STM networks to ATM networks. This allows a slow migration of existing STM technology to ATM.

## 6.7    ATM cells

The ATM cell, as specified by the ANSI T1S1 subcommittee, has 53 bytes, as shown in Figure 6.4. The first five bytes are the header and the remaining bytes are the infor-mation field which can hold 48 bytes of data. Optionally the data can contain a 4-byte ATM adaptation layer and 44 bytes of actual data. A bit in the control field of the header sets the data to either 44 or 48 bytes. The ATM adaptation layer field allows for fragmentation and reassembly of cells into larger packets at the source and destination respectively. The control field also contains bits which specify whether this is a flow control cell or an ordinary data cell, a bit to indicate whether this packet can be deleted in a congested network, and so on.

The ETSI definition of an ATM cell also contains 53 bytes with a 5-byte header and 48 bytes of data. The main differences are the number of bits in the VCI field, the number of bits in the header checksum, and the definitions and position of the control bits.

The IEEE 802.6 standard for the MAC layer of the metropolitan area network (MAN) DQDB (distributed queue dual bus) protocol is similar to the ATM cell.

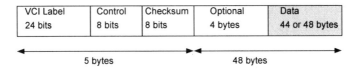

**Figure 6.4**   ATM cell

## 6.8   Routing cell within an ATM network

In STM networks, data can change its position in each time slot in the interchanges over the global network. This can occur in ATM where the VCI label changes between intermediate nodes in the route.

When a transmitting node wishes to communicate through the network it makes contact with the UNI and negotiates parameters such as destination, traffic type, peak and traffic requirements, delay and cell loss requirement, and so on. The UNI forwards this request to the network. From this data the network computes a route based on the specified parameters and determines which links on each leg of the route can best support the requested quality of service and data traffic. It sends a connection set-up request to all the nodes in the path en route to the destination node.

Figure 6.5 shows an example of ATM routing. In this case, User 1 connects to Users 2 and 3. The virtual path set up between User 1 and User 2 is through the ATM switches 2, 3 and 4, whereas User 1 and User 3 connect through ATM switches 1, 5 and 6. A VCI number of 12 is assigned to the path between ATM switches 1 to 2, in the connection between User 1 and User 2. When ATM switch 2 receives a cell with a VCI number of 12 then it sends the cell to ATM switch 3 and gives it a new VCI number of 6. When it gets to ATM switch 3 it is routed to ATM switch 4 and given the VCI number of 22. The virtual circuit for User 1 to User 3 is through ATM switches 1, 5 and 6, and the VCI numbers used are 10 and 15. Once a connection is terminated the VCI labels assigned to the communications are used for other connections.

Certain users, or applications, can be assigned reserved VCI labels for special services that may be provided by the network. However, as the address field only has 24 bits it is unlikely that many of these requests would be granted. ATM does not provide for acknowledgements when the cells arrive at the destination.

Note that as there is a virtual circuit set up between the transmitting and receiving node then cells are always delivered in the same order as they are transmitted. This is because cells cannot take alternative routes to the destination. Even if the cells are buffered at a node, they will still be transmitted in the correct sequence (this is achieved at a higher level).

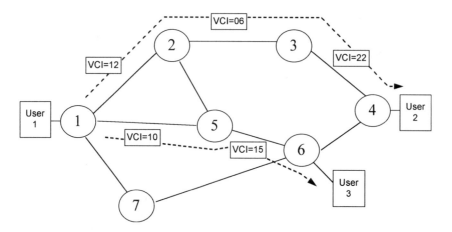

**Figure 6.5** A virtual ATM virtual connection

### 6.8.1  VCI header

The 5-byte ATM user network cell header splits into six main fields:

- GFC (4 bits) which is the generic control bit. It is used only for local significance and is not transmitted from the sender to the receiver.
- VPI (8 bits) which is the path connection identifier (VPI). See next section for an explanation of virtual path.
- VCI (16 bits) which is the virtual path/channel identifier (VCI). Its usage was described in the previous section. Each part of the route is allocated a VCI number.
- PT (3 bits) which is the payload type field. This is used to identify the higher-layer application or data type.
- CLP (1 bit) which is the cell loss priority bit and indicates if a cell is expendable. When the network is busy an expendable cell may be deleted.
- HEC (8 bits) which is the header error control field. This is an 8-bit checksum for the header.

Note that the user to network cell differs from the network to network cell. A network to network cell uses a 12-bit VPI field and does not have a GFC field. Otherwise, it is identical.

## 6.9   Virtual channels and virtual paths

Virtual circuits are set up between two users when a connection is made. Cells then travel over this fixed path through a reserved path. Often several virtual circuits take the same path. These circuits can be grouped together to form a virtual path.

A virtual path is defined as a collection of virtual channels which have the same start and end points, as illustrated in Figure 6.6. These channels will take the same route. This makes the network administration easier and allows new virtual circuits, with the same route, to be easily set up.

Some of the advantages of virtual paths are:

- Network user groups or interconnected networks can be mapped to virtual paths and are thus easily administered.
- Simpler network architecture which consists of groups (virtual paths) with individual connections (virtual circuits).
- Less network administration and shorter connection times arise from fewer set-up connections.

Virtual circuits and virtual paths allows two levels of cell routing through the network. A VC switch routes virtual circuits and a VP switch routes virtual paths. Figure 6.7 shows a VP switch and a VC switch. In this case, the VP switch contains the routing table which maps VP1 to VP2, VP2 to VP3 and VP3 to VP1. This switch does not change the VCI number of the incoming virtual circuits (for example VC1 goes in as VC1 and exits as VC1).

The diagram shows the concepts between both types of switches. The VP switch on the left-hand side redirects the contents of a virtual path to a different virtual path. The virtual connections it contains are unchanged. This is similar to switching an input cable to a different physical cable. In a VC switch the virtual circuits are switched. In the case of Figure 6.7 the routing table will contain VC1 mapped to VC5, VC2 to VC6, and so on. The VC switch thus ignores the VP number and only routes the VC number. Thus the input and output VP number can change.

A connection is made by initially sending routing information cells through the network. When the connection is made, each switch in the route adds a link address for either a virtual path and or a virtual connection.

The combination of VP and VC addressing allows for the support of any addressing scheme, including subscriber telephone numbering or IP addresses. Each of these address can be broken down in a chain of VPI/VCI addresses.

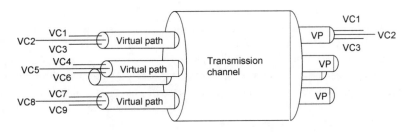

**Figure 6.6** Virtual circuits and virtual paths

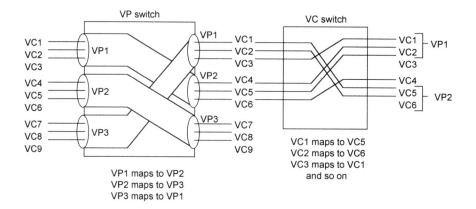

**Figure 6.7** Virtual circuits and virtual paths

## 6.10 Statistical multiplexing

Fast packet switching attempts to solve the problem of unused time slots of STM. This is achieved by statistically multiplexing several connections on the same link based on their traffic characteristics. Applications, such as voice traffic, which requires a constant data transfer are allowed safe routes through the network. Whereas several applications, which have bursts of traffic, may be assigned to the same link in the hope that statistically they will not all generate bursts of data at the same time. Even if some of them were to burst simultaneously, their data could be buffered and sent at a later time. This technique is called statistical multiplexing and allows the average traffic on the network to be evened out over a relatively short time period. This is impossible on an STM network.

## 6.11 ATM flow control

ATM cannot provide for a reactive end-to-end flow control because by the time a message is returned from the destination to the source, large amounts of data could have been sent along the ATM pipe, possibly making the congestion worse. The opposite can occur when the congestion on the network has cleared by the time the flow control message reaches the transmitter. The transmitter will thus reduce the data flow when there is little need. ATM tries to react to network congestion quickly, and it slowly reduces the input data flow to reduce congestion.

This rate-based scheme of flow control involves controlling the amount of data to a specified rate, agreed when the connection is made. It then automatically changes the rate based on the past history of the connection as well as the present congestion state of the network.

Data input is thus controlled by early detection of traffic congestion through closely monitoring the internal queues inside the ATM switches, as shown in Figure 6.8. The network then reacts gradually as the queues lengthen and reduces the traffic into the network from the transmitting UNI. This is an improvement over imposing a complete restriction on the data input when the route is totally congested. In summary, anticipation is better than desperation.

A major objective of the flow control scheme is to try to affect only the streams which are causing the congestion, not the well-behaved streams.

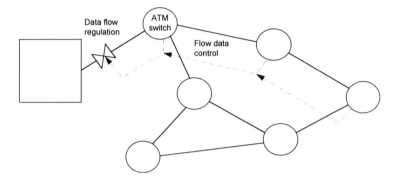

**Figure 6.8**   Flow control feedback from ATM switches

## 6.12   ATM signalling and call set-up

ATM, as with most telecommunications systems, uses a single-pass approach to setting up a connection. Initially, the source connection (the source end-system) communicates a connection request to the destination connection (the destination end-point). The routing protocol manages the routing of the connection request and all subsequent data flow. The call is established with:

- A set-up message. This is initially sent, across the UNI, to the first ATM switch. It contains:

  - Destination end-system address.
  - Desired traffic.
  - Quality of service.
  - Information Elements (IE) defining particular desired higher-layer protocol bindings and so on.

- The initial ATM switch sends back a local call proceeding acknowledgement to the source end-system.
- The initial ATM switch invokes an ATM routing protocol, and propagates a signalling request across the network, it finally reaches the ATM switch connected to the destination end-system.

- The destination ATM switch connected to the destination end-system forwards the set-up message to the end-system, across its UNI.
- The destination end-system either accepts or rejects the connection. If necessary, the destination can negotiate the connection parameters. If the destination end-system rejects the connection request, it returns a release message. This is also sent back to the source end-system and clears the connection, such as clearing any allocated VCI labels. A release message can also be used by any of the end-systems, or by the network, to clear an established connection.
- If the destination end-system accepts the call then the ATM switch, which connects to it, returns a connect message through the network, along the same path.
- When the source end-system receives and acknowledges the connection message, either node can then start transmitting data on the connection (the chain of allocated VCI labels defines the route).

## 6.13 ATM addressing scheme

ATM, like any other network, requires a network address scheme which identifies the source and destination addresses. The ITU-T have developed a standardised, telephone-like, numbering system called E.164 for addressing public ATM networks. Unfortunately, E.164 addresses are public addresses and cannot typically be used within private networks. The ATM Forum have since extended ATM addressing to include private networks. For a private networking scheme in UNI 3.0/3.1 they evaluated two different models. These differ in the way that the ATM protocol layer is viewed in relation to existing protocol layers, such as IP and IPX layers, and are:

- Peer model. This model treats the ATM layer as a peer of existing network layers and uses the same addressing schemes within the ATM networks. Thus, ATM endpoints would be identified by their existing network layer address (such as an IP or an IPX address). The ATM signalling requests would then carry these addresses for the source and destination ATM switch. Also network layer routing protocols, such as RIP, and so on, can be used to route ATM signalling requests using existing network layer addresses. The peer model allows for simplified addressing.
- Overlay model. This model decouples the ATM layer from any existing network protocol and defines a new addressing structure and a new routing protocol. This, as with Ethernet, FDDI and Token Ring which use MAC addresses, allow all existing protocols to operate over an ATM network. For this reason, the model is known as the subnetwork or overlay model. Thus, all ATM switches need an ATM address, and possibly, also a network layer address (such as an IP or IPX address).

The disadvantage with the overlay model is that there needs to be an ATM address resolution protocol which maps network addresses (IP or IPX) to ATM addresses. The peer model does not need address resolution protocols, and, because it uses existing routing protocols.

The ATM Forum decided to implement the overlay model for UNI 3.0/3.1 signalling. This is mainly becauses the peer model would be difficult to implement as they must essentially act as multiprotocol routers and support address tables for all current protocols, as well as all of their existing routing protocols. In addition, currently available routing protocols for LANs and WANs do not map well into the QoS parameter.

The ATM Forum chose a private network addressing scheme based on the OSI Network Service Access Point (NSAP) address. These are not true NSAP addresses, and are either ATM private network addresses or ATM end-point identifiers. They basically are subnetwork points of attachment.

An NSAP ATM address for a private network has 20 bytes, while a public network uses a E.164 address, as defined by the ITU-T. NSAP-based addresses have three main fields:

- Authority and Format Identifier (AFI). This defines the type and format of the Initial Domain Identifier (IDI).
- Initial Domain Identifier (IDI). This defines the address allocation and administration authority.
- Domain Specific Part (DSP). This defines the actual routing information.

There are three formats that private ATM addressing use for different definitions for the AFI and IDI parts. These are:

- NSAP Encoded E.164 format. The E.164 number is contained in the IDI.
- DCC Format. The IDI is a Data Country Code (DCC) which identities the country, as specified in ISO 3166. These addresses are administered, in each country, by the ISO National Member Body.
- ICD Format. The IDI contains the International Code Designator (ICD). The ICD is allocated by the ISO 6523 registration authority. They identify particular international organisations.

### 6.13.1 NSAP

NSAP is defined in ISO/IEC 8348. It divides the address into two main parts: Initial Domain Part (IDP), which splits into the Authority and Format Identifier (AFI), and Initial Domain Identifier (IDI). The format is thus:

```
| IDP       | DSP
| AFI | IDI |
```

In the ISO/IEC 10589 specification, the DSP address includes an ID and SEL (1 byte selector) field which are used by level 1 routing. Typically, the ID part is taken from the ISO/IEC 8802 48-bit MAC address. The format is thus:

```
| IDP       | DSP                    |
| AFI | IDI |           | ID | SEL  |
```

In the UNI-3.1 specification, the ID field is six bytes. It is also defined that the NSAP address format uses a maximum length of 20 bytes.

### 6.13.2 ICD Format

The format of an ICD scheme is:

```
AFI                    47              (1 byte)
ICI                    xxxx            (2 bytes)
Version                xx              (1 byte)
Network                xxxxxx          (3 bytes)
Tele traffic area      xx              (1 byte)
Member identifier      xxxx            (2 byte)
Member access point    xx              (1 byte)
Area                   xx              (1 byte)
Switch                 xx              (1 byte)
MAC-address            xxxxxxxxxxxx    (6 bytes)
Nselector              xx              (1 byte)
```

An example format is:

```
+--+--+--+--+--+--+--+--+--+--+--+--+--+--+--+--+--+--+--+--+
|47|00 23|00|00 00 03|xx|xx xx|xx|xx|xx| ESI MAC address |xx|
+--+--+--+--+--+--+--+--+--+--+--+--+--+--+--+--+--+--+--+--+
```

### 6.13.3 DCC Format

The DCC format is defined by the National Standards Organisation 39528+1100. Its fields include:

```
AFI (39 or 38)      ISO DCC format                  (1 byte)
IDI                                                 (2 bytes)
CFI                 Country Format Identifier       (4 bits)
CDI                 Country Domain Identifier       (12 bits)
SFI                 SURFNet Format Identifier       (4 bits)
        0=CLN S in case of an organizational SDI
        1=in case of a network SDI
        2=ATM in case of an organization SDI
SDI                 SURFNet Domain Identifier       (2 bytes)
                    decimal encoded administrative numbers
ASDI                Additional Domain Identifier    (4 bits)
NYU                 Not yet used                    (5 bytes)
ESI                 End System Identifier           (6 bytes)
SEL                 Selector                        (1 byte)
```

The EaStMAN network uses a 13 byte prefix, in the form:

```
39.826f.1107.16.7000.00.nnmm.ee.ff
```

where 39 is the AFI – ISO DCC, 826f is the IDI (indicating the UK), 1 is the CFI, 107 is the CDI, 1 for the SFI, 107 the SDI (country and domain), 16 for ASNI (for region), 00 (not yet used), nnmm for site code, ee for campus number and ff for switch number.

The nn part represents the institution, these are:

| | | | |
|---|---|---|---|
| 01 | University of Edinburgh | 02 | Moray House |
| 03 | Queen Margaret College | 04 | Napier University |
| 05 | Heriot-Watt University | 06 | Edinburgh College of Art |
| 07 | University of Stirling | | |

and mm is the ring access point. These are assigned in a clockwise direction on the ring, starting from Kings Building (University of Edinburgh). In summary, the nnmm codes are assigned as follows:

University of Edinburgh:

| Kings Buildings | 0101 | Pollock Halls | 0102 |
| Old College | 0103 | New College | 0106 |

Moray House:

| MH-H | 0204 | MH-Cramond | 0209 |

Queen Margaret College:

| QMC-Leith | 0305 | QMC-Corstorphine | 030a |

Napier University:

| Merchiston | 0407 | Sighthill | 040b |

Heriot-Watt:

| Riccarton campus | 0508 |

Edinburgh College of Art:

| ECA-L | 060c | ECA-G | 060d |

University of Stirling:

| Stirling | 070e |

The last two byte values (ee and ff) are allocated by the local institution. Typically, they can be used to identify the campus number (ee) and the switch number within the campus (ff).

### 6.13.4 E.164 Format (ATM Forum/95-0427R1)

The E.164 format provides a geographical scheme, but, as it is derived from the telephone system, the addresses are in short supply. Therefore, the E.164 NSAP format is recommend, which is extensible to ISDN. Its format is:

```
+--+--+--+--+--+--+--+--+--+--+--+--+--+--+--+--+--+--+--+--+
|45| Internat E.164 number |  HO-DSP   |xx xx xx xx xx xx|xx|
+--+--+--+--+--+--+--+--+--+--+--+--+--+--+--+--+--+--+--+--+
```

Where:

45      AFI for E.164 binary syntax

```
IDI        International E.164 number
HO-DSP     Extends the E.164 address to logically identify
           many devices in a single geographical location.
ESI        Similar to HO-DSP, extends the E.164 address.
SEL        Selector
```

## 6.14 ATM and the OSI model

The basic ATM cell fits roughly into the data link layer of the OSI model, but contains some network functions, such as end-to-end connection, flow control, and routing. It thus fits into layers 2 and 3 of the model, as shown in Figure 6.9. The layer 4 software layer, such as TCP/IP (as covered in Chapter 9), can communicate directly with ATM.

The ATM network provides a virtual connection between two gateways and the IP protocol fragments IP packets into ATM cells at the transmitting UNI which are then reassembled back into the IP packets at the destination UNI.

With TCP/IP each host is assigned an IP address as it is the ATM gateway. Once the connection has been made then the cells are fragmented into the ATM network and follow a predetermined route through the network. At the receiver the cells are reassembled using the ATM adaptation layer. This reforms the original IP packet which is then passed to the next layer.

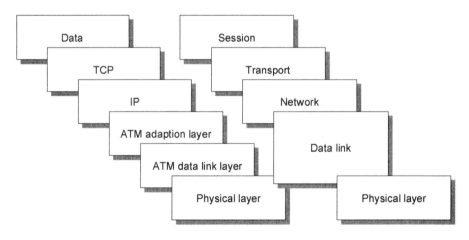

**Figure 6.9** ATM and the OSI model

The functions of the three ATM layers are:

- ATM adaptation layer (AAL) – segmentation and reassembly of data into cells and vice-versa, such as convergence (CS) and segmentation (SAR). It is also involved with quality of service (QOS).
- ATM data link (ADL) – maintenance of cells and their routing through the network, such as generic flow control, cell VPI/VCI translation, and cell multiplex and demultiplex.
- ATM physical layer (PHY) – transmission and physical characteristics, such as cell

rate decoupling, HEC header sequence generation/verification, cell delineation, transmission frame adaptation and transmission frame generation/recovery.

The overlay model corresponds to layer 2 of the OSI model (that is, the data link layer). But, ATM actually has most, if not all, of the characteristics of a layer 3 (this is, the network layer), such as having a hierarchical address space and a complex routing protocol. Unfortunately, the original OSI model did not support overlayed networks, where one network layer overlays on another. This has since been added to the model. Overlayed networks are useful when carrying a certain network protocol (such as TCP/IP or SPX/IPX) between two networks, transparently.

ATM can be used to build simpler networks as ATM addresses can be made to be hierarchical, whereas MAC addresses are flat addresses. A flat address is typically a randomly generated address, which does not give any clues about the physical location of the node. A MAC-level bridge does not require to be set up in the same way as routers are set, because they flood packets through the network.

## 6.15 ATM physical layer

The physical layer is not an explicit part of the ATM definition, but is currently being considered by the standards organisations. T1S1 has standardised on SONET (Synchronous Optical NETwork) as the preferred physical layer, with STS-3c at 155.5 Mbps, STS-12 at 622 Mbps and STS-48 at 2.4 Gbps.

The SONET physical layer specification provides a standard world-wide digital telecommunications network hierarchy, known internationally as the Synchronous Digital Hierarchy (SDH). The base transmission rate, STS-1, is 51.84 Mbps. This is then multiplexed to make up higher bit rate streams, such as STS-3 which is 3 times STS-1, STS-12 which is 12 times STS-1, and so on. The 155 Mbps stream is the lowest bit rate for ATM traffic and is also called STM-1 (synchronous transport module - level 1).

The SDH specifies a standard method on how data is framed and transported synchronously across fibre-optic transmission links without requiring that all links and nodes have the same synchronised clock for data transmission and recovery.

## 6.16 ATM LAN emulation

For ATM to get global acceptance it must support existing LANs and WANs, and must thus support existing network protocols, such as IP and IPX. There are two methods that ATM can use:

- Native mode operation. With this, address resolution techniques are used to map network layer addresses directly into ATM addresses. The network layer packets are then carried across the ATM network. Most network layer protocols can run directly over ATM networks, but only IP and IPX have been extensively implemented. Novell has outlined a protocol known as Connection Oriented IPX (CO-IPX), which allows IPX to be used over ATM networks. The LANE protocol does not fully use the Quality of Service (QoS) parameter and the capability for real-time multimedia applications. It is possible to run applications directly over ATM, without requiring the need for a network or a transport stack (no TCP/IP). This reduces the overhead of the IP and TCP protocols. Unfortunately, it limits the applications to running over purely ATM, which is difficult as long as there are non-ATM networks. In the future, with a totally integrated ATM network, from desktop-to-desktop, this will be possible. One of the main functions of the network layers is to provide network transparency, where the type of network is transparet to the application. If this layer is deleted it does not allow the applications to communicate over different networks.

- LANE (LAN Emulation). With this, network layer packets are carried across the ATM network, so as to emulate a local area network. The LANE protocol defines the techniques to emulate IEEE 802.3 (Ethernet) and IEEE 802.5 (Token Ring) networks. LANE thus encapsulates the data in the appropriate LAN MAC packet format and sends it over the ATM network. The protocol does not, itself, try to emulate the actual media access control protocol of the specific LAN concerned (that is, CSMA/CD for Ethernet or token passing for 802.5). It makes the ATM network look like an Ethemet or Token Ring LAN. The main function of the LANE protocol is to resolve MAC addresses into ATM addresses. This is equivalent to a protocol for MAC bridging on ATM.

### 6.16.1 LANE protocol

The LANE protocol allows for easy interfacing of ATM to existing IP or IPX-based networks, as it presents the same service interface of existing MAC protocols to network layer drivers (for example, an NDIS- or ODI-like driver interface), as illustrated in Figure 6.10.

The LANE protocol can be implement in two ways:

- ATM Network Interface Cards (NICs). The ATM NIC implements LANE, which will present the same software interface as a LAN NIC. This will increase the bandwidth of the LAN, as ATM offers high bit rates.
- Routers and switches. The routers or switches can also use the LANE protocol, as illustrated in Figure 6.11. This is an excellent method of bridging two networks, as the LANE protocol has been designed to bridge across ATM networks.

ATM switches are not directly effected by the LANE protocol, as LANE builds upon the overlay model. Thus, LANE protocols operate transparently over and through ATM switches, using only standard ATM signalling procedures.

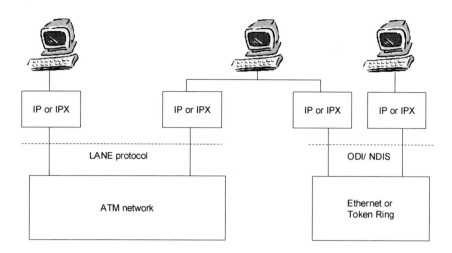

**Figure 6.10**  LANE protocol using NICs

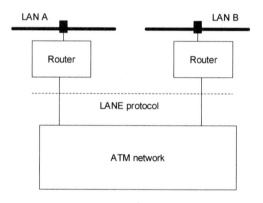

**Figure 6.11**  LAN protocol over routers

### *6.16.2 IP over ATM*

The transport of any network layer protocol over an overlayed ATM network involves: packet encapsulation and address resolution.

**Packet encapsulation**

A node must receive information about what kind of data packet that is contained within the encapsulated packet. There are two main methods used are:

- LLC/SNAP encapsulation. With this, any type of protocol types can be carried across the connection. The LLC/SNAP header is then used from the encapsulated packet to identified the protocol type.
- VC multiplexing. With this, the protocol type is identified when the connection is set up, thus a single protocol is carried across the ATM connection. There will be no multiplexing or packet type field is required or carried within the

packet, though the encapsulated packet may be prefixed with a pad field. The type of encapsulation used by LANE for data packets is actually a form of VC muxing. This type of encapsulation can be used where direct application to application ATM connectivity, bypassing lower level protocols, is desired. Such direct connectivity precludes the possibility of internetworking with nodes outside the ATM network.

**Address resolution**

Implementing IP over an ATM network requires a method of resolving IP addresses to ATM addresses. The address resolution table could be configured manually, but this is not a very scalable solution. The IP-Over-ATM working group has defined a protocol to support automatic address resolution of IP addresses in RFC 1577. This RFC introduces Logical IP Subnet (LIS), which, as a normal IP subnet, consists of a collection of IP nodes that make-up an ATM network and belong to the same IP subnet (just like a normal IP subnet). Then, for addresses resolution of the nodes within the LIS, each LIS has a single ATMARP server. All nodes (LIS clients) within the LIS are configured with the unique ATM address of the ATMARP server.

When an ATM nodes starts up, the following is implemented:

- The LIS client, using the configured address, connects to the ATMARP server.
- The ATMARP server transmits an Inverse ARP request to the LIS client, which requests the IP and ATM addresses of the node.
- ATMARP server adds the IP and ATM addresses of the client to its ATMARP table.
- Nodes then send an ATMARP request to the ATMARP server, which tries to resolve the destination IP address and return back its ATM address. If it cannot resolve it, it returns back an ATM_NAK response.
- On a successful return address, the LIS client has obtained the ATM address it can then communicate with the ATM node.
- The server periodically sends out Inverse ARP requests to client. If they do not respond, the server deletes their entry from its address table.

## 6.17  AAL service levels

The AAL layer uses cells to process data into a cell-based format and to provide information to configure the level of service required.

### 6.17.1 Processing data

The AAL performs two essential functions for processing data as shown: the higher-level protocols present a data unit with a specific format. This data frame is then converted using a convergence sublayer with the addition of a header and trailer that give information on how the data unit should be segmented into cells and reassembled at the destination. The data is then segmented into cells, together with the convergence subsystem information and other management data, and sent through the network.

### 6.17.2 AAL functionality

The AAL layer, as part of the process, also defines the level of service that the user wants from the connection. The following shows the four classes supported. For each class there is an associated AAL (as given in Table 6.2).

Table 6.2    Four basic categories of data

|  | Timing information between source and destination | Bit rate characteristics | Connection mode |
|---|---|---|---|
| Class A | ✓ | Constant | Connection-oriented |
| Class B | ✓ | Variable | Connection-oriented |
| Class C | ✗ | Variable | Connection-oriented |
| Class D | ✗ | Variable | Connectionless |

### 6.17.3 AAL services

Thus class A supports a constant bit rate with a connection and preserves timing information. This is typically used for voice transmission. Class B is similar to A but has a variable bit rate. Typically it is used for video/audio data (such as, over the Internet). Class C also has a variable bit rate and is connection-oriented, although there is no timing information. This is typically used for non-real-time data, such as computer data. Class D is the same as class C, but is connectionless. This means there is no connection between the sender and the receiver before the data is transmitted.

There are four AAL services: AAL1 (for class A), AAL2 (for class B), AAL3/4 or AAL5 (for class C) and AAL3/4 (for class D).

**AAL1**

The AAL1 supports class A and is intended for real-time voice traffic; it provides a constant bit rate and preserves timing information over a connection. The format of the 48 bytes of the data cell consists of 47 bytes of data, such as PCM or ADPCM code and a 1-byte header. Figure 6.12 shows the format of the cell, including the cell header. The 47-byte data field is described as the SAR-PDU (segmentation and reassembly protocol data units). The header consists of:

- SN (4 bits) which is a sequence number.
- SNP (4 bits) which is the sequence number protection.

| 5 bytes | 4 bits | 4 bits | 47 bytes |
|---|---|---|---|
| Cell header | SNP | SNP | SAR-PDU data |

**Figure 6.12**    Cell format

**AAL type 2**

AAL type 2 is under further study.

## AAL type 3/4

Type 3/4 is connection-oriented where the bit rate is variable and there is no need for timing information (Figure 6.13). It uses two main formats:

- SAR (segment and reassemble) which is segments of CPCS PDU with a SAR header and trailer. The extra SAR fields allow the data to be reassembled at the receiver. When the CPCS PDU data has been reassembled the header and trailer are discarded. The fields in the SAR are:
    - Segment type (ST) identifies how the SAR has been segmented. Figure 6.13 shows how the CPCS PDU data has been segmented into five segments: one beginning segment, three continuation segments and one end segment. The ST field has 2 bits and can therefore contain one of four possible types:

        - SSM (single sequence message) identifies that the SAR contains the complete data.
        - BOM (beginning of message) identifies that it is the first SAR PDU in a sequence.
        - COM (continuation of message) identifies that it is an intermediate SAR PDU.
        - EOM (end of message) identifies that it is the last SAR PDU.

    - Sequence number (SN) which is used to reassemble a SAR SDU and thus verify that all of the SAR PDUs have been received.
    - Multiplexing indication (MI) which is a unique identifier associated with the set of SAR PDUs that carry a single SAR SDU.
    - Length indication (LI) which defines the number of bytes in the SAR PDU. It can have a value between 4 and 44. The COM and BOM types will always have a value of 44. If the EOM field contains fewer than 44 bytes, it is padded to fill the remaining bytes. The LI then indicates the number of value bytes. For example if the LI is 20; there are only 20 value bytes in the SAR PDU the other 24 are padding bytes.
    - CRC which is a 10-bit CRC for the entire SAR PDU.

- CPCS (convergence protocol sublayer) takes data from the PDU. As this can be any length, the data is padded so it can be divided by four. A header and trailer are then added and the completed data stream is converted into one or more SAR PDU format cells. Figure 6.14 shows the format of the CPCS-PDU for AAL type 3/4.

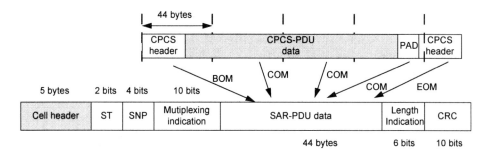

**Figure 6.13** AAL type 3/4 cell format

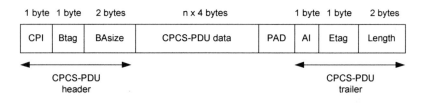

**Figure 6.14** CPCS-PDU type 3/4 frame format

The fields in the CPCS-PDU are:

- CPI (common part indicator) which indicates how the remaining fields are interpreted (currently one version exists).
- Btag (beginning tag) which is a value associated with the CPCS-PDU data. The Etag has the same value as the Btag.
- BASize (buffer allocation size) which indicates the size of the buffer that must be reserved so that the completed message can be stored.
- AI (alignment) a single byte which is added to make the trailer equal to 32 bits.
- Etag (end tag) which is the same as the Btag value.
- Length which gives the length of the CPCS PDU data field.

### AAL type 5

AAL type 5 is a connectionless service; it has no timing information and can have a variable bit rate. It assumes that one of the levels above the AAL can establish and maintain a connection (such as TCP). Type 5 provides stronger error checking with a 32-bit CRC for the entire CPCS PDU, whereas type 3/4 only allows a 10-bit CRC which is error checking for each SAR PDU. The type 5 format is given in Figure 6.15. The fields are:

- CPCS-UU (CPCS user-to-user) indication.
- CPI (common part indicator) which indicates how the remaining fields are interpreted (currently one version exists).
- Length which gives the length of the CPCS-PDU data.
- CRC which is a 32-bit CRC field.

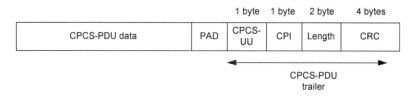

**Figure 6.15** CPCS-PDU type 5 frame format

The type 5 CPCS-PDU is then segmented into groups of 44 bytes and the ATM cell header is added. Thus, type 5 does not have the overhead of the SAR-PDU header and trailer (i.e. it does not have ST, SN, MID, LI or CRC). This means it does not contain any sequence numbers. It is thus assumed that the cells will always be received in the correct order and none of the cells will be lost. Types 3/4 and 5 can be summarised as follows:

Type 3/4: SAR-PDU overhead is 4 bytes, CPCS-PDU overhead is 8 bytes.
Type 5: SAR-PDU overhead is 0 bytes, CPCS-PDU overhead is 8 bytes.

Type 5 can be characterised as:

- Strong error checking.
- Lack of sequence numbers.
- Reduced overhead of the SAR-PDU header and trailer.

## 6.18 Exercises

**6.18.1** The main advantage that ATM has over traditional LAN technologies is:

(a) It is cheaper to implement
(b) It properly supports real-time and non-real-time traffic
(c) It is easier to interface to
(d) It properly supports TCP/IP

**6.18.2** What is the sampling rate for speech:

(a) 4 kHz (b) 8 kHz
(c) 20 kHz (d) 44.1 kHz

**6.18.3** What is the sampling rate for hi-fi audio:

(a) 4 kHz (b) 8 kHz
(c) 20 kHz (d) 44.1 kHz

**6.18.4** Referring to Table 6.2, which class would speech use:

(a) Class A (b) Class B
(c) Class C (d) Class D

**6.18.5** Discuss how ATM connections are more efficient in their transmission than ISDN and PCM-TDM. Also, determine the time between samples for speech (maximum frequency 4 kHz), audio (maximum frequency 20 kHz) and for video (maximum frequency 6 MHz).

**6.18.6** Explain the fields in an ATM cell. Also explain how ATM cells are routed through a network, highlighting why the cells always take a fixed route.

**6.18.7** Explain virtual channels, virtual paths and their uses.

**6.18.8** Explain the AAL service levels and give examples of data types which might use the service levels.

**6.18.9** Explain why computer-type data normally differs in its traffic profile from speech and video data.

**6.18.10** Investigate a local WAN; determine its network topology and its network technology.

**6.18.11** If there is access to an Internet connection, use the WWW to investigate the current status of the EaStMAN network (http://www.eastman.ac.uk).

## 6.19 Note from the author

*Until recently, it seemed unlikely that Ethernet would survive as a provider of network backbones and for campus networks, and its domain would stay, in the short-term, with connections to local computers. The world seemed distended for the global domination of ATM, the true integrator of real-time and non real-time data. This was due to Ethernet's lack of support for real-time traffic and that it does not cope well with traffic rates that approach the maximum bandwidth of a segment (as the number of collisions increases with the amount of traffic on a segment). ATM seemed to be the logical choice as it analyses the type of data being transmitted and reserves a route for the given quality of service. It looked as if ATM would migrate down from large-scale networks to the connection of computers, telephones, and all types analogue/digital communications equipment. But, remember, not always the best technological solution wins the battle for the market, a specialist is normally always trumped by a good all-rounder.*

*Ethernet also does not provide for quality of service and requires other higher-level protocols, such as IEEE 802.1p. These disadvantages, though, are often outweighed by its simplicity, its upgradeability, its reliability and its compatibility. One way to overcome the contention problem is to provide a large enough bandwidth so that the network is not swamped by sources which burst data onto the network. For this, the Gigabit Ethernet standard is likely to be the best solution for most networks.*

*Another advantage that Ethernet has over ATM is in its lack of complexity. Ethernet is simple and well supported by most software and hardware companies. ATM, on the other hand, still has many issues to be resolved, such as routing, ATM addressing and the methods of analysing and providing a given quality of service.*

# 7 Example MANs

## 7.1    Introduction

This chapter investigates some typical Metropolitan Area Networks (MANs) within a country. The UK offers an excellent model as it contains many institutions of Higher Education, which have developed high-speed MANs. Many cities around the UK have developed WANs. These networks are not based on contention networks, such as Ethernet, and are based on FDDI and ATM. Typical MANs in the UK are:

| Network | Universities connected | WWW link |
|---|---|---|
| EASTMAN | Edinburgh, Heriot Watt, Stirling, Napier and Queen Margaret College. | `http://www.eastman.net.uk` |
| FaTMAN | Dundee, St Andrews, Abertay and Northern College | `http://www.dundee.ac.uk/itservices/fatman` |
| AbMAN | Aberdeen, Northern College of Education, Robert Gordons University, Aberdeen College and Scottish Agricultural College. | |
| CLYDENET | University of Glasgow, University of Strathclyde, University of Paisley, Glasgow Caledonian University | `http://greenock-bank.clyde.net.uk` |
| G-MING | UMIST, Manchester | `http://www.g-ming.net.uk/G-MING` |
| London MAN | ULCC, UCL, Telehouse, Greenwich, South Bank, Imperial College | `http://www.lonman.net.uk` |
| Bristol and West of England | Bristol | `http://www.bwe.net.uk/` |
| South Wales MAN | University of Wales University of Glamorgan University of Wales College University of Wales Institute University of Wales College of Medicine Swansea Institute of Higher Education Welsh College of Music and Drama | `http://www.cardiff.ac.uk/uwcc/comp/man.html` |

## 7.2    JANET and SuperJANET

JANET is the UK's academic and research network, which is funded by the JISC (Joint Information Systems Committee) [http://www.jisc.ac.uk/] of the Higher Education Funding Councils of England (HEFCE), SHEFC (Scotland), Wales (HEFCW) and the Department of Education for Northern Ireland (DENI). JANET is managed and developed by UKERNA [http://www.ukerna.ac.uk/].

The JANET network connects to many higher education and research institutes. These are shown in Figure 7.1. It also provides a connect onto the Internet, other National Research Networks (NRNs) in Europe, the US and the rest of the world.

SuperJANET was initiated in 1989 and provided a broadband fibre optic based network. SuperJANET was envisaged as a network of networks formed by a national network complemented by a number of regional networks (MANs) serving areas where several HE institutions are located closely together. The SuperJANET project has transformed the JANET network from one primarily handling data to a network capable of simultaneously transporting video and audio as well as data.

## 7.3    EaStMAN

As mentioned in Chapter 5 a MAN has been set-up around Edinburgh, UK. It consists of two rings on ATM and FDDI, which run around the Edinburgh sites. This also connects to the University of Stirling through a 155 Mbps SDH connection. The main connection to the SuperJANET network, is at the University of Edinburgh. The two different network technologies allow the universities to operate a two-speed network. For computer-type data the well-established FDDI technology provides good reliable communications and the ATM network allows for future exploitation of mixed voice, data and video transmissions.

The JANET and SuperJANET networks provide connections to all UK universities. A gateway out of the network to the rest of the world is located at University College London (UCL).

The 100 Mbps FDDI dual rings link 10 Edinburgh city sites. This ring provides for IP traffic on SuperJANET and also for high-speed metropolitan connections. Initially a 155 Mbps SDH/STM-1 ATM network connected five Edinburgh sites and the University of Stirling. This also connected to the SuperJANET ATM pilot network. Figure 7.2 and Figure 7.3 show the FDDI and ATM connections. The connected sites are:

- University of Edinburgh (King's Buildings/ Old College/ New College/ Pollock Halls).
- Heriot Watt University (Riccarton Campus).
- Napier University (Sighthill/ Merchiston).
- Edinburgh College of Art.
- Moray House (Holyrood Campus).
- Queen Margaret's College (Corstorphine).

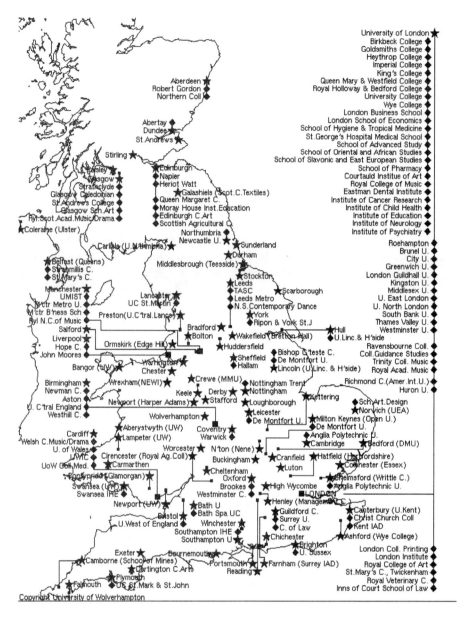

University of London ★
Birkbeck College ◆
Goldsmiths College ◆
Heythrop College ◆
Imperial College ◆
King's College ◆
Queen Mary & Westfield College ◆
Royal Holloway & Bedford College ◆
University College ◆
Wye College ◆
London Business School ◆
London School of Economics ◆
School of Hygiene & Tropical Medicine ◆
St.George's Hospital Medical School ◆
School of Advanced Study ◆
School of Oriental and African Studies ◆
School of Slavonic and East European Studies ◆
School of Pharmacy ◆
Courtauld Institue of Art ◆
Royal College of Music ◆
Eastman Dental Institute ◆
Institute of Cancer Research ◆
Institute of Child Health ◆
Institute of Education ◆
Institute of Neurology ◆
Institute of Psychiatry ◆

Roehampton ◆
Brunel U. ◆
City U. ◆
Greenwich U. ◆
London Guildhall U. ◆
Kingston U. ◆
Middlesex U. ◆
U. East London ◆
U. North London ◆
South Bank U. ◆
Thames Valley U. ◆
Westminster U. ◆

Ravensbourne Coll. ◆
Coll.Guidance Studies ◆
Trinity Coll. Music ◆
Royal Acad. Music ◆

Richmond C.(Amer.Int.U.) ◆
Huron U. ◆

Sch.Art.Design ◆
Norwich (UEA) ★

Bedford (DMU) ◆

Colchester (Essex) ★

Chelmsford (Writtle C.) ◆
Anglia Polytechnic U. ◆

Canterbury (U.Kent) ★
Christ Church Coll ◆
Kent IAD ★
Ashford (Wye College) ◆

London Coll. Printing ◆
London Institute ◆
Royal College of Art ◆
St.Mary's C., Twickenham ◆
Royal Veterinary C. ◆
Inns of Court School of Law ◆

**Figure 7.1**  UK higher education institutes and research organisations

After the great success of the Phase I installation, the network was expanded to
take in other campuses, as well as the connection to other Scottish MANs, such as
FatMAN, AbMAN and ClydeNET. These connections are shown in Figure 7.4. The
connections to the other Scottish MANs is intended to allow a Virtual Campus around
Scotland. With this lectures can be transmitted from one of the sites, and viewed by
students on other campuses and institutions.

114  *Mastering Networks*

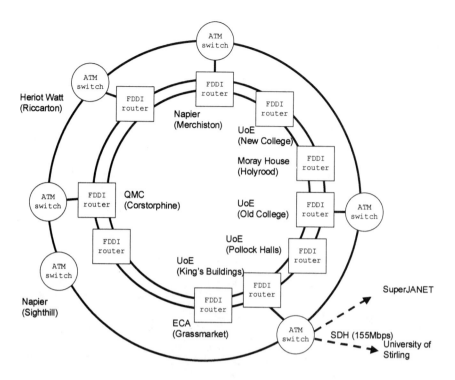

**Figure 7.2**  EaStMAN ring connections Phase I

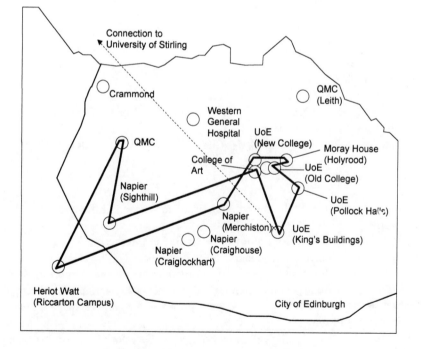

**Figure 7.3**  EaStMAN phase I connections

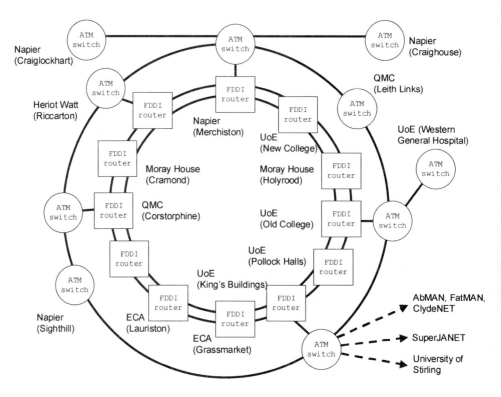

**Figure 7.4**  EaStMAN ring connections Phase II

The total circumference of the EASTMAN ring is 83 km, and the new connected sites in Phase II were:

- Queen Margaret's College (Leith Links).
- Napier University (Craighouse/ Craiglockhart).
- University of Edinburgh (Western General Hospital/ Royal Infirmary).
- Edinburgh College of Art (Lauriston).
- Connections to other Scottish MANs (FatMAN, AbMAN and ClydeMAN).

The potential applications of the MAN include.

- Video Conferencing. Staff connect with academics around Edinburgh, the UK and the world.
- SuperJANET facilities. Connection onto the Global Internet.
- Library applications. Remote connection to libraries.
- Computer-based learning applications. As the bandwidth can support multi-media applications, as well as connection on the Internet, there is thus the potential for computer-based education.
- Visible Human Project.
- Master class teaching. This will allow experts to give tutorial support, or even give lectures over the MAN.

- WWW cache. This allows important WWW pages to be stored locally in a WWW cache.
- USENET News.
- Inter HEI collaboration. This allows academics to contact each other over video conferencing.
- Future connections to business/industrial/government/school networks.

### 7.3.1 *EaStMAN addressing scheme*

The private ATM addressing scheme is defined in Section 6.13.3.

### 7.3.2 *IP addresses*

The IP addresses and DNS names of the FDDI nodes are:

| Site | IP address | DNS name |
|------|-----------|----------|
| UoE (Old College) | 194.81.56.65 | oc2.ed.eastman.net.uk |
| UoE (Pollock Halls) | 194.81.56.66 | ph2.ed.eastman.net.uk |
| UoE (New College) | 194.81.56.67 | nc2.ed.eastman.net.uk |
| Moray House (Cramond) | 194.81.56.77 | gw2.mhie.eastman.net.uk |
| MHIE, Holyrood | 194.81.56.78 | gw1.mhie.eastman.net.uk |
| College of Art (Grassmarket) | 194.81.56.81 | gw1.eca.eastman.net.uk |
| College of Art (Lauriston) | 194.81.56.82 | gw2.eca.eastman.net.uk |
| QMC (Leith Links) | 194.81.56.93 | gw2.qmced.eastman.net.uk |
| QMC (Corstorphine) | 194.81.56.94 | gw1.qmced.eastman.net.uk |
| Napier University (Merchiston) | 194.81.56.97 | me1.napier.eastman.net.uk |
| Napier University ( Sighthill) | 194.81.56.98 | si1.napier.eastman.net.uk |
| Heriot-Watt University (Riccarton) | 194.81.56.110 | gw1.hw.eastman.net.uk |
| SuperJANET | 194.81.56.126 | gw1.sj.eastman.net.uk |

### 7.3.3 *Supporting non-IP protocols*

The EASTMAN network supports the following, non-IP, protocols:

- Novell IPX. Several Universities on the network (University of Edinburgh and Napier University) require the support of Novell IPX services across the MAN. The IPX number used is C25138, and represents the hexadecimal address of the first three bytes of the MAN IP network address (192 decimal is C2 in hex, 81 decimal is 56 in hex). This makes it compatible with Novell's worldwide network number registry. IPX packets are encapsulated with an FDDI frame
- AppleTalk. As with IPX, AppleTalk is required to be transmitted over the EASTMAN network. AppleTalk is encapsulated within IP and is then tunnelled.
- Other protocols. Further development will involve supporting DECnet traffic. This is likely to be encapsulated with frames.

## 7.4  FaTMAN

The FaTMAN (Fife and Tayside Metropolitan Area Network) connects higher education institutions around Fife and Tayside, Scotland. It was one of the first educational MANs within the UK and Phase I cost over £500,000. As with the EASTMAN network it was partially funded by JISC and SHEFC. The institutions connected are:

- University of Abertay, Dundee.
- University of Dundee.
- University of St. Andrews. The cables connecting the University of St. Andrews and the other institutions cross the River Tay.
- Northern College.

Figure 7.5 shows the ATM ring and the FDDI connections. The total ring size for the ATM ring is 47.8km.

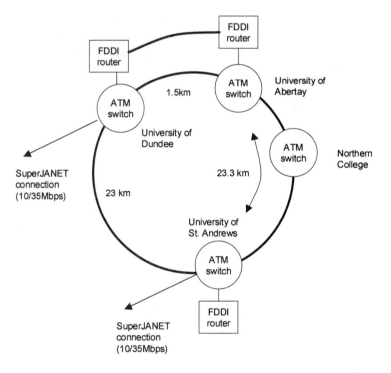

**Figure 7.5** FatMAN ring connections

## 7.5 London MAN

The London MAN connection institutions around London. Figure 7.6 shows the Phase I connections. It includes a 155 Mbps ATM ring, and several connections to satellite institutions, with 34 Mbps links.

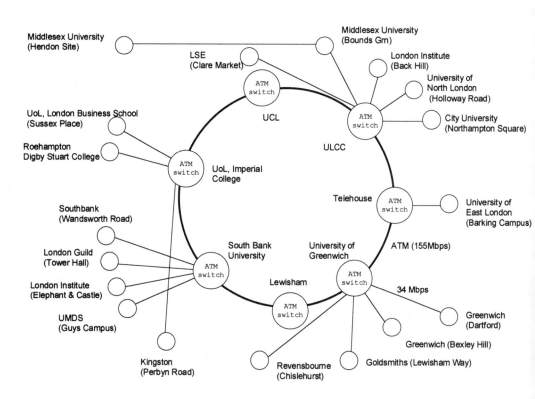

**Figure 7.6** London MAN Phase I

## 7.6 South Wales MAN

The South Wales MAN connects universities and colleges within South Wales. It was partly funded by HEFCW and JISC, and was installed by CableTel (South Wales) Ltd. The project was initiated in 1994 under the leadership of University of Wales, Cardiff. The connected sites are:

- Swansea Institute of Higher Education.
- University of Glamorgan.
- University of Wales College of Medicine.
- University of Wales College, Newport.
- University of Wales Institute, Cardiff.
- University of Wales, Cardiff.
- University of Wales, Swansea.
- Welsh College of Music and Drama.

which includes the following connections:

- University of Wales (UW), Cardiff Cathays Park.
- University of Wales, Swansea, Singleton Park.
- University of Glamorgan, Treforest.
- University of Glamorgan, Glyntaff.
- University of Wales College, Newport, Allt-yr-Yn.
- University of Wales College, Newport, Caerleon.
- University of Wales Institute, Cardiff, Llandaff.
- University of Wales Institute, Cardiff, Colchester Avenue.
- University of Wales College of Medicine (UWCM), Heath Park.
- University of Wales College of Medicine, Llandough Hospital.
- Swansea Institute of Higher Education (SIHE), Town Hill.
- Swansea Institute of Higher Education, Mount Pleasant.
- Welsh College of Music and Drama, Cathays Park.

Initially the network was installed with SDH links of 155 Mbps, this was to be followed up with ATM switches. Its basic architecture is two hubs at University of Wales (Cardiff) and another at University of Wales (Swansea). All of the other institutions involved connect to one of these hubs. Figure 7.7 shows the Phase I connections.

Upgraded connections include the connection to Aberwystwyth, the Welsh Office, the National Museum of Wales, the Higher Education Funding Council for Wales and ten other Further Education sites in South Wales.

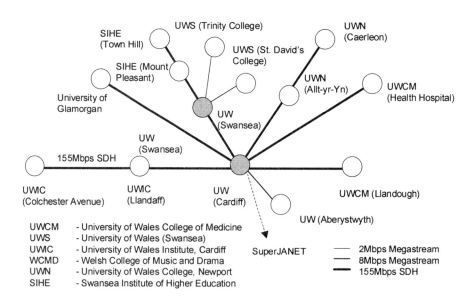

**Figure 7.7**   South Wales MAN connections

ClydeNET covers the geographical area around the River Clyde, in Glasgow, Scotland. The following institutions connect to ClydeNET:

- Glasgow University.
- Strathclyde University.
- The University of Paisley.
- The Glasgow Caledonian University.
- St Andrew's College.
- The Royal Infirmary.
- The Glasgow School of Art.
- The Royal Scottish Academy of Music and Drama.

It is based on 155 Mbps ATM links, and is illustrated in Figure 7.8.

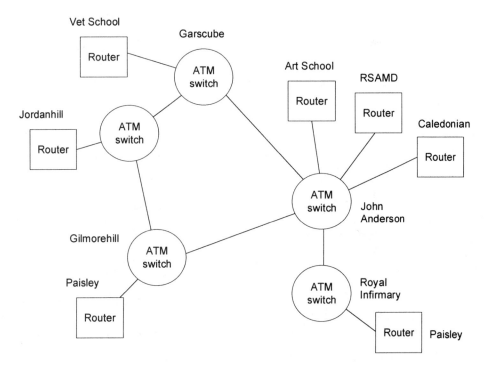

**Figure 7.8**   ClydeMAN connections

## 7.8    Exercises

**7.8.1**       Investigate the MANs around the UK. The main links are:

| | |
|---|---|
| EASTMAN | `http://www.eastman.net.uk` |
| FATMAN | `http://www.dundee.ac.uk/itservices/fatman` |
| ClydeMAN | `http://greenock-bank.clyde.net.uk` |
| G-MING | `http://www.g-ming.net.uk/G-MING` |
| London MAN | `http://www.lonman.net.uk` |
| Bristol and West of England | `http://www.bwe.net.uk` |
| South Wales MAN | `http://www.cardiff.ac.uk/uwcc/comp/man.html` |

**7.8.2** Using the `ping` command, determine the time delay to reach the following nodes on the EASTMAN network:

```
oc2.ed.eastman.net.uk      ph2.ed.eastman.net.uk
nc2.ed.eastman.net.uk      gw2.mhie.eastman.net.uk
gw1.mhie.eastman.net.uk    gw1.eca.eastman.net.uk
gw2.eca.eastman.net.uk     gw2.qmced.eastman.net.uk
gw1.qmced.eastman.net.uk   me1.napier.eastman.net.uk
si1.napier.eastman.net.uk  gw1.hw.eastman.net.uk
gw1.sj.eastman.net.uk
```

**7.8.3** Using the `traceroute` command, determine the route from the network that your node connects to, to the following:

```
www.ed.ac.uk       University of Edinburgh WWW Server
www.hw.ac.uk       Heriot Watt WWW Server
www.napier.ac.uk   Napier University WWW Server
```

From this, identify the route around the EASTMAN network, and to Super-JANET.

**7.8.4** Investigate the MANs around the UK. Use the ping command to determine if they are responding to TCP/IP traffic.

**7.8.5** Investigate MANs around the world. Use the `ping` command to determine if they are responding to TCP/IP traffic. Also, use the `traceroute` command to determine a route to them.

# 8 ISDN

## 8.1 Introduction

A major problem in data communications and networks is the integration of real-time sampled data with non-real-time (normal) computer data. Sampled data tends to create a constant traffic flow whereas computer-type data has bursts of traffic. In addition, sampled data normally needs to be delivered at a given time but computer-type data needs a reliable path where delays are relatively unimportant.

The basic rate for real-time data is speech. It is normally sampled at a rate of 8 kHz and each sample is coded with eight bits. This leads to a transmission bit rate of 64 kbps. ISDN uses this transmission rate for its base transmission rate. Computer-type data can then be transmitted using this rate or can be split to transmit over several 64 kbps channels. The basic rate ISDN service uses two 64 kbps data lines and a 16 kbps control line, as illustrated in Figure 8.1. Table 8.1 summarises the I series CCITT standards.

Typically, modems are used in the home for the transmission of computer-type data. Unfortunately, modems have a maximum bit rate of 56 kbps. With ISDN, this is automatically increased, on a single channel, to 64 kbps. The connections made by a modem and by ISDN are circuit-switched.

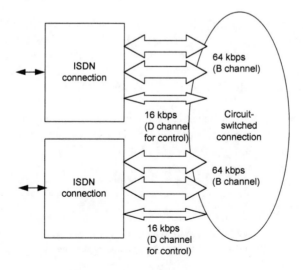

**Figure 8.1** Basic rate ISDN services

**Table 8.1** CCITT standards on ISDN

| CCITT standard number | Description |
|---|---|
| I.1XX | ISDN terms and technology |
| I.2XX | ISDN services |
| I.3XX | ISDN addressing |
| I.430 and I.431 | ISDN physical layer interface |
| I.440 and I.441 | ISDN data layer interface |
| I.450 and I.451 | ISDN network layer interface |
| I.5XX | ISDN internetworking |
| I.6XX | ISDN maintenance |

The great advantage of an ISDN connection is that the type of data transmitted is irrelevant to the transmission and switching circuitry. Thus, it can carry other types of digital data, such as facsimile, teletex, videotex and computer data. This reduces the need for modems, which convert digital data into an analogue form, only for the public telephone network to convert the analogue signal back into a digital form for transmission over a digital link. It is also possible to multiplex the basic rate of 64 kbps to give even higher data rates. This multiplexing is known as $N \times 64$ kbps or Broadband ISDN (B-ISDN).

Another advantage of ISDN is that it is a circuit-switched connection where a permanent connection is established between two nodes. This connection is guaranteed for the length of the connection. It also has a dependable delay time and is thus suited to real-time data.

## 8.2 ISDN channels

ISDN uses channels to identify the data rate, each based on the 64 kbps provision. Typical channels are B, D, H0, H11 and H12. The B-channel has a data rate of 64 kbps and provides a circuit-switched connection between endpoints. A D-channel operates at 16 kbps and it controls the data transfers over the B channels. The other channels provide B-ISDN for much higher data rates. Table 8.2 outlines the basic data rates for these channels.

The two main types of interface are the basic rate access and the primary rate access. Both are based around groupings of B- and D-channels. The basic rate access allows two B-channels and one 16 kbps D-channel.

**Table 8.2** ISDN channels

| Channel | Description |
|---|---|
| B | 64 kbps |
| D | 16 kbps signalling for channel B (ISDN) |
|   | 64 kbps signalling for channel B (B-ISDN) |
| H0 | 384 kbps ($6 \times 64$ kbps) for B-ISDN |
| H11 | 1.536 Mbps ($24 \times 64$ kbps) for B-ISDN |
| H12 | 1.920 Mbps ($30 \times 64$ kbps) for B-ISDN |

Primary rate provides B-ISDN, such as H12 which gives 30 B-channels and a 64 kbps D-channel. For basic and primary rates, all channels multiplex onto a single line by combining channels into frames and adding extra synchronisation bits. Figure 8.3 gives examples of the basic rate and primary rate (See Section 8.7).

The basic rate ISDN gives two B-channels at 64 kbps and a signalling channel at 16 kbps. These multiplex into a frame and, after adding extra framing bits, the total output data rate is 192 kbps. The total data rate for the basic rate service is thus 128 kbps. One or many devices may multiplex their data, such as two devices transmitting at 64 kbps, a single device multiplexing its 128 kbps data over two channels (giving 128 kbps), or by several devices transmitting a sub-64 kbps data rate over the two channels. For example, four 32 kbps devices could simultaneously transmit their data, eight 16 kbps devices, and so on.

For H12, 30 × 64 kbps channels multiplex with a 64 kbps-signalling channel, and with extra framing bits, the resulting data rate is 2.048 Mbps (compatible with European PCM-TDM systems). This means the actual data rate is 1.920 Mbps. As with the basic service this could contain a number of devices with a data rate of less than or greater than a multiple of 64 kbps.

For H11, 24 × 64 kbps channels multiplex with a 64 kbps-signalling channel, and with extra framing bits, it produces a data rate of 1.544 Mbps (compatible with USA PCM-TDM systems). The actual data rate is 1.536 Mbps.

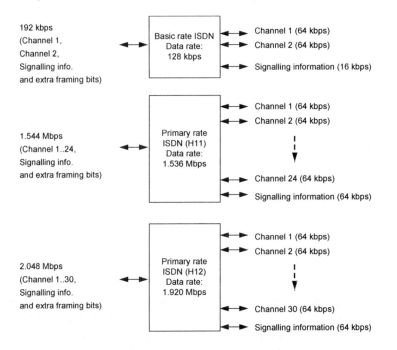

**Figure 8.2** Basic rate, H11 and H12 ISDN services

## 8.3  ISDN physical layer interfacing

The physical layer corresponds to layer 1 of the OSI 7-layer model and is defined in CCITT specifications I.430 and I.431. Pulses on the line are not coded as pure binary, they use a technique called alternate mark inversion (AMI).

### 8.3.1  Alternative mark inversion (AMI) line code

AMI line codes use three voltage levels. In pure AMI, 0 V represents a '0', and the voltage amplitude for each '1' is the inverse of the previous '1' bit. ISDN uses the inverse of this, i.e. 0 V for a '1' and an inverse in voltage for a '0', as shown in Figure 8.3. Normally the pulse amplitude is 0.75 V.

   Inversion of the AMI signal (i.e. inverting a '0' rather than a '1') allows for timing information to be recovered when there are long runs of zeros, which is typical in the idle state. AMI line code also automatically balances the signal voltage, and the average voltage will be approximately zero even when there are long runs of 0's (this is a requirement as the connection to the network is transformer coupled).

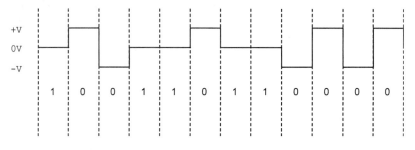

**Figure 8.3**  AMI used in ISDN

### 8.3.2  System connections

In basic rate connections, up to eight devices, or items of termination equipment (TE), can connect to the network termination (NT). They connect over a common four-wire bus using two sets of twisted-pair cables. The transmit output ($T_x$) on each TE connects to the transmit output on the other TEs, and the receive input ($R_x$) on each TE connects to all other TEs. On the NT the receive input connects to the transmit of the TEs, and the transmit output of the NT connects to the receive input of the TEs. A contention protocol allows only one TE to communicate at a time.

   An 8-pin ISO 8877 connector connects a TE to the NT; this is similar to the RJ-45 connector. Figure 8.4 shows the pin connections. Pins 3 and 6 carry the $T_x$ signal from the TE, pins 4 and 5 provide the $R_x$ to the TEs. Pins 7 and 8 are the secondary power supply from the NT and pins 1 and 2 the power supply from the TE (if used). The $T_x/R_x$ lines connect via transformers thus only the AC part of the bitstream transfers into the PCM circuitry of the TE and the NT. This produces a need for a balanced DC line code such as AMI, as the DC component in the bitstream will not pass through the transformers.

### 8.3.3  Frame format

Figures 8.5 and 8.6 show the ISDN frame formats. Each frame is 250 µs long and contains 48 bits; this give a total bit rate of 192 kbps ($48/250 \times 10^{-6}$) made up of two 64 kbps B channels, one 16 kbps D-channel and extra framing, DC balancing and synchronisation bits.

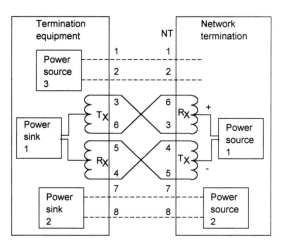

**Figure 8.4** Power supplies between NT and TE

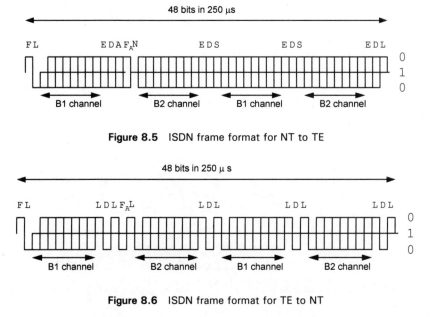

**Figure 8.5** ISDN frame format for NT to TE

**Figure 8.6** ISDN frame format for TE to NT

where
| | | | | | |
|---|---|---|---|---|---|
| F | – | framing bit | N | – | set to a 1 |
| L | – | DC balancing bit | D | – | D-channel bit |
| E | – | D-echo channel bit | $F_A$ | – | auxiliary framing bit ($= 0$) |
| S | – | reserved for future use | A | – | activation bit |
| M | – | multiframing bit | B1 | – | bits for channel 1 |
| B2 | – | bits for channel 2 | | | |

The F/L pair of bits identify the start of each transmitted frame. When transmitting from a TE to an NT there is a 10-bit offset in the return of the frame back to the TE. The E bits echo the D-channel bits back to the TE.

When transmitting from the NT to the TE, the bits after the F/L bits, in the B-channel, have a volition in the first 0. If any of these bits is a 0 then a volition will occur, but if they are 1's then no volition can occur. To overcome this the $F_A$ bit forces a volition. Since it is followed by 0 (the N bit) it will not be confused with the F/L pair. The start of the frame can thus be traced backwards to find the F/L pair.

There are 16 bits for each B-channel, giving a basic data rate of 64 kbps $(16/250 \times 10^{-6})$ and there are 4 bits in the frame for the D-channel, giving a bit rate of 16 kbps $(4/250 \times 10^{-6})$.

The L bit balances the DC level on the line. If the number of 0's following the last balancing bit is odd then the balancing bit is a 0, else it is a 1. When synchronised the NT informs the TEs by setting the A bit.

## 8.4   ISDN data link layer

The data link layer uses a protocol known as the Link Access Procedure for the D-channel (LAPD). Figure 8.7 shows the frame format. The unique bit sequence 01111110 identifies the start and end of the frame. This bit pattern cannot occur in the rest of the frame due to zero bit-stuffing.

The address field contains information on the type of data contained in the frame (the service access point identifier) and the physical address of the ISDN device (the terminal endpoint identifier). The control field contains a supervisory, an unnumbered or an information frame. The frame check sequence provides error detection information.

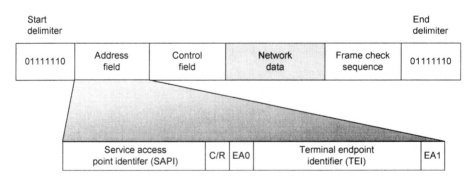

**Figure 8.7**   D-channel frame structure

### 8.4.1   Address field

The data link address only contains addressing information to connect the TE to the NT and does not have network addresses. Figure 8.7 shows the address field format. The SAPI identifies the type of ISDN services. For example, a frame from a telephone would be identified as such, and only telephones would read the frame.

All TEs connect to a single multiplexed bus, thus each has a unique data link address, known as a terminal endpoint identifier (TEI). The user or the network sets this; the ranges of available addresses are:

| | |
|---|---|
| 0–63 | non-automatic assignment TEIs |
| 64–126 | automatic assignment TEIs |
| 127 | global TEI |

The non-automatic assignment involves the user setting the address of each of the devices connected to the network. When a device transmits data it inserts its own TEI address and only receives data which has its TEI address. In most cases devices should not have the same TEI address, as this would cause all devices with the same TEI address, and the SAPI, to receive the same data (although, in some cases, this may be a requirement).

The network allocates addresses to devices requiring automatic assignment before they can communicate with any other devices. The global TEI address is used to broadcast messages to all connected devices. A typical example is when a telephone call is incoming to a group on a shared line where all the telephones would ring until one was answered.

The C/R bit is the command/response bit and EA0/EA1 are extended address field bits.

### 8.4.2 Bit stuffing

With zero bit-stuffing the transmitter inserts a zero into the bitstream when transmitting five consecutive 1's. When the receiver receives five consecutive 1's it deletes the next bit if it is a zero. This stops the unique 01111110 sequence occurring within the frame. For example if the bits to be transmitted are:

10100010101111110000101000101000011111010101010

then with the start and end delimiter this would be:

01111110101000101*01111111*0000101000101000011111010101001111110

It can be seen from this bitstream that the stream to be transmitted contains the delimiter within the frame. This zero bit-insertion is applied to give:

01111110101000101*011111*0*1*00001010001010000111110010101001111110

Notice that the transmitter has inserted a zero when five consecutive 1's occur. Thus the bit pattern 01111110 cannot occur anywhere in the bitstream. When the receiver receives five consecutive 1's it deletes the next bit if it is a zero. If it is a 1 then it is a valid delimiter. In the example the received stream will be:

01111110101000101011111100001010001010000111110101010001111110

### 8.4.3 Control field

ISDN uses a 16-bit control field for information and supervisory frames and an 8-bit field for unnumbered frames, as illustrated in Figure 8.8. Information frames contain sequenced data. The format is 0SSSSSSSXRRRRRRR, where SSSSSSS is the send sequence number and RRRRRRR is the frame sequence number that the sender expects to receive next (X is the poll/final bit). Since the extended mode uses a 7-bit sequence field then information frames are numbered from 0 to 127.

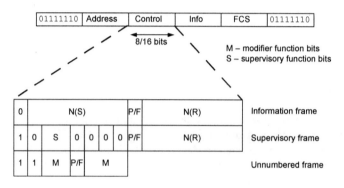

**Figure 8.8** ISDN control field

Supervisory frames contain flow control data. Table 8.3 lists the supervisory frame types and the control field bit settings. The RRRRRRR value represent the 7-bit receive sequence number.

**Table 8.3** Supervisory frame types and control field settings

| Type | Control field setting |
|------|----------------------|
| Receiver ready (RR) | 10000000PRRRRRRR |
| Receiver not ready (RNR) | 10100000PRRRRRRR |
| Reject (REJ) | 10010000PRRRRRRR |

Unnumbered frames set up and clear connections between a node and the network. Table 8.4 lists the unnumbered frame commands and Table 8.5 lists the unnumbered frame responses.

**Table 8.4** Unnumbered frame commands and control field settings

| Type | Control field setting |
|------|----------------------|
| Set asynchronous balance mode extended (SABME) | 1111P110 |
| Unnumbered information (UI) | 1100F000 |
| Disconnect mode (DISC) | 1100P010 |

**Table 8.5** Unnumbered frame responses and control field settings

| Type | Control field setting |
|---|---|
| Disconnect mode (DM) | 1111P110 |
| Unnumbered acknowledgment (UA) | 1100F000 |
| Frame reject (FRMR) | 1110P001 |

In ISDN all connected nodes and the network connection can send commands and receive responses. Figure 8.9 shows a sample connection of an incoming call to an ISDN node (address TEI_1). The SABME mode is set up initially using the SABME command (U[SABME,TEI_1,P=1]), followed by an acknowledgement from the ISDN node (U[UA,TEI_1,F=1]). At any time, either the network or the node can disconnect the connection. In this case the ISDN node disconnects the connection with the command U[DISC,TEI_1,P=1]. The network connection acknowledges this with an unnumbered acknowledgement (U[UA,TEI_1,F=1]).

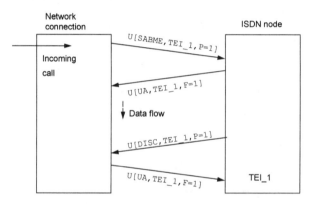

**Figure 8.9** Example connection between a primary/secondary

### 8.4.4 D-channel contention

The D-channel contention protocol ensures that only one terminal can transmit its data at a time. This happens because the start and the end of the D-channel bits have the bitstream 01111110, as shown below:

1111**10111110**XXXXXXXXX...XXXXXXXX**011111110**1111

When idle, each TE floats to a high-impedance state, which is taken as a binary 1. To transmit, a TE counts the number of 1's in the D-channel. A 0 resets this count. After a predetermined number, greater than a predetermined number of consecutive 1's, the TE transmits its data and monitors the return from the NT. If it does not receive the correct D-channel bitstream returned through the E bits then a collision has occurred. When a TE detects a collision it immediately stops transmitting and monitors the line.

When a TE has finished transmitting data it increases its count value for the number of consecutive 1's by 1. This gives other TEs an opportunity to transmit their data.

### 8.4.5 Frame check sequence

The frame check sequence (FCS) field contains an error detection code based on cyclic redundancy check (CRC) polynomials. It uses the CCITT V.41 polynomial, which is $G(x) = x^{16} + x^{12} + x^5 + x^1$.

## 8.5 ISDN network layer

The D-channel carriers network layer information within the LAPD frame. This information establishes and controls a connection. The LAPD frames contain no true data as this is carried in the B-channel. Its function is to set up and manage calls and to provide flow control between connections over the network.

Figure 8.10 shows the format of the layer three signalling message frame. The first byte is the protocol discriminator. In the future, this byte will define different communications protocols. At present it is normally set to 0001000. After the second byte the call reference length value is defined. This is used to identify particular calls with a reference number. The length of the call reference value is defined within the second byte. As it contains a 4-bit value, up to 16 bytes can be contained in the call reference value field. The next byte gives the message type and this type defines the information contained in the proceeding field.

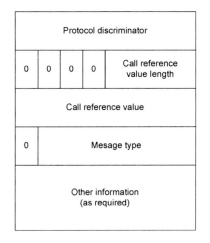

**Figure 8.10** Signalling message structure

There are four main types of message: call establish, call information, call clearing and miscellaneous messages. Table 8.6 outlines the main messages. Figure 8.11 shows an example connection procedure. The initial message sent is SETUP. This may contain some of the following:

- Channel identification – identifies a channel with an ISDN interface.
- Calling party number.

- Calling party subaddress.
- Called party number.
- Called party subnumber.
- Extra data (2–131 bytes).

After the calling TE has sent the SETUP message, the network then returns the SETUP ACK message. If there is insufficient information in the SETUP message then other information needs to flow between the called TE and the network. After this the network sends back a CALL PROCEEDING message and it also sends a SETUP message to the called TE. When the called TE detects its TEI address and SAPI, it sends back an ALERTING message. This informs the network that the node is alerting the user to answer the call. When it is answered, the called TE sends a CONNECT to the network. The network then acknowledges this with a CONNECT ACK message, at the same time it sends a CONNECT message to the calling TE. The calling TE then acknowledges this with a CONNECT ACK. The connection is then established between the two nodes and data can be transferred.

To disconnect the connection the DISCONNECT, RELEASE and RELEASE COMPLETE messages are used.

**Table 8.6** ISDN network messages

| Call establish | Information messages | Call clearing |
|---|---|---|
| ALERTING | RESUME | DISCONNECT |
| CALL PROCEEDING | RESUME ACKNOWLEDGE | RELEASE |
| CONNECT | RESUME REJECT | RELEASE COMPLETE |
| CONNECT ACKNOWLEDGE | SUSPEND | RESTART |
| PROGRESS | SUSPEND ACKNOWLEDGE | RESTART ACKNOWLEDGE |
| SETUP | SUSPEND REJECT | |
| SETUP ACKNOWLEDGE | USER INFORMATION | |

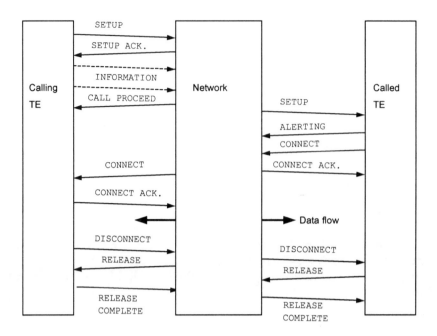

**Figure 8.11** Call establishment and clearing

## 8.6   Speech sampling

With telephone-quality speech the signal bandwidth is normally limited to 4 kHz, thus it is sampled at 8 kHz. If each sample is coded with eight bits then the basic bit rate will be:

Digitised speech signal rate = $8 \times 8$ kbps = 64 kbps

Table 8.7 outlines the main compression techniques for speech. The G.722 standard allows the best-quality signal, as the maximum speech frequency is 7 kHz rather than 4 kHz in normal coding systems; and has the equivalent of 14 coding bits. The G.728 allows extremely low bit rates (16 kbps).

## 8.7   PCM-TDM systems

Multiple channels of speech can be sent over a single line using time division multi-plexing (TDM). In the UK, a 30-channel PCM system is used, whereas the USA uses 24.

**Table 8.7**  Speech compression standards

| ITU standard | Technology | Bit rate | Description |
| --- | --- | --- | --- |
| G.711 | PCM | 64 kbps | Standard PCM |
| G.721 | ADPCM | 32 kbps | Adaptive delta PCM where each value is coded with 4 bits |
| G.722 | SB-ADPCM | 48, 56 and 64 kbps | Subband ADPCM allows for higher-quality audio signals with a sampling rate of 16 kHz |
| G.728 | LD-CELP | 16 kbps | Low-delay code excited linear prediction for low bit rates |

With a PCM-TDM system, several voice band channels are sampled, converted to PCM codes, these are then time division multiplexed onto a single transmission media.

Each sampled channel is given a time slot and all the time slots are built up into a frame. The complete frame usually has extra data added to it such as synchronisation data, and so on. Speech channels have a maximum frequency content of 4 kHz and are sampled at 8 kHz. This gives a sample time of 125 μs. In the UK a frame is built-up with 32 time slots from TS0 to TS31. TS0 and TS16 provide extra frame and synchronisation data. Each of the time slots has 8 bits, therefore the overall bit rate is:

Bits per time slot    =  8
Number of time slots    =  32
Time for frame    =  125 μs

$$\text{Bit rate} = \frac{\text{No of bits}}{\text{Time}} = \frac{32 \times 8}{125 \times 10^{-6}} = 2048 \text{ kbps}$$

In the USA and Japan this bit rate is 1.544 Mbps. These bit rates are known as the primary rate multipliers. Further interleaving of several primary rate multipliers increases the rate to 6.312, 44.736 and 139.264 Mbps (for the USA) and 8.448, 34.368 and 139.264 Mbps (for the UK).

The UK multiframe format is given in Figure 8.12. In the UK format the multiframe has 16 frames. Each frame time slot 0 is used for synchronisation and time slot 16 is used for signaling information. This information is sub-multiplexed over the 16 frames. During frame 0 a multiframe-alignment signal is transmitted in TS16 to identify the start of the multiframe structure. In the following frames, the eight binary digits available are shared by channels 1–15 and 16–30 for signalling purposes. TS16 is used as follows:

Frame    0        0000XXXX
Frames    1–15    1234 5678

where 1234 are the four signalling bits for channels 1, 2, 3, …, 15 in consecutive frames, and 5678 are the four signalling bits for channels 16, 17, 18, … 31 in consecutive frames.

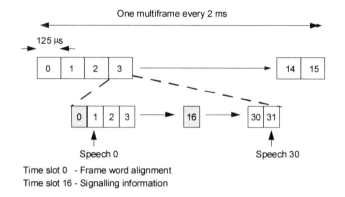

**Figure 8.12**   PCM-TDM multiframe format with 30 speech channels

Thus in the first frame the 0000XXXX code word is sent, in the next frame the first channel and the 16th channel appear in TS16, the next will contain the second and the 17th, and so on. Typical 4-bit signal information is:

1111 – circuit idle/busy
1101 – disconnection

TS0 contains a frame-alignment signal which enables the receiver to synchronise with the transmitter. The frame-alignment signal (X0011011) is transmitted in alternative frames. In the intermediate frames a signal known as a not-word is transmitted (X10XXXXX). The second binary digit is the complement of the corresponding binary digit in the frame-alignment signal. This reduces the possibility of demultiplexed mis-alignment to imitative frame-alignment signals.

Alternative frames:

TS0:   X0011011
TS0:   X10XXXXX

where X stands for don't care conditions.

---

## 8.8   Exercises

**8.8.1**    What is the function of a B-channel in ISDN:

(a)    It transmits data          (b)          It sends control information
(c)    It creates a network      (d)          It emulates a modem

**8.8.2**    What is the function of a D-channel in ISDN:

| (a) | It transmits data | (b) | It sends control information |
|-----|-------------------|-----|------------------------------|
| (c) | It creates a network | (d) | It emulates a modem |

**8.8.3**    What is the bitrate of a single ISDN B-channel:

| (a) | 16kbps | (b) | 64kbps |
|-----|--------|-----|--------|
| (c) | 128kbps | (d) | 256kbps |

**8.8.4**    What is the bitrate of the an ISDN D-channel:

| (a) | 16kbps | (b) | 64kbps |
|-----|--------|-----|--------|
| (c) | 128kbps | (d) | 256kbps |

**8.8.5**    What is the maximum bitrate of an ISDN connection:

| (a) | 16kbps | (b) | 64kbps |
|-----|--------|-----|--------|
| (c) | 128kbps | (d) | 256kbps |

**8.8.6**    Which series of CCITT (ITU-T) specify ISDN specifications:

| (a) | I-series | (b) | X-series |
|-----|----------|-----|----------|
| (c) | T-series | (d) | R-series |

**8.8.7**    What is the base bitrate for a USA PCM-TDM system:

| (a) | 1.544Mbps | (b) | 64kbps |
|-----|-----------|-----|--------|
| (c) | 2.048Mbps | (d) | 2Gbps |

**8.8.8**    What is the base bitrate for a UK PCM-TDM system:

| (a) | 1.544Mbps | (b) | 64kbps |
|-----|-----------|-----|--------|
| (c) | 2.048Mbps | (d) | 2Gbps |

**8.8.9**    How many ISDN channels does the H11 (derived from USA PCM-TDM system) support:

| (a) | 20 | (b) | 24 |
|-----|----|-----|----|
| (c) | 30 | (d) | 32 |

**8.8.10**    How many ISDN channels does the H12 (derived from UK PCM-TDM system) support:

| (a) | 20 | (b) | 24 |
|-----|----|-----|----|
| (c) | 30 | (d) | 32 |

**8.8.11**    How does ISDN AMI (Alternative Mark Inversion):

(a)    Every bit that is sent is inverted
(b)    Every one that is sent has an alternating voltage level, but the zeros are sent as a zero voltage level
(c)    Every zero that is sent has an alternating voltage level, but the ones are sent as a zero voltage level
(d)    Ones are sent as negative voltages, and zeros as positive voltages

**8.8.12**    Why does the 01111110 bit sequence only occur at the start and end of a frame:

(a)    Bit stuffing is used whenever it appears within the data frame
(b)    It is a special code that can never occur within the data
(c)    It is coded with special voltage levels
(d)    It will hardly ever occur, so the occasional error is acceptable

**8.8.13**    Show why speech requires to be transmitted at 64 kbps.

**8.8.14**    If the bandwidth of hi-fi audio is 20 kHz and 16 bits are used to code each sample, determine the required bit rate for single-channel transmission. Hence prove that the bit rate required for professional hi-fi, which is sampled at 44.1kHz is 1.4112 Mbps.

**8.8.15**    Using the rates determined in Question 8.8.14, shows that the basic rate for a CD-ROM drive is 150 kB/s.

**8.8.16**    Explain the format of the ISDN frame.

**8.8.17**    Suppose that an ISDN frame has 48 bits and takes 250 μs to transmit. Show that the bit rate on each D-channel is 16 kbps and that the bit rate of the B-channel is 64 kbps.

**8.8.18**    Explain the different types of frames and show how a connection is made between ISDN nodes.

**8.8.19**    Show how supervisory frames are used to control the flow of data.

**8.8.20**    Discuss the format of the ISDN network layer packet.

**8.8.21**    How does an ISDN node set up and disconnect a network connection.

---

## 8.9    Note from the author

*ISDN is a good short-term fix for transmitting digital data into an integrated digital network. Unfortunately, it creates a circuit-switched connection which means that users are charged for the amount of time that they are connected, and not the amount of data that they transfer. Is ATM the future?*

# 9 TCP/IP

## 9.1 Introduction

Networking technologies such as Ethernet, Token Ring and FDDI provide a data link layer function that is, they allow a reliable connection between one node and another on the same network. They do not provide internetworking where data can be transferred from one network to another or from one network segment to another. For data to be transmitted across a network requires an addressing structure which is read by a bridge, gateway and router. The interconnection of networks is known as internetworking (or an internet). Each part of an internet is a subnetwork (or subnet). Transmission Control Protocol (TCP) and Internet Protocol (IP) are a pair of protocols that allow one subnet to communicate with another. A protocol is a set of rules that allows the orderly exchange of information. The IP part corresponds to the network layer of the OSI model and the TCP part to the transport layer. Their operation is transparent to the physical and data link layers and can thus be used on Ethernet, FDDI or Token Ring networks. This is illustrated in Figure 9.1. The address of the Data Link layer corresponds to the physical address of the node, such as the MAC address (in Ethernet and Token Ring) or the telephone number (for a modem connection). The IP address is assigned to each node on the internet. It is used to identify the location of the network and any subnets.

TCP/IP was originally developed by the US Defense Advanced Research Projects Agency (DARPA). Their objective was to connect a number of universities and other research establishments to DARPA. The resultant internet is now known as the Internet. It has since outgrown this application and many commercial organisations now connect to the Internet. The Internet uses TCP/IP to transfer data. Each node on the Internet is assigned a unique network address, called an IP address. Note that any organisation can have its own internets, but if it is to connect to the Internet then the addresses must conform to the Internet addressing format.

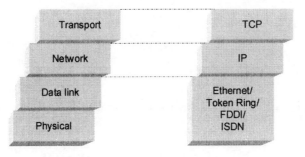

**Figure 9.1**  TCP/IP and the OSI model

The ISO have adopted TCP/IP as the basis for the standards relating to the network and transport layers of the OSI model. This standard is known as ISO-IP. Most currently available systems conform to the IP addressing standard.

Common applications that use TCP/IP communications are remote login and file transfer. Typical programs used in file transfer and login over TCP communication are `ftp` for file transfer program and `telnet` which allows remote log into another computer. The `ping` program determines if a node is responding to TCP/IP communications.

## 9.2  TCP/IP gateways and hosts

TCP/IP hosts are nodes which communicate over interconnected networks using TCP/IP communications. A TCP/IP gateway node connects one type of network to another. It contains hardware to provide the physical link between the different networks and the hardware and software to convert frames from one network to the other. Typically, it converts a Token Ring MAC layer to an equivalent Ethernet MAC layer, and vice versa.

A router connects a network of a similar type to another of the same kind through a point-to-point link. The main operational difference between a gateway, a router, and a bridge is that for a Token Ring and Ethernet network, the bridge uses the 48-bit MAC address to route frames, whereas the gateway and router use the IP network address. As an analogy to the public telephone system, the MAC address would be equivalent to a randomly assigned telephone number, whereas the IP address would contain the information on where the telephone is logically located, such as which country, area code, and so on.

Figure 9.2 shows how a gateway (or router) routes information. It reads the frame from the computer on network A, and reads the IP address contained in the frame and makes a decision whether it is routed out of network A to network B. If it does then it relays the frame to network B.

## 9.3  Function of the IP protocol

The main functions of the IP protocol are to:

- Route IP data frames – which are called internet datagrams – around an internet. The IP protocol program running on each node knows the location of the gateway on the network. The gateway must then be able to locate the interconnected network. Data then passes from node to gateway through the internet.

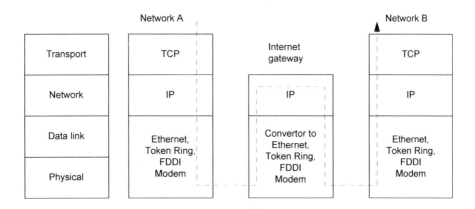

**Figure 9.2** Internet gateway layers

- Fragment the data into smaller units, if it is greater than a given amount (64 kB).
- Report errors. When a datagram is being routed or is being reassembled an error can occur. If this happen then the node that detects the error reports back to the source node. Datagrams are deleted from the network if they travel through the network for more than a set time. Again, an error message is returned to the source node to inform it that the internet routing could not find a route for the datagram or that the destination node, or network, does not exist.

## 9.4 Internet datagram

The IP protocol is an implementation of the network layer of the OSI model. It adds a data header onto the information passed from the transport layer, the resultant data packet is known as an internet datagram. The header contains information such as the destination and source IP addresses, the version number of the IP protocol and so on. Figure 9.3 shows its format.

The datagram can contain up to 65 536 bytes (64 kB) of data. If the data to be transmitted is less than, or equal to, 64 kB, then it is sent as one datagram. If it is more than this then the sender splits the data into fragments and sends multiple datagrams. When transmitted from the source each datagram is routed separately through the internet and the received fragments are finally reassembled at the destination.

The fields in the IP datagram are:

- **Version**. The TCP/IP `version number` helps gateways and nodes interpret the data unit correctly. Differing versions may have a different format. Most current implementations will have a version number of four (IPv4).

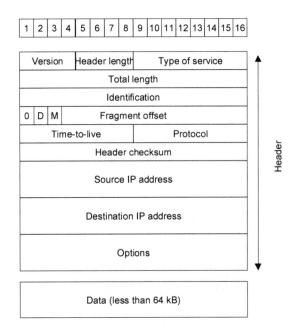

**Figure 9.3** Internet datagram format and contents

- **Type of service**. The `type of service` bit field is an 8-bit bit pattern in the form PPPDTRXX, where PPP defines the priority of the datagram (from 0 to 7). The precedence levels are:

  | | | |
  |---|---|---|
  | 111 (Network control) | 110 (Internetwork control) | 101 (CRITIC/ECP) |
  | 100 (Flash override) | 011 (Flash) | 010 (Immediate) |
  | 001 (Priority) | 000 (Routine) | |

  D sets a low delay service (0 – normal delay, 1 – low delay).
  T sets high throughput (0 – normal throughput, 1 – high throughput).
  R sets high reliability (0 – normal reliability, 1 – high reliability).
  The XX bits are currently not used (and set to 00).

- **Header length** (4 bits). The `header length` defines the size of the data unit in multiplies of four bytes (32 bits). The minimum length is five bytes and the maximum is 65 536 bytes. Padding bytes fill any unused spaces.

- **Identification** (16 bits). A value which is assigned by the sender to aid the assembly of the frames of a datagram.

- **D and M bits**. A gateway may route a datagram and split it into smaller fragments. The D bit informs the gateway that it should not fragment the data and thus it signifies that a receiving node should receive the data as a single unit or not at all. The M bit is the 'more fragments' bit and is used when data is split into fragments. The `fragment offset` contains the fragment number. The bit settings are:

**D** – Don't fragment. 0 – may fragment,   1 – don't fragment.
**M** – Last fragment.  0 – last fragment,   1 – more fragments.

- **Fragment offset** (13 bits). Indicates which datagram this fragment belongs to. The fragment offset is measured in units of eight bytes (64 bits). The first fragment has an offset of zero.

- **Time-to-live** (8 bits). A datagram could propagate through the internet indefinitely. To prevent this, the 8-bit `time-to-live` value is set to the maximum transit time in seconds and is set initially by the source IP. Each gateway then decrements this value by a defined amount. When it becomes zero the datagram is discarded. It also defines the maximum amount of time that a destination IP node should wait for the next datagram fragment.

- **Protocol** (8 bits). Different IP protocols can be used on the datagram. The 8-bit `protocol` field defines the type to be used. A full list is given in Table 9.5 (Section 9.15.1). Typical values are: 1 – ICMP and 6 – TCP.

- **Header checksum** (16 bits). The `header checksum` contains a 16-bit pattern for error detection. Since values within the header change from gateway to gateway (such as the time-to-live field), it must be recomputed every time the IP header is processed. The algorithm is:

  *The 16-bit 1's complement of the 1's complement sum of all the 16-bit words in the header. When calculating the checksum the header checksum field is assumed to be set to a zero.*

- **Source and destination IP addresses** (32 bits). The `source` and `destination IP addresses` are stored in the 32-bit source and destination IP address fields.

- **Options**. The `options` field contains information such as debugging, error control and routing information. See Section 9.15.2 for further information.

## 9.5   ICMP

Messages, such as control data, information data and error recovery data, are carried between Internet hosts using the Internet Control Message Protocol (ICMP). These messages are sent with a standard IP header. Typical messages are:

- Destination unreachable (message type 3) – which is sent by a host on the network to say that a host is unreachable. The message can also include the reason the host cannot be reached.
- Echo request/echo reply (message type 8 or 0) – which is used to check the connectivity between two hosts. The `ping` command uses this message, where it sends an ICMP 'echo request' message to the target host and waits for the destination

host to reply with an 'echo reply' message.

- Redirection (message type 5) – which is sent by a router to a host that is requesting its routing services. This helps to find the shortest path to a desired host.
- Source quench (message type 4) – which is used when a host cannot receive any-more IP packets at the present (or reduce the flow).

An ICMP message is sent within an IP header, with the Version field, Source and Des-tination IP Addresses, and so on. The Type of Service field is set to a 0 and the Protocol field is set to a 1 (which identifies ICMP). After the IP header, follows the ICMP message, which starts with three fields, as shown in Figure 9.4. The message type has eight bits and identifies the type of message; as Table 9.1. The code fields are also eight bits long and a checksum field is 16 bits long. The checksum is the 1's com-plement of the 1's complement sum of all 16-bit words in the header (the checksum field is assumed to be zero in the addition).

The information after this field depends on the type of message, such as:

- For echo request and reply, the message header is followed by an 8-bit identifier, then an 8-bit sequence number followed by the original IP header.
- For destination unreachable, source quelch and time, the message header is fol-lowed by 32 bits which are unused and then the original IP header.
- For timestamp request, the message header is followed by a 16-bit identifier, then by a 16-bit sequence number, followed by a 32-bit originating timestamp.

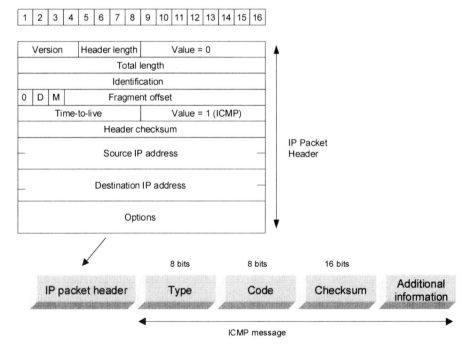

**Figure 9.4** ICMP message format

**Table 9.1** Message type field value

| Value | Description | Code field | Additional information |
|---|---|---|---|
| 0 | Echo Reply Message | 0 | 16-bit Identifier<br>16-bit Sequence Number |
| 3 | Destination Unreachable | 0 – net unreachable<br>1 – host unreachable<br>2 – protocol unreachable<br>3 – port unreachable<br>4 – fragmentation needed and D bit set<br>5 – source route failed | 32 bits unused.<br>Internet Header + 64 bits of Original Data Datagram |
| 4 | Source Quench Message | 0 | 32 bits unused.<br>Internet Header + 64 bits of Original Data Datagram |
| 5 | Redirect Message | 0 – redirect datagram for the network<br>1 – redirect datagram for the host<br>2 – redirect datagram for the type of service and network<br>3 – redirect datagram for the type of service and host | 32 bits Gateway address.<br>Internet Header + 64 bits of Original Data Datagram |
| 8 | Echo Request | 0 | |
| 11 | Time-to-live Exceeded | 0 – time-to-live exceeded in transit<br>1 – fragment reassembly time exceeded | 32 bits unused.<br>Internet Header + 64 bits of Original Data Datagram |
| 12 | Parameter Problem | 0 – pointer indicates the error | 8-bit Pointer.<br>24 bits unused.<br>Internet Header + 64 bits of Original Data Datagram |
| 13 | Timestamp Request | 0 | 16-bit Identifier<br>16-bit Sequence Number<br>32-bit Originate Timestamp<br>32-bit Receive Timestamp<br>32-bit Transmit Timestamp |
| 14 | Timestamp Reply | 0 | As above |
| 15 | Information Request | 0 | 16-bit Identifier<br>16-bit Sequence Number |
| 16 | Information Reply | 0 | As above. |

Where:

- Pointer (8-bit). Identifies the byte location of the parameter error in the original IP header. For example, a value of 9 would identify the Protocol field, and 12 would identify the Source IP address field.
- Identifier (16-bit). Helps the matching of requests and replies (possibly set to zero). It can be used to identify a unique connection.
- Sequence Number (16-bit). Helps in matching request and replies (possibly set to zero).
- Timestamps (32-bit) – This is the time in milliseconds since midnight UT (Universal Time). If this is not possible then it is anytime, as long as the high-order bit of the timestamp is set to a 1 to indicate that it is non-standard time.
- Gateway address (32-bit). The address of the gateway to which network traffic specified in the original datagram should be sent to.
- Internet Header + 64 bits of Data Datagram. This is the original IP header and the first 64 byte of the data part. It is used by the host to match the match to the required high-level application (such as TCP port values).

The descriptions of the messages and replies are:

- Source Quelch Message (4). Sent by a gateway or a destination host when it discards a datagram (possibly through lack of buffer memory), and identifies that the sender should reduce the flow of traffic transmission. The host should then reduce the flow, and gradually increase it, as long as it does not receive any more Source Quelch messages.
- Time Exceeded Message (11). This is sent either by a gateway when a datagram has a Time-to-Live field which is zero and has been deleted, or when a host cannot reassemble a fragmented datagram due to missing fragments, within a certain time limit.
- Parameter Problem Message (12). Sent by a gateway or a host when they encounter a problem with one of the parameters in an IP header.
- Destination Unreachable Message (3). Sent by a gateway to identify that a host cannot be reached or a TCP port process does not exist.
- Redirected Message (5). Sent by a gateway to inform other gateways that there is a better route to a given network destination address.
- Information Reply Message (15). Sent in reply to an Information Request. See Information Request (16) for a typical usage.
- Information Request (16). This request can be sent with a fully specified Source IP address, and a zero Destination IP address. The replying IP gateway then replies with an Information Reply Message with its fully specified IP address. In this way the host can determine the network address that it is connected to.
- Echo Message (8). Requests an echo. See Echo Reply Message (0).
- Echo Reply Message (0). The data received in the Echo Message (8) must be returned in this message.

## 9.6 TCP/IP internets

Figure 9.5 illustrates a sample TCP/IP implementation. A gateway MERCURY provides a link between a Token Ring network (NETWORK A) and the Ethernet network (ETHER C). Another gateway PLUTO connects NETWORK B to ETHER C. The TCP/IP protocol allows a host on NETWORK A to communicate with VAX01.

### 9.6.1 Selecting internet addresses

Each node using TCP/IP communications requires an IP address which is then matched to its Token Ring or Ethernet MAC address. The MAC address allows nodes on the same segment to communicate with each other. In order for nodes on a different network to communicate, each must be configured with an IP address.

Nodes on a TCP/IP network are either hosts or gateways. Any nodes that run application software or are terminals are hosts. Any node that routes TCP/IP packets between networks is called a TCP/IP gateway node. This node must have the necessary network controller boards to physically interface to other networks it connects with.

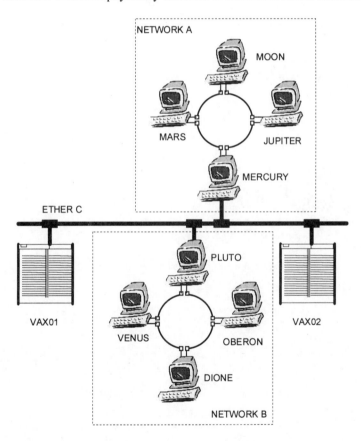

**Figure 9.5** Example internet

### 9.6.2 Format of the IP address

A typical IP address consists of two fields: the left field (or the network number) identifies the network, and the right number (or the host number) identifies the particular host within that network. Figure 9.6 illustrates this.

The IP address is 32 bits long and can address over four million physical addresses ($2^{32}$ or $4\,294\,967\,296$ hosts). There are three main address formats and these are shown in Figure 9.7.

Each of these types is applicable to certain types of networks. Class A allows up to 128 ($2^7$) different networks and up to $16\,777\,216$ ($2^{24}$) hosts on each network. Class B allows up to $16\,384$ ($2^{14}$) networks and up to $65\,536$ ($2^{16}$) hosts on each network. Class C allows up to $2\,097\,152$ ($2^{21}$) networks each with up to 256 ($2^8$) hosts.

The class A address is thus useful where there are a small number of networks with a large number of hosts connected to them. Class C is useful where there are many networks with a relatively small number of hosts connected to each network. Class B addressing gives a good compromise of networks and connected hosts.

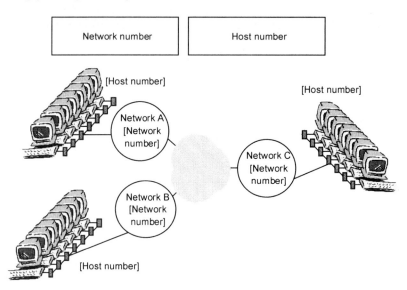

**Figure 9.6** IP addressing over networks

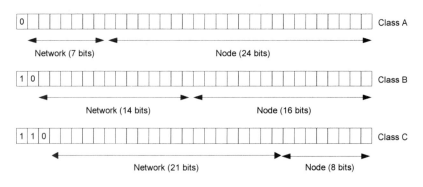

**Figure 9.7** Type A, B and C IP address classes

When selecting internet addresses for the network, the address can be specified simply with decimal numbers within a specific range. The standard DARPA IP addressing format is of the form:

$$W.X.Y.Z$$

where W, X, Y and Z represent 1 byte of the IP address. As decimal numbers they range from 0 to 255. The 4 bytes together represent both the network and host address.

The valid range of the different IP addresses is given in Figure 9.7 and Table 9.2 defines the valid IP addresses. Thus for a class A type address there can be 127 networks and 16 711 680 (256×256×255) hosts. Class B can have 16 320 (64×255) networks and class C can have 2 088 960 (32×256×255) networks and 255 hosts.

Addresses above 223.255.254 are reserved, as are addresses with groups of zeros.

**Table 9.2**   Ranges of addresses for type A, B and C internet address

| Type | Network portion | Host portion |
|------|-----------------|--------------|
| A | 1 - 126 | 0.0.1 - 255.255.254 |
| B | 128.1 - 191.254 | 0.1 - 255.254 |
| C | 192.0.1 - 223.255.254 | 1 - 254 |

### 9.6.3   Creating IP addresses with subnet numbers

Besides selecting IP addresses of internets and host numbers, it is also possible to designate an intermediate number called a subnet number. Subnets extend the network field of the IP address beyond the limit defined by the type A, B, C scheme. They allow a hierarchy of internets within a network. For example, it is possible to have one network number for a network attached to the internet, and various subnet numbers for each subnet within the network. This is illustrated in Figure 9.8.

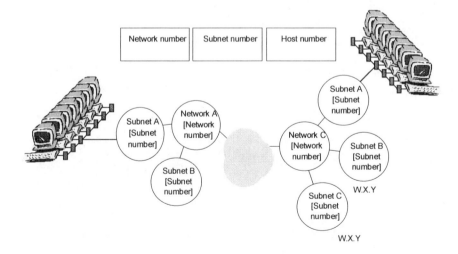

**Figure 9.8**   IP addresses with subnets

For an address W.X.Y.Z and type for a type A address W specifies the network and X the subnet. For type B the Y field specifies the subnet, as illustrated in Figure 9.9.

To connect to a global network a number is normally assigned by a central authority. For the Internet network it is assigned by the Network Information Center (NIC). Typically, on the Internet an organisation is assigned a type B network address. The first two fields of the address specify the organisation network, the third specifies the subnet within the organisation and the final value specifies the host.

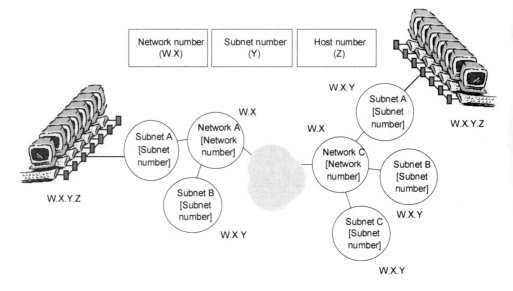

**Figure 9.9** Internet addresses with subnets

### 9.6.4 Specifying subnet masks

If a subnet is used then a bit mask, or subnet mask, must be specified to show which part of the address is the network part and which is the host.

The subnet mask is a 32-bit number that has 1's for bit positions specifying the network and subnet parts and 0's for the host part. A text file called *hosts* is normally used to set up the subnet mask. Table 9.3 shows example subnet masks.

**Table 9.3** Default subnet mask for type A, B and C IP addresses

| Address Type | Default mask |
| --- | --- |
| Class A | 255.0.0.0 |
| Class B | 255.255.0.0 |
| Class C and Class B with a subnet | 255.255.255.0 |

To set up the default mask the following line is added to the *hosts* file.

📄 Hosts file
```
255.255.255.0  defaultmask
```

## 9.7 Domain name system

An IP address can be defined in the form WWW.XXX.YYY.ZZZ, where XXX, YYY, ZZZ and WWW are integer values in the range 0 to 255. On the Internet it is WWW.XXX.YYY that normally defines the subnet and WWW that defines the host. Such names may be difficult to remember. A better method is to use symbolic names rather than IP addresses.

Users and application programs can then use symbolic names rather than the IP addresses. The directory network service on the Internet determines the IP address of the named destination user or application program. This has the advantage that users and application programs can move around the Internet and are not fixed to an IP address.

An analogy relates to the public telephone service. A telephone directory contains a list of subscribers and their associated telephone numbers. If someone looks for a telephone number, first the user name is looked up and then the associated telephone number found. The telephone directory listing maps a user name (symbolic name) to an actual telephone number (the actual address).

Table 9.4 lists some Internet domain assignments for World Wide Web (WWW) servers. Note that domain assignments are not fixed and can change their corresponding IP addresses, if required. The binding between the symbolic name and its address can thus change at any time.

**Table 9.4** Internet domain assignments for web servers

| Web server | Internet domain name | Internet IP address |
|---|---|---|
| NEC | web.nec.com | 143.101.112.6 |
| Sony | www.sony.com | 198.83.178.11 |
| Intel | www.intel.com | 134.134.214.1 |
| IEEE | www.ieee.com | 140.98.1.1 |
| University of Bath | www.bath.ac.uk | 136.38.32.1 |
| University of Edinburgh | www.ed.ac.uk | 129.218.128.43 |
| IEE | www.iee.org.uk | 193.130.181.10 |
| University of Manchester | www.man.ac.uk | 130.88.203.16 |

## 9.8 Internet naming structure

The Internet naming structure uses labels separated by periods; an example is eece.napier.ac.uk. It uses a hierarchical structure where organisations are grouped into primary domain names. These are com (for commercial organisations), edu (for educational organisations), gov (for government organisations), mil (for military organisations), net (Internet network support centers) or org (other organisations). The primary domain name may also define the country in which the host is located, such as uk (United Kingdom), fr (France), and so on. All hosts on the Internet must be registered to one of these primary domain names.

The labels after the primary field describe the subnets within the network. For example in the address eece.napier.ac.uk, the ac label relates to an academic institution within the uk, napier to the name of the institution and eece the subnet within that organisation. An example structure is illustrated in Figure 9.10.

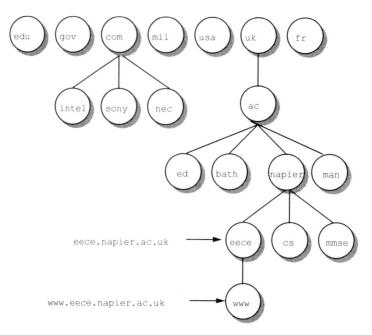

eece.napier.ac.uk ⟶ eece

www.eece.napier.ac.uk ⟶ www

**Figure 9.10**   Example domain naming

---

## 9.9   Domain name server

Each institution on the Internet has a host that runs a process called the domain name server (DNS). The DNS maintains a database called the directory information base (DIB) which contains directory information for that institution. When a new host is added, the system manager adds its name and its IP address. It can then access the Internet.

### 9.9.1   DNS program

The DNS program is typically run on a Linux-based PC with a program called `named` (located in `/usr/sbin`) with an information file of `named.boot`. To run the program the following is used:

```
/usr/bin/named -b /usr/local/adm/named/named.boot
```

The following shows that the DNS program is currently running.

```
$ ps -ax
  PID TTY STAT    TIME COMMAND
  295 con  S      0:00 bootpd
   35 con  S      0:00 /usr/sbin/lpd
  272 con  S      0:00 /usr/sbin/named -b /usr/local/adm/named/named.boot
  264 p 1  S      0:01 bash
  306 pp0  R      0:00 ps -ax
```

In this case the data file `named.boot` is located in the `/usr/local/adm/named` directory. A sample `named.boot` file is:

```
/usr/local/adm/named - soabasefile
              eece.napier.ac.uk -main record of computer names
              net/net144    -reverse look-up database
              net/net145        "        "
              net/net146        "        "
              net/net147        "        "
              net/net150        "        "
              net/net151        "        "
```

This file specifies that the reverse look-up information on computers on the subnets 144, 145, 146, 147, 150 and 151 is contained in the `net144`, `net145`, `net146`, `net147`, `net150` and `net151` files, respectively. These are stored in the `net` subdirectory. The main file which contains the DNS information is, in this case, `eece.napier.ac.uk`.

Whenever a new computer is added onto a network, in this case, the `eece.napier.ac.uk` file and the `net/net1**` (where `**` is the relevant subnet name) are updated to reflect the changes. Finally, the serial number at the top of these data files is updated to reflect the current date, such as 19970321 (for 21st March 1997).

The DNS program can then be tested using `nslookup`. For example:

```
$ nslookup
Default Server:  ees99.eece.napier.ac.uk
Address:  146.176.151.99
> src.doc.ic.ac.uk
Server:  ees99.eece.napier.ac.uk
Address:  146.176.151.99
Non-authoritative answer:
Name:    swallow.doc.ic.ac.uk
Address:  193.63.255.4
Aliases:  src.doc.ic.ac.uk
```

## 9.10  Bootp protocol

The bootp protocol allocates IP addresses to computers based on a table of network card MAC addresses. When a computer is first booted, the bootp server interrogates its MAC address and then looks up the bootp table for its entry. It then grants the corresponding IP address to the computer. The computer then uses it for connections.

### 9.10.1 Bootp program

The bootp program is typically run on a Linux-based PC with the `bootp` program. The following shows that the `bootp` program is currently running on a computer:

```
$ ps -ax
```

```
PID TTY STAT   TIME COMMAND
    1 con S   0:06 init
   31 con S   0:01 /usr/sbin/inetd
14142 con S   0:00 bootpd -d 1
   35 con S   0:00 /usr/sbin/lpd
   49 p 3 S   0:00 /sbin/agetty 38400 tty3
14155 pp0 R   0:00 ps -ax
10762 con S   0:18 /usr/sbin/named -b /usr/local/adm/named/named.boot
```

For the bootp system to operate then a table is required that reconciles the MAC addresses of the card to an IP address. In the previous example this table is contained in the `bootptab` file which is located in the `/etc` directory. The following file gives an example `bootptab`:

## ▤ Contents of bootptab file

```
# /etc/bootptab: database for bootp server
# Blank lines and lines beginning with '#' are ignored.
# Legend:
# first field -- hostname
#        (may be full domain name and probably should be)
# hd -- home directory
# bf -- bootfile
# cs -- cookie servers
# ds -- domain name servers
# gw -- gateways
# ha -- hardware address
# ht -- hardware type
# im -- impress servers
# ip -- host IP address
# lg -- log servers
# lp -- LPR servers
# ns -- IEN-116 name servers
# rl -- resource location protocol servers
# sm -- subnet mask
# tc -- template host (points to similar host entry)
# to -- time offset (seconds)
# ts -- time servers
#
#hostname:ht=1:ha=ether_addr_in_hex:ip=ip_addr_in_dec:tc=allhost:
.default150:\
  :hd=/tmp:bf=null:\
  :ds=146.176.151.99 146.176.150.62 146.176.1.5:\
  :sm=255.255.255.0:gw=146.176.150.253:\
  :hn:vm=auto:to=0:
.default151:\
  :hd=/tmp:bf=null:\
  :ds=146.176.151.99 146.176.150.62 146.176.1.5:\
  :sm=255.255.255.0:gw=146.176.151.254:\
  :hn:vm=auto:to=0:

pc345: ht=ethernet: ha=0080C8226BE2:  ip=146.176.150.2: tc=.default150:
pc307: ht=ethernet: ha=0080C822CD4E:  ip=146.176.150.3: tc=.default150:
pc320: ht=ethernet: ha=0080C823114C:  ip=146.176.150.4: tc=.default150:
pc331: ht=ethernet: ha=0080C823124B:  ip=146.176.150.5: tc=.default150:
pc401: ht=ethernet: ha=0080C82379F7:  ip=146.176.150.6: tc=.default150:
pc404: ht=ethernet: ha=0080C8238369:  ip=146.176.150.7: tc=.default150:
pc402: ht=ethernet: ha=0080C8238467:  ip=146.176.150.8: tc=.default150:
    :        :
pc460: ht=ethernet: ha=0000E8C7BB63:  ip=146.176.151.142: tc=.default151:
pc414: ht=ethernet: ha=0080C8246A84:  ip=146.176.151.143: tc=.default151:
pc405: ht=ethernet: ha=0080C82382EE:  ip=146.176.151.145: tc=.default151:
```

The format of the file is:

```
#hostname:ht=1:ha=ether_addr_in_hex:ip=ip_addr_in_dec:tc=allhost:
```

where hostname is the hostname, the value defined after ha= is the Ethernet MAC address, the value after ip= is the IP address and the name after the tc= field defines the host information script. For example:

```
pc345:  ht=ethernet:  ha=0080C8226BE2:  ip=146.176.150.2:
tc=.default150:
```

defines the hostname of pc345, ethernet indicates it is on an Ethernet network, and shows its IP address is 146.176.150.2. The MAC address of the computer is 00:80:C8: 22:6B:E2 and it is defined by the script .default150. This file defines a subnet of 255.255.255.0 and has associated DNS of

```
146.176.151.99 146.176.150.62 146.176.1.5
```

and uses the gateway at:

```
146.176.150.253
```

## 9.11 Example network

A university network is shown in Figure 9.11. The connection to the outside global Internet is via the Janet gateway node and its IP address is 146.176.1.3. Three sub-nets, 146.176.160, 146.176.129 and 146.176.151, connect the gateway to departmental bridges. The Computer Studies bridge address is 146.176.160.1 and the Electrical Department bridge has an address 146.176.151.254.

The Electrical Department bridge links, through other bridges, to the subnets 146.176.144, 146.176.145, 146.176.147, 146.176.150 and 146.176.151. main bridge into the department connects to two Ethernet networks of PCs (subnets 146.176.150 and 146.176.151) and to another bridge (Bridge 1). Bridge 1 connects to the subnet 146.176.144. Subnet 146.176.144 connects to workstations and X-terminals. It also connects to the gateway Moon that links the Token Ring subnet 146.176.145 with the Ethernet subnet 146.176.144. The gateway Oberon, on the 146.176.145 subnet, connects to an Ethernet link 146.176.146. This then connects to the gateway Dione that is also connected to the Token Ring subnet 146.176.147.

The topology of the Electrical Department network is shown in Figure 9.12. Each node on the network is assigned an IP address. The hosts file for the set up in Figure 9.12 is shown next. For example the IP address of Mimas is 146.176.145.21 and for miranda it is 146.176.144.14. Notice that the gateway nodes, Oberon, Moon and Dione, all have two IP addresses.

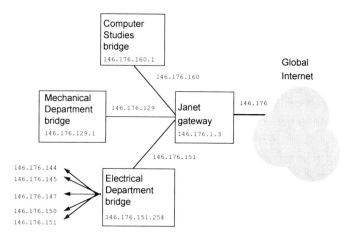

**Figure 9.11**  A university network

---

## 📄 Contents of host file

```
146.176.1.3          janet
146.176.144.10       hp
146.176.145.21       mimas
146.176.144.11       mwave
146.176.144.13       vax
146.176.144.14       miranda
146.176.144.20       triton
146.176.146.23       oberon
146.176.145.23       oberon
146.176.145.24       moon
146.176.144.24       moon
146.176.147.25       uranus
146.176.146.30       dione
146.176.147.30       dione
146.176.147.31       saturn
146.176.147.32       mercury
146.176.147.33       earth
146.176.147.34       deimos
146.176.147.35       ariel
146.176.147.36       neptune
146.176.147.37       phobos
146.176.147.39       io
146.176.147.40       titan
146.176.147.41       venus
146.176.147.42       pluto
146.176.147.43       mars
146.176.147.44       rhea
146.176.147.22       jupiter
146.176.144.54       leda
146.176.144.55       castor
146.176.144.56       pollux
146.176.144.57       rigel
146.176.144.58       spica
146.176.151.254      cubridge
146.176.151.99       bridge_1
146.176.151.98       pc2
146.176.151.97       pc3
           : : : : :
146.176.151.71       pc29
146.176.151.70       pc30
```

```
146.176.151.99      ees99
146.176.150.61      eepc01
146.176.150.62      eepc02
255.255.255.0       defaultmask
```

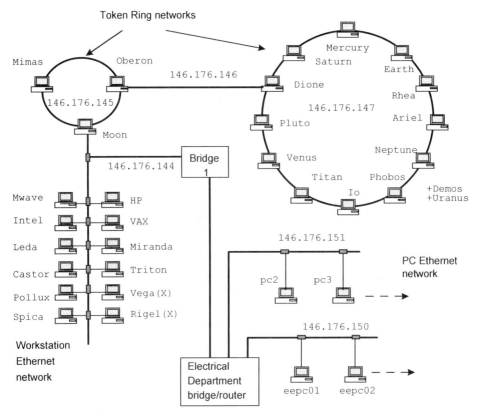

**Figure 9.12** Network topology for the Electrical Department network

## 9.12 ARP

ARP (Address Resolution Protocol) translates IP addresses to Ethernet addresses. This is used when IP packets are sent from a computer, and the Ethernet address is added to the Ethernet frame. A table look-up, called the ARP table, is used to translate the addresses. One column has the IP address and the other has the Ethernet address. The following is an example ARP table:

```
IP address      Ethernet address
146.176.150.2   00-80-C8-22-6BE2
146.176.150.3   00-80-C8-22-CD4E
146.176.150.4   00-80-C8-23-114C
```

A typical conversation is as follows:

- Application sends an application message to TCP.
- TCP sends the corresponding TCP message to the IP module. The destination IP address is known by the application, the TCP module, and the IP module.
- At this point the IP packet has been constructed and is ready to be given to the Ethernet driver, but first the destination Ethernet address must be determined.
- The ARP table is used to look up the destination Ethernet address.

The sequence of determining the Ethernet address is as follows:

1. An ARP request packet with a broadcast Ethernet address (FF-FF-FF-FF-FF-FF) is sent out on the network to every computer. Other typical Ethernet broadcast addresses are given in Section 9.15.3.
2. The outgoing IP packet is queued.
3. All the computers on the network segment read the broadcast Ethernet frame, and examine the Type field to determine if it is an ARP packet. If it is then it is passed to the ARP module.
4. If the IP address of a receiving station matches the IP address in the IP packet then it sends a response directly to the source Ethernet address.
5. The originator then receives the Ethernet frame and checks the Type field to determine if it an ARP packet. If it is then it adds the sender's IP address and Ethernet address to its ARP table.
6. The IP packet can now be sent with the correct Ethernet address.

Each computer has a separate ARP table for each of its Ethernet interfaces.

## 9.13  IP multicasting

Many applications of modern communications require the transmission of IP datagrams to multiple hosts. Typical applications are video conferencing, remote teaching, and so on. This is supported by IP multicasting, where a host group is identified by a single IP address. The main parameters of IP multicasting are:

- The group membership is dynamic.
- Hosts may join and leave the group at any time.
- There is also no limit to the location or number of members in a host group.
- A host may be a member of more than one group at a time.
- A host group may be permanent or transient. Permanent groups are well-known and are administratively assigned a permanent IP address. The group is then dynamically associated with this IP address. IP multicast addresses that are not reserved to permanent groups are available for dynamic assignment to transient groups.

- Multicast routers forward IP multicast datagrams into the Internet.

### 9.13.1 Group addresses

A special group of addresses are assigned to multicasting. These are known as Class D addresses, and they begin with 1110 as their starting 4 bits (Class E addresses with the upper bits of 1111 are reserved for future uses). The Class D addresses thus range from:

224.0.0.0           (11100000 00000000 00000000 00000000)

239.255.255.255    (11101111 11111111 11111111 11111111)

The address 224.0.0.0 is reserved. 224.0.0.1 is also assigned to the permanent group of all IP hosts (including gateways), and is used to address all multicast hosts on the directly connected network. Reserved and allocated addresses are:

| | |
|---|---|
| 224.0.0.0 | Reserved |
| 224.0.0.1 | All Systems on current subnet |
| 224.0.0.2 | All Routers on current subnet |
| 224.0.0.3 | Unassigned |
| 224.0.0.4 | DVMRP Routers |
| 224.0.0.5 | OSPFIGP All Routers |
| 224.0.0.6 | OSPFIGP Designated Routers |
| 224.0.0.7 | ST Routers |
| 224.0.0.8 | ST Hosts |
| 224.0.0.9 | RIP2 Routers |
| 224.0.0.10–224.0.0.255 | Unassigned |
| 224.0.1.0 | VMTP Managers Group |
| 224.0.1.1 | NTP Network Time Protocol |
| 224.0.1.2 | SGI-Dogfight |
| 224.0.1.3 | Rwhod |
| 224.0.1.4 | VNP |
| 224.0.1.5 | Artificial Horizons - Aviator |
| 224.0.1.6 | NSS - Name Service Server |
| 224.0.1.7 | AUDIONEWS - Audio News Multicast |
| 224.0.1.8 | SUN NIS+ Information Service |
| 224.0.1.9 | MTP Multicast Transport Protocol |
| 224.0.1.10–224.0.1.255 | Unassigned |
| 224.0.2.1 | rwho group (BSD) (unofficial) |
| 224.0.2.2 | SUN RPC PMAPPROC_CALLIT |
| 224.0.3.0–224.0.3.255 | RFE Generic Service |
| 224.0.4.0–224.0.4.255 | RFE Individual Conferences |
| 224.1.0.0–224.1.255.255 | ST Multicast Groups |
| 224.2.0.0–224.2.255.255 | Multimedia Conference Calls |
| 232.x.x.x | VMTP transient groups |

All the above addresses are listed in the Domain Name Service under MCAST.NET and 224.IN-ADDR.ARPA. On an Ethernet or IEEE 802 network, the 23 low-order bits of the IP Multicast address are placed in the low-order 23 bits of the Ethernet or IEEE 802 net multicast address.

### 9.13.2 Conformance

There are three levels of conformance:

- Level 0. No IP multicasting support. In this, a Level 0 host ignores, or deletes, all Class D addressed datagrams.
- Level 1. Sending support, but no receiving. In this, a Level 1 host can send multi-cast datagrams, but cannot receive them.
- Level 2: Full multicasting support. In this, a Level 2 host can send and receive IP multicasting. It also requires the implementation of the Internet Group Management Protocol (IGMP).

## 9.14  Exercises

**9.14.1**    Which OSI layer does the IP layer correspond to:

|     |           |     |         |
|-----|-----------|-----|---------|
| (a) | Data link | (b) | Network |
| (c) | Transport | (d) | Session |

**9.14.2**    Which OSI layer does the TCP layer correspond to:

|     |           |     |         |
|-----|-----------|-----|---------|
| (a) | Data link | (b) | Network |
| (c) | Transport | (d) | Session |

**9.14.3**    Which IP version do most TCP/IP hosts use:

|     |           |     |           |
|-----|-----------|-----|-----------|
| (a) | Version 2 | (b) | Version 4 |
| (c) | Version 5 | (d) | Version 6 |

**9.14.4**    How much data can be carried within an IP datagram:

|     |        |     |           |
|-----|--------|-----|-----------|
| (a) | 64 kB  | (b) | 128 kB    |
| (c) | 256 kB | (d) | Unlimited |

**9.14.5**    How many IP addresses are possible:

|     |               |     |                              |
|-----|---------------|-----|------------------------------|
| (a) | 1,048,576     | (b) | 16,777,216                   |
| (c) | 4,294,967,296 | (d) | $3.402823669 \times 10^{38}$ |

**9.14.6**    How are IP datagrams deleted from the network:

- (a) They are deleted when the Time-to-live field becomes zero.
- (b) They are never deleted, and will always be delivered.
- (c) They are buffered on intermediate systems, and then deleted after a given time.

      (d)     They are returned to the originator if they are not deleted, and the originator either resends them or deletes them.

**9.14.7**     Which of the following is a Class A IP address:

      (a)     12.1.14.12      (b)     146.176.151.130
      (c)     194.50.100.1     (d)     224.50.50.1

**9.14.8**     Which of the following is a Class D IP address:

      (a)     12.1.14.12      (b)     146.176.151.130
      (c)     194.50.100.1     (d)     224.50.50.1

**9.14.9**     What are Class D IP addresses used for:

      (a)     Dynamic IP addressing     (b)     Testing networks
      (c)     Static IP addressing      (d)     Multicasting

**9.14.10**    Which of the following is the country domain for Germany:

      (a)     ge     (b)     de     (c)     dr     (d)     gy

**9.14.11**    Which service allows hosts to determine the IP address for a given domain name:

      (a)     TCP     (b)     ICMP
      (c)     ARP     (d)     DNS

**9.14.12**    Which protocol is used by a node to determine the Ethernet address to a host with a given IP address:

      (a)     TCP     (b)     ICMP
      (c)     ARP     (d)     DNS

**9.14.13**    Which Ethernet address is used for broadcast messages:

      (a)     FF-FF-FF-FF-FF-FF     (b)     11-11-11-11-11-11-11
      (c)     00-00-00-00-00-00     (d)     AA-AA-AA-AA-AA-AA

**9.14.14**    Outline how ARP uses the broadcast address and the Type field to identify that an ARP request is being transmitted. Also, discuss a typical ARP conversation.

**9.14.15**    Outline how the protocol is identified in the IP header. Discuss how the format of the data after the header differs with different protocols (such as TCP and ICMP).

**9.14.16**    Explain how ICMP and the Options field would be used to determine the following information:

(i)   Whether a destination node is responding to TCP/IP communications.
(ii)  The route to a destination node.
(iii) The route to a destination node, with the time delay between each gateway.

**9.14.17**   Explain how the Options field can be used to set the route that a datagram can take.

**9.14.18**   Determine the IP addresses, and their type (i.e. class A, B or C), of the following 32-bit addresses:

(i)     `10001100.01110001.00000001.00001001`
(ii)    `01000000.01111101.01000001.11101001`
(iii)   `10101110.01110001.00011101.00111001`

**9.14.19**   Determine the countries which use the following primary domain names:

(a) `de`   (b) `nl`   (c) `it`   (d) `se`   (e) `dk`   (f) `sg`
(g) `ca`   (h) `ch`   (i) `tr`   (j) `jp`   (k) `au`

Determine some other domain names.

**9.14.20**   For a known TCP/IP network determine the names of the nodes and their Internet addresses.

**9.14.21**   For a known TCP/IP network determine how the DNS is implemented and how IP addresses are granted.

**9.14.22**   If a subnet mask on a Class B network is 255.255.240.0, show that there can be 16 connected networks, each with 4095 nodes on a Class B network.

## 9.15  Additional material

### 9.15.1 Assigned Internet Protocol numbers

Table 9.5 outlines the values that are used in the Protocol field of the IP header.

**Table 9.5**   Assigned Internet Protocol Numbers

| Value | Protocol | Value | Protocol |
|-------|----------|-------|----------|
| 0 | Reserved | 18 | Multiplexing |
| 1 | ICMP | 19 | DCN |
| 2 | IGMP (Internet Group Management) | 20 | TAC Monitoring |

| 3 | Gateway-to-Gateway | 21–62 | |
| 4 | CMCC Gateway Monitoring Message | 63 | Any local network |
| 5 | ST | 64 | SATNET and Backroom EXPAK |
| 6 | TCP | 65 | MIT Subnet Support |
| 7 | UCL | 66–68 | Unassigned |
| 8 | EGP (Exterior Gateway Protocol) | 69 | SATNET Monitoring |
| 9 | Secure | 70 | Unassigned |
| 10 | BBN RCC Monitoring | 71 | Internet Packet Core Utility |
| 11 | NVP | 72–75 | Unassigned |
| 12 | PUP | 76 | Backroom SATNET Monitoring |
| 13 | Pluribus | 77 | Unassigned |
| 14 | Telenet | 78 | WIDEBAND Monitoring |
| 15 | XNET | 79 | WIDEBAND EXPAK |
| 16 | Chaos | 80–254 | Unassigned |
| 17 | User Datagram | 255 | Reserved |

### 9.15.2 Options field in an IP header

The Options field in an IP header is an optional field which may or may not appear in the header, and is also variable in length. It is a field which must be implemented by all hosts and gateways. There are two classes of option:

- An option-type byte.
- An option-type byte, followed by an option-length byte, and then the actual option-data bytes. The option-length byte counts all the bytes in the options field.

The option-type byte is the first byte and has three fields, as illustrated in Figure 9.13. The Copied flag indicates that this option is (or is not) copied into all fragments on fragmentation.

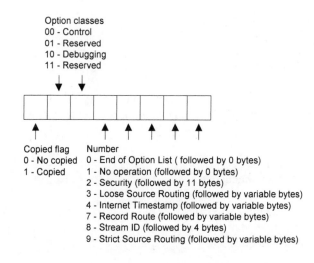

Figure 9.13 Options-type byte

### End of Option List (Type = 0)

This option indicates the end of the option list, but does not necessarily need to coincide with the end of the IP header according to the internet header length. It is used at the end of all options, but not the end of each option. It may be copied, introduced, or deleted on fragmentation, or for any other reason.

### No Operation (Type = 1)

This option may be used between options, and can be used to align the beginning of a subsequent option on a 32-bit boundary. It may be copied, introduced, or deleted on fragmentation, or for any other reason.

### Security (Type = 130)

This option allows hosts to send security, compartmentation, handling restrictions, and TCC (closed user group) parameters. In this option, the Type field is a 2, and the Class field is also a 2. Thus the option-type byte has a value of 130 (0100 0010), and has 11 bytes in total. Its format is:

```
+--------+--------+---...---+---...---+---...---+---...---+
|10000010|00001011|SSS   SSS|CCC   CCC|HHH   HHH|   TCC   |
+--------+--------+---...---+---...---+---...---+---...---+
```

The fields are:

- SSS...SSS. Security (16 bits). These specify one of 16 levels of security, such as:

| | |
|---|---|
| 00000000 00000000 – Unclassified | 11110001 00110101 – Confidential |
| 01111000 10011010 – EFTO | 10111100 01001101 – MMMM |
| 01011110 00100110 – PROG | 10101111 00010011 – Restricted |
| 11010111 10001000 – Secret | 01101011 11000101 – Top Secret |
| 00110101 11100010 – Reserved | 10011010 11110001 – Reserved |
| 01001101 01111000 – Reserved | 00100100 10111101 – Reserved |
| 00010011 01011110 – Reserved | 10001001 10101111 – Reserved |
| 11000100 11010110 – Reserved | 11100010 01101011 – Reserved |

- CCC...CCC. Compartments (16 bits). When this field contains all zero values then the transmitted information is not compartmented, other values can be obtained from the Defense Intelligence Agency.

- HHH...HHH. Handling Restrictions (16 bits). This field is defined in the Defense Intelligence Agency Manual DIAM 65-19.

- TCC. Transmission Control Code (24 bits). This field allows the segragation of traffic and to define controlled communities of interest among subscribers (available from HQ DCA Code 530). Must be copied on fragmentation.

### Loose Source and Record Route (Type = 131)

Loose source and record route (LSRR) allows for the source of an internet datagram to supply routing information to be used by the gateways in forwarding the datagram to the destination. It can also be used to record routing information.

When routing the source host adds the IP addresses of the route to the Route data, and each gateway routes the datagram using the recorded route, and not with its own internal routing table. This allows datagrams to take alternative routes through the Internet. Its format is:

```
+--------+--------+--------+---------...--------+
|10000011| Length | Pointer|    Route data      |
+--------+--------+--------+---------...--------+
```

where:

- Length. This is a single byte which contains the number of bytes in the option field.

- Pointer. This is a pointer, which is relative to this option, into the route data which indicates the byte which begins the next source address to be processed. The smallest value is 4.

- Route data. This is constructed with a number of internet addresses, each of 4 bytes in length. If the pointer is greater than the length, the source route is empty (and the recorded route full) and the routing is to be based on the destination address field.

When reaching the address in the destination address field, and when the pointer is not greater than the length in the route data, then the next address in the source route data replaces the address in the destination field. The pointer is also incremented by 4, to point to the next address. It is loose as the gateways are allowed to use any route to get to the next specified address in the routing table.

It must be copied on fragmentation and occurs, at the most, once in a datagram.

### Strict Source and Record Route (Type = 137)

The SSRR is similar to the LSRR, but the routing must follow, exactly, the addresses in the routing table. It thus cannot use any intermediate routes to get to these addresses. Its format is:

```
+--------+--------+--------+---------...--------+
|10001001| Length | Pointer|    Route data      |
+--------+--------+--------+---------...--------+
```

### Record Route (Type = 7)

The Record Route option records the route of an internet datagram. It can thus be used by such utilities as Traceroute. Its format is:

```
+--------+--------+--------+---------...--------+
|00000111| Length | Pointer|    Route data      |
+--------+--------+--------+---------...--------+
```

where:

- Length. This is a single byte which contains the number of bytes in the option field.
- Pointer. This is a pointer, which is relative to this option, into the route data which

indicates the byte at which the next address should be added to. The smallest value is 4.
- Route data. Contains a list of the route which a datagram has taken. Each entry has 4 bytes. The originating host must reserve enough area for the total number of addresses in the routing table, as the size of this option does not change as it transverses over the Internet. If there is a problem adding the address then an ICMP Parameter Problem can be sent back to the source host.

It is not copied on fragmentation, and goes in the first fragment only. In addition, it occurs, at the most, once in a datagram.

**Internet Timestamp (Type = 68)**

The Internet Timestamp option records a timestamp for each gateway along the route of a datagram. It allows the source host to trace the time that each part of the route takes. Its format is:

```
+--------+--------+--------+--------+
|01000100| Length | Pointer|Ov  |Flg|
+--------+--------+--------+--------+
|            internet address       |
+--------+--------+--------+--------+
|               timestamp           |
+--------+--------+--------+--------+
|                  .                |
                   .
```

where:

- Length. This is a single byte which contains the number of bytes in the option field (maximum is 40).
- Pointer. This is a pointer, which is relative to this option, into the route data which indicates the byte at which the next timestamp should be added to. The smallest value is 5.
- Overflow (Ov). This has four bits and holds the number of IP modules that cannot register timestamps due to lack of space.
- Flag (Flg). This has four bits and defines the format of the timestamp. Valid values are:

  0 – Store only the time stamps as 32-bit words.
  1 – Store IP address followed by a time stamp.
  3 – In this mode the IP addresses are specified in a table. A gateway only adds its timestamp if its IP address is in this table.

- Timestamp. This is a 32-bit value for the number of milliseconds since midnight UT (Universal Time). If this is not possible then it is any time, as long as the high-order bit of the timestamp is set to a 1 to indicate that it is non-standard time.

The originating host must reserve enough area for the total number of timestamps, as the size of this option does not change as it transverses over the Internet. If there is a problem adding the address then an ICMP Parameter Problem can be sent back to the source host. Initially the contents of the timestamp data area is either zero, or has IP addresses with zero time stamps. The timestamp area is full when the pointer is greater than the length.

It is not copied on fragmentation, and goes in the first fragment only. Also, it occurs, at the most, once in a datagram.

### Stream Identifier (Type =136)

This option allows for a 16-bit SATNET stream identifier to be carried through networks that do not support the stream concept. Its format is:

```
+--------+--------+--------+--------+
|10001000|00000010|    Stream ID   |
+--------+--------+--------+--------+
```

### 9.15.3 Ethernet Multicast/Broadcast Addresses

The following is a list of typical Ethernet Multicast addresses:

| Ethernet address | Type field | Usage |
|---|---|---|
| 01-00-5E-00-00-00 | 0800 | Internet Multicast (RFC-1112) |
| 01-80-C2-00-00-00 | 0802 | Spanning tree (for bridges) |
| 09-00-09-00-00-01 | 8005 | HP Probe |
| 09-00-09-00-00-04 | 8005 | HP DTC |
| 09-00-1E-00-00-00 | 8019 | Apollo DOMAIN |
| 09-00-2B-00-00-03 | 8038 | DEC Lanbridge Traffic Monitor (LTM) |
| 09-00-4E-00-00-02 | 8137 | Novell IPX |
| 0D-1E-15-BA-DD-06 | ???? | HP |
| CF-00-00-00-00-00 | 9000 | Ethernet Configuration Test protocol |

The following is a list of typical Ethernet Broadcast addresses:

| Ethernet address | Type field | Usage |
|---|---|---|
| FF-FF-FF-FF-FF-FF | 0600 | XNS packets, Hello or gateway search. |
| FF-FF-FF-FF-FF-FF | 0800 | IP (such as RWHOD with UDP) |
| FF-FF-FF-FF-FF-FF | 0804 | CHAOS |
| FF-FF-FF-FF-FF-FF | 0806 | ARP (for IP and CHAOS) as needed |
| FF-FF-FF-FF-FF-FF | 0BAD | Banyan |
| FF-FF-FF-FF-FF-FF | 1600 | VALID packets. Hello or gateway search. |
| FF-FF-FF-FF-FF-FF | 8035 | Reverse ARP |
| FF-FF-FF-FF-FF-FF | 807C | Merit Internodal (INP) |
| FF-FF-FF-FF-FF-FF | 809B | EtherTalk |

## 9.16  Note from the author

*Which two people have done more for world unity than anyone else? Well, Prof. TCP and Dr. IP must be somewhere in the Top 10. They have done more to unify the world than all the diplomats in the world have. They do not respect national borders, time zones, cultures, industrial conglomerates or anything like that. They allow the sharing of information around the world, and are totally open for anyone to use. Top marks to Prof. TCP and Dr. IP, the true champions of freedom and democracy.*

# 10 TCP/UDP

## 10.1 Introduction

TCP, ICMP and IP are extremely important protocols as they allow hosts to communicate over the Internet in a reliable way. The TCP layer is defined by RFC793 and RFC1122, ICMP by RFC792 and IP layer by RFC791. TCP provides a connection between two hosts and supports error handling. This chapter discusses TCP in more detail and shows how a connection is established then maintained. An important concept of TCP/IP communications is the usage of ports and sockets. A port identifies the process type (such as FTP, TELNET, and so on) and the socket identifies a unique connection number. In this way, TCP/IP can support multiple simultaneous connections of applications over a network.

The IP header is added to higher-level data. This header contains a 32-bit IP address of the destination node. Unfortunately, the standard 32-bit IP address is not large enough to support the growth in nodes connecting to the Internet. Thus a new standard, IP Version 6, has been developed to support a 128-bit address, as well as additional enhancements.

## 10.2 Transmission control protocol

In the OSI model, TCP fits into the transport layer and IP fits into the network layer. TCP thus sits above IP, which means that the IP header is added onto the higher-level information (such as transport, session, presentation and application). The main function of TCP is to provide a robust and reliable transport protocol. It is characterised as a reliable, connection-oriented, acknowledged and datastream-oriented server. IP, itself, does not support the connection of two nodes, whereas TCP does. With TCP, a connection is initially established and is then maintained for the length of the transmission.

The main aspects of TCP are:

- Data Transfer. Data is transmitted between two applications by packaging the data within TCP packets. This data is buffered and forwarded whenever necessary. A push function can be used when the data is required to be sent immediately.
- Reliability. TCP uses sequence numbers and positive acknowledgements (ACK) to keep track of transmitted packets. Thus, it can recover from data that is damaged, lost, duplicated, or delivered out of order, such as:

- Time-outs. The transmitter waits for a given time (the timeout interval), and if it does not receive an ACK, the data is retransmitted.
- Sequence numbers. The sequence numbers are used at the receiver to correctly order the packets and to delete duplicates.
- Error detection and recovery. Each packet has a checksum, which is checked by the receiver. If it is incorrect the receiver discards it, and can use the acknowledgements to indicate the retransmission of the packets.

- Flow Control. TCP returns a window with every ACK. This window indicates a range of acceptable sequence numbers beyond the last segment successfully received. This window also indicates the number of bytes that the sender can transmit before receiving further acknowledgements.
- Multiplexing. To support multiple connections to a single host, TCP provides a set of ports within each host. This, along with the IP addresses of the source and destination, makes a socket. Each connection is uniquely identified by a pair of sockets. Ports are normally associated with various services and allow service programs to listen for defined port numbers.
- Connections. A connection is defined by the sockets, sequence numbers and window sizes. Each host must maintain this information for the length of the connection. When the connection is closed, all associated resources are freed. As TCP connections can be made with unreliable hosts and over unreliable communication channels, TCP uses a handshake mechanism with clock-based sequence numbers to avoid inaccurate connection initialisation.
- Precedence and Security. TCP allows for different security and precedence levels.

TCP information contains simple acknowledgement messages and a set of sequential numbers. It also supports multiple simultaneous connections using destination and source port numbers, and manages them for both transmission and reception. As with IP, it supports data fragmentation and reassembly, and data multiplexing/demultiplexing.

The set-up and operation of TCP is as follows:

1. When a host wishes to make a connection, TCP sends out a request message to the destination machine that contains unique numbers, called a socket number and a port number. The port number has a value which is associated with the application (for example a TELNET connection has the port number 23 and an FTP connection has the port number 21). The message is then passed to the IP layer, which assembles a datagram for transmission to the destination.
2. When the destination host receives the connection request, it returns a message containing its own unique socket number and a port number. The socket number and port number thus identify the virtual connection between the two hosts.
3. After the connection has been made the data can flow between the two hosts (called a data stream).

After TCP receives the stream of data, it assembles the data into packets, called TCP segments. After the segment has been constructed, TCP adds a header (called the protocol data unit) to the front of the segment. This header contains information such as a checksum, port number, destination and source socket numbers, socket number of both machines and segment sequence numbers. The TCP layer then sends the packaged segment down to the IP layer, which encapsulates it and sends it over the network as a datagram.

### 10.2.1 Ports and sockets

As previously mentioned, TCP adds a port number and socket number for each host. The port number identifies the required service, whereas the socket number is a unique number for that connection. Thus, a node can have several TELNET connections with the same port number but each connection will have a different socket number. A port number can be any value but there is a standard convention that most systems adopt. Table 10.1 defines some of the most common values. Standard applications normally use port values from 0 to 255, while unspecified applications can use values above 255. Section 10.12 outlines the main ports.

**Table 10.1**   Typical TCP port numbers

| Port | Process name | Notes |
|------|-------------|-------|
| 20 | FTP-DATA | File Transfer Protocol - data |
| 21 | FTP | File Transfer Protocol - control |
| 23 | TELNET | Telnet |
| 25 | SMTP | Simple Mail Transfer Protocol |
| 49 | LOGIN | Login Protocol |
| 53 | DOMAIN | Domain Name Server |
| 79 | FINGER | Finger |
| 161 | SNMP | SNMP |

### 10.2.2 TCP header format

The sender's TCP layer communicates with the receiver's TCP layer using the TCP protocol data unit. It defines parameters such as the source port, destination port, and so on, and is illustrated in Figure 10.1. The fields are:

- Source and destination port number – which are 16-bit values that identify the local port number (source number and destination port number or destination port).
- Sequence number – which identifies the current sequence number of the data segment. This allows the receiver to keep track of the data segments received. Any segments that are missing can be easily identified. The sequence number of the first data byte in this segment (except when SYN is present). If SYN is present the sequence number is the initial sequence number (ISN) and the first data octet is ISN+1.
- Acknowledgement number – When the ACK bit is set, it contains the value of the next sequence number the sender of the packet is expecting to receive. This is always set after the connection is made.
- Data offset – which is a 32-bit value that identifies the start of the data. It is defined as the number of 32-bit words in the header (as the TCP header always has a multiple number of 32-bit words).
- Flags – the flag field is defined as UAPRSF, where U is the urgent flag (URG), A the acknowledgement flag (ACK), P the push function (PSH), R the reset flag (RST), S the sequence synchronise flag (SYN) and F the end-of-transmission flag (FIN).

- Window – which is a 16-bit value and gives the number of data bytes that the receiving host can accept at a time, beginning with the one indicated in the acknowledgement field of this segment.
- Checksum – which is a 16-bit checksum for the data and header. It is the 1's complement of the 1's complement sum of all the 16 bit words in the TCP header and text. The checksum is assumed to be a zero when calculating the checksum.
- UrgPtr – which is the urgent pointer and is used to identify an important area of data (most systems do not support this facility). It is only used when the URG bit is set. This field communicates the current value of the urgent pointer as a positive offset from the sequence number in this segment.
- Options. See Section 10.2.3.
- Padding (variable) – The TCP header padding is used to ensure that the TCP header ends and data begins on a 32-bit boundary. The padding is composed of zeros.

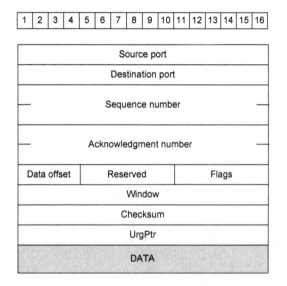

**Figure 10.1** TCP header format

In TCP, a packet is termed as the complete TCP unit, that is, the header and the data. A segment is a logical unit of data, which is transferred between two TCP hosts. Thus a packet is made up of a header and a segment.

### 10.2.3 Options

Like IP, the Option field can precede the DATA. It is variable in length and the content of the header beyond the End-of-Option option must be header padding. It must be implement by all hosts and gateways. There are two classes of option, these are:

- An option-type byte.
- An option-type byte, followed by an option-length byte, and then the actual option-data bytes. The option-length byte counts all the bytes in the options field.

Supported types are:

| Type | Length | Description |
|------|--------|-------------|
| 0 | | End of option list |
| 1 | | No operation |
| 2 | 4 | Maximum Segment Size |

### 10.2.4 End of Option List (Type=0)

The End of Option List indicates the end of all the options, not just the end of each option. It may not necessarily coincide with the end of the TCP header (according to the Data Offset field). It is only needed if the end of the options would not otherwise coincide with the end of the TCP header. Its format is:

```
+--------+
|00000000|
+--------+
```

### 10.2.5 No-Operation (Type=1)

The No-Operation can be used between options. A typical application is to align the beginning of a subsequent option, so that it is on a 32-bit word boundary. Its format is:

```
+--------+
|00000001|
+--------+
```

### 10.2.6 Maximum Segment Size (Type=2, Length=4)

In this option the maximum receive segment size is defined, and is preceeded by a 16-bit maximum segment size. It is only sent in an initial connection request, that is, when the SYN control bit is set. If it is not included, then any segment size is allowed. Its format is:

```
+--------+--------+---------+--------+
|00000010|00000100|    max seg size  |
+--------+--------+---------+--------+
```

## 10.3 UDP

TCP allows for a reliable connection-based transfer of data. The User Datagram Protocol (UDP) is an unreliable connection-less approach, where datagrams are sent into the network without an acknowledgements or connections. It is defined in RFC768 and uses IP as its underlying protocol. It has the advantage over TCP in that it has a minimal protocol mechanism, but does not guarantee delivery of any of the data. Figure 10.2 shows its format. The fields are:

- Source port. This is an optional field is set to a zero if not used. It identifies the local port number which should be used when the destination host requires to contact the originator.

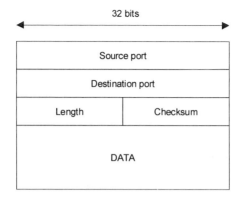

**Figure 10.2** UDP header format

- Destination Port to connect to on the destination.
- Length. Number of bytes in the datagram, including the UDP header and the data.
- Checksum. The 16-bit 1's complement of the 1's complement sum of the IP header, the UDP header, the data (which, if necessary, is padded with zero bytes at the end, to make an even number of bytes).

When used with IP the UDP/IP header is shown in Figure 10.3. The Protocol field is set to 17 to identify UDP.

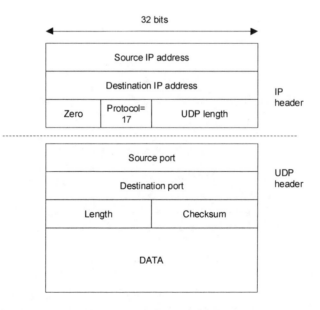

**Figure 10.3** UDP/IP header format

## 10.4 TCP specification

TCP is made reliable with the following:

- Sequence numbers. Each TCP packet is sent with a sequence number. Theoretically, each data byte is assigned a sequence number. The sequence number of the first data byte in the segment is transmitted with that segment and is called the segment sequence number (SSN).
- Acknowledgements. Packets contain an acknowledgement number, which is the sequence number of the next expected transmitted data byte in the reverse direction. On sending, a host stores the transmitted data in a storage buffer, and starts a timer. If the packet is acknowledged then this data is deleted, else, if no acknowledgement is received before the timer runs out, the packet is retransmitted.
- Window. With this, a host sends a window value which specifies the number of bytes, starting with the acknowledgement number, that the host can receive.

### 10.4.1 Connection establishment, clearing and data transmission

The main interfaces in TCP are shown in Figure 10.4. The calls from the application program to TCP include:

- OPEN and CLOSE. To open and close a connection.
- SEND and RECEIVE. To send and receive.
- STATUS. To receive status information.

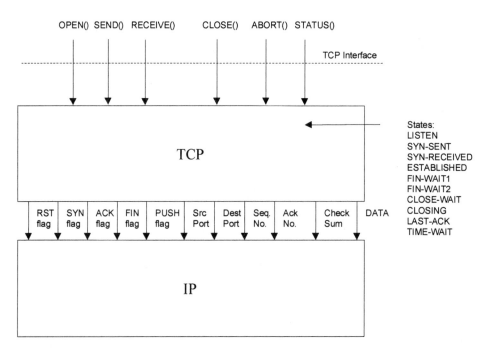

**Figure 10.4**  TCP interface

The OPEN call initiates a connection with a local port and foreign socket arguments. A Transmission Control Block (TCB) stores the information on the connection. After a successful connection, TCP adds a local connection name by which the application program refers to the connection in subsequent calls.

The OPEN call supports two different types of call, as illustrated in Figure 10.5. These are:

- Passive OPEN. TCP waits for a connection from a foreign host, such as from an active OPEN. In this case, the foreign socket is defined by a zero. This is typically used by servers, such as TELNET and FTP servers. The connection can either be from a fully specified or an unspecified socket.
- Active OPEN. TCP actively connects to a foreign host, typically a server (which is opened with a passive OPEN). Two processes which issue active OPENs to each other, at the same time, will also be connected.

A connect is established with the transmission of TCP packets with the SYN control flag set and uses a three-way handshake (see Section 10.6). A connection is cleared by the exchange of packets with the FIN control flag set. Data flows in a stream using the SEND call to send data and RECEIVE to receive data.

The PUSH flag is used to send data in the SEND immediately to the recipient. This is required as a sending TCP is allowed to collect data from the sending application program and sends the data in segments when convenient. Thus, the PUSH flag forces it to be sent. When the receiving TCP sees the PUSH flag, it does not wait for any more data from the sending TCP before passing the data to the receiving process.

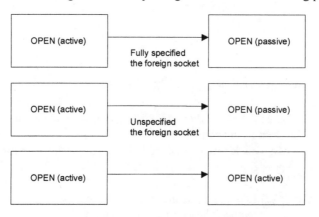

**Figure 10.5** TCP connections

# 10.5 TCB parameters

Table 10.2 outlines the send and receive packet parameters, as well as the current segment parameter, which are stored in the TCB. Along with this, the local and remote port number require to be stored.

**Table 10.2** TCB parameters

| Send Sequence Variables | Receive Sequence Variables | Current Packet Variable |
| --- | --- | --- |
| SND.UNA   Send unacknowledged | RCV.NXT   Receive next | SEG.SEQ segment sequence number |
| SND.NXT  Send next | RCV.WND  Receive window | SEG.ACK segment acknowledgement number |
| SND.WND Send window | RCV.UP Receive urgent pointer | |
| SND.UP Send urgent pointer | IRS Initial receive sequence number | SEG.LEN segment length |
| SND.WL1 Segment sequence number used for last window update | | SEG.WND segment window |
| | | SEG.UP segment urgent pointer |
| SND.WL2 Segment acknow-ledgement number used for last window update | | SEG.PRC segment precedence value |
| ISS Initial send sequence num-ber | | |

## 10.6  Connection states

Figure 10.6 outlines the states in which the connection goes into, and the events which cause them. The events from applications programs are: OPEN, SEND, RECEIVE, CLOSE, ABORT, and STATUS, and the events from the incoming TCP packets include the SYN, ACK, RST and FIN flags. The definition of each of the connection states are:

- LISTEN. This is the state in which TCP is waiting for a remote connection on a given port.
- SYN-SENT. This is the state where TCP is waiting for a matching connection request after it has sent a connection request.
- SYN-RECEIVED. This is the state where TCP is waiting for a confirming connection request acknowledgement after having both received and sent a connection request.
- ESTABLISHED. This is the state that represents an open connection. Any data received can be delivered to the application program. This is the normal state for data to be transmitted.
- FIN-WAIT-1. This is the state in which TCP is waiting for a connection termination request, or an acknowledgement of a connection termination, from the remote TCP.
- FIN-WAIT-2. This is the state in which TCP is waiting for a connection termination request from the remote TCP.
- CLOSE-WAIT. This is the state where TCP is waiting for a connection termination request from the local application.
- CLOSING. This is the state where TCP is waiting for a connection termination

request acknowledgement from the remote TCP.

- LAST-ACK. This is the state where TCP is waiting for an acknowledgement of the connection termination request previously sent to the remote TCP.
- TIME-WAIT. This is the state in which TCP is waiting for enough time to pass to be sure the remote TCP received the acknowledgement of its connection termination request.
- CLOSED. This is the fictional state, which occurs after the connection has been closed.

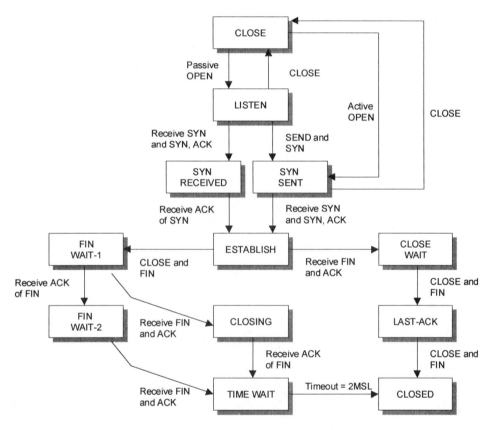

**Figure 10.6** TCP connection states

### 10.6.1 Sequence Numbers

TCP packets contain a 32-bit sequence number (0 to 4,294,967,295), which relates to every byte sent. It uses a cumulative acknowledgement scheme, where an acknowledgement with a value of VAL, validates all bytes up to, but not including, byte VAL. The number of bytes which the packet starts at the first data byte and are then numbered consecutively.

When sending data, TCP should receive acknowledgements for the transmitted data. The required TCB parameters will be:

| SND.UNA | Oldest unacknowledged sequence number. |
|---|---|
| SND.NXT | Next sequence number to send. |
| SEG.ACK | Acknowledgement from the receiving TCP (next sequence number expected by the receiving TCP). |
| SEG.SEQ | First sequence number of a segment. |
| SEG.LEN | Number of bytes in the TCP packet. |
| SEG.SEQ+SEG.LEN−1 | Last sequence number of a segment. |

One receiving data, the following TCB parameters are required:

| RCV.NXT | Next sequence number expected on an incoming segments, and is the left or lower edge of the receive window. |
|---|---|
| RCV.NXT+RCV.WND−1 | Last sequence number expected on an incoming segment, and is the right or upper edge of the receive window. |
| SEG.SEQ | First sequence number occupied by the incoming segment. |
| SEG.SEQ+SEG.LEN−1 | Last sequence number occupied by the incoming segment. |

### 10.6.2 ISN selection

The Initial Sequence Number (ISN) is selected so that previous sockets are not confused with new sockets. Typically, this can happen when a host application crashes and then quickly re-establishes the connection before the other side can time-out the connection. To avoid this a 32-bit initial sequence number (ISN) generator is created when the connection is made. It is generated by a 32-bit clock, which is incremented approximately every $4\,\mu s$ (giving a ISN cycle of 4.55 hours). Thus, within 4.55 hours, each ISN will be unique.

As each connection has a send and receive sequence number, there is an initial send sequence number (ISS) and an initial receive sequence number (IRS). When establishing a connection, the two TCPs synchronise their initial sequence numbers. This is done by exchanging connection establishing packets, with the SYN bit set and with the initial sequence numbers (these packets are typically called SYNs). Thus four packets must be initially exchanged; these are:

- A sends to B. SYN with $A_{SEQ}$.
- B sends to A. ACK of the sequence number ($A_{SEQ}$).
- B sends to A. SYN with $B_{SEQ}$.
- A sends to B. ACK of the sequence number ($B_{SEQ}$).

Note that the two intermediate steps can be combined into a single message. This is sometimes knows as a three-way handshake. This handshake is necessary as the sequence numbers are not tied to a global clock, only to local clocks, and has many advantages, including the fact that old packets will be discarded as they occurred in a previous time.

To makes sure that a sequence number is not duplicated, a host must wait for a maximum segment lifetime (MSL) before starting to retransmit packets (segments) after start-up or when recovering from a crash. An example MSL is 2 minutes. Although, if it is recovering, and it has a memory of the previous sequence numbers, it may not need to wait for the MSL, as it can use sequence numbers which are much greater than the previously used sequence numbers.

## 10.7 Opening and closing a connection

Figure 10.7 shows a basic three-way handshake. The steps are:

1.  The initial state on the initiator is CLOSED and, on the recipient, it is LISTEN (the recipient is waiting for a connection).
2.  The initiator goes into the SYN-SENT state and sends a packet with the SYN bit set and indicates that the starting sequence number will be 999 (the current sequence number, thus the next number sent will be 1000). When this is received the recipient goes into the SYN-RECEIVED state.
3.  The recipient sends back a TCP packet with the SYN and ACK bits set (which identifies that it is a SYN packet and also that it is acknowledging the previous SYN packet). In this case, the recipient tells the originator that it will start transmitting at a sequence number of 100. The acknowledgement number is 1000, which is the sequence number that the recipient expects to receive next. When this is received, the originator goes into the ESTABLISHED state.
4.  The originator sends back a TCP packet with the SYN and ACK bits set and the acknowledgement number is 101, which is the sequence number it expects to see next.
5.  The originator transmits data with the sequence number of 1000.

| **Originator** | | | | **Recipient** |
|---|---|---|---|---|
| 1. CLOSED | | | | LISTEN |
| 2. SYN-SENT | → | <SEQ=999><CTL=SYN> | | SYN-RECEIVED |
| 3. ESTABLISHED | | <SEQ=100><ACK=1000> | <CTL=SYN,ACK> ← | SYN-RECEIVED |
| 4. ESTABLISHED | → | <SEQ=1000><ACK=101> | <CTL=ACK> | ESTABLISHED |
| 5. ESTABLISHED | → | <SEQ=1000><ACK=101> | <CTL=ACK><DATA> | ESTABLISHED |

**Figure 10.7** TCP connection

Note that the acknowledgement number acknowledges every sequence number up to, but not including the acknowledgement number.

Figure 10.8 shows how the three-way handshake prevents old duplicate connection initiations from causing confusion. In state 3, a duplicate SYN has received, which is from a previous connection. The Recipient sends back an acknowledgement for this (4), but when this is received by the Originator, the Originator sends back a RST (reset) packet. This causes the Recipient to go back into a LISTEN state. It will then receive the SYN packet sent in 2, and after acknowledging it, a connection is made.

TCP connections are half-open if one of the TCPs has closed or aborted, and the other end is still connected. It can also occurs if the two connections have become desynchronised because of a system crash. This connection is automatically reset if data is sent in either direction. This is because the sequence numbers will be incorrect, otherwise the connection will time-out.

A connection is normally closed with the CLOSE call. A host who has closed cannot continue to send, but can continue to RECEIVE until it is told to close by the other side. Figure 10.9 shows a typical sequence for closing a connection. Normally the application program sends a CLOSE call for the given connection. Next, a TCP packet is sent with the FIN bit set, the originator enters into the FIN-WAIT-1 state. When the other TCP has acknowledged the FIN and sent a FIN of its own, the first TCP can ACK this FIN.

| **Originator** | | **Recipient** |
|---|---|---|
| 1. CLOSED | | LISTEN |
| 2. SYN-SENT | → <SEQ=999><CTL=SYN> | |
| 3. (duplicate) | → <SEQ=900><CTL=SYN> | |
| 4. SYN-SENT | <SEQ=100><ACK=901> <CTL=SYN,ACK> ← | SYN-RECEIVED |
| 5. SYN-SENT | → <SEQ=901><CTL=RST> | LISTEN |
| 6. | (packet 2 received) → | |
| 7. SYN-SENT | <SEQ=100><ACK=1000><CTL=SYN,ACK ← | SYN-RECEIVED |
| 8. ESTABLISHED | → <SEQ=1000><ACK=101><CTL=ACK><DATA> | ESTABLISHED |

**Figure 10.8**  TCP connection with duplicate connections

| **Originator** | | **Recipient** |
|---|---|---|
| 1. ESTABLISHED | | ESTABLISHED |
| (*CLOSE call*) | | |
| 2. FIN-WAIT-1 | → <SEQ=1000><ACK=99> <CTL=SFIN,ACK> | CLOSE-WAIT |
| 3. FIN-WAIT-2 | <SEQ=99><ACK=1001><CTL=ACK> ← | CLOSE-WAIT |
| 4. TIME-WAIT | <SEQ=99><ACK=101><CTL=FIN,ACK> ← | LAST-ACK |
| 5. TIME-WAIT | → <SEQ=1001><ACK=102><CTL=ACK> | CLOSED |

**Figure 10.9**  TCP close connection

## 10.8  TCP User commands

The commands in this section characterise the interface between TCP and the application program. Their actual implementation depends on the operating system. Section 10.9 discusses the WinSock implementation and Chapter 24 shows a Java implementation (Java is somewhat restricted in what it can do with sockets).

### 10.8.1 OPEN

The OPEN call initiates an active or a passive TCP connection. The basic parameters passed and returned from the call are given next. Parameters in brackets are optional.

| Parameters passed: | local port, foreign socket, active/passive  [, timeout] [, precedence] [, security/compartment] [, options]) |
|---|---|
| Parameters returned: | local connection name |

These parameters are defined as:

- Local port. The local port to be used.
- Foreign socket. The definition of the foreign socket.
- Active/passive. A passive flag causes TCP to LISTEN, else it will actively seek a

connection.

- Timeout. If present, this parameter allows the caller to set up a timeout for all data submitted to TCP. If the data is not transmitted successfully within the timeout period the connection is aborted.
- Security/compartment. Specifies the security of the connection.
- Local connection name. A unique connection name is returned which identifies the socket.

### 10.8.2 SEND

The SEND call causes the data in the output buffer to be sent to the indicated connection. Most implementations return immediately from the SEND call, even if the data has not been sent, although some implementation will not return until either there is a timeout or the data has been sent. The basic parameters passed and returned from the call are given next. Parameters in brackets are optional.

Parameters passed:         local connection name, buffer address, byte count, PUSH flag, URGENT flag [,timeout]

These parameters are defined as:

- Local connection name. A unique connection name which identifies the socket.
- Buffer address. Address of data buffer.
- Byte count. Number of bytes in the buffer.
- PUSH flag. If this flag is set then the data will be transmitted immediately, else the TCP may wait until it has enough data.
- URGENT flag. Sets the urgent pointer.
- Timeout. Sets a new timeout for the connection.

### 10.8.3 RECEIVE

The RECEIVE call allocates a receiving buffer for the specified connection. Most implementations return immediately from the RECEIVE call, even if the data has not been received, although some implementation will not return until either there is a timeout or the data has been received. The basic parameters passed and returned from the call are given next. Parameters in brackets are optional.

Parameters passed:         local connection name, buffer address, byte count
Parameters returned:       byte count, URGENT flag, PUSH flag

These parameters are defined as:

- Local connection name. A unique connection name which identifies the socket.
- Buffer address. Address of the receive data buffer.
- Byte count. Number of bytes received in the buffer.
- PUSH flag. If this flag is set then the PUSH flag has been set on the received data.
- URGENT flag. If this flag is set then the URGENT flag has been set on the received data.

### 10.8.4 CLOSE

The CLOSE call closes the connections and releases associated resources. All pending SENDs will be transmitted, but after the CLOSE call has been implement, no further SENDs can occur. RECEIVEs can occur until the other host has also closed the connection. The basic parameters passed and returned from the call are given next.

Parameters passed:        local connection name

### 10.8.5 STATUS

The STATUS call determines the current status of a connection, typically listing the TCBs. The basic parameters passed and returned from the call are given next.

Parameters passed:        local connection name
Parameters returned:        status data

The returned information should include status information on the following:

- local socket, foreign socket, local connection name;
- receive window, send window, connection state;
- number of buffers awaiting acknowledgement, number of buffers pending receipt;
- urgent state, precedence, security/compartment;
- transmission timeout.

### 10.8.6 ABORT

The ABORT call causes all pending SENDs and RECEIVEs to be aborted. All TCBs are also removed and a RESET message to sent to the other TCP. The basic parameters passed and returned from the call are given next. Parameters in brackets are optional.

Parameters passed:        local connection name

---

## 10.9 WinSock

### 10.9.1 Introduction

The Windows Sockets specification describes a common interface for networked Windows programs. WinSock uses TCP/IP communications and provides for binary and source code compatibility for different network types.

The Windows Sockets API (WinSock API, or WSA) is a library of functions that implement the socket interface by the Berkley Software Distribution of UNIX. WinSock augments the Berkley socket implementation by adding Windows-specific extensions to support the message-driven nature of Windows system.

The basic implementation normally involves:

- Opening a socket. This allows for multiple connections with multiple hosts. Each socket has a unique identifier. It normally involves defining the protocol suite, the socket type and the protocol name. The API call used for this is `socket()`.
- Naming a socket. This involves assigning location and identity attributes to a socket. The API call used for this is `bind()`.
- Associate with another socket. This involves either listening for a connection or actively seeking a connection. The API calls used in this are `listen()`, `connect()` and `accept()`.
- Send and receive between socket. The API calls used in this are `send()`, `sendto()`, `recv()` and `recvfrom()`.
- Close the socket. The API calls used in this are `close()` and `shutdown()`.

### 10.9.2 Windows Sockets

The main WinSock API calls are:

| | |
|---|---|
| `socket().` | Creates a socket. |
| `accept().` | Accepts a connection on a socket. |
| `connect().` | Establishes a connection to a peer. |
| `bind().` | Associates a local address with a socket. |
| `listen().` | Establishes a socket to listen for incoming connection. |
| `send().` | Sends data on a connected socket. |
| `sendto().` | Sends data on an unconnected socket. |
| `recv().` | Receives data from a connected socket. |
| `recvfrom().` | Receives data from an unconnected socket. |
| `shutdown().` | Disables send or receive operations on a socket. |
| `closesocket().` | Closes a socket. |

Figure 10.10 shows the operation of a connection of a client to a server. The server is defined as the computer which waits for a connection, the client is the computer which initially makes contact with the server.

On the server the computer initially creates a socket with the `socket()` function, and this is bound to a name with the `bind()` function. After this, the server listens for a connection with the `listen()` function. When the client calls the `connect()` function the server then accepts the connection with `accept()`. After this the server and client can send and receive data with the `send()` or `recv()` functions. When the data transfer is complete the `closesocket()` is used to close the socket.

### socket()

The `socket()` function creates a socket. Its syntax is:

```
SOCKET socket ( int af, int type, int protocol)
```

where

| | |
|---|---|
| *af* | A value of `PF_INET` specifies the ARPA Internet address format specification (others include `AF_IPX` for SPX/IPX and `AF_APPLETALK` for AppleTalk). |
| *type* | Socket specification, which is typically either `SOCK_STREAM` or |

SOCK_DGRAM. The SOCK_STREAM uses TCP and provides a sequenced, reliable, two-way, connection-based stream. SOCK_DGRAM uses UDP and provides for connectionless datagrams. This type of connection is not recommended. A third type is SOCK_RAW, for types other than UDP or TCP, such as for ICMP.

*protocol*        Defines the protocol to be used with the socket. If it is zero then the caller does not wish to specify a protocol.

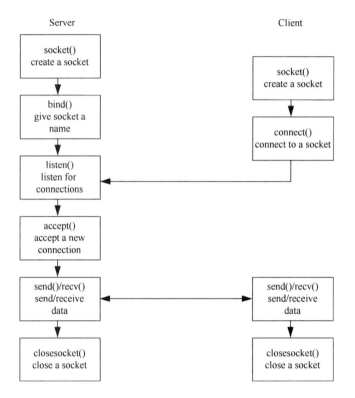

**Figure 10.10** WinSock connection

If the socket function succeeds then the return value is a descriptor referencing the new socket. Otherwise, it returns SOCKET_ERROR, and the specific error code can be tested with WSAGetLastError. An example creation of a socket is given next:

```
SOCKET s;

s=socket(PF_INET,SOCK_STREAM,0);
if (s == INVALID_SOCKET)
{
    cout << "Socket error"
}
```

**bind()**

The bind() function associates a local address with a socket. It is before called before the `connect` or `listen` functions. When a socket is created with `socket`, it exists in a name space (address family), but it has no name assigned. The `bind` function gives the socket a local association (host address/port number). Its syntax is:

```
int bind(SOCKET s, const struct sockaddr FAR * addr, int namelen);
```
where

| | |
|---|---|
| *s* | A descriptor identifying an unbound socket. |
| *namelen* | The length of the *addr*. |
| *addr* | The address to assign to the socket. The `sockaddr` structure is defined as follows: |

```
struct sockaddr
{
        u_short     sa_family;
        char        sa_data[14];
};
```

In the Internet address family, the `sockadd_in` structure is used by Windows Sockets to specify a local or remote endpoint address to which to connect a socket. This is the form of the `sockaddr` structure specific to the Internet address family and can be cast to `sockaddr`. This structure can be filled with the `sockaddr_in` structure which has the following form:

```
struct SOCKADDR_IN
{
    short               sin_family;
    unsigned short      sin_port;
    struct              in_addr  sin_addr;
    char                sin_zero[8];
}
```

where

| | |
|---|---|
| `sin_family` | must be set to `AF_INET`. |
| `sin_port` | IP port. |
| `sin_addr` | IP address. |
| `sin_zero` | Padding to make structure the same size as `sockaddr`. |

If an application does not care what address is assigned to it, it may specify an Internet address equal to `INADDR_ANY`, a port equal to 0, or both. An Internet address equal to `INADDR_ANY` causes any appropriate network interface be used. A port value of 0 causes the Windows Sockets implementation to assign a unique port to the application with a value between 1024 and 5000.

If no error occurs then it returns a zero value. Otherwise, it returns `INVALID_SOCKET`, and the specific error code can be tested with `WSAGetLastError`. If an application needs to bind to an arbitrary port outside of the range 1024 to 5000 then the following outline code can be used:

```
#include <windows.h>
#include <winsock.h>
```

```
int main(void)
{

SOCKADDR_IN    sin;
SOCKET         s;
  s = socket(AF_INET,SOCK_STREAM,0);

  if (s == INVALID_SOCKET)
  {
      // Socket failed
  }

  sin.sin_family = AF_INET;
  sin.sin_addr.s_addr = 0;

  sin.sin_port = htons(100); // port=100

  if (bind(s, (LPSOCKADDR)&sin, sizeof (sin)) == 0)
  {
      // Bind failed
  }
  return(0);
}
```

The Windows Sockets `htons` function converts an unsigned short (`u_short`) from host byte order to network byte order.

### connect()

The `connect()` function establishes a connection with a peer. If the specified socket is unbound then unique values are assigned to the local association by the system and the socket is marked as bound. Its syntax is:

```
int connect (SOCKET s, const struct sockaddr FAR * name,
             int namelen)
```

where

|          |                                                       |
|----------|-------------------------------------------------------|
| *s*      | Descriptor identifying an unconnected socket.         |
| *name*   | Name of the peer to which the socket is to be connected. |
| *namelen* | Name length.                                         |

If no error occurs then it returns a zero value. Otherwise, it returns SOCKET_ERROR, and the specific error code can be tested with WSAGetLastError.

### listen()

The `listen()` function establishes a socket which listens for an incoming connection. The sequence to create and accept a socket is:

* `socket()`. Creates a socket.
* `listen()`. This creates a queue for incoming connections and is typically used by a server that can have more than one connection at a time.
* `accept()`. These connections are then accepted with accept.

The syntax of `listen()` is:

```
int listen (SOCKET s, int backlog)
```

where

> *s*        Describes a bound, unconnected socket.
>
> *backlog* Defines the queue size for the maximum number of pending connections may grow (typically a maximum of 5).

If no error occur then it returns a zero value. Otherwise, it returns SOCKET_ERROR, and the specific error code can be tested with WSAGetLastError.

```c
#include <windows.h>
#include <winsock.h>

int main(void)
{

SOCKADDR_IN    sin;
SOCKET         s;

  s = socket(AF_INET,SOCK_STREAM,0);
  if (s == INVALID_SOCKET)
  {
      // Socket failed
  }

  sin.sin_family = AF_INET;
  sin.sin_addr.s_addr = 0;

  sin.sin_port = htons(100); // port=100

  if (bind(s, (struct sockaddr FAR *)&sin, sizeof (sin))==SOCKET_ERROR)
  {
      // Bind failed
    }
  if (listen(s,4)==SOCKET_ERROR)
  {
      // Listen failed
  }
  return(0);
}
```

## accept()

The `accept()` function accepts a connection on a socket. It extracts any pending connections from the queue and creates a new socket with the same properties as the specified socket. Finally, it returns a handle to the new socket. Its syntax is:

```
SOCKET accept(SOCKET s, struct sockaddr FAR *addr, int FAR *addrlen );
```

where

> *s*        Descriptor identifying a socket that is in listen mode.

*addr*      Pointer to a buffer that receives the address of the connecting entity, as known to the communications layer.

*addrlen*   Pointer to an integer which contains the length of the address *addr*.

If no error occurs then it returns a zero value. Otherwise, it returns INVALID_SOCKET, and the specific error code can be tested with WSAGetLastError.

```
#include <windows.h>
#include <winsock.h>

int main(void)
{

SOCKADDR_IN    sin;
SOCKET         s;
int            sin_len;
  s = socket(AF_INET,SOCK_STREAM,0);
  if (s == INVALID_SOCKET)
  {
      // Socket failed
  }

  sin.sin_family = AF_INET;
  sin.sin_addr.s_addr = 0;
  sin.sin_port = htons(100); // port=100

  if (bind(s, (struct sockaddr FAR *)&sin, sizeof (sin))==SOCKET_ERROR)
  {
      // Bind failed
  }

  if (listen(s,4)<0)
  {
      // Listen failed
  }
  sin_len = sizeof(sin);
  s=accept(s,(struct sockaddr FAR *) & sin,(int FAR *) &sin_len);
  if (s==INVALID_SOCKET)
  {
      // Accept failed
  }
  return(0);
}
```

### send()

The send() function sends data to a connected socket. Its syntax is:

```
int send (SOCKET s, const char FAR *buf, int len, int flags)
```

where

      *s*     Connected socket descriptor.
      *buf*   Transmission data buffer.
      *len*   Buffer length.
      *flags* Calling flag.

The *flags* parameter influences the behavior of the function. These can be:

MSG_DONTROUTE    Specifies that the data should not be subject to routing.
MSG_OOB             Send out-of-band data.

If send() succeeds then the return value is the number of characters sent (which can be less than the number indicated by *len*). Otherwise, it returns SOCKET_ERROR, and the specific error code can be tested with WSAGetLastError.

```
#include <windows.h>
#include <winsock.h>
#include <string.h>
#define   STRLENGTH 100

int main(void)
{

SOCKADDR_IN     sin;
SOCKET          s;
int sin_len;
char    sendbuf[STRLENGTH];
  s = socket(AF_INET,SOCK_STREAM,0);
  if (s == INVALID_SOCKET)
  {
      // Socket failed
  }
  sin.sin_family = AF_INET;
  sin.sin_addr.s_addr = 0;
      sin.sin_port = htons(100); // port=100
  if (bind(s, (struct sockaddr FAR *)&sin, sizeof (sin))==SOCKET_ERROR)
  {
      // Bind failed
  }

  if (listen(s,4)<0)
  {
      // Listen failed
  }
  sin_len = sizeof(sin);

  s=accept(s,(struct sockaddr FAR *) & sin,(int FAR *) &sin_len);

  if (s<0)
  {
      // Accept failed
  }

  while (1)
  {
      // get message to send and put into sendbuff
      send(s,sendbuf,strlen(sendbuf),80);
  }
  return(0);
}
```

**recv()**

The recv() function receives data from a socket. It waits until data arrives and its syntax is:

```
int recv(SOCKET s, char FAR *buf, int len, int flags)
```

where

> s    Connected socket descriptor.
> buf   Incoming data buffer.
> len   Buffer length.
> flags  Specifies the method by which the data is received.

If `recv()` succeeds then the return value is the number of bytes received (a zero identifies that the connection has been closed). Otherwise, it returns `SOCKET_ERROR`, and the specific error code can be tested with `WSAGetLastError`.

The flags parameter may have one of the following values:

> `MSG_PEEK` Peek at the incoming data. Any received data is copied into the buffer, but not removed from the input queue.
> `MSG_OOB` Process out-of-band data.

```c
#include <windows.h>
#include <winsock.h>

#define  STRLENGTH 100

int main(void)
{

SOCKADDR_IN    sin;
SOCKET         s;
int            sin_len, status;
char           recmsg[STRLENGTH];

  s = socket(AF_INET,SOCK_STREAM,0);

  if (s == INVALID_SOCKET)
  {
      // Socket failed
  }

  sin.sin_family = AF_INET;
  sin.sin_addr.s_addr = 0;

      sin.sin_port = htons(100); // port=100

  if (bind(s, (struct sockaddr FAR *)&sin, sizeof (sin))==SOCKET_ERROR)
  {
      // Bind failed
  }

  if (listen(s,4)<0)
  {
      // Listen failed
  }
  sin_len = sizeof(sin);

  s=accept(s,(struct sockaddr FAR *) & sin,(int FAR *) &sin_len);

  if (s<0)
  {
      // Accept failed
```

```
    }
    while (1)
    {
        status=recv(s,recmsg,STRLENGTH,80);

        if (status==SOCKET_ERROR)
        {
            // no socket
            break;
        }

        recmsg[status]=NULL; // terminate string
        if (status)
        {
            // szMsg contains received string
        }
        else
        {
            break;
            // connection broken
        }
    }
    return(0);
}
```

### shutdown()

The shutdown() function disables send or receive operations on a socket and does not close any opened sockets. Its syntax is:

```
int shutdown(SOCKET s, int how);
```

where

> *s*   Socket descriptor.
> *how*  Flag that identifies operation types that will no longer be allowed. These are:
> 0 – Disallows subsequent receives.
> 1 – Disallows subsequent sends.
> 2 – Disables send and receive.

If no error occurs then it returns a zero value. Otherwise, it returns INVALID_SOCKET, and the specific error code can be tested with WSAGetLastError.

### closesocket()

The closesocket() function closes a socket. Its syntax is:

```
int closesocket (SOCKET s);
```

where

> *s*   Socket descriptor.

If no error occurs then it returns a zero value. Otherwise, it returns INVALID_SOCKET, and the specific error code can be tested with `WSAGetLastError`.

## 10.10 Visual Basic socket implementation

Visual Basic supports a WinSock control and allows the connection of hosts over a network. It supports both UDP and TCP. Figure 10.11 shows a sample Visual Basic screen with a WinSock object (in this case, it is named Winsock1). To set the Procotol used then either select the Properties window on the WinSock object, click Protocol and select either sckTCPProtocol, or sckUDPProtocol. Otherwise, within the code it can be set to TCP with:

```
Winsock1.Protocol = sckTCPProtocol
```

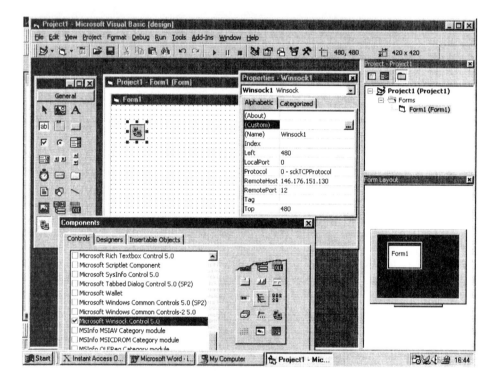

**Figure 10.11** WinSock object

The WinSock object has various properties, such as:

*obj*.RemoteHost    Defines the IP address or domain name of the remote host.
*obj*.LocalPort    Defines the local port number

The methods that are used with the WinSock object are:

| *obj*.Connect | Connects to a remote host (client invoked). |
|---|---|
| *obj*.Listen | Listens for a connection (server invoked). |
| *obj*.GetData | Reads data from the input steam. |
| *obj*.SendData | Sends data to an output stream. |

The main events are:

| ConnectionRequest | Occurs when a remote host wants to make a connection with a server. |
|---|---|
| DataArrival | Occurs when data has arrived from a connection (data is then read with GetData). |

### 10.10.1 Creating a server

A server must listen for connection. To do this, do the following:

1 Create a new Standard EXE project.
2 Change the name of the default form to myServer.
3 Change the caption of the form to "Server Application" (see Figure 10.12).
4 Put a Winsock control on the main form and change its name to myTCPServer.
5 Add two TextBox controls to the form. Name the first SendTextData, and the second ShowText (see Figure 10.12).
6 Add the code given below to the form.

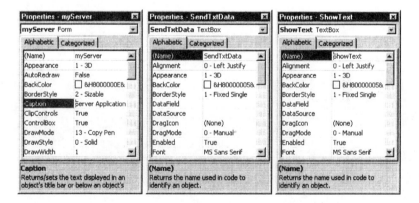

**Figure 10.12** Server set-ups

```
Private Sub Form_Load()
    ' Set the local port to 1001 and listen for a connection
    myTCPServer.LocalPort = 1001
    myTCPServer.Listen
    myClient.Show
End Sub

Private Sub myTCPServer_ConnectionRequest (ByVal requestID As Long)
    ' Check state of socket, if it is not closed then close it.
    If myTCPServer.State <> sckClosed Then myTCPServer.Close
    ' Accept the request with the requestID parameter.
    myTCPServer.Accept  requestID
```

```
End Sub

Private Sub SendTextData_Change()
    ' SendTextData contains the data to be sent.
    ' This data is setn using the SendData method
    myTCPServer.SendData = SendTextData.Text
End Sub

Private Sub myTCPServer_DataArrival (ByVal bytesTotal As Long)
    ' Read incoming data into the str variable,
    ' then display it to ShowText
    Dim str As String
    myTCPServer.GetData = str
    ShowText.Text = str
End Sub
```

Figure 10.13 shows the server setup.

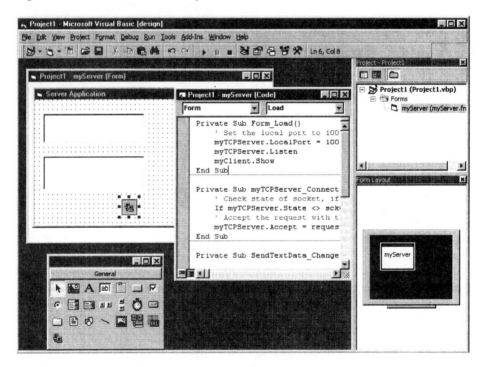

**Figure 10.13**   Server form

### 10.10.2   Creating a client

The client must actively seek a connection. To create a client, do the following:

1   Add a new form to the project, and name it myClient.
2   Change the caption of the form to "Client Application".
3   Add a Winsock control to the form and name it myTCPClient.
4   Add two TextBox controls to the form. Name the first SendTextData, and the second ShowText.

5  Draw a CommandButton control on the form and name it cmdConnect.

6  Change the caption of the CommandButton control to Connect.

7  Add the code given below to the form.

```
Private Sub Form_Load()
    ' In this case it will connect to 146.176.151.130
    ' change this to the local IP address or DNS of the local computer
    myTCPClient.RemoteHost = "146.176.151.130"
    myTCPClient.RemotePort = 1001
End Sub

Private Sub cmdConnect_Click()
    ' Connect to the server
    myTCPClient.Connect
End Sub

Private Sub SendTextData_Change()
    tcpClient.SendData txtSend.Text
End Sub

Private Sub tcpClient_DataArrival (ByVal bytesTotal As Long)
    Dim str As String
    myTCPClient.GetData str
    ShowText.Text = str
End Sub
```

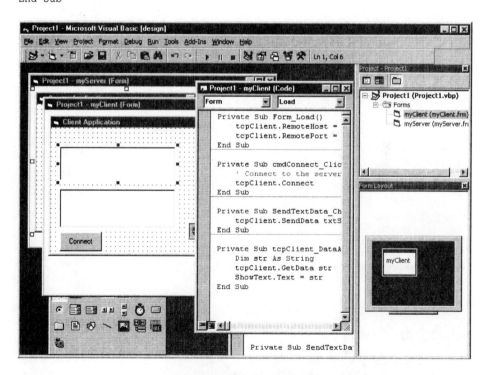

**Figure 10.14**  Client form

The program, when it is run, will act as a client and a server. Any text typed in the SendTxtData TextBox will be sent to the ShowText TextBox on the other form.

### 10.10.3 Multiple connections

In Visual Basic, it is also possible to create multiple connections to a server. This is done by creating multiple occurances of the server object. A new one is created every time there is a new connection (with the Connection_Request event). Each new server accepts the incoming connection. The following code, which has a Winsock control on a form called multServer, is given below.

```
Private ConnectNo As Long

Private Sub Form_Load()
    ConnectNo = 0
    multServer(0).LocalPort = 1001
    multServer(0).Listen
End Sub

Private Sub multServer_ConnectionRequest _
                    (Index As Integer, ByVal requestID As Long)
    If Index = 0 Then
        ConnectNo = ConnectNo + 1
        Load multServer(ConnectNo)
        multServer(ConnectNo).LocalPort = 0
        multServer(ConnectNo).Accept requestID
        Load txtData(ConnectNo)
    End If
End Sub
```

### 10.10.4 Connect event

The Connect event connects to a server. If an error occurs then a flag (ErrorOccurred) is set to True, else it is False. Its syntax is:

```
Private Sub object.Connect(ErrorOccurred As Boolean)
```

### 10.10.5 Close event

The Close event occurs when the remote computer closes the connection. Applications should use the Close method to correctly close their connection. Its syntax is:

```
object_Close()
```

### 10.10.6 DataArrival event

The DataArrival event occurs when new data arrives, and returns the number of bytes read (bytesTotal). Its syntax is:

```
object_DataArrival (bytesTotal As Long)
```

### 10.10.7 Bind method

The Bind method specifies the Local port (LocalPort) and the Local IP address (LocalIP) to be used for TCP connections. Its syntax is:

```
object.Bind LocalPort, LocalIP
```

### 10.10.8 Listen method

The Listen method creates a socket and goes into listen mode (for server applications). Its stays in this mode until a ConnectionRequest event occurs, which indicates an incoming connection. After this, the Accept method should be used to accept the connection. Its syntax is:

*object*.Listen

### 10.10.9 Accept method

The Accept method accepts incoming connections after a ConnectionRequest event. Its syntax is:

*object*.Accept requestID

The requestID parameter is passed into the ConnectionRequest event and is used with the Accept method.

### 10.10.10 Close method

The Close method closes a TCP connection. Its syntax is:

*object*.Close

### 10.10.11 SendData method

The SendData methods sends data (Data) to a remote computer. Its syntax is:

*object*.SendData *Data*

### 10.10.12 GetData method

The GetData method gets data (Data) from an object. Its syntax is:

*object*.GetData *data*, [*type*,] [*maxLen*]

## 10.11 Exercises

10.11.1    Which of the following is not part of a TCP header:

   (a)    Host IP address          (b)    Time-to-live field
   (c)    Host port number         (d)    Acknowledgement number

10.11.2    Which port does a TELNET server listen to:

   (a)    21                       (b)    25
   (c)    25                       (d)    80

**10.11.3**   Which port does an Email server (using SMTP) listen to:

(a)   21                          (b)   25
(c)   25                          (d)   80

**10.11.4**   Which port does a WWW server (using HTTP) listen to:

(a)   21                          (b)   25
(c)   25                          (d)   80

**10.11.5**   Which port does a FTP server listen to:

(a)   21                          (b)   25
(c)   25                          (d)   80

**10.11.6**   What is the main difference between UDP and TCP:

(a)   TCP uses sequence numbers, makes a connections and uses ac-
        knowledgements
(b)   They uses different addressing schemes
(c)   They use different port allocations
(d)   UDP only supports one-way traffic, while TCP support multiplexed
        traffic.

**10.11.7**   What is the main method that TCP uses to create a reliable connection:

(a)   Enhanced error correction
(b)   Specially coded data
(c)   Encrypted data
(d)   Sequence numbers and acknowledgements

**10.11.8**   How is the initial sequence number of a TCP packet generated:

(a)   Randomly
(b)   From a 32-bit clock which is updated every 4 µs
(c)   From a universal Internet-based clock
(d)   From the system clock

**10.11.9**   How many packets are exchanged in setting up an established TCP connection:

(a)   1          (b)   2
(c)   3          (d)   4

**10.11.10**   Outline the operation of the three-way handshaking.

**10.11.11**   What advantages does TCP have over UDP. Investigate server applications
which use UDP.

**10.11.12** If possible, implement a basic client/server application with either C++ or Visual Basic. As a test, run the client and the server on the same computer. (note the IP address of the computer as this is required by the client).

**10.11.13** Change the program in Exercise 10.11.12 so that the client and the server run on different computers (note the IP address of the server as this is required by the client). If possible, run the program on different network segments.

*For the following questions, download a program from the WWW which connects to a specified port on a specified server.*

**10.11.14** Connect to a WWW server using port 13. This port should return back the current date and time.

**10.11.15** Connect to a WWW server using port 19. This port should return the current date and time.

**10.11.16** Connect two computers over a network and set up a chat connection. One of the computers should be the chat server and the other the chat client. Modify it so that the server accepts calls from one or many clients.

## 10.12 TCP/IP services reference

| Port | Service | Comment | Port | Service | Comment |
|---|---|---|---|---|---|
| 1 | TCPmux | | 7 | echo | |
| 9 | discard | Null | 11 | systat | Users |
| 13 | daytime | | 15 | netstat | |
| 17 | qotd | Quote | 18 | msp | Message send protocol |
| 19 | chargen | ttytst source | 21 | ftp | |
| 23 | telnet | | 25 | smtp | Mail |
| 37 | time | Timserver | 39 | rlp | Resource location |
| 42 | nameserver | IEN 116 | 43 | whois | Nicname |
| 53 | domain | DNS | 57 | mtp | Deprecated |
| 67 | bootps | BOOTP server | 67 | bootps | |
| 68 | bootpc | BOOTP client | 69 | tftp | |
| 70 | gopher | Internet Gopher | 77 | rje | Netrjs |
| 79 | finger | | 80 | www | WWW HTTP |
| 87 | link | Ttylink | 88 | kerberos | Kerberos v5 |
| 95 | supdup | | 101 | hostnames | |
| 102 | iso-tsap | ISODE | 105 | csnet-ns | CSO name server |
| 107 | rtelnet | Remote Telnet | 109 | pop2 | POP version 2 |
| 110 | pop3 | POP version 3 | 111 | sunrpc | |
| 113 | auth | Rap ID | 115 | sftp | |
| 117 | uucp-path | | 119 | nntp | USENET |
| 123 | ntp | Network Timel | 137 | netbios-ns | NETBIOS Name Service |

| | | | | | |
|---|---|---|---|---|---|
| 138 | netbios-dgm | NETBIOS | 139 | netbios-ssn | NETBIOS session |
| 143 | imap2 | | 161 | snmp | SNMP |
| 162 | snmp-trap | SNMP trap | 163 | cmip-man | ISO management over IP |
| 164 | cmip-agent | | 177 | xdmcp | X Display Manager |
| 178 | nextstep | NeXTStep | 179 | bgp | BGP |
| 191 | prospero | | 194 | irc | Internet Relay Chat |
| 199 | smux | SNMP Multiplexer | 201 | at-rtmp | AppleTalk routing |
| 202 | at-nbp | AppleTalk name binding | 204 | at-echo | AppleTalk echo |
| 206 | at-zis | AppleTalk zone information | 210 | z3950 | NISO Z39.50 database |
| 213 | ipx | IPX | 220 | imap3 | Interactive Mail Access |
| 372 | ulistserv | UNIX Listserv | 512 | exec | Comsat 513 login |
| 513 | who | Whod | 514 | shell | No passwords used |
| 514 | syslog | | 515 | printer | Line printer spooler |
| 517 | talk | | 518 | ntalk | |
| 520 | route | RIP | 525 | timed | Timeserver |
| 526 | tempo | Newdate | 530 | courier | Rpc |
| 531 | conference | Chat | 532 | netnews | Readnews |
| 533 | netwall | Emergency broadcasts | 540 | uucp | Uucp daemon |
| 543 | klogin | Kerberized 'rlogin' (v5) | 544 | kshell | Kerberized 'rsh' (v5) |

## 10.13 Note from the author

*TCP is amazing. In fact, so is IP. How many people have been amazed by how easy it is to run several different network applications, all at the same time. For example, a user could be downloading a file in one window, accessing the WWW in another window and sending an electronic mail in another. TCP does its job so silently, but effectively. It allows for application programmers to talk directly to other application programs, over a network, without having to worry about any of the other applications that are running on the computer. The TCP layer obviously relies heavily on the IP layer to route data from the local computer to the remote computer. If IP does its job effectively then all the TCP layer has to worry about is the connection and transmission of application data between the local computer and the remote computer.*

*TCP is also amazing in that it does not care about the computer system it is running on. It could be a computer, a fax, a printer, its really doesn't matter. Imagine a world which was dominated by industrial standards. TCP and IP have greatly reduced this problem. A PC will happily talk to a UNIX workstation, a computer in Japan can communicate with a printer in France, an electronic mail message can be sent from one user to another, purely by putting a simple address. Amazing. But it works. So don't knock it.*

*About twenty years ago the computer industry was dominated by large industrial corporations, who dominated the industry by enforcing their own standards. These days TCP and IP have made it virtually impossible for any company to dominate the networking market. It has also made it easier for non-computer systems to intercommunicate. Maybe some day IP addresses and domain names will replace telephone numbers and TCP will allow us to speak to many people, all at the same time (maybe not, but it's a nice thought).*

# TCP/IP Commands and IPv6

## 11.1  Introduction

This chapter discusses some of the TCP/IP programs which can be used to connect to other hosts and also to determine routing information.

## 11.2  TCP/IP commands

There are several standard programs available over TCP/IP connections. The example sessions is this section relate to the network outlined in Figure 9.12. These applications may include:

- FTP (File Transfer Protocol) – transfers file between computers.
- HTTP (Hypertext Transfer Protocol) – which is the protocol used in the World Wide Web (WWW) and can be used for client-server applications involving hypertext.
- MIME (Multipurpose Internet Mail Extension) – gives enhanced electronic mail facilities over TCP/IP.
- SMTP (Simple Mail Management Protocol) – gives simple electronic mail facilities.
- TELNET – allows remote login using TCP/IP.
- PING – determines if a node is responding to TCP/IP communications.

### 11.2.1 ping

The `ping` program (Packet Internet Gopher) determines whether a node is responding to TCP/IP communication. It is typically used to trace problems in networks and uses the Internet Control Message Protocol (ICMP) to send a response request from the target node. Sample run 11.1 shows that `miranda` is active and `ariel` isn't.

---

🖳  Sample run 11.1: Using PING command

```
C:\WINDOWS>ping miranda
miranda (146.176.144.14) is alive
C:\WINDOWS>ping ariel
no reply from ariel (146.176.147.35)
```

---

The `ping` program can also be used to determine the delay between one host and an-

other, and also if there are any IP packet losses. In Sample run 11.2 the local host is
`pc419.eece.napier.ac.uk` (which is on the `146.176.151` segment); the host `miranda`
is tested (which is on the `146.176.144` segment). It can be seen that, on average, the
delay is only 1 ms and there is no loss of packets.

---

🖥  Sample run 11.2: Using PING command

```
225 % ping miranda
PING miranda.eece.napier.ac.uk: 64 byte packets
64 bytes from 146.176.144.14: icmp_seq=0. time=1. ms
64 bytes from 146.176.144.14: icmp_seq=1. time=1. ms
64 bytes from 146.176.144.14: icmp_seq=2. time=1. ms
3 packets transmitted, 3 packets received, 0% packet loss
round-trip (ms)  min/avg/max = 1/1/1
```

---

In Sample run 11.3 the destination node (`www.napier.ac.uk`) is located within the
same building but is on a different IP segment (`147.176.2`). It is also routed through a
router. It can be seen that the packet delay has increased to between 9 and 10 ms.
Again, there is no packet loss.

---

🖥  Sample run 11.3: Using PING command

```
226 % ping www.napier.ac.uk
PING central.napier.ac.uk: 64 byte packets
64 bytes from 146.176.2.3: icmp_seq=0. time=9. ms
64 bytes from 146.176.2.3: icmp_seq=1. time=9. ms
64 bytes from 146.176.2.3: icmp_seq=2. time=10. ms
3 packets transmitted, 3 packets received, 0% packet loss
round-trip (ms)  min/avg/max = 9/9/10
```

---

Sample run 11.4 shows a connection between Edinburgh and Bath in the UK (`www.
bath.ac.uk` has an IP address of `138.38.32.5`). This is a distance of approximately
500 miles and it can be seen that the delay is now between 30 and 49 ms. This time
there is 25% packet loss.

---

🖥  Sample run 11.4: Using PING command

```
222 % ping www.bath.ac.uk
PING jess.bath.ac.uk: 64 byte packets
64 bytes from 138.38.32.5: icmp_seq=0. time=49. ms
64 bytes from 138.38.32.5: icmp_seq=2. time=35. ms
64 bytes from 138.38.32.5: icmp_seq=3. time=30. ms
4 packets transmitted, 3 packets received, 25% packet loss
round-trip (ms)  min/avg/max = 30/38/49
```

---

Finally, in Sample run 11.5 the `ping` program tests a link between Edinburgh, UK, and
a WWW server in the USA (`home.microsoft.com`, which has the IP address of
`207.68.137.51`). It can be seen that in this case, the delay is between 447 and 468 ms,
and the loss is 60%.

A similar utility program to `ping` is `spray` which uses Remote Procedure Call
(RPC) to send a continuous stream of ICMP messages. It is useful when testing a network connection for its burst characteristics. This differs from `ping`, which waits for a
predetermined amount of time between messages.

Sample run 11.5: Ping command with packet loss

```
224 % ping home.microsoft.com
PING home.microsoft.com: 64 byte packets
64 bytes from 207.68.137.51: icmp_seq=2. time=447. ms
64 bytes from 207.68.137.51: icmp_seq=3. time=468. ms
----home.microsoft.com PING Statistics----
5 packets transmitted, 2 packets received, 60% packet loss
```

### 11.2.2 ftp (file transfer protocol)

The `ftp` program uses the TCP/IP protocol to transfer files to and from remote nodes. If necessary, it reads the `hosts` file to determine the IP address. Once the user has logged into the remote node, the commands that can be used are similar to DOS commands such as `cd` (change directory), `dir` (list directory), `open` (open node), `close` (close node), `pwd` (present working directory). The `get` command copies a file from the remote node and the `put` command copies it to the remote node.

The type of file to be transferred must also be specified. This file can be ASCII text (the command `ascii`) or binary (the command `binary`).

### 11.2.3 telnet

The `telnet` program uses TCP/IP to remotely log in to a remote node.

### 11.2.4 nslookup

The `nslookup` program interrogates the local `hosts` file or a DNS server to determine the IP address of an Internet node. If it cannot find it in the local file then it communicates with gateways outside its own network to see if they know the address. Sample run 11.6 shows that the IP address of `www.intel.com` is `134.134.214.1`.

🖳 Sample run 11.6: Example of nslookup

```
C:\> nslookup
Default Server:  ees99.eece.napier.ac.uk
Address:  146.176.151.99
> www.intel.com
Server:  ees99.eece.napier.ac.uk
Address:  146.176.151.99
Name:   web.jf.intel.com
Address:  134.134.214.1
Aliases:  www.intel.com
230 % nslookup home.microsoft.com
Non-authoritative answer:
Name:   home.microsoft.com
Addresses:  207.68.137.69, 207.68.156.11, 207.68.156.14, 207.68.156.56
207.68.137.48, 207.68.137.51
```

### 11.2.5 netstat (network statistics)

On a UNIX system the command `netstat` can be used to determine the status of the network. The `-r` option shown in Sample run 11.7 shows that this node uses `moon` as a gateway to another network.

```
[54:miranda :/net/castor_win/local_user/bill_b ] % netstat -r
Destination      Gateway            Flags   Refs      Use  Interface
localhost        localhost          UH        0    27306  lo0
default          moon               UG        0  1453856  lan0
146.176.144      miranda            U         8  6080432  lan0
146.176.1        146.176.144.252    UGD       0       51  lan0
146.176.151      146.176.144.252    UGD      11     5491  lan0
```

### 11.2.6 traceroute

The traceroute program traces the route of an IP packet through the Internet. It uses the IP protocol time-to-live field and attempts to get an ICMP TIME_EXCEEDED response from each gateway along the path to a defined host. The default probe datagram length is 38 bytes (although the sample runs use 40 byte packets by default). Sample run 11.8 shows an example of traceroute from a PC (pc419. eece.napier.ac.uk). It can be seen that initially it goes through a bridge (pcbridge.eece.napier.ac.uk) and then to the destination (miranda. eece.napier.ac.uk).

Sample run 11.9 shows the route from a PC (pc419.eece.napier.ac.uk) to a destination node (www.bath.ac.uk). Initially, from the originator, the route goes through a gateway (146.176.151.254) and then goes through a routing switch (146.176.1.27) and onto EaStMAN ring via 146.176.3.1. The route then goes round the EaStMAN to a gateway at the University of Edinburgh (smds-gw.ed.ja.net). It is then routed onto the SuperJanet network and reaches a gateway at the University of Bath (smds-gw.bath.ja.net). It then goes to another gateway (jips-gw.bath.ac.uk) and finally to its destination (jess.bath.ac.uk). Figure 11.15 shows the route the packet takes.

⌨ Sample run 11.8: Example traceroute

```
www:~/www$ traceroute miranda
traceroute to miranda.eece.napier.ac.uk (146.176.144.14), 30 hops max,
   40 byte packets
1  pcbridge.eece.napier.ac.uk (146.176.151.252)  2.684 ms  1.762 ms
1.725 ms
2  miranda.eece.napier.ac.uk (146.176.144.14)  2.451 ms  2.554 ms
2.357 ms
```

Note that gateways 4 and 8 hops away either don't send ICMP 'time exceeded' messages or send them with time-to-live values that are too small to be returned to the originator.

Sample run 11.10 shows an example route from a local host at Napier University, UK, to the USA. As before, it goes through the local gateway (146.176.151.254) and then goes through three other gateways to get onto the SMDS SuperJANET connection. The data packet then travels down this connection to University College, London (gw5.ulcc.ja.net). It then goes onto high speed connects to the USA and arrives at a US gateway (mcinet-2.sprintnap.net). Next, it travels to core2-hssi2-0.WestOrange.mci.net before reaching the Microsoft Corporation gateway in Seattle (microsoft.Seattle.mci.net). It finally finds it way to the destination (207.68.145.53). The total journey time is just less than half a second.

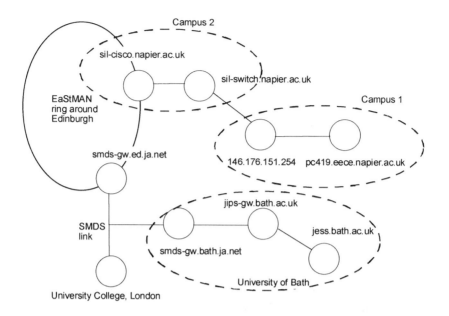

**Figure 11.1** Route between local host and the University of Bath

---

### Sample run 11.9: Example traceroute

```
www:~/www$ traceroute www.bath.ac.uk
traceroute to jess.bath.ac.uk (138.38.32.5), 30 hops max, 40 byte pack-
ets
1   146.176.151.254 (146.176.151.254)  2.806 ms  2.76 ms  2.491 ms
2   sil-switch.napier.ac.uk (146.176.1.27)  19.315 ms  11.29 ms  6.285 ms
3   sil-cisco.napier.ac.uk (146.176.3.1)  6.427 ms  8.407 ms  8.872 ms
4   * * *
5   smds-gw.ed.ja.net (193.63.106.129)  8.98 ms  30.308 ms  398.623 ms
6   smds-gw.bath.ja.net (193.63.203.68)  39.104 ms  46.833 ms  38.036 ms
7   jips-gw.bath.ac.uk (146.97.104.2)  32.908 ms  41.336 ms  42.429 ms
8   * * *
9   jess.bath.ac.uk (138.38.32.5)  41.045 ms  *  41.93 ms
```

---

### Sample run 11.10: Example traceroute

```
> traceroute home.microsoft.com
 1   146.176.151.254 (146.176.151.254)  2.931 ms  2.68 ms  2.658 ms
 2   sil-switch.napier.ac.uk (146.176.1.27)  6.216 ms  8.818 ms  5.885 ms
 3   sil-cisco.napier.ac.uk (146.176.3.1)  6.502 ms  6.638 ms  10.218 ms
 4   * * *
 5   smds-gw.ed.ja.net (193.63.106.129)  18.367 ms  9.242 ms  15.145 ms
 6   smds-gw.ulcc.ja.net (193.63.203.33)  42.644 ms  36.794 ms  34.555 ms
 7   gw5.ulcc.ja.net (128.86.1.80)  31.906 ms  30.053 ms  39.151 ms
 8   icm-london-1.icp.net (193.63.175.53)  29.368 ms  25.42 ms  31.347 ms
 9   198.67.131.193 (198.67.131.193)  119.195 ms  120.482 ms  67.479 ms
10   icm-pen-1-H2/0-T3.icp.net (198.67.131.25)  115.314 ms  126.152 ms
     149.982 ms
11   icm-pen-10-P4/0-OC3C.icp.net (198.67.142.69)  139.27 ms  197.953 ms
     195.722 ms
12   mcinet-2.sprintnap.net (192.157.69.48)  199.267 ms  267.446 ms
287.834 ms
```

```
13  core2-hssi2-0.WestOrange.mci.net (204.70.1.49)  216.006 ms   688.139
ms 228.968 ms
14  microsoft.Seattle.mci.net (166.48.209.250)  310.447 ms  282.882 ms
    313.619 ms
15  * microsoft.Seattle.mci.net (166.48.209.250)  324.797 ms  309.518 ms
16  * 207.68.145.53 (207.68.145.53)  435.195 ms *
```

## 11.3  IPv6

The IP header (IP Ver4) is added to higher-level data (as defined in RFC791). This header contains a 32-bit IP address of the destination node. Unfortunately, the standard 32-bit IP address is not large enough to support the growth in nodes connecting to the Internet. Thus a new standard, IP Version 6 (IP Ver6, aka, IP, The Next Generation, or IPng), has been developed to support a 128-bit address, as well as additional enhancements, such as authentication and data encryption.

The main techniques being investigated are:

- TUBA (TCP and UDP with bigger addresses).
- CATNIP (common architecture for the Internet).
- SIPP (simple Internet protocol plus).

It is likely that none of these will provide the complete standard and the resulting standard will be a mixture of the three. The RFC1883 specification outlines the main changes as:

- Expanded Addressing Capabilities.  The size of the IP address will be increased to 128 bits, rather than 32 bits. This will allow for more levels of addressing hierarchy, an increased number of addressable nodes and a simpler auto-configuration of addresses.  With multicast routing, the scalability is improved by adding a scope field to the multicast addresses. As well as this, an anycast address has been added so that packets can be sent to any one of a group of nodes.
- Improved IP Header Format. This tidies the IPv4 header fields by dropping the least used options, or making them optional.
- Improved Support for Extensions and Options. These allow for different encodings of the IP header options, and thus allows for variable lengths and increased flexibility for new options.
- Flow Labelling Capability. A new capability is added to enable the labelling of packet belonging to particular traffic *flows* for which the sender requests special handling, such as non-default quality of service or *real-time* service.
- Authentication and Privacy Capabilities. Extensions to support authentication, data integrity, and (optional) data confidentiality are specified for IPv6.

### 11.3.1 IPv6 header format

Figure 11.2 shows the basic format of the IPv6 header. The main fields are:

- Version number (4 bits) – contains the version number, such as 6 for IP Ver6. It is used to differentiate between IPv4 and IPv6. See Section 11.3.2.
- Priority (4 bits) – indicates the priority of the datagram, and gives 16 levels of priority (0 to 15). The first eight values (0 to 7) are used where the source is providing congestion control (which is traffic that backs-off when congestion occurs), these are:
  - 0 defines no priority.
  - 1 defines background traffic (such as netnews).
  - 2 defines unattended transfer (such as email).
  - 3 (reserved)
  - 4 defines attended bulk transfer (FTP, NFS).
  - 5 (reserved)
  - 6 defines interactive traffic (such as telnet, X-windows).
  - 7 defines control traffic (such as routing protocols, SNMP).

  The other values are used for traffic that will not back off in response to congestion (such as real-time traffic). The lowest priority for this is 8 (traffic which is the most willing to be discarded) and the highest is 15 (traffic which is the least willing to be discarded).

- Flow label (24 bits) – still experimental, but will be used to identify different data flow characteristics. It assigned by the source and can be used to label packets which require special handling by IPv6 routers, such as defined QoS (Quality of Service) or real-time services. See Section 11.3.3.
- Payload length (16 bits) – defines the total size of the IP datagram (and includes the IP header attached data).
- Next header – this field indicates which header follows the IP header (it uses the same IPv4). For example:

  - 0 defines IP information.
  - 1 defines ICMP information.
  - 6 defines TCP information.
  - 80 defines ISO-IP.

- Hop limit – defines the maximum number of hops that the datagram takes as it traverses the network. Each router decrements the hop limit by 1; when it reaches 0 it is deleted. This has been renamed from IPv4, where it was called Time-to-live, as it better describes the parameter.
- IP addresses (128 bits) – defines IP address. There will be three main groups of IP addresses: unicast, multicast and anycast. A unicast address identifies a particular host, a multicast address enables the hosts within a particular group to receive the same packet, and the anycast address will be addressed to a number of interfaces on a single multicast address.

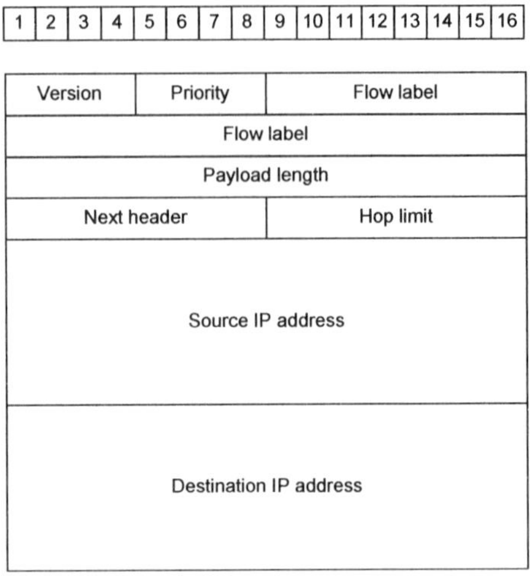

| 1 | 2 | 3 | 4 | 5 | 6 | 7 | 8 | 9 | 10 | 11 | 12 | 13 | 14 | 15 | 16 |
|---|---|---|---|---|---|---|---|---|----|----|----|----|----|----|----|

| Version | Priority | Flow label | |
|---------|----------|-----------|--|
| Flow label | | | |
| Payload length | | | |
| Next header | | Hop limit | |
| Source IP address | | | |
| Destination IP address | | | |

**Figure 11.2**   IP Ver6 header format

### 11.3.2 IP version label

There are various assigned values for the IP version label. These are:

| Value | Keyword | Description |
|-------|---------|-------------|
| 0 | | Reserved |
| 1-3 | | Unassigned |
| 4 | IP | Internet Protocol (RFC791) |
| 5 | ST | ST Datagram Mode (RFC1190) |
| 6 | SIP | Simple Internet Protocol |
| 7 | TP/IX | TP/IX: The Next Internet |
| 8 | PIP | The P Internet Protocol |
| 9 | TUBA | TUBA |
| 10-14 | | Unassigned |
| 15 | | Reserved |

### 11.3.3 Flow labels

A flow is defined as a sequence of packets sent from a particular source to a particular (unicast or multicast) destination, which require special handling by intervening routers. There can possibly be many active flows from a source to a destination, as well as other, non-associated traffic. Flow are uniquely identified by the combination of their source address and a non-zero flow label (1h to FFFFFFh). Packets that are not part of a flow are given a zero label.

All packets in the same flow have the same flow label, as well as having the same source and destination addresses, and priority level. The flow-handling lifetime must be setup as part of the set-up mechanism. A label is initially assigned pseudo-randomly and then are assigned sequentially. A source should not re-use a flow label for a new flow within the lifetime of any flow-handling state that could have been established in recent history of the lifetime of a flow. Thus a host must be careful when it restarts from a crash that it is not using a previously defined flow label, that is still within its lifetime. Typically, this is overcome by storing a table of previously assigned flow labels.

## 11.4 Exercises

**11.4.1** Which TCP/IP command allows a user to test to see if a node is responding to TCP/IP communications:

(a)   nslookup          (b)   telnet

(c)   ping               (d)   ftp

**11.4.2** Which TCP/IP command allows a user to determine the IP address of a host address:

(a)   nslookup          (b)   telnet

(c)   ping               (d)   ftp

**11.4.3** What is the size of the IP address in IPv6:

(a)   32 bits          (b)   64 bits

(c)   128 bits        (d)   Any size

**11.4.4** Using the `ping` program determine if the following nodes are responding:

(i)     www.eece.napier.ac.uk

(ii)   home.microsoft.com

(iii)  www.intel.com

**11.4.5** Using the `traceroute` program determine the route from your local host to the following destinations:

(i)     www.napier.ac.uk

(ii)   home.microsoft.com

(iii)  www.intel.com

Identify each part of the route and note the timing information.

**11.4.6** Outline how IPv6 uses priority levels to different between traffic that can back-off and of which not willing to back-off. How is the priority level of real-time traffic deal with?

**11.4.7** Describe how IPv6 uses flow labels to route traffic.

**11.4.8** An example trace for a computer on the `146.176.150` segment to a computer at `hotmail.com` gives:

```
146.176.150.253      eece_1.eece.napier.ac.uk
146.176.151.254      Unavailable
146.176.7.250        Unavailable
146.176.9.1          Unavailable
194.81.56.126        scot-x-gw.eastman.net.uk
146.97.253.33        scot-pop.ja.net
146.97.254.41        leeds-core.ja.net
146.97.254.54        external-gw.ja.net
128.86.1.80          tglobe.gw2.ja.net
193.62.157.10        ppt-gw.ja.net
207.45.215.165       gin-ppt-bb2.Teleglobe.net
207.45.223.42        gin-mtt-core1.Teleglobe.net
207.45.223.109       gin-nyy-core1.Teleglobe.net
207.45.215.165       bbr05-p1-1.jrcy01.exodus.net
207.45.215.165       bbr02-p6-1.jrcy01.exodus.net
207.45.215.165       bbr02-p0-1.sntc01.exodus.net
```

Determine the routers on the local network, the EASTMAN networks, the
JANET network and the connection between the UK and the USA. If possible, trace the route to the `scot-x-gw.eastman.net.net` router.

# 12 SPX/IPX

## 12.1 Introduction

Novell NetWare is one of the most popular network operating systems for PC LANs and provides file and print server facilities. Its default network protocol is normally SPX/IPX. This can also be used with Microsoft Windows to communicate with other Microsoft Windows nodes and with Novell NetWare networks. The Internet Packet Exchange (IPX) protocol is a network layer protocol for transportation of data between computers on a NetWare network. IPX is very fast and has a small connectionless datagram protocol (just like IP). The Sequenced Packet Interchange (SPX) provides a communications protocol which supervises the transmission of the packet and ensures its successful delivery (just like TCP).

NetWare is typically used in organisations and works well on a local network. Network traffic which travels out on the Internet or that communicates with UNIX networks must be in TCP/IP form. IP tunnelling encapsulates the IPX packet within the IP packet. This can then be transmitted into the Internet network. When the IP packet is received by the destination NetWare gateway; the IP encapsulation is stripped off. IP tunnelling thus relies on a gateway into each IPX-based network that also runs IP. The NetWare gateway is often called an IP tunnel peer.

## 12.2 NetWare architecture

NetWare provides many services, such as file sharing, printer sharing, security, user administration and network management. The interface between the network interface card (NIC) and the SPX/IPX stack is ODI (Open Data-link Interface). NetWare clients run software which connects them to the server, the supported client operating systems are DOS, Microsoft Windows, UNIX, OS/2 and Macintosh.

With NetWare Version 3, DOS and Windows 3.x clients use a NetWare shell called NETx.COM. This shell is executed when the user wants to log into the network and stays resident. It acts as a command redirector and processes requests which are either generated by application programs or from the keyboard. It then decides whether they should be handled by the NetWare network operating system or passed to the client's local DOS operating system. NETx builds its own tables to keep track of the location of network-attached resources rather than using DOS tables. Figure 12.1 illustrates the relationship between the NetWare shell and DOS, in a DOS-based client. Note that Windows 3.x uses the DOS operating system, but Windows 95/98/NT/2000 have their own operating systems and only emulate DOS. Thus, Windows 95/98/NT/2000 do not need to use the NETx program.

The ODI allows NICs to support multiple transport protocols, such as TCP/IP and IPX/SPX, simultaneously. Also, in an Ethernet interface card, the ODI allows simultaneous support of multiple Ethernet frame types such as Ethernet 802.3, Ethernet 802.2, Ethernet II, and Ethernet SNAP. Figure 12.2 shows a configuration of the frame type for IPX/SPX protocol.

To install NetWare, the server must have a native operating system, such as DOS or Microsoft Windows, and it must be installed on its own disk partition. NetWare then adds a partition in which the NetWare partition is added. This partition is the only area of the disk that the NetWare kernel can access.

### 12.2.1 NetWare loadable modules (NLMs)

NetWare allows enhancements from third-party suppliers using NLMs. The two main categories are:

- Operating systems enhancements – these allow extra operating system functions, such as a virus checker and also client hardware specific modules, such as a network interface drivers.
- Application programs – these programs actually run on the NetWare server rather than on the client machine.

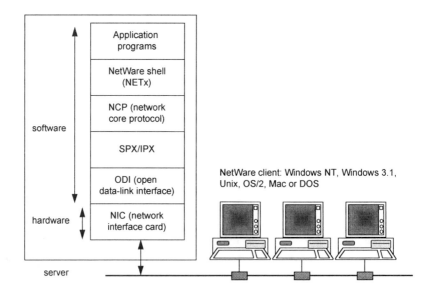

**Figure 12.1**  NetWare architecture

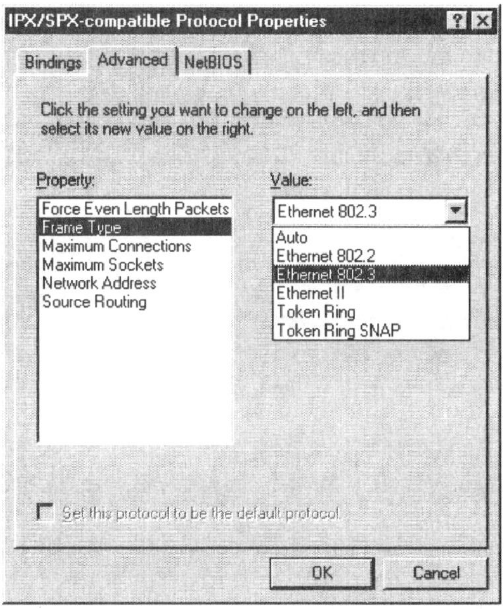

**Figure 12.2** IPX/SPX frame types

## 12.2.2 Bindery services

NetWare must keep track of users and their details. Typically, NetWare must keep track of:

- User names and passwords.
- Groups and group rights.
- File and directory rights.
- Print queues and printers.
- User restrictions (such as allowable login times, and the number of times a user can simultaneously log in to the network).
- User/group administration and charging (such as charging for user login).
- Connection to networked peripherals.

This information is kept in the bindery files. Whenever a user logs in to the network their login details are verified against the information in the bindery files.

The bindery is organised with objects, properties and values. Objects are entities that are controlled or managed, such as users, groups, printers (servers and queues), disk drives, and so on. Each object has a set of properties, such as file rights, login restrictions, restrictions to printers, and so on. Each property has a value associated with it. Here are some examples:

| Object | Property | Value |
|--------|----------|-------|
| User | Login restriction | Wednesday 9 am till 5pm |
| User | Simultaneous login | 2 |
| Group | Access to printer | No |

Objects, properties and values are stored in three separate files which are linked by pointers on every NetWare server:

1. NET$OBJ.SYS (contains object information).
2. NET$PROP.SYS (contains property information).
3. NET$VAL.SYS (contains value information).

If multiple NetWare servers exist on a network then bindery information must be exchanged manually between the servers so that the information is the same on each server. In a multiserver NetWare 3.x environment, the servers send SAP (service advertising protocol) information between themselves to advertise available services. Then the bindery services on a particular server update their bindery files with the latest information regarding available services on other reachable servers. This synchronisation is difficult when just a few servers exist but is extremely difficult when there are many servers. Luckily, NetWare 4.1 has addressed this problem with NetWare directory services.

## 12.3  NetWare protocols

NetWare uses IPX (Internet Packet Exchange) for the network layer and either SPX (Sequenced Packet Exchange) or NCP (NetWare Core Protocols) for the transport layer. The routing information protocol (RIP) is also used to transmit information between NetWare gateways. These protocols are illustrated in Figure 12.3.

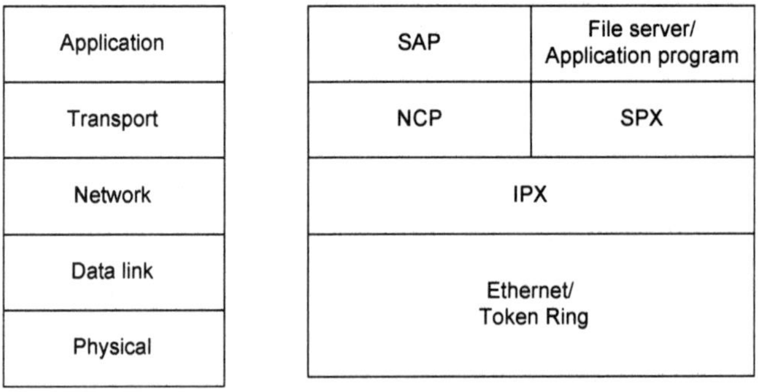

| Application | | SAP | File server/ Application program |
| --- | --- | --- | --- |
| Transport | | NCP | SPX |
| Network | | IPX | |
| Data link | | Ethernet/ Token Ring | |
| Physical | | | |

**Figure 12.3**  NetWare reference model

### 12.3.1 IPX

IPX performs a network function that is similar to IP. The higher information is passed to the IPX layer which then encapsulates it into IPX envelopes. It is characterised by:

- A Connectionless connection – each packet is sent into the network and must find its own way through the network to the final destination (connections are established with SPX).

- It is unreliable – as there is only basic error checking and no acknowledgement (acknowledgements are achieved with SPX).

IPX uses a 12-byte station address (whereas IP uses a 4-byte address). The IPX fields are:

- Checksum (2 bytes) – this field is rarely used in IPX, as error checking is achieved in the SPX layer. The lower-level data link layer also provides an error detection scheme (both Ethernet and Token Ring support a frame check sequence).
- Length (2 bytes) – this gives the total length of the packet in bytes (i.e. header+DATA). The maximum number of bytes in the DATA field is 546, thus the maximum length will be 576 bytes ($2+2+1+1+12+12+546$).
- Transport control (1 byte) – this field is incremented every time the frame is processed by a router. When it reaches a value of 16 it is deleted. This stops packets from traversing the network for an infinite time. It is also typically known as the time-to-live field or hop counter.
- Packet type (1 byte) – this field identifies the upper layer protocol so that the DATA field can be properly processed.
- Addressing (12 bytes) – this field identifies the address of the source and destination station. It is made up of three fields: a network address (4 bytes), a host address (6 bytes) and a socket address (2 bytes). The 48-bit host address is the 802 MAC LAN address. NetWare supports a hierarchical addressing structure where the network and host addresses identify the host station and the socket address identifies a process or application and thus supports multiple connections (up to 50 per node).

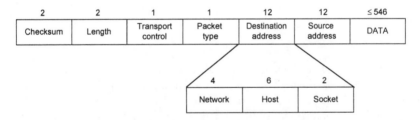

**Figure 12.4** IPX packet format

### 12.3.2 SPX

On a NetWare network the level above IPX is either NCP or SPX. The SPX protocol sets up a virtual circuit between the source and the destination (just like TCP). Then all SPX packets follow the same path and will thus always arrive in the correct order. This type of connection is described as connection-oriented.

SPX also allows for error checking and an acknowledgement to ensure that packets are received correctly. Each SPX packet has flow control and also sequence numbers. Figure 12.5 illustrates the SPX packet.

The fields in the SPX header are:

- Connection control (1 byte) – this is a set of flags which assist the flow of data. These flags include an acknowledgement flag and an end-of-message flag.

- Datastream type (1 byte) – this byte contains information which can be used to determine the protocol or information contained within the SPX data field.
- Destination connection ID (2 bytes) – the destination connection ID allows the routing of the packet through the virtual circuit.
- Source connection ID (2 bytes) – the source connection ID identifies the source station when it is transmitted through the virtual circuit.
- Sequence number (2 bytes) – this field contains the sequence number of the packet sent. When the receiver receives the packet, the destination error checks the packet and sends back an acknowledgement with the previously received packet number in it.
- Acknowledgement number (2 bytes) – this acknowledgement number is incremented by the destination when it receives a packet. It is in this field that the destination station puts the last correctly received packet sequence number.
- Allocation number (2 bytes) – this field informs the source station of the number of buffers the destination station can allocate to SPX connections.
- DATA (up to 534 bytes).

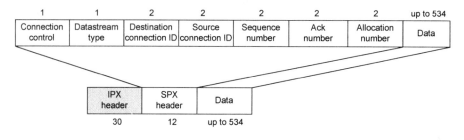

**Figure 12.5**   SPX packet format

### 12.3.3 RIP

The NetWare Routing Information Protocol (RIP) is used to keep routers updated on the best routes through the network. RIP information is delivered to routers within IPX packets. Figure 12.6 illustrates the information fields in an RIP packet. The RIP packet is contained in the field which would normally be occupied by the SPX packet.

Routers are used within networks to pass packets from one network to another in an optimal way (and error-free with a minimal time delay). A router reads IPX packets and examines the destination address of the node. If the node is on another network then it routes the packet in the required direction. This routing tends not to be fixed as the best route will depend on network traffic at given times. Thus the router needs to keep the routing tables up to date; RIP allows routers to exchange their current routing tables with other routers.

The RIP packet allows routers to request or report on multiple reachable networks within a single RIP packet. These routes are listed one after another (Figure 12.6 shows two routing entries). Thus each RIP packet has only one operation field, but has multiple entries of the network number, the number of router hops, and the number of tick fields, up to the length limit of the IPX packet. RIP packets add to the general network traffic as each router broadcasts its entire routing table every 60 seconds. This shortcoming has been addressed by NetWare 4.1.

The fields are:

- Operation (2 bytes) – this field indicates that the RIP packet is either a request or a response.
- Network number (4 bytes) – this field defines the assigned network address number to which the routing information applies.
- Number of router hops (2 bytes) – this field indicates the number of routes that a packet must go through in order to reach the required destination. Each router adds a single hop.
- Number of ticks (2 bytes) – this field indicates the amount of time (in 1/18 second) that it takes a packet to reach the given destination. Note that a route which has the fewest hops may not necessarily be the fastest.

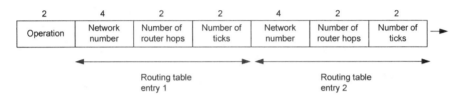

**Figure 12.6** RIP packet format

### 12.3.4 SAP

Every 60 seconds each server transmits a SAP (Service Advertising Protocol) packet which gives its address and tells other servers which services it offers. These packets are read by special agent processes running on the routers which then construct a database that defines which servers are operational and where they are located.

When the client node is first booted it transmits a request to the network asking for the location of the nearest server. The agent on the router then reads this request and matches it up to the best server. This choice is then sent back to the client. The client then establishes an NCP (NetWare Core Protocol) connection with the server, from which the client and server negotiate the maximum packet size. After this, the client can access the networked file system and other NetWare services.

Figure 12.7 illustrates the contents of a SAP packet. It can be seen that each SAP packet contains a single operation field and data on up to seven servers. The fields are:

- Operation type (2 bytes) – defines whether the SAP packet is server information request or a broadcast of server information.
- Server type (2 bytes) – defines the type of service offered by a server. These services are identified by a binary pattern, such as:

| | | | |
|---|---|---|---|
| File server | 0000 1000 | Job server | 0000 1001 |
| Gateway | 0000 1010 | Print server | 0000 0111 |
| Archive server | 0000 1001 | SNA gateway | 0010 0001 |
| Remote bridge server | 0010 0100 | TCP/IP gateway | 0010 0111 |
| NetWare access server | 1001 1000 | | |

- Server name (48 bytes) – which identifies the actual name of the server or host offering the service defined in the service type field.
- Network address (4 bytes) – which defines the address of the network to which the server is attached.
- Node Address (6 bytes) – which defines the actual MAC address of the server.
- Socket address (6 bytes) – which defines the socket address on the server assigned to this particular type of service.
- Hops to server (2 bytes) – which indicates the number of hops to reach the particular service.

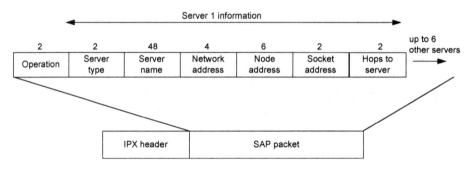

**Figure 12.7**   SAP packet format

## 12.3.5 NCP

The clients and servers communicate using the NetWare Core Protocols (NCPs). They have the following operation:

- The NETx shell reads the application program request and decides whether it should direct it to the server.
- If it does redirect, then it sends a message within an NCP packet, which is then encapsulated within an IPX packet and transmitted to the server.

Figure 12.8 illustrates the packet layout and encapsulation of an NCP packet. The fields are:

- Request type (2 bytes) – which gives the category of NCP communications. Among the possible types are:

| | |
|---|---|
| Busy message | 1001 1001 1001 1001 |
| Create a service | 0001 0001 0001 0001 |
| Service request from workstation | 0010 0010 0010 0010 |
| Service response from server | 0011 0011 0011 0011 |
| Terminate a service connection | 0101 0101 0101 0101 |

For example, the create-a-service request is initiated at login time and a terminate-a-connection request is sent at logout.

- Sequence number (1 byte) – which contains a request sequence number. The client reads the sequence number so that it knows the request to which the server is responding to.
- Connection number (1 byte) –a unique number which is assigned when the user logs into the server.
- Task number (1 byte) – which identifies the application program on the client which issued the service request.
- Function code (1 byte) – which defines the NCP message or commands. Example codes are:

| | | | |
|---|---|---|---|
| Close a file | 0100 0010 | Create a file | 0100 1101 |
| Delete a file | 0100 0100 | Get a directory entry | 0001 1111 |
| Get file size | 0100 0000 | Open a file | 0100 1100 |
| Rename a file | 0100 0101 | Extended functions | 0001 0110 |

Extended functions can be defined after the 0001 0110 field.

- NCP message (up to 539 bytes) – the NCP message field contains additional information which is passed between the clients and servers. If the function code contains 0001 0110 then this field will contain subfunction codes.

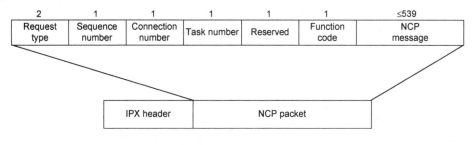

**Figure 12.8** NCP packet format

## 12.4 Novel NetWare set-up

NetWare 3.x and 4.1 use the Open Data-Link Interface (ODI) to interface NetWare to the NIC. Figure 12.9 shows how the NetWare 3.x fits into the OSI model. ODI is similar to NDIS in Microsoft Windows and was developed jointly between Apple and Novell. It provides a standard vendor-independent method to interface the software and the hardware (Figure 12.10 shows that Microsoft Windows can choose between NDIS2 and ODI).

A typical login procedure for a NetWare 3.x network is:

```
LSL.COM
NE2000
```

```
IPXODI
NETx /PS=EECE_1
F:
LOGIN
```

The program LSL (link support layer) provides a foundation for the MAC layer to communicate with multiple protocols. An interface adapter driver (in this case NE2000) provides a MAC layer driver and is used to communicate with the interface card. This driver is known as a multilink interface driver (MLID). After this driver is installed, the program IPXODI is then installed. This program normally communicates with LSL and applications.

The NETx program communicates with the server and sets up a connection with the server EECE_1. This then sets up a local disk partition of F: (onto which the user's network directory will be mounted). Next, the user logs into the network with the command LOGIN.

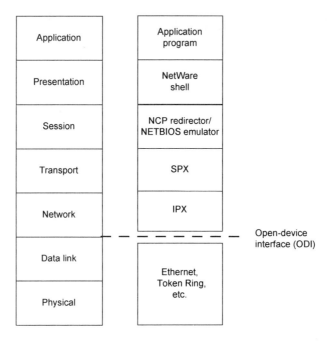

**Figure 12.9**   OSI model and NetWare 3.x

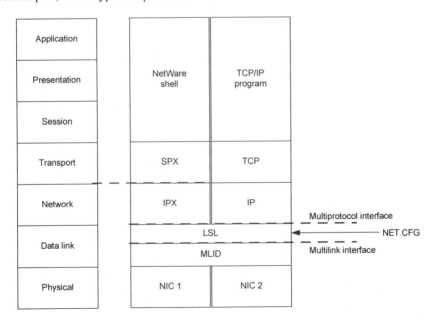

**Figure 12.10** Network adapter driver

### 12.4.1 ODI

ODI allows users to load several protocol stacks (such as TCP/IP and SPX/IPX) simultaneously for operation with a single NIC. It also allows support to link protocol drivers to adapter drivers. Figure 12.11 shows the architecture of the ODI interface. The LSL layer supports multiple protocols and it reads from a file NET.CFG, which contains information on the network adapter and the protocol driver, such as the interface adapter, frame type and protocol.

| | | |
|---|---|---|
| Application | NetWare shell | TCP/IP program |
| Presentation | | |
| Session | | |
| Transport | SPX | TCP |
| Network | IPX | IP |
| Data link | LSL | |
| | MLID | |
| Physical | NIC 1 | NIC 2 |

Multiprotocol interface
NET.CFG
Multilink interface

**Figure 12.11** ODI architecture

Here is a sample NET.CFG file:

```
Link Driver NE2000
  Int #1 11
  Port #1 320
  Frame Ethernet_II
  Frame Ethernet_802.3
  Protocol IPX 0 Ethernet_802.3
        Protocol Ethdev 0 Ethernet_II
```

This configuration file defines the interface adapter as using interrupt line 11, having a base address of 320h, operating IPX, Ethernet 802.3 frame type and following the Ethernet II protocol. Network interface card drivers (such as NE2000, from the previous set-up) are referred to as a multilink interface driver (MLID).

## 12.5  Exercises

12.5.1     For a known Novell NetWare network determine the following:

    (a)    Its version number.
    (b)    Its architecture.
    (c)    The connected peripherals (such as printers, tape backups, and so on).
    (d)    The number of user logins.
    (e)    File servers.
    (f)    The connections it makes with other NetWare servers.
    (g)    The connections it makes with the Internet.
    (h)    The location of bridges, routers or gateways.

12.5.2     Discuss the format of an IPX packet.

12.5.3     Discuss the format of an SPX packet.

12.5.4     Discuss the RIP, SAP and NCP packets.

## 12.6  Further references

For further reference on Novell NetWare and NDS, refer to:

W.Buchanan, Mastering Microsoft Windows, Novell NetWare and UNIX, *Macmillan.*

# 13 WWW

## 13.1 Introduction

The World-Wide Web (WWW) and the Internet have more jargon words and associated acronyms than anything else in modern life. Words, such as

gopher, ftp, telnet, TCP/IP stack, intranets, Web servers, clients, browsers, hypertext, URLs, Internet access providers, dial-up connections, UseNet servers, firewalls

have all become common in the business vocabulary.

The WWW was initially conceived in 1989 by CERN, the European particle physics research laboratory in Geneva, Switzerland. Its main objective was:

*to use the hypermedia concept to support the interlinking of various types of information through the design and development of a series of concepts, communications protocols, and systems*

One of its main characteristics is that stored information tends to be distributed over a geographically wide area. The result of the project has been the world-wide acceptance of the protocols and specifications used. A major part of its success was due to the full support of the National Center for Supercomputing Applications (NCSA), which developed a family of user interface programs known collectively as Mosaic.

The WWW, or Web, is basically an infrastructure of information. This information is stored on the WWW on Web servers and it uses the Internet to transmit data around the world. These servers run special programs that allow information to be transmitted to remote computers which are running a Web browser, as illustrated in Figure 13.1. The Internet is a common connection in which computers can communicate using a common addressing mechanism (IP) with a TCP/IP connection.

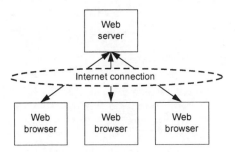

**Figure 13.1** Web servers and browsers

The information is stored on Web servers and is accessed by means of pages. These pages can contain text and other multimedia applications such as graphic images, digitised sound files and video animation. There are several standard media files (with typical file extensions):

- GIF or JPEG files for compressed images (GIF or JPG).
- QuickTime movies for video (QT or MOV).
- Postscript files (PS or EPS).
- MS video (AVI).
- Audio (AU, SND or WAV).
- MPEG files for compressed video (MPG).
- Compressed files (ZIP, Z or GZ).
- JavaScript (JAV, JS or MOCHA).
- Text files (TEX or TXT).

Each page contains text known as hypertext, which has specially reserved keywords to represent the format and the display functions. A standard language known as HTML (Hypertext Markup Language) has been developed for this purpose.

Hypertext pages, when interpreted by a browser program, display an easy-to-use interface containing formatted text, icons, pictorial hot spots, underscored words, and so on. Each page can also contain links to other related pages.

The topology and power of the Web now allows for distributed information, where information does not have to be stored locally. To find information on the Web the user can use powerful search engines to search for related links. Figure 13.2 shows an example of Web connections. The user initially accesses a page on a German Web server, this then contains a link to a Japanese server. This server contains links to UK and USA servers. This type of arrangement leads to the topology that resembles a spider's web, where information is linked from one place to another.

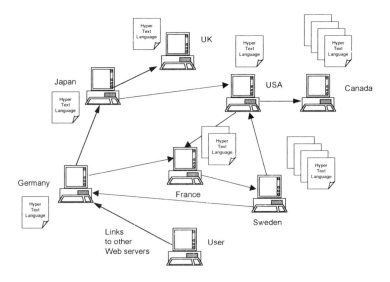

**Figure 13.2** Example Web connections

## 13.2 Advantages and disadvantages of the WWW

The WWW and the Internet tend to produce a polarisation of views. Thus, before analysing the WWW for its technical specification, a few words must be said on some of the subjective advantages and disadvantages of the WWW and the Internet. It should be noted that some of these disadvantages can be seen as advantages to some people, and vice versa. For example, freedom of information will be seen as an advantage to a freedom-of-speech group but often a disadvantage to security organisations. Table 13.1 outlines some of the advantages and disadvantages.

**Table 13.1** Advantages and disadvantages of the Internet and the WWW

| | Advantages | Disadvantages |
|---|---|---|
| Global information flow | Less control of information by the media, governments and large organisations. | Lack of control on criminal material, such as certain types of pornography and terrorist activity. |
| Global transmission | Communication between people and organisations in different countries which should create the Global Village. | Data can easily get lost or state secrets can be easily transmitted over the world. |
| Internet connections | Many different types of connections are possible, such as dial-up facilities (perhaps over a modem or with ISDN) or through frame relays. The user only has to pay for the service and the local connection. | Data once on the Internet is relatively easy to tap into and possibly easy to change. |
| Global information | Creation of an ever-increasing global information database. | Data is relatively easy to tap into and possibly easy to change. |
| Multimedia integration | Tailor-made applications with good presentation tools. | Lack of editorial control leads to inferior material, which is hacked together. |
| Increasing WWW usage | Helps to improve its chances of acceptance into the home. | Increased traffic swamps the global information network and slows down commercial traffic. |
| WWW links | Easy to set up and leads users from one place to the next in a logical manner. | WWW links often fossilise where the link information is out-of-date or doesn't even exist. |
| Education | Increased usage of remote teaching with full multimedia education. | Increase in surface learning and lack of deep research. It may lead to an increase in time-wasting (too much surfing and too little learning). |

## 13.3  Client/server architecture

The WWW is structured with clients and servers, where a client accesses services from the server. These servers can either be local or available through a global network connection. A local connection normally requires the connection over a local area network but a global connection normally requires connection to an Internet provider. These providers are often known as Internet access providers (IAPs), sometimes as Internet connectivity providers (ICP) or Internet Service Providers (ISPs). They provide the mechanism to access the Internet and have the required hardware and software to connect from the user to the Internet. This access is typically provided through one of the following:

- Connection to a client computer though a dial-up modem connection (typically at 28.8 kbps or 56 kbps).
- Connection to a client computer though a dial-up ISDN connection (typically at 64 kbps or 128 kbps).
- Connection of a client computer to a server computer which connects to the Internet though a frame relay router (typically 56 kbps or 256 kbps).
- Connection of a client computer to a local area network which connects to the Internet though a T-1, 1.544 Mbps router.

These connections are illustrated in Figure 13.3. A router automatically routes all traffic to and from the Internet whereas the dial-up facility of a modem or ISDN link requires a connection to be made over a circuit-switched line (that is, through the public telephone network). Home users and small businesses typically use modem connections (although ISDN connections are becoming more common). Large corporations which require global Internet services tend to use frame routers. Note that an IAP may be a commercial organisation (such as CompuServe or America On-line) or a support organisation (such as giving direct connection to government departments or educational institutions). A commercial IAP organisation is likely to provide added services, such as electronic mail, search engines, and so on.

An Internet Presence Provider (IPP) allows organisations to maintain a presence on the Internet without actually having to invest in the Internet hardware. The IPPs typically maintain WWW pages for a given charge (they may also provide sales and support information).

## 13.4  Web browsers

Web browsers interpret special hypertext pages which consist of the hypertext markup language (HTML) and JavaScript. They then display it in the given format. There are currently four main Web browsers:

- Netscape Navigator – Navigator is one of the most widely used WWW browsers and is available in many different versions on many systems. It runs on PCs (running Microsoft Windows), UNIX workstations and Macintosh computers. Figure 13.4 shows Netscape Navigator Version 4. It has become the standard WWW browser and has many add-ons and enhancements, which have been added through continual development by Netscape. The basic package also has many compatible software plug-ins which are developed by third-party suppliers. These add extra functionality such as video players and sound support.

- NSCA Mosaic – Mosaic was originally the most popular Web browser when the Internet first started. It has now lost its dominance to Microsoft Internet Explorer and Netscape Navigator. NSCA Mosaic was developed by the National Center for Supercomputing Applications (NCSA) at the University of Illinois.

- Lynx – Lynx is typically used on UNIX-based computers with a modem dial-up connection. It is fast to download pages but does not support many of the features supported by Netscape Navigator or Mosaic.

- Microsoft Internet Explorer – Explorer now comes as a standard part of Microsoft Windows and as this has become the most popular computer operating system then so will this browser.

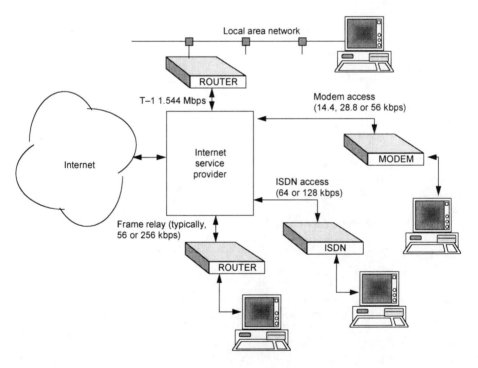

**Figure 13.3** Example connections to the Internet

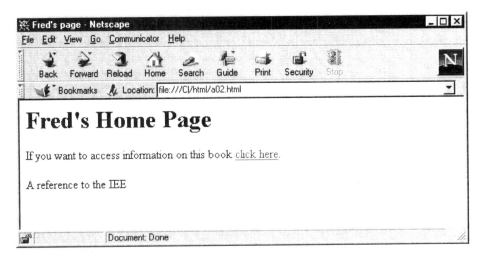

**Figure 13.4** Netscape Navigator Version 4.0

## 13.5 Internet resources

The Internet expands by the day as the amount of servers and clients which connect to the global network increases and the amount of information contained in the network also increases. The three major services which the Internet provides are:

- The World Wide Web.
- Global electronic mail.
- Information sources.

The main information sources, apart from the WWW, are from FTP, Gopher, WAIS and UseNet servers. These different types of servers which will be discussed in the next section.

## 13.6 Universal resource locators (URLs)

Universal resource locators (URLs) are used to locate a file on the WWW. They provide a pointer to any object on a server connected over the Internet. This link could give FTP access, hypertext references, and so on. URLs contain:

- The protocol of the file (the scheme).
- The server name (domain).
- The pathname of the file.
- The filename.

URL standard format is:

*<scheme>:<scheme-specific-part>*

and can be broken up into four parts. These are:

```
aaaa://bbb.bbb.bbb/ccc/ccc/ccc?ddd
```

where

`aaaa:` is the access method and specifies the mechanism to be used by the browser to communicate with the resource. The most popular mechanisms are:

- `http:`. HyperText Transfer Protocol. This is the most commonly used mechanism and is typically used to retrieve an HTML file, a graphic file, a sound file, an animation sequence file, a file to be executed by the server, or a word processing file.
- `https:`. HyperText Transfer Protocol. It is a variation on the standard access method and can be used to provide some level of transmission security.
- `file:`. Local File Access. This causes the browser to load the specified file from the local disk.
- `ftp:`. File Transport Protocol. This method allows files to be downloaded using an FTP connection.
- `mailto:`. E-Mail Form. This method allows access to a destination e-mail address. Normally the browser automatically generates an input form for entering the e-mail message.
- `news:`. USENET News. This method defines the access method for a news group.
- `nntp:`. Local Network News Transport Protocol.
- `wais:`. Wide Area Information Servers.
- `gopher:`. GOPHER protocol.
- `telnet:`. TELNET. The arguments following the access code are the login arguments to the telnet session as `user[:password]@host`.
- `cid:`. Content identifiers for MIME body part.
- `mid:`. Message identifiers for electronic mail.
- `afs:`. AFS File Access.
- `prospero:`. Prospero Link.
- `x-exec:`. Executable Program.

`//bbb.bbb.bbb` is the Internet node and specifies the node on the Internet where the file is located. If a node is not given then the browser defaults to the computer which is running the browser. A colon may follow the node address and the port number (most browsers default to port 80, which is also the port that most servers use to reply to the browser).

`/ccc/ccc/ccc` is the file path (including subdirectories and the filename). Typically systems restrict the access to a system by allocating the root directory as a subdirectory of the main file system.

?ddd is the argument which depend upon the access method, and the file accessed. For example, with an HTML document a '#' identifies the fragment name internal to an HTML document which is identified by the A element with the NAME attribute.

An example URL is:

```
http://www.toytown.anycor.co/fred/index.html
```

where `http` is the file protocol (Hypertext Translation Protocol), `www.toytown.anycor.co` is the server name, `/fred` is the path of the file and the file is named `index.html`.

### 13.6.1 Files

A file URL scheme allows files to be assessed. It takes the form:

```
file://<host>/<path>
```

where *<host>* is the fully qualified domain name of the system to be accessed, *<path>* is the full path name, and takes the form of a directory path, such as *<directory>/<directory>/.../<name>*.

For a file:

```
C:\DOCS\NOTES\NETWORKS\NET_CHAP13.DOC
```

would be accessed as from `dummy.com` with:

```
file://dummy.com/C|DOCS/NOTES/NETWORKS/NET_CHAP13.DOC
```

Note, that if the host is defined as `localhost` or is an empty string then the host is assumed to be the local host. The general format is:

```
fileurl = "file://" [ host | "localhost" ] "/" fpath
```

### 13.6.2 Electronic mail address

The `mailto` scheme defines a link to an Internet email address. An example is:

```
mailto: fred.bloggs@toytown.ac.uk
```

When this URL is selected then an email message will be sent to the email address `fred.bloggs@toytown.ac.uk`. Normally, some form of text editor is called and the user can enter the required email message. Upon successful completion of the text message it is sent to the addressee.

### 13.6.3 File Transfer Protocol (FTP)

The `ftp` URL scheme defines that the files and directories specified are accessed using the FTP protocol. In its simplest form it is defined as:

```
ftp://<hostname>/<directory-name>/<filename>
```

The FTP protocol normally requests a user to log into the system. For example, many public domain FTP servers use the login of:

```
anonymous
```

and the password can be anything (but it is normally either the user's full name or their Internet email address). Another typical operation is changing directory from a starting directory or the destination file directory. To accommodate this, a more general form is:

ftp://<*user*>:<*password*>@<*hostname*>:<*port*>/<*cd1*>/<*cd2*>/
.../<*cdn*>/<*filename*>

where the user is defined by <*user*> and the password by <*password*>. The host name, <*hostname*>, is defined after the @ symbol and change directory commands are defined by the *cd* commands. The node name may take the form //user [:password]@host. Without a user name, the user anonymous is used.

For example the reference to the standard related to HTML Version 2 can be downloaded using the URL:

```
ftp://ds.internic.net/rfc/rfc1866.txt
```

and draft Internet documents from:

```
ftp://ftp.isi.edu/internet-drafts/
```

The general format is:

```
ftpurl    =  "ftp://" login [ "/" fpath [ ";type=" ftptype ]]
fpath     =  fsegment *[ "/" fsegment ]
fsegment  =  *[ uchar | "?" | ":" | "@" | "&" | "=" ]
ftptype   =  "A" | "I" | "D" | "a" | "i" | "d"
```

### 13.6.4 Hypertext Transfer Protocol (HTTP)

HTTP is the protocol which is used to retrieve information connected with hypermedia links. The client and server initially perform a negotiation procedure before the HTTP transfer takes place. This negotiation involves the client sending a list of formats it can support and the server replying with data in the required format.

Users generally move from a link on one server to another server. Each time the user moves from one server to another, the client sends an HTTP request to the server. Thus the client does not permanently connect to the server, and the server views each transfer as independent from all previous accesses. This is known as a stateless protocol.

An HTTP URL takes the form:

http://<*host*>:<*port*>/<*path*>?<*searchpart*>

Note that, if the <*port*> is omitted, port 80 is automatically used (HTTP service), <*path*> is an HTTP selector and <*searchpart*> is a query string.

The general format is:

```
httpurl    = "http://" hostport [ "/" hpath [ "?" search ]]
hpath      = hsegment *[ "/" hsegment ]
hsegment   = *[ uchar | ";" | ":" | "@" | "&" | "=" ]
search     = *[ uchar | ";" | ":" | "@" | "&" | "=" ]
```

### 13.6.5 Gopher Protocol

Gopher is widely used over the Internet and is basically a distribution system for the retrieval and delivery of documents. Users retrieve documents through a series of hierarchical menus, or through keyword searches. Unlike HTML documents they are not based on the hypertext concept.

### 13.6.6 Wide area information servers (WAIS)

WAIS is a public domain, fully text-based, information retrieval system over the Internet which performs text-based searches. The communications protocol used is based on the ANSI standard Z39.50, which is designed for networking library catalogues.

WAIS services include index generation and search engines. An indexer generates multiple indexes for organisations or individuals that offer services over the Internet. A WAIS search engine searches for particular words or text string indexes located across multiple Internet-attached information servers of various types.

### 13.6.7 News

UseNet or NewsGroup servers are part of the increasing use of general discussion news groups which share text-based news items. The news URL scheme defines a link to either a news group or individual articles with a group of UseNet news.

A news URL takes one of two forms:

news:*<newsgroup-name>*
news:*<message-id>*

where *<newsgroup-name>* is a period-delimited hierarchical name, such as 'news.inter', and *<message-id>* takes the full form of the message-ID, such as:

*<message-ID>*@*<full_domain_name>*

The general form is:

```
newsurl    = "news:" grouppart
grouppart  = "*" | group | article
group      = alpha *[ alpha | digit | "-" | "." | "+" | "_" ]
article    = 1*[ uchar | ";" | "/" | "?" | ":" | "&" | "=" ] "@" host
```

### 13.6.8 NNTP

The nntp URL scheme gives an alternative method of reviewing news articles. Its format is:

nntp://*<host>*:*<port>*/*<newsgroup-name>*/*<article-number>*

Note that, if the :*<port>* is omitted then the port defaults to 119. The *<newsgroup-name>* is the group's name, and the *<article-number>* is the numeric ID of the article.

### 13.6.9 TELNET

The `telnet` URL allows users to interactively perform a telnet operation, where a user must login to the referred system. Its standard format is:

`telnet://`*<user>*:*<password>*@*<host>*:*<port>*/

Note that, if :<port> is omitted, the default port is 23.

## 13.7  Universal resource identifier

The universal resource identifier (URI) is defined as a generically designated string of characters which refers to objects on the WWW. A URL is an example of a URI, with a designated access protocol and a specific Internet address.

Specifications have still to be completed, but URIs will basically be used to define the syntax for encoding arbitrary naming or addressing schemes. This should decouple the name of a resource from its location and also from its access method. For example, the file:

`MYPIC.HTM`

would be automatically associated with the HTTP protocol.

## 13.8  Web browser design

The Web browser is a carefully engineered software package which allows the user to efficiently find information on the WWW. Most are similar in their approach, but differ in their presentation. Figure 13.5 shows the tool bar for Microsoft Internet Explorer. This has been designed to allow the user to smoothly move through the WWW.

| File | Edit | View | Go | Favorites | Help | | | | | | |
|---|---|---|---|---|---|---|---|---|---|---|---|
| Back | Forward | Stop | Refresh | Home | Search | Favorites | History | Channels | Fullscreen | Mail |
| Address C:\billwww\EXAM~1.HTM | Links | Best of the Web | Channel Guide | Customize Links | Internet Explorer | | | | | | |

**Figure 13.5**  Microsoft Explorer tool bar

The Back and Forward options allow the user to traverse backwards and forwards through links. This allows the user to trace back to a previous link and possibly follow it.

The **Stop** option is used by the user to interrupt the current transfer. It is typically used when the user does not want to load the complete page. This often occurs when the browser is loading a graphics image.

The Web browser tries to reduce data transfer by holding recently accessed pages in a memory cache. This cache is typically held on a local disk. The **Refresh** forces the browser to re-load the page from the remote location.

Often a user wishes to restart a search and can use the **Home** option to return to it. The home page of the user is set up by one of the options.

The **Search** option is used to connect to a page which has access to the search programs. Microsoft Explorer typically connects to `http://home.microsoft.com/access/allinone.asp` which displays most of the available search engines. An example screen from Microsoft search facility is given in Figure 13.6. It can be seen that this links to the most commonly used search engines, such as Yahoo, Lycos, Magallan and eXcite.

Often a user has a list of favourite Web pages. This can be automatically called from the **Favorites** option. A new favourite can be added with the **Add To Favorites** .. option. These favourites can either be select from the Favorites menu option (such as **Internet Start**) or from within folders (such as **Channels** and **Links**). The favourites are organised using the **Organise Favorites...** option.

Other typically accessed sites can be recalled from Links, such as:

where the options are typically linked to the following:

Best of the Web: `http://home.microsoft.com/access/allinone.asp`
Today's Links: `http://home.microsoft.com/links/link.asp`
Web Gallery: `http://home.microsoft.com/isapi/`

Product news:  http://home.microsoft.com/ie
Microsoft:  http://home.microsoft.com/

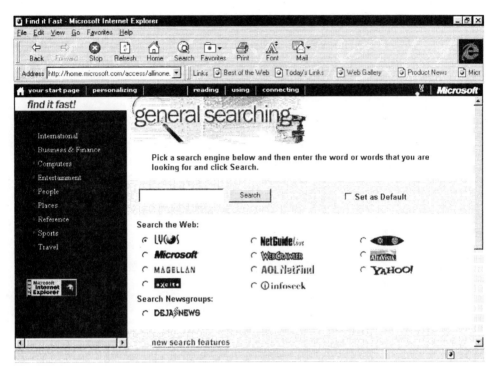

**Figure 13.6**  Microsoft search facility

## 13.9 Exercises

The following questions are multiple choice. Please select from a–d.

**13.9.1**  Where was the WWW first conceived:

    (a)    UCL        (b)    UMIST
    (c)    MIT         (d)    CERN

**13.9.2**  An MPEG file is what type of file:

    (a)    Image        (b)    Motion video
    (c)    Sound file    (d)    Generally compressed file

**13.9.3**  A GIF file is what type of file:

    (a)    Image        (b)    Motion video
    (c)    Sound file    (d)    Generally compressed file

**13.9.4** A ZIP file is what type of file:

    (a)    Image     (b)    Motion video
    (c)    Sound file     (d)    Generally compressed file

**13.9.5** An AU file is what type of file:

    (a)    Image     (b)    Motion video
    (c)    Sound file     (d)    Generally compressed file

**13.9.6** Where is the information on the Web stored:

    (a)    Web clients and servers     (b)    Web clients
    (c)    Web servers     (d)    Web gateways

## 13.10 Tutorial

**13.10.1** If possible, search for the following subjects on the Internet:

    (a)    Ethernet     (b)    EaStMAN     (c)    Edinburgh
    (d)    Napier     (e)    Taxation     (f)    Intel
    (g)    FDDI

**13.10.2** If possible, access the following WWW servers:

| Site | Accessed (YES/NO) | Comments |
|------|-------------------|----------|
| http://www.microsoft.com | | |
| http://www.intel.com | | |
| http://www.ieee.com | | |
| http://www.winzip.com | | |
| http://www.netscape.com | | |
| http://www.realaudio.com | | |
| http://www.cyrix.com | | |
| http://www.compaq.com | | |
| http://www.psion.com | | |
| http://www.amd.com | | |

| | | |
|---|---|---|
| http://www.cnn.com | | |
| http://www.w3.org | | |
| http://www.macromedia.com | | |
| http://www.epson.co.uk | | |
| http://www.euronec.com | | |
| http://www.casio.com | | |
| http://www.hayes.com | | |
| http://www.lotus.com | | |
| http://www.adobe.com | | |
| http://www.corel.com | | |
| http://www.symantec.co.uk | | |
| http://www.fractal.com | | |
| http://www.quarterdeck.com | | |
| http://www.guinness.ie | | |

**13.10.3**   Discuss the methods that users use to find information on the Web.

## 13.11 Research

The WWW and the Internet are powerful tools, but in Education they must be used with caution. Investigate the current uses of the WWW and the Internet within your own organisation, and possibly within other organisations. Typical questions that can be asked are:

| Sample Question | Possible options (delete, as necessary) | Comments |
|---|---|---|
| Does your organisation (University/ College/ Business/ etc) have its own WWW site? If not, visit another site, until you find one. | [YES]/[NO] | Name of site (eg, www.mysite.edu): |

| Is there education material on the WWW site? | [YES]/[NO] | Sample locations (eg `www.mysite.edu/~fred`): |
|---|---|---|
| Are the Lecturers/ Teachers/ Trainers available to be contacted by email? | [YES]/[NO] | Sample email addresses (eg `fred@mysite.edu`): |
| What is the quality of the education material? | Rating (best is 10): [1] [2] [3] [4] [5] [6] [7] [8] [9] [10] | Sample page (eg `www.mysite.edu/edu1.html`): |
| What is the main content source of the education material? | [HTML] [HTML/Java] [PDF] [Documents] [Other] | Example page (eg `www.mysite.edu/java.html`): |
| Does the organisation have a formal policy on WWW-based material, or is it left to individuals to generate the education material? | [YES][NO][N/A] | |
| Does the material integrate with traditional teaching methods (such as Lecturers/ Tutorials/ Experiments) | Rating (best is 10): [1] [2] [3] [4] [5] [6] [7] [8] [9] [10] | Example of integration (eg `www.mysite.edu/course1.html`): |
| Does the education material actually enhance the education learning? | Rating (best is 10): [1] [2] [3] [4] [5] [6] [7] [8] [9] [10] [Don't Know] | Good example (eg `www.mysite.edu/tele.html`): |
| Can the WWW-based material be accessed by people who are external to the organisation? | [YES][NO][N/A] | |
| What percentage of Lecturer/ Teachers/Trainers have WWW-based material? | [0–10%] [10–20%] [30–40%] [40–50%] [60–70%] [80–90%] [90–100%] | Names (eg `Fred Bloggs`): |

| | | |
|---|---|---|
| Find a site which, in your opinion, has excellent education material. What characteristics does it have and is it clear how it integrates into existing courses/programmes? | | Name of site (eg, `www.mysite.edu`):<br><br>Reason it is excellent: |
| Find a site which, in your opinion, has poor education material. What characteristics does it have? | | Name of site (eg, `www.mysite.edu`):<br><br>Reason it is poor: |
| Are there multi-media files (such as sound and video)? Do they enhance the understanding, of the subject? | | Example file (eg `www.mysite.edu/demo.avi`): |
| What are the main usages of the local Internet connection? | | |
| What would be the main recommendations on changing/enhancing the educational material on the WWW site? | | |

## 13.12 Surveys

1. Section 13.2 outlines some of the advantages and disadvantages of the WWW and the Internet. The usage of WWW/Internet by companies and individuals varies from one to the next. Conduct a survey within a class, University/College, workplace, etc, on the best applications of the WWW/Internet. Each person is allowed 12 votes. Ten points should be allocated to their favourite application, five for their second favourite, three for their third, two for their fourth and one for their fifth. People should also give –3 to their three least favourite applications. Total the votes and fill in the table given next, and thus determine the Top 10 favourite applications of the WWW/Internet.

| Application | Vote | Application | Vote | Application | Vote |
|---|---|---|---|---|---|
| Electronic Mail | | Downloading Hardware Drivers | | Video Conferencing | |
| Distributed information | | Multimedia Education | | Remote Access (such as, TELNET) | |
| Application Software Downloads | | Client/server Processing | | News Groups | |
| Product Information | | Remote Control/ Transmission of Data | | Chat Programs | |
| Daily News Events | | Information Archives | | On-line Libraries | |
| Electronic Commerce | | Search Facilities (Educational) | | Search Facilities (Product Information) | |
| Search Facilities (People/White Pages) | | General WWW Surfing | | Sampling Material (such as Music Tracks, Videos, etc) | |
| Source Code Download (Basic/ C/etc) | | Direct Access to Experts (such as through email) | | Special Interest Groups (Chess/etc) | |
| On-line Help | | Software Registration | | Distributed Databases | |
| Bulletin Boards | | Internet Telephone | | On-line Games | |

2. Conduct a survey of the main disadvantages of the WWW/Internet. Every person is allowed 12 votes. Ten points should be allocated to, in their opinion, the main disadvantage, five for their second, three for their third, two for their fourth and one for their fifth. Total the votes and determine the Top 10 disadvantages of the WWW/Internet.

| Application | Vote | Application | Vote | Application | Vote |
|---|---|---|---|---|---|
| Hacking | | Time wastage | | Poor Presentation of Material in Many WWW Sites | |
| Lack of Good Educational Material | | Access to Pornography and Related Material | | Too Much Remote Access | |
| Spying on Electronic Mail | | Spying on WWW/Internet usage | | Fossilisation of Links | |
| Poor On-line Support | | Search Facilities are Swamped by Non-related Material | | Security of Electronic Commerce | |
| Security of All Transmissions | | Lack of Speed | | Cost of Internet Service Provider | |

| | | | | | |
|---|---|---|---|---|---|
| On-line Internet Costs (such as Telephone Bills/ Network Mainte-nance/etc) | | Lack of Interaction | | Lack of Parental Control on WWW accesses | |
| Incompatibility of WWW Browsers | | Incompatibility of WWW pages (such as Java/HTML incompatibilities) | | Difficult to Locate Expert Help | |
| Lack of Real-Time Control | | Poor Quality Video Conferencing | | Poor Quality Audio | |
| Connection Varies in its Responsiveness | | Lack of Editorial Control on Material | | Cost (Physical and Time) of Maintain-ing a WWW Site | |
| Lack of Government Control | | Lack of Organisational Control | | Increased Alienation of People | |
| Too Much Surface Learning, Not Enough Deep Learning | | Reduction in Educational Standards (through Remote Teaching/ On-line Help/etc) | | Difficult to Learn from a Computer Screen | |
| Access to Violent Material | | Other: | | Other: | |

3.  Construct your own survey of the main advantages of the WWW/Internet.

## 13.13 Note from the author

*Good old port 80. Without it, and TCP/IP we would not have had the WWW. The WWW has grown over the past few years. In this short time, WWW pages have evolved from pages which contained a few underlined hypertext links to complex pages which contain state-of-art graphics, animations, menus and even sound files. HTML led to JavaScript, which has led to Java, which provides a platform-independent method of running programs. So what's next? More, and better, Java, probably.*

*The tools for developing WWW pages are still not perfect but they are evolving fast. The design of many computer packages is now based on hypertext design and many use a browser-like layout (such as with navigation buttons and hypertext links). For example, documentation is typically distributed using HTML pages.*

# ⬡14 Security

## 14.1 Introduction

Security involves protecting the system hardware and software from both internal attack and from external attack (hackers). An internal attack normally involves uneducated users causing damage, such as deleting important files or crashing systems. This effect can be minimised if the system manager properly protects the system. Typical actions are to limit the files that certain users can access and also the actions they can perform on the system.

Most system managers have seen the following:

- Users sending a file of the wrong format to the system printer (such as sending a binary file). Another typical one is where there is a problem on a networked printer (such as lack of paper), but the user keeps re-sending the same print job.
- Users deleting the contents of sub-directories, or moving files from one place to another (typically, these days, with the dragging of a mouse cursor). This problem can be reduced by regular backups.
- Users deleting important system files (in a PC, these are normally AUTOEXEC.BAT and CONFIG.SYS). This can be overcome by the system administrator protecting important system files, such as making them read-only or hidden.
- Users telling other people their user passwords or not changing a password from the initial default one. This can be overcome by the system administrator forcing the user to change their password at given time periods.

Security takes many forms, such as:

- Data protection. This is typically where sensitive or commercially important information is kept. It might include information databases, design files or source code files. One method of reducing this risk to encrypt important files with a password and/or some form of data encryption.
- Software protection. This involves protecting all the software packages from damage or from being misconfigured. A misconfigured software package can cause as much damage as a physical attack on a system, because it can take a long time to find the problem.
- Physical system protection. This involves protecting systems from intruders who might physically attack the systems. Normally, important systems are locked in rooms and then within locked rack-mounted cabinets.
- Transmission protection. This involves a hacker tampering with a transmission

connection. It might involve tapping into a network connection or total disconnection. Tapping can be avoided by many methods, including using optical fibres which are almost impossible to tap into (as it would typically involve sawing through a cable with hundreds of fibre cables, which would each have to be connected back as they were connected initially). Underground cables can avoid total disconnection, or its damage can be reduced by having redundant paths (such as different connections to the Internet).

## 14.2  Hacking methods

The best form of protection is to disallow hackers into the network in the first place. Organisational networks are hacked for a number of reasons and in a number of ways. The most common methods are:

- IP spoofing attacks. This is where the hacker steals an authorised IP address, as illustrated in Figure 14.1. Typically, it is done by determining the IP address of a computer and waiting until there is no-one using that computer, then using the unused IP address. Several users have been accused of accessing unauthorised material because other users have used their IP address. A login system which monitors IP addresses and the files that they are accessing over the Internet cannot be used as evidence against the user, as it is easy to steal IP addresses.

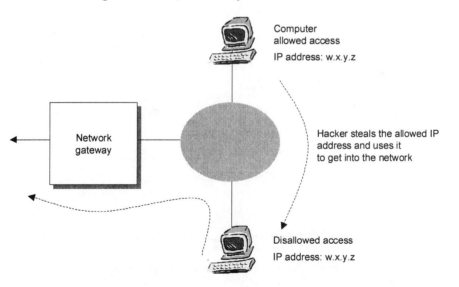

**Figure 14.1**  IP spoofing

- Packet-sniffing. This is where the hacker listens to TCP/IP packets which come out of the network and steals the information in them. Typical information includes user logins, e-mail messages, credit card number, and so on. This method is typically used to steal an IP address, before an IP spoofing attack. Figure 14.2 shows an example where a hacker listens to a conversation between a server and a client. Most TELNET and FTP programs actually transmit the user name and password as text values; these can be easily viewed by a hacker, as illustrated in Figure 14.3.

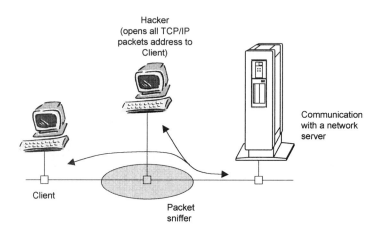

**Figure 14.2**  Packet sniffing

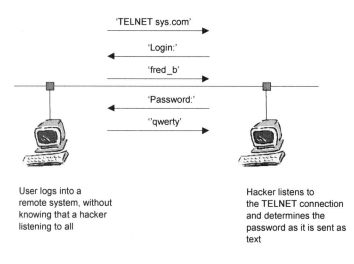

**Figure 14.3**  Packet sniffing on a TELNET connection

- Passwords attacks. This is a common weak-point in any system, and hackers will generally either find a user with a easy password (especially users which have the same password as their login name) or will use a special program which cycles through a range of passwords. This type of attack is normally easy to detect. The worst nightmare of this type of attack is when a hacker determines the system administrator password (or a user who has system privileges). This allows the hacker to change system set-ups, delete files, and even change user passwords.

- Sequence number prediction attacks. Initially, in a TCP/IP connection, the two computers exchange a start-up packet which contains sequence numbers (Section 10.7). These sequence numbers are based on the computer's system clock and then run in a predictable manner, which can be determined by the hacker.
- Session hi-jacking attacks. In this method, the hacker taps into a connection between two computers, typically between a client and a server. The hacker then simulates the connection by using its IP address.
- Shared library attacks. Many systems have an area of shared library files. These are called by applications when they are required (for input/output, networking, graphics, and so on). A hacker may replace standard libraries for ones that have been tampered with, which allows the hacker to access system files and to change file privileges. Figure 14.4 illustrates how a hacker might tamper with dynamic libraries (which are called as a program runs), or with static libraries (which are used when compiling a program). This would allow the hacker to possibly do damage to the local computer, send all communications to a remote computer, or even view everything that is viewed on the user screen. The hacker could also introduce viruses and cause unpredictable damage to the computer (such as remotely rebooting it, or crashing it at given times).
- Social engineering attacks. This type of attack is aimed at users who have little understanding of their computer system. A typical attack is where the hacker sends an email message to a user, asking for their password. Many unknowing users are tricked by this attack. A few examples are illustrated in Figure 14.5. From the initial user login, the hacker can then access the system and further invade the system.
- Technological vulnerability attack. This normally involves attacking some part of the system (typically the operating system) which allows a hacker to be access to the system. A typical one is for the user to gain access to a system and then run a program which reboots the system or slows it down by running a processor intensive program. This can be overcome in operating systems such as Microsoft Windows and UNIX by granting re-boot rights only to the system administrator.

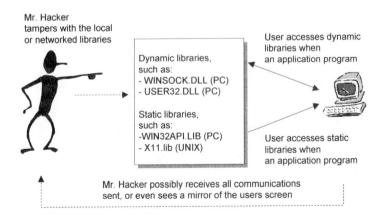

**Figure 14.4** Shared library attack

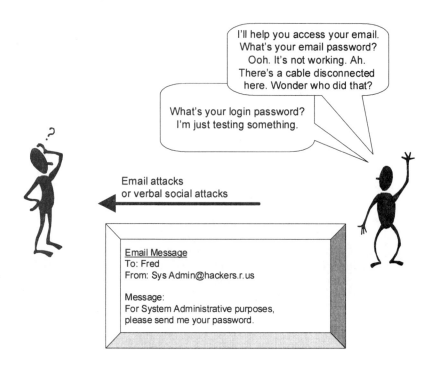

**Figure 14.5**   Social Engineering attack

- Trust-access attacks. This allows a hacker to add their system to the list of systems which are allowed to log into the system without a user password. In UNIX this file is the *.rhosts* (trusted hosts) which is contained in the user's home directory. A major problem is when the trusted hosts file is contained in the root directory, as this allows a user to log in as the system administrator.

## 14.3  Security policies

A well-protected system depends mainly on the system manager. It is up to the manager to define security policies which define how users can operate the system. A good set of policies would be:

- Restrictions on users who can use a given account. The system administrator needs to define the users who can login on a certain account.
- Password requirements and prohibitions. This defines the parameters of the password, such as minimum password size, time between password changes, and so on.
- Internet access/restrictions. This limits whether or not a user is allowed access to the Internet.
- User account deletion. The system administrator automatically deletes user accounts which are either not in use or moved to another system.

- Application program rules. This defines the programs which a user is allowed to run (typically games can be barred for some users).
- Monitoring consent. Users should be informed about how the system monitors their activities. It is important, for example, to tell users that their Internet accesses are being monitored. This gives the user no excuse when they are found to be accessing restricted sites.

## 14.4 Passwords

Passwords are normally an important part of any secure network. They can be easily hacked with the use of a program which continually tries different passwords within a given range (normally called directory-based attacks). These can be easily overcome by only allowing a user three bad logins before the system locks the user out for a defined time. Novell NetWare and Windows NT/2000 both use this method, but UNIX does not. The system manager, though, can determine if an attack has occurred with the BADLOG file. This file stores a list of all the bad logins for a user and the location of the user.

Passwords are a basic system for provide security on a network, and they are only as secure as the user makes them. Good rules for passwords are:

- Use slightly unusual names, such as *vinegarwine, dancertop* or *helpcuddle*. Do not use names of a wife, husband, child or pet. Many users, especially ones who know the user, can easily guess the user's password.
- Use numbers after the name, such as *vinedrink55* and *applefox32*. This makes the password difficult to crack as users are normally only allowed a few chances to login correctly before they are logged out (and a bad login event written to a bad login file).
- Have serveral passwords which are changed at regular intervals. This is especially important for system managers. Every so often, these passwords should be changed to new ones.
- Make the password at least six characters long. This stops 'hackers' from watching the movement of the user's fingers when they login, or from running a program which tries every permutation of characters. Every character added, multiplies the number of combinations by a great factor (for example, if just the characters from 'a' to 'z' and '0' to '9' are taken then every character added increases the number of combinations by a factor of 36).
- Change some letters for numbers, or special characters. Typically, 'o' becomes a 0 (zero), 'i' becomes 1 (one), 's' becomes 5 (five), spaces become '$', 'b' becomes '6', and so on. So a password of 'silly password' might become '5illy$pa55w0rd' (the user makes a rule for 's' and 'o'). The user must obviously remember the rule that has been used for changing the letters to other characters. This method overcomes the technique of hackers and hacker programs, where combinations of words from a dictionary are hashed to try and make the hashed password.

The two main protocols used are:

- Password Authentication Protocol (PAP). This provides for a list of encrypted passwords.
- Challenge Handshake Authentication Protocol (CHAP). This is a challenge-response system which requires a list of unencrypted passwords. When a user logs into the system a random key is generated and sent to the user for encrypting the password. The user then uses this key to encrypt the password, and the encrypted password is sent back to the system. If it matches its copy of the encrypted password then it lets the user log into the system. The CHAP system then continues to challenge the user for encrypted data. If the user gets these wrong then the system disconnects the login.

### 14.4.1 Administrator user name

The administrator account has the highest privileges and will thus be the most highly prized hackable account. If it is hacked into then the whole system is vulnerable to attack until it can be proved that there are no hidden traps. One method of reducing the risk of being hacked is to change the name of the administrator from time to time. The administrator password should be totally secure with a relatively large password size.

### 14.4.2 Password security

The US Government defines certain security levels: D, C1, C2, B1, B2, B3 and A1, which are published in the *Trusted Computer Security Evaluation Criteria* books (each which have different coloured cover to define their function), these include:

- Orange book. Describes system security.
- Red book. Interpretation of the Orange book in a network context.
- Blue book. Application of Orange book to systems not covered in the original book.

Microsoft Windows NT/2000 uses the C2 security level. It has the following features:

- Object control. Users own certain objects and they have control over how they are accessed.
- User names and passwords.
- No object reuse. Once a user or a group has been deleted, the user and group numerical IDs are not used again. New users or groups are granted a new ID number.
- Security auditing system. This allows the system administrator to trace security aspects, such as user login, bad logins, program access, file access, and so on.
- Defined keystroke for system access. In Windows NT, the CNTRL-ALT-DEL keystroke is used by a user to log into the system.

### 14.4.3 Password hacking programs

There are many password cracking hacking programs, especially for UNIX and Windows NT, these include:

- Crack. This is a freely available program which can be used on Windows NT/2000 or UNIX systems. For example a password such as `mouse1` can be cracked within 5 minutes on a reasonable specification computer. This is because Crack searches a through a library of common words and tries these in different combinations. Operating systems such as Linux display a warning when the user enters a password which is typically found in a dictionary.

- PwDump. This utility allows the user to view the encrypted password file for a local or a remote Windows NT/2000 system. These encoded passwords can then be used to hack into the system.
- ScanNT. This is a commercial package for Windows NT.

With PwDump the encoded (hashed) passwords are sent back to user, such as:

```
Administrator:500:EF10EDD3421010325A3B2178::Sys Admin::
Fred:501:32FAB36412032188:...:Fred Bloggs::
```

These encoded passwords can be used to hack into the system because the login process is as follows:

- Server contacts the clients and sends a random nonsense (nonce) message.
- Client then encrypts the nonce and user account name using the encoded password.
- Client sends the result and the text username to the server.
- Server validates this response using the encoded user password.

Many systems are prone to the man in the middle attack, where a hacker sends a forged challenge to the server. Next, the hacker waits for a real request by same user that is to be used to hack into the system. The hacker then sends a challenge to the user, as if it was the server, and incepts the response. This response can then be sent onto the server, from which the hacker can log in. If the hacker already knows the encoded password then there is no need to wait on a response from the hacked user as it can be impersonated immediately with the encoded password.

## 14.5 Hardware security

Passwords are a simple method of securing a system. A better method is to use a hardware-restricted system which either bar users from a specific area or even restrict users from login into a system. Typical methods are:

- Smart cards. With this method a user can only gain access to the system after they have inserted their personal smart card into the computer and then entered their PIN code.
- Biometrics. This is a better method than a smart card where a physical feature of the user is scanned. The scanned parameter requires to be unchanging, such as fingerprints or retina images.

## 14.6 Hacker problems

Once a hacker has entered into a system, there are many methods which can be used to further penetrate into the system, such as:

- Modifying search paths. All systems set up a search path in which the system looks into to find the required executable. For example, in a UNIX system, a typical search path is /bin, /usr/bin, and so on. A hacker can change the search paths for a user and then replace standard programs with ones that have been modified. For example, the hacker could replace the email program for one that sends emails directly to the hacker or any directory listings could be sent to the hacker's screen.
- Modifying shared libraries. As discussed previously.
- Running processor intensive task which slows the system down; this task will be run in the background and will generally not be seen by the user. The hacker can further attack the system by adding the processor intensive task to the system start-up file (such as the rc file on a UNIX system).
- Running network intensive tasks which will slow the network down, and typically slow down all the connected computers. As with the processor intensive task, the networking intensive task can be added to the system start-up file.
- Infecting the system with a virus or worm.

Most PCs have now virus scanners which test the memory and files for viruses and thus virus are easy to detect. A more sinister virus is spread over the Internet, such as the Internet worm which was released on November 1988. This is a program which runs on a computer and creates two threads. A thread in a program is a unit of code that can get a time slice from the operating system to run concurrently with other code units. Each process consists of one or more execution threads that identify the code path flow as it is run on the operating system. This enhances the running of an application by improving throughput and responsiveness. With the worm, the first thread searches for a network connection and when it finds a connection it copies itself to that computer. Next, the worm makes a copy of itself and runs it on the system. Thus a single copy will become two, then four, eight, and so on. This will then continue until the system, and the other connected systems, will be shutdown. The only way to stop the worm is to shutdown all the effected computers at the same time and then restart them.

## 14.7 Network security

Hackers into network come in many forms. The least determined hacker will simply be put off by simple security measures, whereas a determined hacker might attack the network in a number of ways. The main methods of security are:

- Hub security. Hub is configured so that it only recognises authorised MAC addresses.
- Switch security. Switch is configured to filter given types, such as MAC address or protocol.

- Router security. Routers give certain filtering types, such as IP addresses, subnets, and so on.

## Hub Security

Hubs with a management module can be configured with intruder prevention and eavesdrop prevention. Intruder prevention can be set in a number of ways. At the highest level of intruder prevention, a single device (identified by its hard-wired station address) is authorised to use a particular port on the hub. If another device attempts to transmit through that port, the hub disables the port and notifies the network administrator. Thus if an intruder connects on to the cables of a hub it will start transmitting with a different MAC address to the authorised node. The hub will detect this and disconnect the port from the network. This means that an intruder could listen to the traffic coming to the authorised node, but couldn't actively explore the network. Figure 14.6 shows an example of an intruder connected to the connection from node A to the hub.

In eavesdrop prevention the hub examines the destination address in each packet. It sends the packet in its original form only to the port attached to the destination node and sends a meaningless string of 1s and 0s to the other ports. Thus, in Figure 14.6, nodes B to E can communicate with each other without the frames getting sent to node A.

## Switch Security

Switch security operates by filtering. This is achieved by the switch examining incoming packets for certain characteristics and discarding any packets that fail to meet preestablished filtering criteria. Many switches use address filtering and make use of the address table that the switch maintains. Filters can be specified of the following types:

- Multicast (the default).
- Protocol.
- Source port.
- Source MAC.

For MAC address filtering the network administrator makes a permanent entry in the bridge's address table that will cause the switch to discard any packets from the specified address.

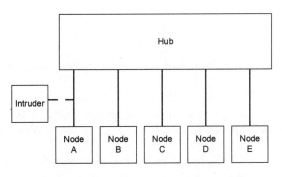

**Figure 14.6** Hub with a connected intruder

### 14.7.1 Router Security

Router security is similar to switch security where it operates by filtering packets. Routers are more complex devices than switches and thus offer an increased number of filters (these depend on the routing protocol being used).

Routing protocols extend filtering beyond that provided by bridges by allowing filtering based on the origin's subnet address. This thus provides for firewall protection and allows keep traffic local within certain parts of a network. They may also support authentication methods including SecurID, CHAP and PAP.

## 14.8 Exercises

The following questions are multiple choice. Please select from a–d.

14.8.1    Which, with respect to a dictionary-based password hacking program, of the following is the least secure password:

(a)    foxmilk           (b)    ele_phant_forest
(c)    aaapppllle        (d)    g00d%pa55w0rd
(e)    ant_fox           (f)    ugrangwad

14.8.2    Assuming an alphabet of 26 letters ('a' to 'z') and a password of 4 letters, how many password permutations are possible:

(a)    26                      (b)    $10^4$ ($26 \times 4$)
(c)    456976 ($26 \times 26 \times 26 \times 26$)    (d)    358800 ($26 \times 25 \times 24 \times 23$)

14.8.3    Modify the following passwords so that they are difficult to crack with a dictionary-based cracking program (Hints: change letters to numbers, spaces to other characters, mix upper and lower case letters, and so on):

(a)    apple tree              (b)    hard disk drive
(c)    simple password         (d)    keyboard connector

## 14.9 Research

1. Search on the Internet for information on the Data Protection (either for individuals or organisations).

2. Search on the Internet for information on security breaches, and the methods that where used to hack into the system.

3. Security policies are important in protecting the system from abuse. For a known system, if possible, investigate the following:

| Subject | Typical questions |
| --- | --- |
| Restrictions on users who can use a given account | Are their individual logins or global logins?<br><br>Have groups been defined? |
| Password requirements and prohibitions | Is there a minimum limit on the number of characters in a password?<br><br>Does a password have a given lifetime?<br><br>Is the user allowed to change their password so that it's the same as the previous one? |
| Internet access/restrictions | Is external Internet access allowed?<br><br>Are their any restrictions on the types of access? |
| Application program rules | What applications are available over the network?<br><br>Are there any restrictions on their usage? |
| Monitoring | Is network accesses monitored?<br><br>Is Internet accesses monitored?<br><br>Is WWW accesses monitored? |

## 14.10 Survey

Many users use easy-to-remembers names for their password. These are typically names of spouses, car types, and so on. Conduct a survey within a class, University/College, workplace, etc, to see if their current, or previous, passwords fits one of the following given below (ignore extra numbers and characters). Total the votes and fill-in the table given next, and thus determine the Top 10 favourite password classifications. NOTE: Don't tell anyone your current password, and withhold your current password's classification, if you want.

| Password classification | Vote | Password classification | Vote |
|---|---|---|---|
| Name of a pet (eg Fido, Tiddles) | | Car type or manufacturer (eg, Ford, Mustang) | |
| Nonsense word (eg rippleworden) | | Computer type or manufacturer (eg IBM) | |
| Default password which was initially allocated (eg QWERTY) | | Parent's/Spouse's name (eg Bert) | |
| Name of a friend/ relation (eg Martin) | | Pop group/ singer (eg Beatles) | |
| Movie star name (eg M_Monroe) | | Film title (eg Casablanca) | |
| Computer game (eg Doom) | | Cartoon Character (eg Bugs_Bunny) | |
| Computer game character (eg Sonic) | | Historical event (eg world_war) | |
| City/ town (eg Edinburgh) | | Sport team name (eg Celtic) | |
| Government Administration Number (LL 123 456 A) | | Country name (eg England) | |
| Children's names (eg Lisa) | | Historical character (eg Shakespeare) | |
| TV program (eg Simpsons) | | Transport (eg Train) | |
| Children's book (eg WillyWonka) | | Other books (eg Cuckoo'sNest) | |
| Comedian (eg Crosby) | | Composer (eg Beethoven) | |
| Old/current school-related name (eg GraemeHigh) | | Old/current college/ university/ company-related name (eg Cambridge) | |

| Church-related name (eg priest) | | Musical Instrument (eg guitar) | |
|---|---|---|---|
| Animal name (eg tiger) | | Food name (eg spaghetti) | |
| Sports Person (eg Pele) | | Computer peripherals (eg diskdrive) | |
| Someone's date of birth (27/11/90) | | Bank details (eg 114466) | |
| Other: | | Other: | |
| Other: | | Other: | |
| Other: | | Other: | |

## 14.11 Note from the author

*To be able to protect a network, either from misuse or from external hackers, it is important to understand the methods that users and hackers use to damage a network.*

*A few words of advice for someone thinking of hacking into a network:*

*'Don't do it'*

*as you will probably get caught and risk being thrown off your course or sacked from your work. It happened at Intel when a part-time System Administrator ran a program which tested the security of user passwords. He was immediately sacked when it was found out that he had run the program (as he had no authorisation to run it).*

*Hacking into a network can be just as damaging in term of money, as someone doing physical damage to a building or a computer system. In fact, many companies see it as a more serious crime (most buildings and computer hardware are insured and easily rebuild or repurchased, but corrupted data or misconfigured systems can take a lot of time and energy to repair)*

*Another thing to remember that a hint of hacking can lead to accusations of much more serious damage. For example, a user could determine the password of another user. If at the same time there is a serious error on the other user's data then the hacker may be accused of actually causing the damage. I have seen many occurrences of this type of situation.*

*Remember. You're a professional. Act like one.*

# 15 Firewalls, Tunnels and Routers

## 15.1 Introduction

An organisation may experience two disadvantages in having a connection to the WWW and the Internet:

- The possible usage of the Internet for non-useful applications (by employees).
- The possible connection of non-friendly users from the global connection into the organisations local network.

For these reasons many organisations have shied away from connection to the global network and have set up intranets. These are in-house, tailor-made internets for use within the organisation and provide limited access (if any) to outside services and also limit the external traffic into the intranet (if any). An intranet might have access to the Internet but there will be no access from the Internet to the organisation's Intranet.

Organisations which have a requirement for sharing and distributing electronic information normally have three choices:

- Use a propriety groupware package, such as Lotus Notes.
- Set up an intranet.
- Set up a connection to the Internet.

Groupware packages normally replicate data locally on a computer whereas intranets centralise their information on central servers which are then accessed by a single browser package. The stored data is normally open and can be viewed by any compatible WWW browser. Intranet browsers have the great advantage over groupware packages in that they are available for a variety of clients, such as PCs, UNIX workstations, Macs, and so on. A client browser also provides a single GUI interface which offers easy integration with other applications, such as electronic mail, images, audio, video, animation, and so on.

The main elements of an intranet are:

- Intranet server hardware.
- Intranet server software.
- TCP/IP stack software on the clients and server.
- WWW browsers.
- A firewall.

256

Typically the intranet server consists of a PC running the Linux (PC-based UNIX-like) operating system. The TCP/IP stack is software installed on each computer and allows communications between a client and a server using TCP/IP.

A firewall is the routing computer which isolates the intranet from the outside world. Another method is to use an intermediate system which isolates the intranet from the external Internet. These intermediate system include:

- A proxy.
- A gateway.
- A tunnel.

Each intermediate system is connected by a TCP and acts as a relay for the request to be sent out and returned to the client. Figure 15.1 shows the set-up of the proxies and gateways.

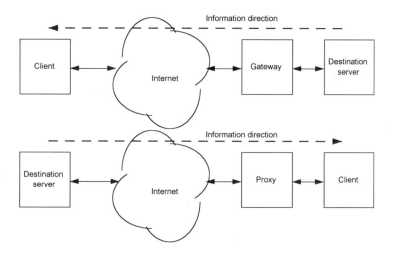

**Figure 15.1**   Usage of proxies and gateways

## 15.2  Proxy server

A proxy connects to a number of clients; it acts on behalf of other clients and sends requests from the clients to a server. It thus acts as a client when it communicates with a server, but as a server when communicating with a client. A proxy is typically used for security purposes where the client and server are separated by a firewall. The proxy connects to the client side of the firewall and the server to the other side of the firewall. Thus the server must authenticate itself to the firewall before a connection can be made with the proxy. Only after this has been authenticated will the proxy pass requests through the firewall. A proxy can also be used to convert between different version of the protocols about TCP/IP, such as HTTP.

## 15.3  Firewalls

A firewall (or security gateway) protects a network against intrusion from outside sources. They tend to differ in their approach, but can be characterised as follows:

- Firewalls which block traffic.
- Firewalls which permit traffic.

They can be split into three main types:

- Network-level firewalls (packet filters). This type of firewalls examines the parameters of the TCP/IP packet to determine if it should dropped or not. This can be done by examining the destination address, the source address, the destination port, the source port, and so on. The firewall must thus contain a list of barred IP addresses or allowable IP addresses. Typically a system manager will determine IP addresses of sites which are barred and add them to the table. Certain port numbers will also be barred, typically TELNET and FTP ports are barred and SMTP is allowed, as this allows mail to be routed into and out of the network, but no remote connections.
- Application-level firewalls. This type of firewall uses an intermediate system (a proxy server) to isolate the local computer from the external network. The local computer communicates with the proxy server, which in turns communicates with the external network, the external computer then communicates with the proxy which in turn communicates with the local computer. The external network never actually communicates directly with the local computer. The proxy server can then be set-up to be limited to certain types of data transfer, such as allowing HTTP (for WWW access), SMTP (for electronic mail), outgoing FTP, but blocking incoming FTP.
- Circuit-level firewalls. A circuit-level firewall is similar to an application-level firewall but it does not bother about the transferred protocol.

### 15.3.1 Network-level firewalls

The network-level firewall (or packet filter) is the simplest form of firewall and are also known as screen routers. It basically keeps a record of allowable source and destination IP addresses, and deletes all packets which do not have them. This technique is known as address filtering. The packet filter keeps a separate source and destination table for both directions, that is, into and out of the intranet. This type of method is useful for companies which have geographically spread sites, as the packet filter allows incoming traffic from other friendly sites, but blocks other non-friendly traffic. This is illustrated by Figure 15.2.

Unfortunately, this method suffers from the fact that IP addresses can be easily forged. For example, a hacker might determine the list of good source addresses and then add one of them to any packets which are addressed to the intranet. This type of attack is known as address spoofing and is the most common method of attacking a network.

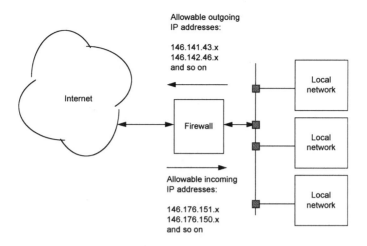

Figure 15.2 Packet filter firewalls

### 15.3.2 Application-level firewall

The application-level firewall uses a proxy server to act as an intermediate system between the external network and the local computer. Normally the proxy only supports a given number of protocols, such as HTTP (for WWW access) or FTP. It is thus possible to block certain types of protocols, typically outgoing FTP (Figure 15.3).

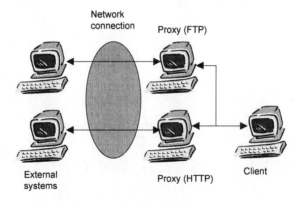

Figure 15.3 Application-level firewall

The proxy server thus isolates the local computer from the external network. The local computer communicates with the proxy server, which in turn communicates with the external network, the external computer then communicates with the proxy, which in turn, communicates with the local computer. The external network never actually communicates directly with the local computer. Figure 15.4 shows a WWW browser is set up to communicate with a proxy server to get its access. In the advanced options (Figure 15.5) different proxy servers can be specified. In this case, for HTTP (WWW access), FTP, Gopher, Secure and Socks (Windows Sockets). It can also be seen that a proxy server can be bypassed by specifying a number of IP addresses (or DNS).

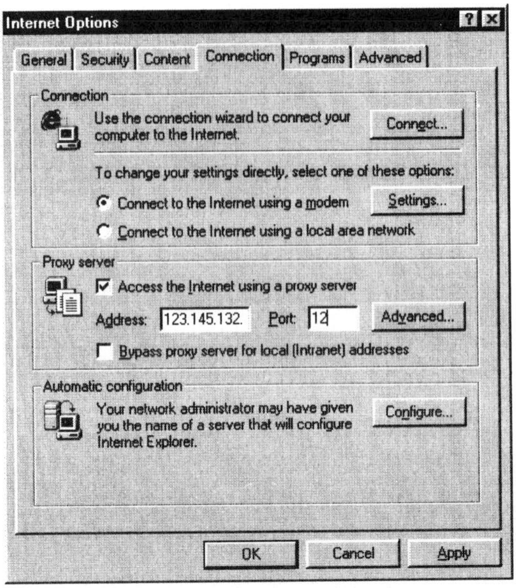

**Figure 15.4** Internet options showing proxy server selection

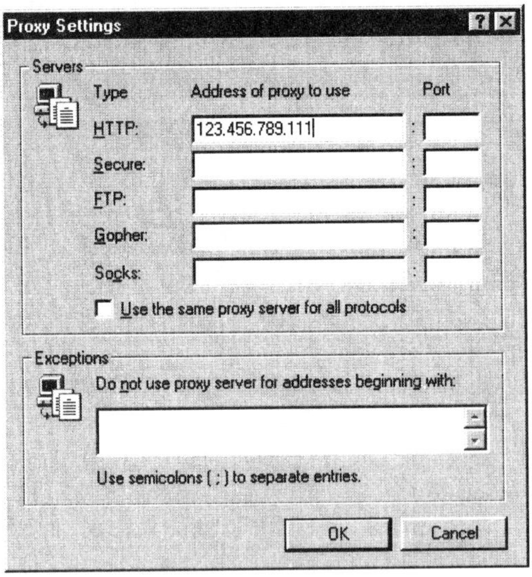

**Figure 15.5** Proxy settings

## 15.4 Firewall architectures

The three main types of firewall are shown in Figure 15.6. These are:

- Dual-homed host firewall. With this type of firewalls a dedicated computer isolates the local network from the external network (typically, the Internet). It contains two network cards to connect to the two networks and should not run any routing software, and must rely on application-layer routing. This type of firewall is fairly secure and easy to maintain.

- Screen-host firewall. With this method, a router is placed between the external network and the firewall. Users on the local network connect to the firewall and the firewall only communicates with the router. There is thus no direct connection between the external network and the firewall (as all communications must go through the router). The security of this method is better than that of the dual-homed type, as there is no direct electrical connection to the external network.
- Screened-subnet firewall. With this method, a router is placed on either side of the firewall. The firewall is thus isolated from the two connected networks. One router filters traffic between the local network and the firewall, and the other filters traffic between the external network and firewall. This provides the greatest level of security for both incoming and outgoing traffic.

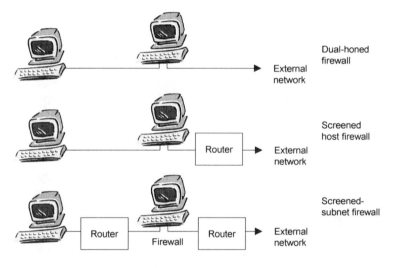

**Figure 15.6** Firewall types

## 15.5 Security ratings

The Orange Book produced by the US Department of Defense (DOD) defines levels of security for systems. It is an important measure of a firewall's security. There are four main divisions, which split into seven main security ratings. Division D is the lowest security level and Division A is the highest. The ratings are:

- Division D. This rating provides no protection on files or for users. For example, a DOS-based computer has no real security on files and users, thus it has a Division D rating.

- Division C. This rating splits into two groups: C1 rating and C2 rating. C1 contains a trust computing base (TCB) which separates users and data. It suffers from the fact that all the data on the system has the same security level. Thus, users cannot make distinctions between highly secure data and not-so secure data. A C1 system has user names and passwords, as well as some form of control of users and objects. C2 has a higher level of security and provides for some form of accountability and audit. This allows events to be logged and traced, for example, it might contain a list of user logins, network address logins, resource accesses, bad logins, and so on.
- Division B. This rating splits into three groups: B1, B2 and B3. Division B rated systems have all the security of a C2 rating, but have more security because they have a different level of security for all system accesses. For example, each computer can have a different security level, each printer can also have different security levels, and so on. Each object (such as a computer, printer, and so on) has a label associated with it. It is with this label that the security is set by. Non-labelled resources cannot be connected to the system. In a B2 rated system, users are notified of any changes of an object that they are using. The TCB also includes separate operator and administrator functions. In a B3 rated system the TCB excludes information which is not related to security. The system should also be designed to be simple to trace, but also well tested to prevent external hackers. It should also have a full-time administrator, audit trails and system recovery methods.
- Division A. This is the highest level of security. It is similar to B3, but has formal methods for the systems security policy. The system should also have a security manager, who should document the installation of the system, and any changes to the security model.

## 15.6 Application level gateways

Application-level gateways provide an extra layer of security when connecting an intranet to the Internet. They have three main components:

- A gateway node.
- Two firewalls which connect on either side of the gateway and only transmit packets which are destined for or to the gateway.

Figure 15.7 shows the operation of an application level gateway. In this case, Firewall A discards anything that is not addressed to the gateway node, and discards anything that is not sent by the gateway node. Firewall B, similarly discards anything from the local network that is not addressed to the gateway node, and discards anything that is not sent by the gateway node. Thus, to transfer files from the local network into the global network, the user must do the following:

- Log onto the gateway node.
- Transfer the file onto the gateway.
- Transfer the file from the gateway onto the global network.

To copy a file from the network, an external user must:

- Log onto the gateway node.
- Transfer from the global network onto the gateway.
- Transfer the file from the gateway onto the local network.

A common strategy in organisations is to allow only electronic mail to pass from the Internet to the local network. This specifically disallows file transfer and remote login. Unfortunately, electronic mail can be used to transfer files. To overcome this problem the firewall can be designed specifically to disallow very large electronic mail messages, so it will limit the ability to transfer files. This tends not to be a good method as large files can be split up into small parts, then sent individually.

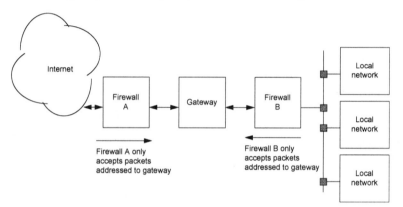

**Figure 15.7**　Application level gateway

## 15.7　Encrypted tunnels

Packet filters and application level gateways suffer from insecurity, which can allow non-friendly users into the local network. Packet filters can be tricked with fake IP addresses and application level gateways can be hacked into by determining the password of certain users of the gateway then transferring the files from the network to the firewall, on to the gateway, on to the next firewall and out. The best form of protection for this type of attack is to allow only a limited number of people to transfer files onto the gateway.

The best method of protection is to encrypt the data leaving the network then to decrypt it on the remote site. Only friendly sites will have the required encryption key to receive and send data. This has the extra advantage that the information cannot be easily tapped-into.

Only the routers which connect to the Internet require to encrypt and decrypt, as illustrated in Figure 15.8. Typically, remote users connect to a corporation intranet by connecting over a modem which is connected to the corporation intranet, and using a standard Internet connection protocol, such as Point-to-Point Protocol (PPP). This can be expensive in both phone calls or in providing enough modems for all connected users. These costs can be drastically reduced if the user connects to an ISP, as they provide local rate charges. For this a new protocol, called Point-to-Point Tunneling Protocol (PPTP) has been developed to allow remote users connections to intranets from a remote connection (such as from a modem or ISDN). It operates as follows:

- Users connect to an ISP, using a protocol such as Point-to-Point Protocol (PPP) and requests that the information is sent to an intranet. The ISP has special software and hardware to handle PPTP.
- The data send to the ISP, using PPTP, is encrypted before it is sent into the Internet.
- The ISP sends the encrypted data (wrapped in an IP packet) to the Intranet.
- Data is passed through the firewall, which has the software and hardware to process PPTP packets.
- Next, the user logs in using Password Authentication Protocol (PAP) or Challenge Handshake Authentication (CHAP).
- Finally, the intranet server reads the IP packet and decrypts the data.

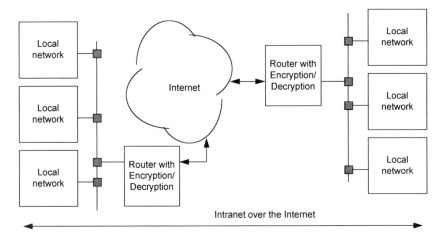

**Figure 15.8**   Encryption tunnels

## 15.8  Filtering routers

Filtering routers run software which allows many different parameters of the incoming and outgoing packets to be examined, as illustrated in Figure 15.9, such as:

- Source IP address. The router will have a table of acceptable source IP addresses.

This will limit the access to the external network as only authorised users will be granted IP addresses. This unfortunately is prone to IP spoofing, where a local user can steal an authorised IP address. Typically, it is done by determining the IP address of a computer and waiting until there is no-one using that computer, then using the unused IP address. Several users have been accused of accessing unauthorised material because other users have used their IP address. A login system which monitors IP addresses and the files that they are accessing over the Internet cannot be used as evidence against the user, as it is easy to steal IP addresses.

- Destination IP address. The router will have a table of acceptable outgoing destination IP addresses, addresses which are not in the table are blocked. Typically, this will be used to limit the range of destination addresses to the connected organisational intranet, or to block certain addresses (such as pornography sites).
- Protocol. The router holds a table of acceptable protocols, such as TCP and/or UDP.
- Source port. The router will have a table of acceptable TCP ports. For example, electronic mail (SMTP) on port 25 could be acceptable, but remote login on port 543 will be blocked.
- Destination port. The router will have a table of acceptable TCP ports. For example, ftp on port 21 could be acceptable, but telnet connections on port 23 will be blocked.
- Rules. Other rules can be added to the system which define a mixture of the above. For example, a range of IP addresses can be allowed to transfer on a certain port, but another range can be blocked for this transfer.

| IP | TCP/UDP | | INCOMING | | OUTGOING | |
|----|---------|---|----------|-----------|----------|-----------|
| | | | Allowed | Disallowed | Allowed | Disallowed |
| | | Protocol (TCP/UDP) | | | | |
| | | Source Port | | | | |
| | | Destination Port | | | | |
| | | Source IP address | | | | |
| | | Destination IP address | | | | |

**Figure 15.9** Filtering routers

Filter routers are either tightly bound when they are installed and then relaxed, or are relaxed and then bound. The type depends on the type of organisation. For example, a financial institution will have a very strict router which will allow very little traffic, apart from the authorised traffic. The router can be opened-up when the systems have been proved to be secure (they can also be closed quickly when problems occur).

An open organisation, such as an education institution will typically have an open system, where users are allowed to access any location on any port, and external users are allowed any access to the internal network. This can then be closed slowly when internal or external users breach the security or access unauthorised information. For example, if a student is accessing a pornographic site consistently then the IP address for that site could be blocked (this method is basically closing the door after the horse has bolted).

To most users the filtering router is an excellent method of limited traffic access, but to the determined hacker it can be easily breached, as the hacker can fake both IP addresses and also port addresses. It is extremely easy for a hacker to write their own TCP/IP driver software to address whichever IP address, and port numbers that they want.

## 15.9 Extranets

Extranets (external Intranets) allow two or more companies to share parts of their Intranets related to joint projects. For example, two companies may be working on a common project, an Extranet would allow them to share files related with the project.

## 15.10 Exercises

The following questions are multiple choice. Please select from a–d.

**15.10.1** Which of the following best describes an Intranet:

    (a)    A company specific network using company designed tools
    (b)    A local internet which is isolated from the Internet
    (c)    A totally incompatible system to the Internet
    (d)    A faster version of the Internet

**15.10.2** The main function of a firewall is:

    (a)    To disallow unwanted users into the network and allow wanted traffic
    (b)    To allow users access to the Internet
    (c)    To allow faster transfer of data between the Intranet and the Internet

(d)     Convert one type of network to connect to another type

**15.10.3**   Which of the following best describes a proxy:

(a)     It connects to a number of clients and acts on behalf of other
        clients and sends requests from the clients to a server
(b)     A server that acts as if it is the destination server
(c)     It passes messages to the client or server without modifying them
(d)     It stores responses

**15.10.4**   Which of the following best describes a gateway:

(a)     It connects to a number of clients and acts on behalf of other
        clients and sends requests from the clients to a server
(b)     A server that acts as if it is the destination server
(c)     It passes messages to the client or server without modifying them
(d)     It stores responses

**15.10.5**   Which of the following best describes a tunnel:

(a)     It connects to a number of clients and acts on behalf of other
        clients and sends requests from the clients to a server
(b)     A server that acts as if it is the destination server
(c)     It passes messages to the client or server without modifying them
(d)     It stores responses

**15.10.6**   Which TCP/IP application would be blocked if port 23 was blocked:

(a)     TELNET              (b)     FTP
(c)     WWW (HTTP)          (d)     Electronic Mail (SMTP)

**15.10.7**   Which TCP/IP application would be blocked if port 80 was blocked:

(a)     TELNET              (b)     FTP
(c)     WWW (HTTP)          (d)     Electronic Mail (SMTP)

**15.10.8**   Which is the best method of securing transmitted/received data:

(a)     Firewalls           (b)     Encryption
(c)     Proxy servers       (d)     Leased lines

# 16 HTTP

## 16.1 Introduction

Chapter 13 discussed the WWW. The foundation protocol of the WWW is the Hypertext Transfer Protocol (HTTP) which can be used in any client/server application involving hypertext. It is used on the WWW for transmitting information using hypertext jumps and can support the transfer of plaintext, hypertext, audio, images, or any Internet-compatible information. The most recently defined standard is HTTP 1.1, which has been defined by the IETF standard.

HTTP is a stateless protocol where each transaction is independent of any previous transactions. The advantage of being stateless is that it allows the rapid access of WWW pages over several widely distributed servers. It uses the TCP protocol to establish a connection between a client and a server for each transaction then terminates the connection once the transaction completes.

HTTP also supports many different formats of data. Initially a client issues a request to a server which may include a prioritised list of formats that it can handle. This allows new formats to be easily added and also prevents the transmission of unnecessary information.

A client's WWW browser (the user agent) initially establishes a direct connection with destination server which contains the required WWW page. To make this connection the client initiates a TCP connection between the client and the server. After this is established the client then issues an HTTP request, such as the specific command (the method), the URL, and possibly extra information such as request parameters or client information. When the server receives the request, it attempts to perform the requested action. It then returns an HTTP response, which includes status information, a success/error code, and extra information itself. After the client receives this, the TCP connection is closed.

## 16.2 Caches, tunnels and user agents

In a computer system, a cache is an area of memory that stores information likely to be accessed in a fast access memory area. For example, a cache controller takes a guess on which information the process is likely to access next. When the processor wishes to access the disk then, if it has guessed right it will load, the cache controller will load from the electronic memory rather than loading it from the disk. A WWW cache stores cacheable responses so that there is a reduction in network traffic and an improvement in access times.

Tunnels are intermediary devices which act as a blind relay between two connections. When the tunnel becomes active, it is not seen to be part of the HTTP communications. When the connection is closed by both sides, the tunnel ceases to exit.

A user agent, in HTTP, is a client which initiates requests to a server. Typically this is a WWW browser or a WWW spider (an automated WWW trailing program).

## 16.3 HTTP messages

HTTP messages are either requests from clients to servers or responses from servers to clients. The message is either a simple-request, a simple-response, full-request or a full-response. HTTP Version 0.9 defines the simple request/ response messages whereas HTTP Version 1.1 defines full requests/responses.

### 16.3.1 Simple requests/responses

The simple request is a GET command with the requested URI such as:

```
GET  /info/dept/courses.html
```

The simple response is a block containing the information identified in the URI (called the entity-body).

### 16.3.2 Full requests/responses

Very few security measures or enhanced services are built into the simple requests/responses. HTTP Version 1.0/1.1 improves on the simple requests/ responses by adding many extra requests and responses, as well as adding extra information about the data supported. Each message header consists of a number of fields which begin on a new line and consist of the field name followed by a colon and the field value. This follows the format of RFC 822 (as shown in Section 22.5.4) and allows for MIME encoding. It is thus similar to MIME-encoded email. A full request starts with a request line command (such as GET, MOVE or DELETE) and is then followed by one or more of the following:

- General-headers which contain general fields that do not apply to the entity being transferred (such as MIME version, date, and so on).
- Request-headers which contain information on the request and the client (e.g. the client's name, its authorisation, and so on).
- Entity-headers which contain information about the resource identified by the request and entity-body information (such as the type of encoding, the language, the title, the time when it was last modified, the type of resource it is, when it expires, and so on).
- Entity-body which contains the body of the message (such as HTML text, an image, a sound file, and so on).

A full response starts with a response status code (such as OK, Moved Temporarily, Accepted, Created, Bad Request, and so on) and is then followed by one or more of the following:

- General-headers, as with requests, contain general fields which do not apply to the entity being transferred (MIME version, date, and so on).
- Response-headers which contain information on the response and the server (e.g. the server's name, its location and the time the client should retry the server).
- Entity-headers, as with request, which contain information about the resource identified by the request and entity-body information (such as the type of encoding, the language, the title, the time when it was last modified, the type of resource it is, when it expires, and so on).
- Entity-body, as with requests, which contains the body of the message (such as HTML text, an image, a sound file, and so on).

The following example shows an example request. The first line is always the request method, in this case it is GET. Next there are various headers. The general-header field is Content-Type, the request-header fields are If-Modified-Since and From. There are no entity parts to the message as the request is to get an image (if the command had been to PUT then there would have been an attachment with the request). Notice that a single blank line delimits the end of the message as this indicates the end of a request/response. Note that the headers are case sensitive, thus Content-Type with the correct types of letters (and GET is always in uppercase letters).

---

📖 **Example HTTP request**

```
GET mypic.jpg
Content-Type: Image/jpeg
If-Modified-Since: 06 Mar 1997 12:35:00
From: Fred Bloggs <FREDB@ACOMP.CO.UK>
```

---

**Request messages**

The most basic request message is to GET a URI. HTTP/1.1 adds many more requests including:

| | | | | |
|------|--------|---------|-------|------|
| COPY | DELETE | GET | HEAD | POST |
| LINK | MOVE | OPTIONS | PATCH | PUT |
| TRACE | UNLINK | WRAPPED | | |

As before, the GET method requests a WWW page. The HEAD method tells the server that the client wants to read only the header of the WWW page. If the If-Modified-Since field is included then the server checks the specified date with the date of the URI and verifies whether it has not changed since then.

A PUT method requests storage of a WWW page and POST appends to a named resource (such as electronic mail). LINK connects two existing resources and UNLINK breaks the link. A DELETE method removes a WWW page.

The request-header fields are mainly used to define the acceptable type of entity that can be received by the client; they include:

| | | |
|--------|----------------|-----------------|
| Accept | Accept-Charset | Accept-Encoding |

```
Accept-Language        Authorization          From
Host                   If-Modified-Since      Referer
Proxy-Authorization    Range
Unless                 User-Agent
```

The `Accept` field is used to list all the media types and ranges that client can accept. An `Accept-Charset` field defines a list of character sets acceptable to the server and `Accept-Encoding` is a list of acceptable content encodings (such as the compression or encryption technique). The `Accept-Language` field defines a set of preferred natural languages.

The `Authorization` field has a value which authenticates the client to the server. A `From` field defines the email address of the user who is using the client (e.g. `From: fred.blogg@anytown.uk`) and the `Host` field specifies the name of the host of the resource being requested.

A useful field is the `If-Modified-Since` field, used with the `GET` method. It defines a date and time parameter and specifies that the resource should not be sent if it has not been modified since the specified time. This is useful when a client has a local copy of the resource in a local cache and, rather than transmitting the unchanged resource, it can use its own local copy.

The `Proxy-Authorization` field is used by the client to identify itself to a proxy when the proxy requires authorisation. A `Range` field is used with the `GET` message to get only a part of the resource.

The `Referer` field defines the URI of the resource from which the `Request-URI` was obtained and enables the server to generate lists of back-links. An `Unless` field is used to make a comparison based on any entity-header field value rather than a date/time value (as with `GET` and `If-Modified-Since`).

The `User-Agent` field contains information about the user agent originating this request.

## Response messages

In HTTP/0.9 the response from the server was either the entity or no response. HTTP/1.1 includes many other responses. These include:

```
Accepted                         Bad Gateway
Bad Request                      Conflict
Continue                         Created
Forbidden                        Gateway Timeout
Gone                             Internal Server Error
Length Required                  Method Not Allowed
Moved Permanently                Moved Temporarily
Multiple Choices                 No Content
Non-Authoritative Info           None Acceptable
Not Found                        Not Implemented
Not Modified                     OK
Partial Content                  Payment Required
Proxy Authorization Required     Request Timeout
Reset Content                    See Other
Service Unavailable              Switching Protocols
Unauthorized                     Unless True
Use Proxy
```

These responses can be put into five main groupings:

- Client error – Bad Request, Conflict, Forbidden, Gone, Payment required, Not Found, Method Not Allowed, None Acceptable, Proxy Authentication Required, Request Timeout, Length Required, Unauthorized, Unless True.
- Informational – Continue, Switching Protocol.
- Redirection – Moved Permanently, Moved Temporarily, Multiple Choices, See Other, Not Modified, User Proxy.
- Server error – Bad Gateway, Internal Server Error, Not Implemented, Service Unavailable, Gateway Timeout.
- Successful – Accepted, Created, OK, Non-Authoritative Info. The OK field is used when the request succeeds and includes the appropriate response information.

The response header fields are:

```
Location          Proxy-Authenticate        Public
Retry-After       Server                    WWW-Authenticate
```

The Location field defines the location of the resource identified by the Request-URI. A Proxy-Authenticate field contains the status code of the Proxy Authorization Required response.

The Public field defines non-standard methods supported by this server. A Retry-After field contains values which define the amount of time a service will be unavailable (and is thus sent with the Service Unavailable response).

The WWW-Authenticate field contains the status code for the Unauthorized response.

### General-header fields

General-header fields are used either within requests or within responses; they include:

```
Cache-Control    Connection      Date      Forwarded
Keep-Alive       MIME-Version    Pragma    Upgrade
```

The Cache-Control field gives information on the caching mechanism and stops the cache controller from modifying the request/response. A Connection field specifies the header field names that apply to the current TCP connection.

The Date field specifies the date and time at which the message originated; this is obviously useful when examining the received message as it gives an indication of the amount of time the message took to arrive at is destination. Gateways and proxies use the Forwarded field to indicate intermediate steps between the client and the server. When a gateway or proxy reads the message, it can attach a Forwarded field with its own URI (this can help in tracing the route of a message).

The Keep-Alive field specifies that the requester wants a persistent connection. It may indicate the maximum amount of time that the sender will wait for the next request before closing the connection. It can also be used to specify the maximum number of additional requests on the current persistent connection.

The MIME-Version field indicates the MIME version (such as MIME-Version: 1.0). A Pragma field contains extra information for specific applications.

In a request the Upgrade field specifies the additional protocols that the client supports and wishes to use, whereas in a response it indicates the protocol to be used.

**Entity-header fields**

Depending on the type of request or response, an entity-header can be included:

```
Allow                Content-Encoding         Content-Language
Content-Length       Content-MD5              Content-Range
Content-Type         Content-Version          Derived-From
Expires              Last-Modified            Link
Title                Transfer-encoding
URI-Header extension-header
```

The Allow field defines the supported methods supported by the resource identified in the Request-URI. A Content-Encoding field indicates content encodings, such as ZIP compression, that have been applied to the resource (Content-Encoding: zip).

The Content-Language field identifies natural language(s) of the intended audience for the enclosed entity (e.g. Content-language: German) and the Content-Length field defines the number of bytes in the entity.

The Content-Range field designates a portion of the identified resource that is included in this response, while Content-Type indicates the media type of the entity body (such as Content-Type=text/html, Content-Type=text/plain, Content-Type=image/gif or Content-type=image/jpeg). The version of the entity is defined in the Content-Version field.

The Expires field defines the date and time when the entity is considered stale. The Last-Modified field is the date and time when the resource was last modified.

The Link field defines other links and the Title field defines the title for the entity. A Transfer-Encoding field indicates the transformation type that is applied so the entity can be transmitted.

## 16.4 Exercises

**16.4.1** Which field is used to define the media type (such as JPEG, GIF, MPEG, and so on) of the entity:

    (a)   Content-Encoding    (b)   Content-Range
    (c)   Content-Type    (d)   Content-Language

**16.4.2** Which field is used to define the additional compression (zip) that has been applied to the entity:

|     |                  |     |                  |
|-----|------------------|-----|------------------|
| (a) | Content-Encoding | (b) | Content-Range    |
| (c) | Content-Type     | (d) | Content-Language |

**16.4.3** Which field does the GET method use to determine if a resource has changed since it was last accessed:

|     |                 |     |                  |
|-----|-----------------|-----|------------------|
| (a) | Accept          | (b) | If-Modified-Since |
| (c) | Accept-Encoding | (d) | Authorization    |

**16.4.4** Discuss the limitation of simple requests and responses with HTTP.

**16.4.5** Discuss request messages and the fields that are set.

**16.4.6** Discuss response messages and the fields that are set.

## 16.5 HTTP reference

### 16.5.1 Method definitions

The main methods are:

- GET. Retrieves the information that is defined in the Request-URI. If the request message includes an If-Modified-Since header field, the GET is conditional on the date and time that is defined in the If-Modified-Since header. Conditional GETs allow cached system to be refreshed only when resources have been updated.
- HEAD. Identical to GET, but the server should not return any Entity-Body in the response. It can be used for obtaining information on the resource without actually receiving the Entity-Body. It can be used to test links for the accessibility, validity, and so on.
- POST. Used to request that the destination server accept the entity enclosed in the request as a subordinate of a resource. Typical applications are annotation existing resources and posting message to bulletin boards, newsgroups, and so on.
- PUT. Requests that the enclosed entity is stored under the supplied Request-URI. If the Request-URI is an existing resource, the enclosed entity is a considered as a modified version of the existing resource, else it is treated as a new resource.
- DELETE. Requests that the server deletes the resource identified by the Request-URI.
- LINK. Establishes one or more links between the existing resources and resources identified by the Request-URI.
- UNLINK. Opposite of LINK.

### 16.5.2 HTTP message

HTTP messages are text-based and are either requests from the client to the server, or are responses from the server to the client. The can either be Simple-

Requests/Responses (HTTP/0.9), such as:

GET   &lt;SPACE&gt; Request-URI      &lt;CRLF&gt;

or Full-Requests/Responses (HTTP/1.0 or HTTP/1.1), such as:

GET &lt;SPACE&gt; Request-URI &lt;SPACE&gt; HTTP-Version &lt;CRLF&gt;
HEAD &lt;SPACE&gt; Request-URI &lt;SPACE&gt; HTTP-Version &lt;CRLF&gt;
POST &lt;SPACE&gt; Request-URI &lt;SPACE&gt; HTTP-Version &lt;CRLF&gt;

Simple-Request format is discouraged as it prevents a server from identifying the media type of the returned entity. Both types can include optional header fields and an entity body. Entity bodies are separated from the headers by a null line.

HTTP header fields consist of a name followed by a colon (':'), then a space followed by the field values. They include:

- General-Headers. These are applicable for both request and response messages, but they do not apply to the entity being transferred.
- Request-Header. These allow clients to pass extra information about the request, and about itself, to the server. They act as request modifiers.
- Entity-Header. These define optional metainformation about the Entity-Body.
- Response-Header. These allow the server to pass additional information about the response which cannot be placed in the Status-Line.

### Date (General header)

The Date field represents the date and time of the transmitted message (in the same format as RFC822). An example is:

Date: Wed, 30 Dec 1998 15:22:15 GMT

### Pragma (General header)

The Pragma field is used to include implementation-specific directives that may apply to any recipient along the request/response chain. An example is:

pragma-directive = no-cache

which allows a client to refresh a cached copy which is known to be corrupted or stale.

### Authourization (Request-Header)

The Authourization field authenticates a user agent to a server. The server sends a challenge to the user agent, based on a user-ID and a password for each realm (a sting). The user agent must return back a valid user-ID and password for the Request-URI (this is the basic authentication scheme).

When the server receives an unauthorised request for a URI, the server responds with a challenge, such as:

WWW-Authenticate: Basic realm="FredServer"

where "FredServer" is the realm to identify the protection space of the Request-URI. The client must then send back its user-ID and password, separated by a single colon character, and using base64 encoded (see Section 22.7.4). An example may be:

Authorization: Basic A=IYaacZZP===GSpKQarcc3 1pacbu

### From (Request-Header)

The From field contains an Internet e-mail address of the owner of the requesting user agent, such as:

From: fred_b@myserver.com

It is typically used for logging purposes.

### If-Modified-Since (Request-header)

The If-Modified-Since field is used with the GET to define that a GET is conditional on the date that the resource was last modified. If it was not modified since the specified data then the resource is not sent in the Entity-Body and a 304 response (Not Modified) is sent. An example of this field is:

If-Modified-Since: Wed, 30 Dec 1998 15:22:15 GMT

### Referer (Request-Header)

The Referer field allows the client to specify the address (URI) from which it from which the Request-URI was obtained. This allows the server to trace referenced links. An example of this field is:

Referer: http://www.w3.org/hypertext/DataSources/Overview.html

### User-Agent (Request-Header)

The User-Agent field contains information about the user agent originating the request. It is normal used for tracing and logging purposes.

### Location (Response-header)

The Location field defines the resource location that was specified in the Request-URI. An example of this field is:

Location: http://www.myserver.com/test/newlink.html

### Server (Response-header)

The Server field contains information about the software which is used by the origin server to handle the request. An example of this field is:

Server: CERN/3.0 libwww/2.17

## WWW-Authenticate (Response-header)

See Authorization.

## Allow (Entity-header)

The Allow field lists the set of methods supported by the resource identified by the Request-URI. An example of this field is:

Allow: GET, HEAD

## Content-Encoding (Entity-header)

The Content-Encoding field describes the type of encoding used in the entity. It indicates the additional content coding has been applied to the resource. In most cases the encoding is 'gzip' or 'x-compress' (or 'x-gzip' and 'compress'). The Content-Type header field defines the underlying content. An example of this field is:

Content-Encoding: x-gzip
Content-Type=text/plain

where the content type is plain text, which has been zipped with gzip (a Lempel-Ziv based compression program). The x-compress program uses Lempel-Ziv-Welsh (LZW) compression.

## Content-Length (Entity-header)

The Content-Length field defines the number of bytes in the Entity-Body. An example is:

Content-Length: 4095

## Content-Type (Entity-header)

The Content-Type field defines the media type of the Entity-Body sent to the recipient An example of the field is:

Content-type: text/plain; charset=ISO-8859-1

Content-Types are of the format *type/subject*. Typical types are 'application', 'image', 'text', 'audio' and 'video', and example content types are:

```
text/plain                  text/enriched           image/gif
image/jpeg                  audio/basic             video/mpeg
application/octet-stream    application/postscript
application/msword          application/rtf
```

## Expires (Entity-header)

The Expires field defines the date and time after which the entity should be considered as stale. An example of the field is:

Expires: Wed, 30 Dec 1998 15:22:15 GMT

### Last-Modified (Entity-header)

The Last-Modified indicates the date and time the resource was last modified. An example of the field is:

Last-Modified: Wed, 23 Dec 1998 03:20:25 GMT

### Content-language (Entity-header)

The Language field defines the language of the resource. It format is *Language-tag*, where *Language* is the language (such as en for English), and *tag* is the dialect. For example:

Content-type: audio/basic
Content-Language: en-scottish

### *16.5.3 Status codes*

### Informational 1xx

The Informational status codes indicate a provisional response. They are typically used for experimental purposes.

### Successful 2xx

The successful status codes indicate that a client's request has been successful. These include:

| | |
|---|---|
| 200 (OK) | Request succeeded. Information returned depends on the method used. With GET, the requested entity is sent in the response. |
| 201 (Created) | New resource has been created. The new created resource is defined in the URI returned in the entity of the response. |
| 202 (Accepted) | Request has been accepted for processing, but the processing is continuing. |
| 204 (No Content) | Successful implementation, but there is no new information to be sent back. |

### Redirection 3xx

The redirection status code indicates that further action is required to fulfil the request. These include:

| | |
|---|---|
| 300 (Multiple Choices) | Request resource is available from one or more locations. If the server has a preference it add a Location field with the preferred URL. |

301 (Moved Permanently)

        Requested resource has been assigned a new permanent URL. Future references should be made to the specified URL, which is located in the Location field.

302 (Moved Temporarily)

        Requested resource has temporarily move to another URL. The calling agent should still use the URI given in the Request-URI.

304 (Not Modified)  This is sent when the client issues a GET request with the If-Modified-Since field is set to a given time, and the document has not modified since the time specified.

## Client Error 4xx

The client error status codes indicate that an error has occurred on the client. These include:

400 (Bad Request)  Request cannot be understood by the server due to bad syntax.

401 (Unauthorized)  Request requires user authentication. A response includes the WWW-Authenticate header field, which contains a challenge for the requested resource. The client must then repeat the request with a suitable Authorization header field.

403 (Forbidden)  Server will not fulfil the request. It is typically used when the server does not want to reveal the reason why it is not fulfilling the request.

404 (Not Found)  Server did not find the required Request-URI.

## Server Error 5xx

The server error status codes indicate that there is an error with the server.

500 (Internal Server Error)

        Unexpected server condition in fulfilling the request.

501 (Not Implemented)

        Server does not support the request.

502 (Bad Gateway)  Server, while acting as a gateway or proxy, received an invalid response from the upstream server it accessed in attempting to fulfil the request.

503 (Service Unavailable)

        Server is currently unable, possibly because of server maintenance or overloading.

# 17 Data Encryption Principles

## 17.1 Introduction

The increase in electronic mail has also increased the need for secure data transmission. An electronic mail message can be easily incepted as it transverses the world's communication networks. Thus there is a great need to encrypt the data contained in it. Traditional mail messages tend to be secure as they are normally taken by a courier or postal service and transported in a secure environment from source to destination. Over the coming years more individuals and companies will be using electronic mail systems and these must be totally secure.

Data encryption involves the science of cryptographics (note that the word *crytopgraphy* is derived from the Greek words which means hidden, or secret, writing). The basic object of cryptography is to provide a mechanism for two people to communicate without any other person being able to read the message.

Encryption is mainly applied to text transmission as binary data can be easily scrambled so it becomes almost impossible to unscramble. This is because text-based information contains certain key pointers:

- Most lines of text have the words 'the', 'and', 'of' and 'to'.
- Every line has a full stop.
- Words are separated by a space (the space character is the most probable character in a text document).
- The characters 'e', 'a' and 'i' are more probable than 'q', 'z' and 'x'.

Thus to decode a message an algorithm is applied and the decrypted text is then tested to determine whether it contains standard English (or the required language).

## 17.2 Government pressure

Many institutions and individuals read data which is not intended for them; they include:

- Government departments. Traditionally governments around the world have reserved the right to tap into any communications which they think may be against the national interest.
- Spies who tap into communications for industrial or governmental information.
- Individuals who like to read other people's messages.
- Individuals who 'hack' into systems and read secure information.

280

- Criminals who intercept information in order to use it for crime, such as intercepting PIN numbers on bankcards.

Governments around the world tend to be against the use of encryption as it reduces their chances to tap into information and determine messages. It is also the case that governments do not want other countries to use encryption because it also reduces their chances of reading their secret communications (especially military manoeuvres). In order to reduce this threat they must do either of the following:

- Prevent the use of encryption.
- Break the encryption code.
- Learn everyone's cryptographic keys.

Many implementations of data encryption are in hardware, but increasingly it is implemented in software (especially public-key methods). This makes it easier for governments to control their access. For example the US government has proposed to beat encryption by trying to learn everyone's cryptographic key with the Clipper chip. The US government keeps a record of all the serial numbers and encryption keys for each Clipper chip manufactured.

## 17.3 Cryptography

The main object of cryptography is to provide a mechanism for two (or more) people to communicate without anyone else being able to read the message. Along with this it can provide other services, such as:

- Giving a reassuring integrity check – this makes sure the message has not been tampered with by non-legitimate sources.
- Providing authentication – this verifies the sender identity.

Initially plaintext is encrypted into ciphertext, it is then decrypted back into plaintext, as illustrated in Figure 17.1. Cryptographic systems tend to use both an algorithm and a secret value, called the key. The requirement for the key is that it is difficult to keep devising new algorithms and also to tell the receiving party that the data is being encrypted with the new algorithm. Thus, using keys, there are no problems with everyone having the encryption/decryption system, because without the key it is very difficult to decrypt the message.

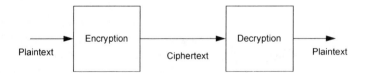

**Figure 17.1** Encryption/decryption process

### 17.3.1 Public key versus private key

The encryption process can either use a public key or a secret key. With a secret key the key is only known to the two communicating parties. This key can be fixed or can be passed from the two parties over a secure communications link (perhaps over the postal network or a leased line). The two most popular private key techniques are DES (Data Encryption Standard) and IDEA (International Data Encryption Algorithm).

In public-key encryption, each user has both a public and a private key. The two users can communicate because they know each other's public keys. Normally in a public-key system, each user uses a public enciphering transformation which is widely known and a private deciphering transform which is known only to that user. The private transformation is described by a private key, and the public transformation by a public key derived from the private key by a one-way transformation. The RSA (after its inventors Rivest, Shamir and Adleman) technique is one of the most popular public-key techniques and is based on the difficulty of factoring large numbers. It is discussed in more detail in Chapter 18.

### 17.3.2 Computational difficulty

Every code is crackable and the measure of the security of a code is the amount of time it takes persons not addressed in the code to break that code. Normally to break the code a computer tries all the possible keys until it finds a match. Thus a 1-bit code would only have 2 keys, a 2-bit code would have 4 keys, and so on. Table 17.1 shows the number of keys as a function of the number of bits in the key. It can be seen that a 64-bit code has:

18 400 000 000 000 000 000

different keys. If one key is tested every 10 μs then it would take $1.84 \times 10^{14}$ seconds ($5.11 \times 10^{10}$ hours or $2.13 \times 10^{8}$ days or 5 834 602 years). So, for example, if it takes 1 million years for a person to crack the code then it can be considered safe. Unfortunately the performance of computer systems increases by the year. For example if a computer takes 1 million years to crack a code, then assuming an increase in computing power of a factor of 2 per year, then it would only take 500 000 years the next year. Table 17.2 almost shows that after almost 20 years it would take only 1 year to decrypt the same message.

The increasing power of computers is one factor in reducing the processing time, another is the increasing usage of parallel processing. Data decryption is well suited to parallel processing as each processor or computer can be assigned a number of keys to check the encrypted message. Each of them can then work independently of the other (this differs from many applications in parallel processing which suffer from interprocess(or) communication). Table 17.3 gives typical times, assuming a doubling of processing power each year, for processor arrays of 1, 2, 4 ... 4096 elements. It can be seen that with an array of 4096 processing elements it takes only 7 years before the code is decrypted within 2 years. Thus an organisation which is serious about decripering messages will have the resources to invest in large arrays of processors or networked computers. It is likely that many governments have computer systems with thousands or tens of thousands of processors operating in parallel. A prime use of these systems will be in decrypting messages.

**Table 17.1** Number of keys related to the number of bits in the key

| Code size | Number of keys | Code size | Number of keys | Code size | Number of keys |
|---|---|---|---|---|---|
| 1 | 2 | 12 | 4 096 | 52 | $4.5 \times 10^{15}$ |
| 2 | 4 | 16 | 65 536 | 56 | $7.21 \times 10^{16}$ |
| 3 | 8 | 20 | 1 048 576 | 60 | $1.15 \times 10^{18}$ |
| 4 | 16 | 24 | 16 777 216 | 64 | $1.84 \times 10^{19}$ |
| 5 | 32 | 28 | $2.68 \times 10^{8}$ | 68 | $2.95 \times 10^{20}$ |
| 6 | 64 | 32 | $4.29 \times 10^{9}$ | 72 | $4.72 \times 10^{21}$ |
| 7 | 128 | 36 | $6.87 \times 10^{10}$ | 76 | $7.56 \times 10^{22}$ |
| 8 | 256 | 40 | $1.1 \times 10^{12}$ | 80 | $1.21 \times 10^{24}$ |
| 9 | 512 | 44 | $1.76 \times 10^{13}$ | 84 | $1.93 \times 10^{25}$ |
| 10 | 1 024 | 48 | $2.81 \times 10^{14}$ | 88 | $3.09 \times 10^{26}$ |

**Table 17.2** Time to decrypt a message assuming an increase in computing power

| Year | Time to decrypt (years) | Year | Time to decrypt (years) |
|---|---|---|---|
| 0 | 1 million | 10 | 977 |
| 1 | 500 000 | 11 | 489 |
| 2 | 250 000 | 12 | 245 |
| 3 | 125 000 | 13 | 123 |
| 4 | 62 500 | 14 | 62 |
| 5 | 31 250 | 15 | 31 |
| 6 | 15 625 | 16 | 16 |
| 7 | 7 813 | 17 | 8 |
| 8 | 3 907 | 18 | 4 |
| 9 | 1 954 | 19 | 2 |

**Table 17.3** Time to decrypt a message with increasing power and parallel processing

| Processors | Year 0 | Year 1 | Year 2 | Year 3 | Year 4 | Year 5 | Year 6 | Year 7 |
|---|---|---|---|---|---|---|---|---|
| 1 | 1 000 000 | 500 000 | 250 000 | 125 000 | 62 500 | 31 250 | 15 625 | 7 813 |
| 2 | 500 000 | 250 000 | 125 000 | 62 500 | 31 250 | 15 625 | 7 813 | 3 907 |
| 4 | 250 000 | 125 000 | 62 500 | 31 250 | 15 625 | 7 813 | 3 907 | 1 954 |
| 8 | 125 000 | 62 500 | 31 250 | 15 625 | 7 813 | 3 907 | 1 954 | 977 |
| 16 | 62 500 | 31 250 | 15 625 | 7 813 | 3 907 | 1 954 | 977 | 489 |
| 32 | 31 250 | 15 625 | 7 813 | 3 907 | 1 954 | 977 | 489 | 245 |
| 64 | 15 625 | 7 813 | 3 907 | 1 954 | 977 | 489 | 245 | 123 |
| 128 | 7 813 | 3 907 | 1 954 | 977 | 489 | 245 | 123 | 62 |
| 256 | 3 906 | 1 953 | 977 | 489 | 245 | 123 | 62 | 31 |
| 512 | 1 953 | 977 | 489 | 245 | 123 | 62 | 31 | 16 |
| 1 024 | 977 | 489 | 245 | 123 | 62 | 31 | 16 | 8 |
| 2 048 | 488 | 244 | 122 | 61 | 31 | 16 | 8 | 4 |
| 4 096 | 244 | 122 | 61 | 31 | 16 | 8 | 4 | 2 |

## 17.4  Legal issues

Patent laws and how they are implemented vary around the world. Like many good ideas, patents cover most of the cryptographic techniques. The main commercial techniques are:

- DES (Data Encryption Standard) which is patented but royalty-free.
- IDEA (International Data Encryption Algorithm) which is also patented and royalty-free for the non-commercial user.

Access to a global network normally requires the use of a public key. The most popular public-key algorithm is one developed at MIT and is named RSA (after its inventors Rivest, Shamir and Adleman). All public-key algorithms are patented, and most of the important patents have been acquired by Public Key Partners (PKP). As the US government funded much of the work, there are no license fees for US government use. RSA is only patented in the US, but Public Key Partners (PKP) claim that the international Hellman-Merkle patent also covers RSA. The patent on RSA runs out in the year 2000. Public keys are generated by licensing software from a company called RSA Data Security Inc. (RSADSI).

The other widely used technique is Digital Signature Standard (DSS). It is freely licensable but in many respects it is technically inferior to RSA. The free licensing means that it is not necessary to reach agreement with RSADSI or PKP. Since it was announced, PKP have claimed the Helleman-Merkle patent covers all public-key cryptography. It has also strengthened its position by acquiring rights to a patent by Schnorr which is closely related to DSS.

## 17.5  Cracking the code

A cryptosystem converts plaintext into ciphertext using a key. There are several methods that a hacker can use to crack a code, including:

- Known plaintext attack. Where the hacker knows part of the ciphertext and the corresponding plaintext. The known ciphertext and plaintext can then be used to decrypt the rest of the ciphertext.
- Chosen-ciphertext. Where the hacker sends a message to the target, this is then encrypted with the target's private-key and the hacker then analyses the encrypted message. For example, a hacker may send an email to the encryption file server and the hacker spies on the delivered message.
- Exhaustive search. Where the hacker uses brute force to decrypt the ciphertext and tries every possible key.
- Active attack. Where the hacker inserts or modifies messages.
- Man-in-the-middle. Where the hacker is hidden between two parties and impersonates each of them to the other.
- The replay system. Where the hacker takes a legitimate message and sends it into the network at some future time.

- Cut and paste. Where the hacker mixes parts of two different encrypted messages and, sometimes, is able to create a new message. This message is likely to make no sense, but may trick the receiver into doing something that helps the hacker.
- Time resetting. Some encryption schemes use the time of the computer to create the key. Resetting this time or determining the time that the message was created can give some useful information to the hacker.
- Time attack. This involves determining the amount of time that a user takes to de-crypt the message, from this the key can be found.

## 17.6 Random number generators

One way to crack a code is to exploit a weakness in the generation of the encryption key. The hacker can then guess which keys are more likely to occur. This is known as a statistical attack.

Many programming languages use a random number generator which is based on the current system time (such as rand()). This method is no good in data encryption as the hacker can simply determine the time that the message was encrypted and the algorithm used.

An improved source of randomness is the time between two keystrokes (as used in PGP – pretty good privacy). However this system has been criticised as a hacker can spy on a user over a network and determine the time between keystrokes. Other sources of true randomness have also been investigated, including noise from an electronic device and noise from an audio source.

## 17.7 Letter probabilities

The English language has a great deal of redundancy in it, thus common occurrences in text can be coded with short bit sequences. The probability of each letter also varies. For example the letter 'e' occurs many more times than the letter 'z'. Program 17.1 determines the number of occurrences of the characters from 'a' to 'z' in an example text input. Sample run 17.1 shows a sample run with an example piece of text. It can be seen that the most common character in the text is an 'e' (30 occurrences), followed by a 't' (22 occurrences), followed by 'a' (17 occurrences).

📄 **Program 17.1**
```
#include    <stdio.h>
#include    <string.h>

int   get_occurances(char c, char txt[]);

int   main(void)
{
char  ch, text[BUFSIZ];
int   occ;
```

```
printf("Enter text >>");
gets(text);

for (ch='a';ch<='z';ch++)
{
    occ=get_occurances(ch,text);
    printf("%c %d\n",ch,occ);
}
return(0);
}

int    get_occurances(char c, char txt[])
{
int    occ=0,i;

for (i=0;i<strlen(txt);i++)
    if (c==txt[i]) occ++;
return(occ);
}
```

---

🖥 **Sample run 17.1**

```
Enter text >>  this is an example text input to determine the number of
occurrences of a character within a piece of text. it shows how the
characters used in the english language vary in their occurrences. the e
character is the most common character in the english language.
a 17
b 1
c 16
d 2
e 30
f 3
g 6
h 17
i 15
j 0
k 0
l 5
m 5
n 15
o 11
p 3
q 0
r 16
s 12
t 22
u 7
v 1
w 3
x 3
y 1
z 0
```

---

Program 17.8 in Section 17.11 gives a simple C program which determines the probability of letters within a text file. This program can be used to determine typical letter probabilities. Sample run 17.2 shows a sample run using some sample text. It can be seen that the highest probability is with the letter 'e', which occurs, on average, 94.3 times every 1000 letters. Table 17.4 lists the letters in order of their probability. Notice that the letters which are worth the least in the popular board game Scrabble (such as, 'e', 't', 'a', and so on) are the most probable and the letters with the highest scores (such as 'x', 'z' and 'q') are the least probable.

```
Char. Occur. Prob.
  a    1963   0.0672
  b     284   0.0097
  c     914   0.0313
  d     920   0.0315
  e    2752   0.0943
  f     471   0.0161
  g     473   0.0162
  h     934   0.0320
  i    1680   0.0576
  j      13   0.0004
  k      96   0.0033
  l     968   0.0332
  m     724   0.0248
  n    1541   0.0528
  o    1599   0.0548
  p     443   0.0152
  q      49   0.0017
  r    1410   0.0483
  s    1521   0.0521
  t    2079   0.0712
  u     552   0.0189
  v     264   0.0090
  w     383   0.0131
  x      57   0.0020
  y     278   0.0095
  z      44   0.0015
  .     292   0.0100
 SP    4474   0.1533
  ,     189   0.0065
```

**Table 17.4** Letters and their occurrence in a sample text file

| Character | Occurrences | Probability | Character | Occurrences | Probability |
|-----------|-------------|-------------|-----------|-------------|-------------|
| SPACE | 4474 | 0.1533 | g | 473 | 0.0162 |
| e | 2752 | 0.0943 | f | 471 | 0.0161 |
| t | 2079 | 0.0712 | p | 443 | 0.0152 |
| a | 1963 | 0.0672 | w | 383 | 0.0131 |
| i | 1680 | 0.0576 | . | 292 | 0.0100 |
| o | 1599 | 0.0548 | b | 284 | 0.0097 |
| n | 1541 | 0.0528 | y | 278 | 0.0095 |
| s | 1521 | 0.0521 | v | 264 | 0.0090 |
| r | 1410 | 0.0483 | , | 189 | 0.0065 |
| l | 968 | 0.0332 | k | 96 | 0.0033 |
| h | 934 | 0.0320 | x | 57 | 0.0020 |
| d | 920 | 0.0315 | q | 49 | 0.0017 |
| c | 914 | 0.0313 | z | 44 | 0.0015 |
| m | 724 | 0.0248 | j | 13 | 0.0004 |
| u | 552 | 0.0189 | | | |

## 17.8 Basic encryption principles

Encryption codes have been used for many centuries. They have tended to be used in military situations where secret messages have to be sent between troops without the risk of them being read by the enemy.

### 17.8.1 Alphabet shifting

A simple encryption code is to replace the letters with a shifted equivalent alphabet. For example moving the letters two places to the right gives:

```
ABCDEFGHIJKLMNOPQRSTUVWXYZ
YZABCDEFGHIJKLMNOPQRSTUVWX
```

Thus a message:

```
THE BOY STOOD ON THE BURNING DECK
```

would become:

```
RFC ZMW QRMMB ML RFC ZSPLGLE BCAI
```

This code has the problem of being reasonably easy to decode, as there are only 26 different code combinations. The first documented use of this type of code was by Julius Caesar who used a 3-letter shift.

### 17.8.2 Code mappings

Code mappings have no underlying mathematical relationship; they simply use a code-book to represent the characters, often known as a monoalphabetic code. An example could be:

```
Input:       abcdefghijklmnopqrstuvwxyz
Encrypted:   mgqoafzbcdiehxjklntqrwsuvy
```

Program 17.2 shows a C program which uses this code mapping to encrypt entered text and Sample run 17.3 shows a sample run.

The number of different character maps can be determined as follows:

- Take the letter 'A' then this can be mapped to 26 different letters.
- If 'A' is mapped to a certain letter then 'B' can only map to 25 letters.
- If 'B' is mapped to a certain letter then 'C' can be mapped to 24 letters.
- Continue until the alphabet is exhausted.

Thus, in general, the number of combinations will be:

$$26 \times 25 \times 24 \times 23 \dots 4 \times 3 \times 2 \times 1$$

Thus the code has 26! different character mappings (approximately $4.03 \times 10^{26}$). It suffers from the fact that the probabilities of the mapped characters will be similar to those in normal text. Thus if there is a large amount of text then the character having the highest probability will be either an 'e' or a 't'. The character with the lowest probability will tend to be a 'z' or a 'q' (which is also likely be followed by the character map for a 'u').

📄 **Program 17.2**

```
#include <stdio.h>
#include <ctype.h>

int    main(void)
{
int    key,ch,i=0,inch;
char   text[BUFSIZ];
char   input[26]="abcdefghijklmnopqrstuvwxyz";
char   output[26]="mgqoafzbcdiehxjklntqrwsuvy";

  printf("Enter text >>");
  gets(text);

  ch=text[0];
  do
  {
      if (ch!=' ')    inch=output[(tolower(ch)-'a')];
      else inch='#';

      putchar(inch);
      i++;
      ch=text[i];
  } while (ch!=NULL);
  return(0);
}
```

💻 **Sample run 17.3**

```
Enter text >> This is an example piece of text
qbct#ct#mx#aumhkea#kcaqa#jf#qauq
```

A code mapping encryption scheme is easy to implement but unfortunately, once it has been 'cracked', it is easy to decrypt the encrypted data. Normally this type of code is implemented with an extra parameter which changes its mapping, such as changing the code mapping over time depending on the time of day and/or date. Only parties which are allowed to decrypt the message know the mappings of the code to time and/or date. For example, each day of the week could have a different code mapping.

### 17.8.3 Applying a key

To make it easy to decrypt, a key is normally applied to the text. This makes it easy to decrypt the message if the key is known, but difficult to decrypt the message if the key is not known. An example of a key operation is to take each of the characters in a text message and then exclusive-OR (XOR) the character with a key value. For example the ASCII character 'A' has the bit pattern:

100 0001

and if the key had a value of 5 then 'A' exclusive-OR'ed with 5 would give:

| | |
|---|---|
| 'A' | 100 0001 |
| Key (5) | 000 0101 |
| Ex-OR | 100 0100 |

The bit pattern 100 0100 would be encrypted as character 'D'. Program 17.3 is a C program which can be used to display the alphabet of encrypted characters for a given key. In this program the ^ operator represents exclusive-OR. Sample run 17.4 shows a sample run with a key of 5. The exclusive-OR operator has the advantage that when applied twice it results in the original value (it thus changes a value, but does not loose any information when it operates on it).

🖹 **Program 17.3**

```c
#include <stdio.h>

int    main(void)
{
int    key,ch;

  printf("Enter key value >>");
  scanf("%d",&key);

  for (ch='A';ch<='Z';ch++)
      putchar(ch^key);

  return(0);
}
```

---

🖥 **Sample run 17.4**

```
Enter key value >> 5
DGFA@CBMLONIHKJUTWVQPSR]\_
```

---

Program 17.4 is an encryption program which reads some text from the keyboard, then encrypts it with a given key and saves the encrypted text to a file. Program 17.5 can then be used to read the encrypted file for a given key; only the correct key will give the correct results.

🖹 **Program 17.4**

```c
/* Encryt.c */
#include <stdio.h>

int    main(void)
{
FILE *f;
char   fname[BUFSIZ],str[BUFSIZ];
int    key,ch,i=0;

  printf("Enter output file name >>");
  gets(fname);

  if ((f=fopen(fname,"w"))==NULL)
  {
      puts("Cannot open input file");
      return(1);
  }
```

```
    printf("Enter text to be save to file>>");
    gets(str);

    printf("Enter key value >>");
    scanf("%d",&key);

    ch=str[0];

    do
    {
        ch=ch^key; /* Exclusive-OR character with itself */
        putc(ch,f);
        i++;
        ch=str[i];
    } while (ch!=NULL); /* test if end of string */
    fclose(f);
    return(0);
}
```

---

```
Enter output filename >> out.dat
Enter text to be saved to file>> The boy stood on the burning deck
Enter key value >> 3
```

---

File listing 17.1 gives a file listing for the saved encrypted text. One obvious problem with this coding is that the SPACE character is visible in the coding. As the SPACE character is 010 0000, the key can be determined by simply XORing 010 0000 with the '#' character, thus:

| | |
|---|---|
| SPACE | 010 0000 |
| '#' | <u>010 0011</u> |
| Key | <u>000 0011</u> |

Thus the key is 000 0011 (decimal 3).

---

📑 **File listing 17.1**
```
Wkf#alz#pwllg#lm#wkf#avqmjmd#gf`h
```

---

📄 **Program 17.5**
```
/* Decryt.c */
#include <stdio.h>
#include <ctype.h>
int   main(void)
{
FILE  *f;
char  fname[BUFSIZ];
int   key,ch;

    printf("Enter encrypted filename >>");
    gets(fname);
    if ((f=fopen(fname,"r"))==NULL)
    {
        puts("Cannot open input file");
        return(1);
    }
```

```
printf("Enter key value >>");
scanf("%d",&key);

do
{
    ch=getc(f);
    ch=ch^key;
    if (isascii(ch)) putchar(ch); /* only print ASCII char */
} while (!feof(f));
fclose(f);
return(0);
}
```

Program 17.6 uses the exclusive-OR operator and reads from an input file and outputs to an output file. The format of the run (assuming that the source code file is called key.c) is:

key *infile.dat outfile.enc*

where *infile.dat* is the name of the input file (text or binary) and *outfile.enc* is the name of the output file.

The great advantage of this program is that the same program is used for encryption and for decryption. Thus:

key *outfile.enc newfile.dat*

converts the encrypted file back into the original file.

📄 **Program 17.6**
```
#include <stdio.h>

int main(int argc, char *argv[])
{
FILE *in,*out;
char fname[BUFSIZ],key,ch,fout[BUFSIZ],fext[BUFSIZ],*str;

  printf("Enter key >>");
  scanf("%c",&key);

  if ((in=fopen(argv[1],"rb"))==NULL)
  {
      printf("Cannot open");
      return(1);
  }

  out=fopen(argv[2],"wb");

  do
  {
      fread(&ch,1,1,in); /* read a byte from the file */
      ch=((ch & 0xff) ^ (key & 0xff)) & 0xff;
      if (!feof(in)) fwrite(&ch,1,1,out); /* write a byte */

  } while (!feof(in));

  fclose(in); fclose(out);
}
```

### 17.8.4 *Applying a bit shift*

A typical method used to encrypt text is to shift the bits within each character. For example ASCII characters only use the lower 7 bits of an 8-bit character. Thus, shifting the bit positions one place to the left will encrypt the data to a different character. For a left shift a 0 or a 1 can be shifted into the least significant bit; for a right shift the least significant bit can be shifted into the position of the most significant bit. When shifting more than one position a rotate left or rotate right can be used. Note that most of the characters produced by shifting may not be printable, thus a text editor (or viewer) cannot be viewed them. For example, in C the characters would be processed with:

```
ch=ch << 1;
```

which shifts the bits of ch one place to the left, and decrypted by:

```
ch=ch >> 1;
```

which shifts the bits of ch one place to the right.

Program 17.7 gives an example of a program that reads in a text file (or any file), and reads it one byte at a time. For each byte the program rotates the bits 2 places to the left (with rot_left) and saves the byte.

📄 **Program 17.7**
```c
#include <stdio.h>

unsigned char rot_left(unsigned char ch);
unsigned char rot_right(unsigned char ch);

int main(int argc, char *argv[])
{
unsigned char ch;
int i;
FILE *in,*out;
char fname[BUFSIZ],fout[BUFSIZ],fext[BUFSIZ],*str;

  if ((in=fopen(argv[1],"rb"))==NULL)
  {
      printf("Cannot open");
      return(1);
  }

  out=fopen(argv[2],"wb");

  do
  {
      fread(&ch,1,1,in);    /* read a byte from the file */
      ch=rot_left(ch);      /* perform two left rotates */
      ch=rot_left(ch);
      if (!feof(in)) fwrite(&ch,1,1,out); /* write a byte */
  } while (!feof(in));

  fclose(in); fclose(out);
}

// rotate bits to the left
unsigned char rot_left(unsigned char ch)
{
```

```
unsigned char bit8;

  bit8=(ch & 0x80) & 0x80;
  ch=ch << 1;
  ch = ch | ((bit8>>7) & 0x01);
  return(ch);
}
/* rotate bits to the right */
unsigned char rot_right(unsigned char ch)
{
unsigned char bit1;

  bit1=(ch & 1) & 0x01;
  ch=ch >> 1;
  ch = ch | ((bit1<<7) & 0x80);
  return(ch);
}
```

For example the text:

```
Hello. This is some sample text.

Fred.
```

becomes:

```
! • ±±½ ˌ☐Q¡¥Í☐¥Í☐Í½µ • ☐Í…µÁ± • ☐Ñ • áÑ ˌ 4 (4 (☐É • ` ˌ
```

This can then be decrypted by changing the left rotates (rot_left) to right rotates (rot_right).

---

## 17.9  Message hash

A message hash is a simple technique which basically mixes up the bits within the message, using exclusive-OR operations, bit-shifts or character substitutions.

- Base-64 encoding. This is used in electronic mail, and it typically used to change a binary file into a standard 7-bit ASCII form. It takes 6-bit characters and converts them to a printable character, as given in Table 22.5.
- MD5. This is used in several encryption and authentication methods. See Section 20.5.3 for more information. An example conversion is from:

```
Hello, how are you?
Are you felling well?

Fred.
```

to:

```
518bb66a80cf187a20e1b07cd6cef585
```

## 17.10 Exercises

**17.10.1** What bitwise operator is used in encryption, as it always preserves the contents of the information:

    (a)    Exclusive-OR        (b)    AND
    (c)    NOR                (d)    OR

**17.10.2** What happens when a value is Exclusive-OR'ed by the same value, twice:

    (a)    Value becomes all 0's    (b)    Value becomes all 1's
    (c)    Same value results      (d)    Double the value

**17.10.3** Using a shifted alphabet, which is the encrypted message for 'help'

    (a)    gdho           (b)    ifnq
    (c)    ebim           (d)    qatp

**17.10.4** If it takes 100 days to crack an encrypted message, and assuming that computing speed increases by 100% each year, determine how long it will take to crack the message after 2 years:

    (a)    25 days        (b)    44.44... days
    (c)    50 days        (d)    100 days

**17.10.5** If it takes 100 days to crack an encrypted message, and assuming that computing speed increases by 50% each year, determine how long it will take to crack the message after 2 years:

    (a)    25 days        (b)    44.44... days
    (c)    50 days        (d)    100 days

**17.10.6** Create your own encryption algorithm and implement it. For example, an example could be to:

- Read file, one byte at a time.
- Exclusive-OR the byte with a value of AAh (0xAA, in C).
- Rotate bits by 2 positions to the right.
- Exclusive-OR the byte with a value of 73h.
- Rotate bits by 3 positions to the left.
- Save byte.
- Read next byte.
- and so on.

Note that when decrypting the file, the reverse should be implemented, that is:

- Read file, one byte at a time.
- Rotate bits by 3 positions to the right
- Exclusive-OR the byte with 73h.
- Rotate bits by 2 positions to the left.
- Exclusive-OR the byte with AAh.
- Save byte.
- Read next byte.
- and so on.

An outline is:

```
fread(&ch,1,1,in); /* read a byte from the file */
ch=((ch & 0xff) ^ 0xAA) & 0xff; /* X-OR with AAh */
ch=rot_right(ch); /* perform two right rotates */
ch=rot_right(ch);
/*********** Add code here ************/
if (!feof(in)) fwrite(&ch,1,1,out); /* write a byte */
```

**17.10.7**  If it currently takes 1 million years to decrypt a message then complete Table 17.5 assuming a 40% increase in computing power each year.

**Table 17.5**  Time to decrypt a message assuming an increase in computing power

| Year | Time to decrypt (years) | Year | Time to decrypt (years) |
|------|-------------------------|------|-------------------------|
| 0 | 1 million | 10 | |
| 1 | 714,286 | 11 | |
| 2 | | 12 | |
| 3 | | 13 | |
| 4 | | 14 | |
| 5 | | 15 | |
| 6 | | 16 | |
| 7 | | 17 | |
| 8 | | 18 | |
| 9 | | 19 | |

**17.10.8**  The following messages were encrypted using the code mapping:

Input:       abcdefghijklmnopqrstuvwxyz
Encrypted:   mgqoafzbcdiehxjklntqrwsuvy

(i)   qnv#mxo#oaqjoa#qbct#hattmza
(ii)  zjjogva#mxo#fmnasaee#jxa#mxo#mee
(iii) oaqjoa#qbct#mx#vjr#bmwa#fcxctbao#qbct#lratqcjx

Decrypt them and determine the message. (Note that a '#' character has been used as a SPACE character.)

**17.10.9** The following messages were encrypted using a shifted alphabet. Decrypt them by determining the number of shifts. (Note that a '#' character has been used as a SPACE character.)

(i)    XLMW#MW#ER#IBEQTPI#XIBX
(ii)   ROVZ#S#KW#NBYGXSXQ#SX#DRO#COK
(iii)  ZVOKCO#MYWO#AESMU#WI#RYECO#SC#YX#PSBO
(iv)   IJ#D#YJ#IJO#RVIO#OJ#BJ#OJ#OCZ#WVGG

**17.10.10** The following messages were encrypted using a numeric key and the XOR operation. Decrypt them by identifying the SPACE character.

(i)    ]a`z)`z)hg)lqhdyel)}lq}       Hint: ')' is a SPACE
(ii)   Onv!v`ri!xnts!i`oer/          Hint: '!' is a SPACE
(iii)  Xhddir+Odd'+|cnyn+jyn+rd~     Hint: '+' is a SPACE
(iv)   Cftclagf"Fcvc"Amooq#          Hint: '"' is a SPACE

**17.10.11** If you have access to a software development package, write a program in which the user enters a line of text. Encrypt it by shifting the bits in each character one position to the left. Save them to a file. Also write a decryption program.

**17.10.12** The following text is a character-mapped encryption. The common 2-letter words in the text are:

*to   it   is   to   in   as   an*

and the common 3-letter words are:

*for   and   the*

and the only 1-letter word is *a*. Table 17.4 gives a table of letter probabilities from a sample piece of text. If required, this table can be compared with the probabilities in the encrypted text.

```
tzf hbcq boybqtbmf ja ocmctbe tfqzqjejmv jyfl bqbejmrf cn tzbt ocmctbe
ncmqben blf efnn baafqtfo gv qjcnf. bqv rqwbqtfo ocntjltcjq boofo tj b
ncmqbe cn ofnqlcgfo bn qjcnf. tzcn qjreo gf mfqflbtfo gv futflqbe
firckhfqt kljorcqm bclgjlqf ntbtcq, aljh jtzfl ncmqben qjrkecqm cqtj
tzf ncmqbe'n kbtz (qljnn-tbed), aljh wctzcq fefqtlcqbe qjhkjqfqtn, aljh
lfqjlocqm bqo kebvgbqd hfocb, bqo nj jq. b qjhkblbtjl jrtkrtn b zcmz
efyfe ca tzf ncmqbe yjetbmf cn mlfbtfl tzbq tzf tzlfnzjeo yjetbmf, fenf
ct jrtkrtn b ejw. ca tzf qjcnf yjetbmf cn efnn tzbq tzf tzlfnzjeo
yjetbmf tzfq tzf qjcnf wcee qjt baafqt tzf lfqjyflfo ncmqbe. fyfq ca tzf
qjcnf cn mlfbtfl tzbq tzcn tzlfnzjeo tzflf blf tfqzqcirfn wzcqz qbq
lforqf ctn faafqt. ajl fubhkef, futlb gctn qbq gf boofo tj tzf obtb
fctzfl tj oftfqt flljln jl tj qjllfqt tzf gctn cq flljl.
    eblmf bhjrqtn ja ntjlbmf blf lfirclfo ajl ocmctbe obtb. ajl fubhkef,
nfyfqtv hcqrtfn ja zcac irbectv hrncq lfirclfn jyfl ncu zrqolfo hfmgvtfn
ja obtb ntjlbmf. tzf obtb jqqf ntjlfo tfqon tj gf lfcbgef bqo wcee qjt
ofmlbof jyfl tchf (futlb obtb gctn qbq bqc gf boofo tj boofo tj qjllfqt jl
```

oftfqt bqv flljln). tvkcqbeev, tzf obtb cn ntjlfo fctzfl bn hbmqftcq
acfeon jq b hbmqftcq ocnd jl bn kctn jq bq jktcqbe ocnd. tzf bqqrlbqv ja
ocmctbe nvntfhn ofkfqon jq tzf qrhgfl ja gctn rnfo ajl fbqz nbhkef,
wzflfbn bq bqbejmrf nvntfh'n bqqrlbqv ofkfqon jq qjhkjqfqt tjeflbqqf.
bqbejmrf nvntfhn benj kljorqf b ocaaflcqm lfnkjqnf ajl ocaaflfqt nvntfhn
wzflfbn b ocmctbe nvntfh zbn b ofkfqobgef lfnkjqnf.

ct cn yflv ocaacqret (ca qjt chkjnncgef) tj lfqjyfl tzf jlcmcqbe
bqbejmrf ncmqbe batfl ct cn baafqtfo gv qjcnf (fnkfqcbeev ca tzf qjcnf
cn lbqojh). hjnt hftzjon ja lforqcqm qjcnf cqyjeyf njhf ajlh ja
acetflcqm jl nhjjtzcqm ja tzf ncmqbe.  b mlfbt boybqtbmf ja ocmctbe
tfqzqjejmv cn tzbt jqqf tzf bqbejmrf obtb zbn gffq qjqyfltfo tj ocmctbe
tzfq ct cn lfebtcyfev fbnv tj ntjlf ct wctz jtzfl krlfev ocmctbe obtb.
jqqf ntjlfo cq ocmctbe ct cn lfebtcyfev fbnv tj kljqfnn tzf obtb gfajlf
ct cn qjqyfltfo gbqd cqtj bqbejmrf.

bq boybqtbmf ja bqbejmrf tfqzqjejmv cn tzbt ct cn lfebtcyfev fbnv tj
ntjlf. ajl fubhkef, ycofj bqo brocj ncmqben blf ntjlfo bn hbmqftcq
acfeon jq tbkf bqo b kcqtrlf cn ntjlfo jq kzjtjmlbkzcq kbkfl. tzfnf
hfocb tfqo tj boo qjcnf tj tzf ncmqbe wzfq tzfv blf ntjlfo bqo wzfq
lfqjyflfo (nrqz bn tbkf zcnn). rqajltrqbtfev, ct cn benj qjt kjnncgef tj
oftfqt ca bq bqbejmrf ncmqbe zbn bq flljl cq ct.

**17.10.13** The following is a piece of character-mapped encrypted text. The common
2-letter words in the text are:

*to   it   is   to   in   as   an*

and the common 3-letter words are:

*for   and   the*

ixq rnecq ja geie bjhhrtqbeiqjtn etg bjhkriqw tqisjwzn qn qyqw
qtbwqenqtc. qi qn jtq ja ixq aqs iqbxtjmjcqbem ewqen sxqbx fwqtcn
fqtqaqin ij hjni ja ixq bjrtiwqqn etg ixq kqjkmqn ja ixq sjwmg. sqixjri
qi hetv qtgrniwqqn bjrmg tji quqni. qi qn ixq jfdqbiqyq ja ixqn fjjz ij
gqnbrnn geie bjhhrtqbeiqjtn qt e wqegefmq ajwh ixei nirgqtin etg
kwjaqnnqjtemn emm jyqw ixq sjwmg bet rtgqwnietg.

qt ixq keni, hjni qmqbiwjtqb bjhhrtqbeiqjt nvniqhn iwetnhqiiqg
etemjcrq nqctemn. jt et etemjcrq iqmqkxjtq nvniqh ixq yjmiecq mqyqm awjh
ixq kxjtq yewqqn sqix ixq yjqbq nqctem. rtsetiqg nqctemn awjh quiqwtem
njrwbqn qenqmv bjwwrki ixqnq nqctemn. qt e gqcqiem bjhhrtqbeiqjt nvniqh
e nqwqqn ja gqcqiem bjgqn wqkwqnqtin ixq etemjcrq nqctem. ixqnq ewq ixqt
iwetnhqiiqg en jtqn etg oqwjn. gqcqiem qtajwheiqjt qn mqnn mqzqmv ij fq
eaaqbiqg fv tjqnq etg xen ixrn fqbjhq ixq hjni kwqgjhqteti ajwh ja
bjhhrtqbeiqjtn.

gqcqiem bjhhrtqbeiqjt emnj jaaqwn e cwqeiqw trhfqw ja nqwyqbqn,
cwqeiqw iweaaqb etg emmjsn ajw xqcx nkqqg bjhhrtqbeiqjtn fqisqqt gqcqiem
qlrqkhqti. ixq rnecq ja gqcqiem bjhhrtqbeiqjtn qtbmrgqn befmq iqm-
qyqnqjt, bjhkriqw tqisjwzn, aebnqhqmq, hjfqmq gqcqiem wegqj, gqcqiem ax
wegqj etg nj jt.

**17.10.14** Implement a program which converts a text file using Base-64 encoding.

# 17.11 Letter probability program

📄 **Program 17.8**

```c
#include <stdio.h>
#include <string.h>
#include <ctype.h>

#define  NUM_LETTERS 29

int    get_occurances(char c, char txt[]);

int    main(void)
{
char   ch, fname[BUFSIZ];
int    occ[NUM_LETTERS]={0,0,0,0,0,0,0,0,0,0,0,0,0,0,0,0,
                         0,0,0,0,0,0,0,0,0,0,0,0,0};
unsigned int   total,i;
FILE           *in;

  printf("Enter text file>>");
  gets(fname);

  if ((in=fopen(fname,"r"))==NULL)
  {
      printf("Can't find file %s\n",fname);
      return(1);
  }
  do
  {
      ch=tolower(getc(in));

      if (isalpha(ch))
      {
         (occ[ch-'a'])++;
         total++;
      }
      else if (ch=='.') { occ[NUM_LETTERS-3]++; total++; }
      else if (ch==' ') { occ[NUM_LETTERS-2]++; total++; }
      else if (ch==',') { occ[NUM_LETTERS-1]++; total++; }
  } while (!feof(in));

  fclose(in);

  puts("Char. Occur. Prob.");

  for (i=0;i<NUM_LETTERS;i++)
  {
      printf("  %c  %5d %5.4f\n",'a'+i,occ[i],
                             (float)occ[i]/(float)total);
  }

  return(0);
}

int    get_occurances(char c, char txt[])
{
int    occ=0,i;

  for (i=0;i<strlen(txt);i++)
      if (c==txt[i]) occ++;

  return(occ);
}
```

# 18 Private-Key Encryption

## 18.1 Introduction

Encryption techniques can use either public keys or secret keys. Secret-key encryption techniques use a secret key which is only known by the two communicating parities, as illustrated in Figure 18.1. This key can be fixed or can be passed from the two parties over a secure communications link (for example over the postal network or a leased line). The two most popular private-key techniques are DES (Data Encryption Standard) and IDEA (International Data Encryption Algorithm) and a popular public-key technique is RSA (named after its inventors, Rivest, Shamir and Adleman). Public-key encryption uses two keys, one private and the other public.

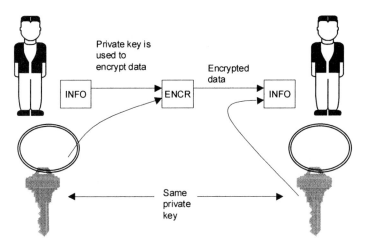

**Figure 18.1**  Private key encryption/decryption process

## 18.2  Survey of private-key cryptosystems

### 18.2.1 DES

DES (Data Encryption Standard) is a block cipher scheme which operates on 64-bit block sizes. The private key has only 56 useful bit as eight of its bits are used for parity. This gives $2^{56}$ or $10^{17}$ possible keys. DES uses a complex series of permutations and substitutions, the result of these operations is XOR'ed with the input. This is then repeated 16 times using a different order of the key bits each time. DES is a very strong code and has never been broken, although several high-powered computers are now available which, using brute force, can crack the code. A possible solution is 3DES (or triple DES) which uses DES three times in a row. First to encrypt, next to decrypt and finally to encrypt. This system allows a key-length of more than 128 bits.

### 18.2.2 MOSS

MOSS (MIME object security service) is an Internet RFC and is typically used for sound encryption. It uses symmetric encryption and the size of the key is not specified. The only public implementation is TIS/MOSS 7.1, which is basically an implementation of 56-bit DES code with a violation.

### 18.2.3 IDEA

IDEA (International Data Encryption Algorithm) is discussed in Section 18.3.2 and is similar to DES. It operates on 64-bit blocks of plaintext, uses a 128-bit key, and has over 17 rounds with a complicated mangler function. During decryption this function does not have to be reversed and can simply be applied in the same way as during encryption (this also occurs with DES). IDEA uses a different key expansion for encryption and decryption, but every other part of the process is identical. The same keys are used in DES decryption but in the reverse order.

The key is devised in eight 16-bit blocks; the first six are used in the first round of encryption the last two are used in the second run. It is free for use in non-commercial version and appears to be a strong cipher.

### 18.2.4 RC4/RC5

RC4 is a cipher designed by RSA Data Security, Inc and was a secret until information on it appeared on the Internet. The Netscape secure socket layer (SSL) uses RC4. It uses a pseudo random number generator where the output of the generator is XOR'ed with the plaintext. It is has a fast algorithm and can use any key-length. Unfortunately the same key cannot be used twice. Recently a 40-bit key version was broken in 8 days without special computer power.

RC5 is a fast block cipher designed by Rivest for RSA Data Security. It has a parameterised algorithm with a variable block size (32, 64 or 128 bits), a variable key size (0 to 2048 bits) and a variable number of rounds (0 to 255).

It has a heavy use of data dependent rotations and the mixture of different operations. This assures that RC5 is secure. Kaliski and Yin found that RC5 with a 64-bit block size and 12 or more rounds gives good security.

### 18.2.5 SAFER

SAFER (Secure and Fast Encryption Routine) is a non-proprietary block-cipher developed by Massey in 1993. It operates on a 64-bit block size and has a 64-bit or 128-bit key size. SAFER has up to 10 rounds (although a minimum of 6 is recommended). Unlike most recent block ciphers, SAFER has a slightly different encryption and decryption procedure. The algorithm operates on single bytes at a time and it thus can be implemented on systems with limited processing power, such as on smart-cards applications.

A typical implementation is SAFER K-64 which uses a 40-bit key and has been shown that it is immune from most attacks when the number of rounds is greater than 6.

### 18.2.6 SKIPJACK

Skipjack is new block cipher which operates on 64-bit blocks. It uses an 80-bit key and has 32 rounds. The NSA have classified details of Skipjack and its algorithm is only available in hardware implementation called Clipper Chips. The name Clipper derives from an earlier implementation of the algorithm. Each transmission contains the session key encrypted in the header. The licensing of clipper chips allows US government to decrypt all SKIPJACK messages.

## 18.3  Private-key encryption

### 18.3.1 Data Encryption Standard (DES)

In 1977, the National Bureau of Standards (now the National Institute of Standards and Technology) published the DES for commercial and unclassified US government applications. DES is based on an algorithm known as the Lucifer cipher designed by IBM. It maps a 64-bit input block to a 64-bit output block and uses a 56-bit key. The key itself is actually 64 bits long but as 1 bit in each of the 8 bytes is used for odd parity on each byte, the key only contains 56 meaningful bits.

### DES overview

The main steps in the encryption process are as follows:

- Initially the 64-bit input is permuted to obtain a 64-bit result (this operation does little to the security of the code).
- Next, there are 16 iterations of the 64-bit result and the 56-bit key. Only 48 bits of the key are used at a time. The 64-bit output from each iteration is used as an input to the next iteration.
- After the 16th iteration, the 64-bit output goes through another permutation, which is the inverse of the initial permutation.

Figure 18.2 shows the basic operation of DES encryption.

### Permutation of the data

Before the first iteration and after the last iteration, DES performs a permutation on the data. The permutation is as follows:

Initial permutation:

```
58 50 42 34 26 18 10 2   60 52 44 36 28 20 12 4   62 54 46 38 30 22 14 6
64 56 48 40 32 24 16 8   57 49 41 33 25 17 9  1   59 51 43 35 27 19 11 3
61 53 45 37 29 21 13 5   63 55 47 39 31 23 15 7
```

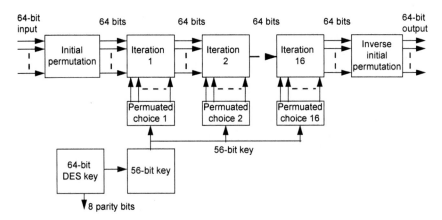

**Figure 18.2** Overview of DES operation

Final permutation:

```
40 8   48 16 56 24 64 32 39 7   47 15 55 23 63 31 38 6   46 14 54 22 62 30
37 5   45 13 53 21 61 29 36 4   44 12 52 20 60 28 35 3   43 11 51 19 59 27
34 2   42 10 50 18 58 26 33 1   41 9  49 17 57 25
```

These numbers specify the bit numbers of the input to the permutation and the order of the numbers corresponds to the output bit position. Thus, input permutation:

- Input bit 58 moves to output bit 1 (58 is in the 1st bit position).
- Input bit 50 moves to output bit 2 (50 is in the 2nd bit position).
- Input bit 42 moves to output bit 3 (42 is in the 3rd bit position).
- Continue until all bits are exhausted.

In addition, the final permutation could be:

- Input bit 58 moves to output bit 1 (1 is in the 58th bit position).
- Input bit 50 moves to output bit 2 (2 is in the 50th bit position).
- Input bit 42 moves to output bit 3 (3 is in the 42nd bit position).
- Continue until all bits are exhausted.

Thus, the input permutation is the reverse of the output permutation. Arranged as blocks of 8 bits, it gives:

```
58 50 42 34 26 18 10 2
60 52 44 36 28 20 12 4
62 54 46 38 30 22 14 6
 :               :
61 53 45 37 29 21 13 5
63 55 47 39 31 23 15 7
```

It can be seen that the first byte of input gets spread into the 8th bit of each of the other bytes. The second byte of input gets spread into the 7th bit of each of the other bytes, and so on.

## Generating the per-round keys

The DES key operates on 64-bit data in each of the 16 iterations. The key is made of a 56-bit key used in the iterations and 8 parity bits. A 64-bit key of:

$$k_1 k_2 k_3 k_4 k_5 k_6 k_7 k_8 k_9 k_{10} k_{11} k_{12} k_{13} \ldots k_{64}$$

contains the parity $k_8$, $k_{16}$, $k_{32} \ldots k_{64}$. The iterations are numbered $I_1$, $I_2$, ... $I_{16}$. The initial permutation of the 56 useful bits of the key is used to generate a 56-bit output. It divides into two 28-bit values, called $C_0$ and $D_0$. $C_0$ is specified as:

$$k_{57} k_{49} k_{41} k_{33} k_{25} k_{17} k_9 k_1 k_{58} k_{50} k_{42} k_{34} k_{26} k_{18} k_{10} k_2 k_{59} k_{51} k_{43} k_{35} k_{27} k_{19} k_{11} k_3 k_{60} k_{52} k_{44} k_{36}$$

And $D_0$ is:

$$k_{63} k_{55} k_{47} k_{39} k_{31} k_{23} k_{15} k_7 k_{62} k_{54} k_{46} k_{38} k_{30} k_{22} k_{14} k_6 k_{61} k_{53} k_{45} k_{37} k_{29} k_{21} k_{13} k_5 k_{28} k_{20} k_{12} k_4$$

Thus the 28-bit $C_0$ key will contain the 57th bit of the DES key as the first bit, the 49th as the second bit, and so on. Notice that none of the 28-bit values contains the parity bits.

Most of the rounds have a 2-bit rotate left shift, but rounds 1, 2, 9 and 16 have a single-bit rotate left (ROL). A left rotation moves all the bits in the key to the left and the bit which is moved out of the left-hand side is shifted into the right-hand end.

The key for each iteration ($K_i$) is generated from $C_i$ (which makes the left half) and $D_i$ (which makes the right half). The permutations of $C_i$ that produces the left half of $K_i$ is:

$$c_{14} c_{17} c_{11} c_{24} c_1 c_5 c_3 c_{28} c_{15} c_6 c_{21} c_{10} c_{23} c_{19} c_{12} c_4 c_{26} c_8 c_{16} c_7 c_{27} c_{20} c_{13} c_2$$

and the right half of $K_i$ is:

$$d_{41} d_{52} d_{31} d_{37} d_{47} d_{55} d_{30} d_{40} d_{51} d_{45} d_{33} d_{48} d_{44} d_{49} d_{39} d_{56} d_{34} d_{53} d_{46} d_{42} d_{50} d_{36} d_{29} d_{32}$$

Thus the 56-bit key is made up of:

$$c_{14} c_{17} c_{11} c_{24} c_1 c_5 c_3 c_{28} c_{15} c_6 c_{21} c_{10} c_{23} c_{19} c_{12} c_4 c_{26} c_8 c_{16} c_7 c_{27} c_{20} c_{13} c_2 d_{41} d_{52} d_{31} d_{37} d_{47} d_{55}$$
$$d_{30} d_{40} d_{51} d_{45} d_{33} d_{48} d_{44} d_{49} d_{39} d_{56} d_{34} d_{53} d_{46} d_{42} d_{50} d_{36} d_{29} d_{32}$$

Figure 18.3 illustrates the process (note that only some of the bit positions have been shown).

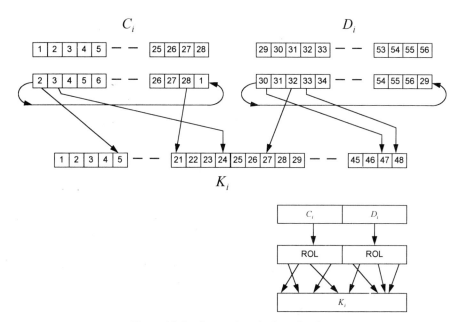

**Figure 18.3** Generating the iteration key

### Iteration operations

Each iteration takes the 64-bit output from the previous iteration and operates on it with a 56-bit per iteration key. Figure 18.4 shows the operation of each iteration. The 64-bit input is split into two parts, $L_i$ and $R_i$. $R_i$ is operated on with an expansion/permutation (E-table) to give 48 bits. The output from the E-table conversion is then exclusive-OR'ed with the permuated 48-bit key. Next a substitute/ choice stage (S-box) is used to transform the 48-bit result to 32 bits. These are then XORed with $L_i$ to give the resulting $R_{i+1}$ (which is $R_i$ for the next iteration). The operation of expansion/XOR/substitution is often known as the mangler function. The $R_i$ input is also used to produce $L_{i+1}$.

The mangler function takes the 32-bit $R_i$ and the 48-bit $K_i$ and produces a 32-bit output (which when XORed with $L_i$ produces $R_i+1$). It initially expands $R_i$ from 32 bits to 48 bits. This is done by splitting $R_i$ into eight 4-bit chunks and then expanding each of the chunks into 6 bits by taking the adjacent bits and concatenating them onto the chunk. The leftmost and rightmost bits of $R$ are considered adjacent. For example, if $R_i$ is:

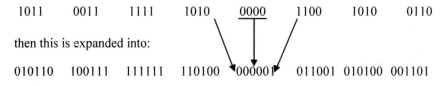

then this is expanded into:

010110   100111   111111   110100   000001   011001 010100 001101

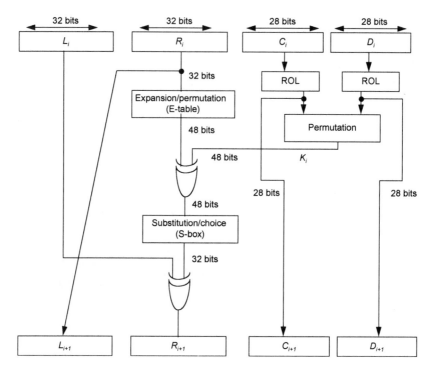

**Figure 18.4** Iteration step

The output from the expansion is then XORed with $K_i$ and the output of this is fed into the S-box. Each 6-bit chunk of the 48-bit output from the XOR operation is then substituted with a 4-bit chunk using a lookup table. An S-box table for the first 6-bit chunk is given in Table 18.1. Thus, for example, the input bit sequence of:

000000 000001 *XXXXXX* ...

would be converted to:

1110 0000 *xxxx* ...

### Concluding remarks

The design of the DES scheme was constructed behind closed doors so there are few pointers to the reasons for the construction of the encryption. One of the major weaknesses of the scheme is the usage of a 56-bit key, which means there are only $2^{56}$ or $7.2 \times 10^{16}$ keys. Thus, as the cost of hardware reduces and the power of computers increases, the time taken to exhaustively search for a key becomes smaller each year.

In the past, there was concern about potential weaknesses in the design of the eight S-boxes. This appears to have been misplaced as no one has found any weaknesses yet. Indeed several researchers have found that swapping the S-boxes significantly reduces the security of the code.

**Table 18.1** S-box conversion for first 6-bit chunk

| Input | Output | Input | Output | Input | Output | Input | Output |
|-------|--------|-------|--------|-------|--------|-------|--------|
| 000000 | 1110 | 010000 | 0011 | 100000 | 0100 | 110000 | 1111 |
| 000001 | 0000 | 010001 | 1010 | 100001 | 1111 | 110001 | 0101 |
| 000010 | 0100 | 010010 | 1010 | 100010 | 0001 | 110010 | 1100 |
| 000011 | 1111 | 010011 | 0110 | 100011 | 1100 | 110011 | 1011 |
| 000100 | 1101 | 010100 | 0100 | 100100 | 1110 | 110100 | 1001 |
| 000101 | 0111 | 010101 | 1100 | 100101 | 1000 | 110101 | 0011 |
| 000110 | 0001 | 010110 | 1100 | 100110 | 1000 | 110110 | 0111 |
| 000111 | 0100 | 010111 | 1011 | 100111 | 0010 | 110111 | 1110 |
| 001000 | 0010 | 011000 | 0101 | 101000 | 1101 | 111000 | 0011 |
| 001001 | 1110 | 011001 | 1001 | 101001 | 0100 | 111001 | 1010 |
| 001010 | 1111 | 011010 | 1001 | 101010 | 0110 | 111010 | 1010 |
| 001011 | 0010 | 011011 | 0101 | 101011 | 1001 | 111011 | 0000 |
| 001100 | 1011 | 011100 | 0000 | 101100 | 0010 | 111100 | 0101 |
| 001101 | 1101 | 011101 | 0011 | 101101 | 0001 | 111101 | 0110 |
| 001110 | 1000 | 011110 | 0111 | 101110 | 1011 | 111110 | 0000 |
| 001111 | 0001 | 011111 | 1000 | 101111 | 0111 | 111111 | 1101 |

A new variant, called Triple DES, has been proposed by Tuchman and has been standardised in financial applications. The technique uses two keys and three executions of the DES algorithm. A key, $K_1$, is used in the first execution, then $K_2$ is used and finally $K_1$ is used again. These two keys give an effective key length of 112 bits, that is $2 \times 64$ key bits minus 16 parity bits. The Triple DES process is illustrated in Figure 18.5.

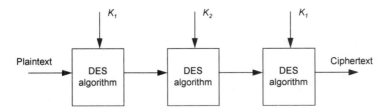

**Figure 18.5** Triple DES process

### 18.3.2 IDEA

IDEA (International Data Encryption Algorithm) is a private-key encryption process which is similar to DES. It was developed by Xuejia Lai and James Massey of ETH Zuria and is intended for implementation in software. IDEA operates on 64-bit blocks of plaintext; using a 128-bit key, it converts them into 64-bit blocks of ciphertext. Figure 18.6 shows the basic encryption process.

IDEA operates over 17 rounds with a complicated mangler function. During decryption this function does not have to be reversed and can simply be applied in the same way as during encryption (this also occurs with DES). IDEA uses a different key expansion for encryption and decryption, but every other part of the process is identical. The same keys are used in DES decryption but in the reverse order.

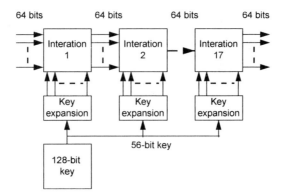

**Figure 18.6** IDEA encryption

## Operation

Each primitive operation in IDEA maps two 16-bit quantities into a 16-bit quantity. IDEA uses three operations, all easy to compute in software, to create a mapping. The three basic operations are:

- Exclusive-OR ($\oplus$).
- Slightly modified add (+), and ignore any bit carries.
- Slightly modified multiply ($\otimes$) and ignore any bit carries. Multiplying involves first calculating the 32-bit result, then taking the remainder when divided by $2^{16}+1$ (mod $2^{16}+1$).

## Key expansions

The 128-bit key is expanded into fifty-two 16-bit keys, $K_1$, $K_2$, ... $K_{52}$. The key is generated differently for encryption than for decryption. Once the 52 keys are generated, the encryption and decryption processes are the same.

The 52 encryption keys are generated as follows:

- Keys 1–8: write out the 128-bit key and, starting from the left, chop off 16 bits at a time. This generates eight 16-bit keys. Thus the 128-bit key of $AAAAAAAAAAAAAAAA...HHHHHHHHHHHHHHHH$ will generate eight keys of $AAAAAAAAAAAAAAAA$, $BBBBBBBBBBBBBBBB$, and so on.
- Keys 9–16: the next eight keys are generated at bit 25, and wrapped around to the beginning when at the end.
- Keys 17–24: the next eight keys are generated at bit 50, and wrapped around to the beginning when at the end.
- The rest of the keys are generated by offsetting by 25 bits and wrapped around to the beginning until the end.

The 64-bit (or 32-bit) per round, keys used are made up of 4 (or 2) of the encryption keys:

Key 1: $K_1K_2K_3K_4$      Key 2: $K_5K_6$      Key 3: $K_7K_8K_9K_{10}$

| Key 4: | $K_{11}K_{12}$ | Key 5: | $K_{13}K_{14}K_{15}K_{16}$ | Key 6: | $K_{17}K_{18}$ |
|--------|----------------|--------|-----------------------------|--------|----------------|

Key 4: $K_{11}K_{12}$     Key 5: $K_{13}K_{14}K_{15}K_{16}$   Key 6: $K_{17}K_{18}$

Key 7: $K_{19}K_{20}K_{21}K_{22}$    Key 8: $K_{23}K_{24}$             Key 9: $K_{25}K_{26}K_{27}K_{28}$

Key 10: $K_{29}K_{30}$         Key 11: $K_{31}K_{32}K_{33}K_{34}$   Key 12: $K_{35}K_{36}$

Key 13: $K_{37}K_{38}K_{39}K_{40}$   Key 14: $K_{41}K_{42}$           Key 15: $K_{43}K_{44}K_{45}K_{46}$

Key 16: $K_{47}K_{48}$         Key 17: $K_{49}K_{50}K_{51}K_{52}$

### 18.3.3 Iteration

Odd rounds have a different process to even rounds. Each odd round uses a 64-bit key and even rounds use a 32-bit key.

Odd rounds are simple; the process is:

If the input is a 64-bit key of $I_1 I_2 I_3 I_4$, where the $I_1$ is the most significant 16 bits, $I_2$ is the next most significant 16 bits, and so on. The output of the iteration is also a 64-bit key of $O_1 O_2 O_3 O_4$ and the applied key is $K_a K_b K_c K_d$. The iteration for the odd iteration is then:

$$O_1 = I_1 \otimes K_a$$
$$O_2 = I_3 + K_c$$
$$O_3 = I_2 + K_b$$
$$O_4 = I_4 \otimes K_d$$

An important feature is that this operation is totally reversible: multiplying $O_1$ by the inverse of $K_a$ gives $I_1$, and multiplying $O_4$ by the inverse of $K_d$ gives $I_4$. Adding $O_2$ to the negative of $K_c$ gives $I_3$, and adding $O_3$ to the negative of $K_b$ gives $I_2$.

Even rounds are less simple, the process is as follows. Suppose the input is a 64-bit key of $I_1 I_2 I_3 I_4$, where $I_1$ is the most significant 16 bits, $I_2$ is the next most significant 16 bits, and so on. The output of the iteration is also a 64-bit key of $O_1 O_2 O_3 O_4$ and the applied key is 32 bits of $K_a K_b$. The iteration for the even round performs a mangler function of:

$$A = I_1 \otimes I_2 \qquad\qquad B = I_3 \otimes I_4$$
$$C = ((K_a \otimes A) + B)) \otimes K_b) \qquad D = (K_a \otimes A) + C$$

$$O_1 = I_1 \oplus C \qquad\qquad O_2 = I_2 \oplus C$$
$$O_3 = I_3 \oplus D \qquad\qquad O_4 = I_4 \oplus D$$

The most amazing thing about this iteration is that the inverse of the function is simply the function itself. Thus, the same keys are used for encryption and decryption (this differs from the odd round, where the key must be either the negative or the inverse of the encryption key.

### 18.3.4 IDEA security

There are no known methods that can be used to crack IDEA, apart from exhaustive search. Thus, as it has a 128-bit code it is extremely difficult to break, even with modern high-performance computers.

# 18.4 Exercises

**18.4.1** How many keys are used in the private-key system:

   (a)   1                    (b)   3
   (c)   2                    (d)   4

**18.4.2** How many keys are used in the public-key system:

   (a)   1                    (b)   3
   (c)   2                    (d)   4

**18.4.3** A typical private-key system is:

   (a)   IDE              (b)   IDA
   (c)   PGP            (d)   IDEA

**18.4.4** How many possible keys are there with a 16-bit key:

   (a)   16              (b)   65,536
   (c)   256           (d)   4,294,967,296

**18.4.5** How many possible keys are there with a 32-bit key:

   (a)   32              (b)   1,048,576
   (c)   1024         (d)   4,294,967,296

**18.4.6** How many actual encryption key bits does IDEA have:

   (a)   56              (b)   64
   (c)   128           (d)   256

**18.4.7** If it takes 10 ns ($10 \times 10^{-9}$ s) to test a key, determine the amount of time it would take, on average, to decrypt a message with a 32-bit key:

   (a)   21.48 seconds    (b)   43 seconds
   (c)   21.48 minutes    (d)   43 minutes

**18.4.8** Show that it will take 5849 years to search all the keys for a 64-bit encryption key. Assume it takes 10 ns ($10 \times 10^{-9}$ s) to test a key. How might this time be drastically reduced?

**18.4.9** Show, by an example, that if $C = A \oplus B$ then $B = A \oplus C$. Use an 8-bit example, a 16-bit example and a 32-bit example.

# 19 Public-Key Encryption

## 19.1 Introduction

Public-key algorithms use a secret element and a public element to their code. One of the main algorithms is RSA. Compared with DES it is relatively slow but it has the advantage that users can choose their own key whenever they need one. The most commonly used public-key cryptosystems are covered in the next sections.

Private-key systems are not feasible for large-scale networks, such as the Internet or electronic commerce, as this would involve organisations creating hundreds or thousands of different private keys. Each conversation with an organisation or even an individual within a company would require a separate key. Thus, public- key methods are much better suited to the Internet and, therefore, Intranets.

Figure 19.1 shows that a public-key system has two key, a private key and a public key. The private key is secret to the user and is used to decrypt messages that have been encrypted with the users public key. The public key is made available to anyone who wants to send an encrypted message to the person. Someone sending a message to the user will use the users public key to encrypt the message and it can only be decrypted using the users private key (as the private and public keys are linked in a certain way). Once the message has been encrypted not even the sender can decrypt it.

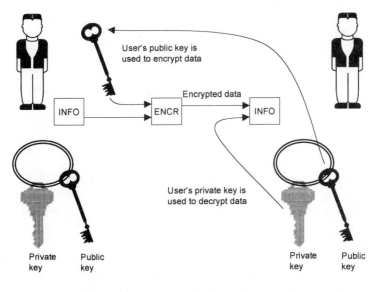

**Figure 19.1** Overview of public-key systems

### 19.1.1 RSA

RSA stands for Rivest, Shamir and Adelman, and is the most commonly used public-key cryptosystem. It is patented only in the USA and is secure for key-length of over 728 bits. The algorithm relies of the fact that it is difficult to factorise large numbers. Unfortunately, it is particularly vulnerable to chosen plaintext attacks and a new timing attack (spying on keystroke time) was announced on the 7 December 1995. This attack would be able to break many existing implementations of RSA.

### 19.1.2 Elliptic curve

Elliptic curve is a new kind of public-key cryptosystem. It suffers from speed problems, but this has been overcome with modern high-speed computers.

### 19.1.3 DSS

DSS (digital signature standard) is related to the DSA (digital signature algorithm). This standard has been selected by the NIST and the NSA, and is part of the Capstone project. It uses 512-bit or 1024-bit key size. The design presents some lack in key-exchange capability and is slow for signature-verification.

### 19.1.4 Diffie-Hellman

Diffie-Hellman is commonly used for key-exchange. The security of this cipher relies on both the key-length and the discrete algorithm problem. This problem is similar to the factorising of large numbers. Unfortunately, the code can be cracked and the prime number generator must be carefully chosen.

### 19.1.5 LUC

Peter Smith developed LUC which is a public-key cipher that uses Lucas functions instead of exponentiation. Four other algorithms have also been developed, these are:

- LUCDIF (a key-negotiation method).
- LUCELG PK (equivalent to EL Gamel encryption).
- LUCELG DS (equivalent to EL Gamel data signature system).
- LUCDSA (equivalent to the DSS).

## 19.2 RSA

### 19.2.1 RSA

RSA is a public-key encryption/decryption algorithm and is much slower than IDEA and DES. The key length is variable and the block size is also variable. A typical key length is 512 bits. RSA uses a public-key and a private key, and uses the fact that large prime numbers are extremely difficult to factorise. The following steps are taken to generate the public and private keys:

1. Select two large prime numbers, $a$ and $b$ (each will be roughly 256 bits long). The factors $a$ and $b$ remain secret and $n$ is the result of multiplying them together. Each of the prime numbers is of the order of $10^{100}$.

2. Next, the public-key is chosen. To do this a number $e$ is chosen so that $e$ and $(a-1) \times (b-1)$ are relatively prime. Two numbers are relatively prime if they have no common factor greater than 1. The public-key is then $<e,n>$ and results in a key which is 512 bits long.

3. Next the private key for decryption, $d$, is computed so that:

$$d = e^{-1} \bmod [(a-1) \times (b-1)]$$

This then gives a private key of $<d,n>$. The values $a$ and $b$ can then be discarded (but should never be disclosed to anyone).

The encryption process to ciphertext, $c$, is then defined by:

$$c = m^e \bmod n$$

The message, $m$, is then decrypted with:

$$m = c^d \bmod n$$

It should be noted that the message block $m$ must be less than $n$. When $n$ is 512 bits then a message which is longer than 512 bits must be broken up into blocks of 512 bits.

### 19.2.2 Encryption/decryption keys

When two parties, $P_1$ and $P_2$, are communicating they encrypt data using a pair of public/private key pairs. Party $P_1$ encrypts their message using $P_2$'s public-key. Then party $P_2$ uses their private key to decrypt this data. When party $P_2$ encrypts a message it sends to $P_1$ using $P_1$'s public-key and $P_1$ decrypts this using their private key. Notice that party $P_1$ cannot decrypt the message that it has sent to $P_2$ as only $P_2$ has the required private key.

A great advantage of RSA is that the key has a variable number of bits. It is likely that, in the coming few years, powerful computer systems will determine all the factors to 512-bit values. Luckily the RSA key has a variable size and can easily be changed. Many users are choosing keys with 1024 bits.

### 19.2.3 Simple RSA example

Initially the PARTY1 picks two prime numbers. For example:

$a=11$ and $b=3$

Next, the $n$ value is calculated. Thus:

$$n = a \times b = 11 \times 3 = 33$$

Next $PHI$ is calculated by:

$$PHI = (a-1)(b-1) = 20$$

The public exponent $e$ is then generated so that the greatest common divisor of $e$ and PHI is 1 ($e$ is relatively prime with PHI). Thus, the smallest value for $e$ is:

$$e = 3$$

The $n$ (33) and the $e$ (3) values are the public keys. The private key ($d$) is the inverse of $e$ modulo PHI.

$$d = e^{-1} \mod [(a-1) \times (b-1)]$$

This can be calculated by using extended Euclidian algorithm, to give the private key, $d$ of 7.

Thus $n=33$, $e=3$ and $d=7$.

The PARTY2 can be given the public keys of $e$ and $n$, so that PARTY2 can encrypt the message with them. PARTY1, using $d$ and $n$ can then decrypt the encrypted message.

For example, if the message value to decrypt is 4, then:

$$c = m^e \mod n = 4^3 \mod 33 = 31$$

Therefore, the encrypted message ($c$) is 31.

The encrypted message ($c$) is then decrypted by PARTY1 with:

$$m = c^d \mod n = 31^7 \mod 33 = 4$$

which is equal to the message value.

### 19.2.4 Simple RSA program

An example program which has a limited range of prime numbers is given next.

```c
#include <stdio.h>
#include <math.h>

#define   TRUE  1
#define   FALSE 0

void   get_prime( long *val);
long   getE( long PHI);
long   get_common_denom( long e, long PHI);
long   getD( long e,  long PHI);
long   decrypt(long c,long n, long d);

int    main(void)
{
long   a,b,n,e,PHI,d,m,c;
```

```
    get_prime(&a);
    get_prime(&b);
    n=a*b;
    PHI=(a-1)*(b-1);
    e=getE(PHI);

    d= getD(e,PHI);
    printf("Enter input value >> "); scanf("%ld",&m);

    printf("a=%ld b=%ld n=%ld PHI=%ld\n",a,b,n,PHI);

    c=(long)pow(m,e) % n; /* note, this may overflow with large numbers */
                          /* when e is relatively large */

    printf("e=%ld d=%ld c=%ld\n",e,d,c);

    m=decrypt(c,n,d);   /* this function required as c to      */
                        /*the power of d causes an overflow    */
    printf("Message is %ld ",m);
    return(0);
}

long  decrypt(long c,long n, long d)
{
long  i,g,f;

if (d%2==0) g=1; else g=c;

  for (i=1;i<=d/2;i++)
  {
      f=c*c % n;
      g=f*g % n;
  }
 return(g);
}

long getD( long e,  long PHI)
{
long u[3]={1,0,PHI};
long v[3]={0,1,e};
long q,temp1,temp2,temp3;

  while (v[2]!=0)
  {
      q=floor(u[2]/v[2]);
      temp1=u[0]-q*v[0];
      temp2=u[1]-q*v[1];
      temp3=u[2]-q*v[2];
      u[0]=v[0];
      u[1]=v[1];
      u[2]=v[2];
      v[0]=temp1;
      v[1]=temp2;
      v[2]=temp3;
  }
  if (u[1]<0) return(u[1]+PHI);
  else return(u[1]);
}

long  getE( long PHI)
{
 long great=0, e=2;

  while (great!=1)
  {
      e=e+1;
```

```
        great = get_common_denom(e,PHI);
  }
  return(e);
}

long get_common_denom(long e, long PHI)
{
long great,temp,a;

  if (e >PHI)
  {
      while (e % PHI != 0)
      {
          temp= e % PHI;
          e =PHI;
          PHI = temp;
      }
      great = PHI;
  } else
  {
      while (PHI % e != 0)
      {
          a = PHI % e;
          PHI = e;
          e = a;
      }
      great = e;
  }
  return(great);
}

void  get_prime( long *val)
{
#define NO_PRIMES 11
long  primes[NO_PRIMES]={3,5,7,11,13,17,19,23,29,31,37};
long  prime,i;
  do
  {
      prime=FALSE;
      printf("Enter a prime number >> ");
      scanf("%ld",val);
      for (i=0;i<NO_PRIMES;i++)
          if (*val==primes[i]) prime=TRUE;
  } while (prime==FALSE);
}
```

A sample run of the program is given next.

```
Enter a prime number >> 11
Enter a prime number >> 3
Enter input value >> 4
a=11 b=3 n=33 PHI=20
e=3 d=7 c=31
Message is 4
```

## 19.3 PGP

PGP (Pretty Good Privacy) uses the RSA algorithm with a 128-bit key. It was developed by Phil Zimmermann and gives encryption, authentication, digital signatures and compression. Its source code is freely available over the Internet and its usage is also free of charge, but it has encountered two main problems:

- The source code is freely available on the Internet causing the US government to claim that it violates laws which relate to the export of munitions. Current versions have since been produced outside of the US to overcome this problem.
- It uses algorithms which have patents, such as RSA, IDEA and MD5.

Figure 19.2 shows the basic encryption process.

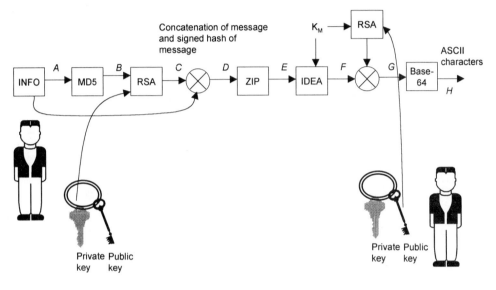

**Figure 19.2** PGP encryption

The steps taken are:

A. Sender hashes the information using the MD5 algorithm.
B. Hashed message is the encrypted using RSA with the sender's private key (this is used to authenticate the sender as the senders public key will be used to decrypt this part of the message).
C. Encrypted message is then concatenated with the original message.
D. Message is compressed using LZ compression.
E. A 128-bit IDEA key ($K_M$) is generated by some random input, such as the content of the message and the typing speed.
F. $K_M$ is then used with the IDEA encryption. $K_M$ is also encrypted with the receiver's public key.
G. Output from IDEA encryption and the encrypted $K_M$ key are concatenated together.
H. Output is encoded as ASCII characters using Base-64 (See Section 22.7.4 on Electronic Mail).

To decrypt the message the receiver goes through the following steps:

A. Receiver reverses the Base-64 conversion.
B. The receiver decrypts the $K_M$ key using their own private RSA key.
C. The $K_M$ key is then used with the IDEA algorithm to decode the message.
D. The message is then decompressed using an UNZIP program.
E. The two fragments produced after the uncompression will be the plaintext message and an MD5/RSA encrypted message. The plaintext message is the original message, whereas the MD5/RSA encrypted message can be used to authenticate the sender. This is done by applying the sender's public key to the uncompressed encrypted part of the message. This should produce the original plaintext message.

PGP allows for three main RSA key sizes. There are:

- 384 bits. This is intended for the casual user and can be cracked by serious crackers.
- 512 bits. This is intended for the commercial user and can only be cracked by organisations with a large budget and extensive computing facilities.
- 1024 bits. This is intended for military uses and, at present, cannot be cracked by anyone. This is the recommend key size for most users of reasonably powerful computers (386/486/Pentium/*etc*). In the future, a 2048-bit code may be used.

## 19.4 Example PGP encryption

The Pretty Good Privacy (PGP) program developed by Philip Zimmermann is widely available over the WWW. It runs as a stand-alone application, and uses various options to use the package. Table 19.1 outlines some of the options.

**Table 19.1** PGP options

| Option | Description |
| --- | --- |
| pgp -e textfile her_userid [other userids] | Encrypts a plaintext file with the recipent's public key. In this case, it produces a file named textfile.pgp. |
| pgp -s textfile [-u your_userid] | Sign a plaintext file with a secret key. In this case, it produces a file named textfile.pgp. |
| pgp -es textfile her_userid [other userids] [-u your_userid] | Signs a plaintext file with the senders secret key, and then encrypt it with recipient's public key. In this case, it produces a file named textfile.pgp. |
| pgp -c textfile | Encrypt with conventional encryption only. |
| pgp ciphertextfile [-o plaintextfile] | Decrypt or check a signature for a ciphertext (.pgp) file. |

To produce output in ASCII for email or to publish over the Internet, the –a option is used with other options. Table 19.2 shows the key management functions.

**Table 19.2**  PGP key management options

| Option | Description |
|---|---|
| pgp –kg | Generate a unique public and private key. |
| pgp –ka keyfile [keyring] | Adds key file's contents to the user's public or secret key ring. |
| pgp –kr userid [keyring] | Removes a key or a user ID from the user's public or secret key ring. |
| pgp –ke your_userid [keyring] | Edit user ID or pass phrase. |
| pgp –kx userid keyfile [keyring] | Extract a key from the public or secret key ring. |
| pgp –kv[v] [userid] [keyring] | View the contents of the public key ring. |
| pgp –kc [userid] [keyring] | Check signatures on the public key ring. |
| pgp –ks her_userid [–u your_userid] [keyring] | Sign someone else's public key on your public key ring. |
| pgp –krs userid [keyring] | Remove selected signatures from a userid on a keyring. |

### 19.4.1 RSA Key Generation

Both the public and the private keys are generated with:

```
pgp -kg
```

Initially, the user is asked about the key sizes. The larger the key the more secure it is. A 1024 bit key is very secure.

```
C:\pgp> pgp -kg
Pretty Good Privacy(tm) 2.6.3i - Public-key encryption for the masses.
(c) 1990-96 Philip Zimmermann, Phil's Pretty Good Software. 1996-01-18
International version - not for use in the USA. Does not use RSAREF.
Current time: 1998/12/29 23:13 GMT

Pick your RSA key size:
    1)    512 bits- Low commercial grade, fast but less secure
    2)    768 bits- High commercial grade, medium speed, good security
    3)   1024 bits- "Military" grade, slow, highest security
Choose 1, 2, or 3, or enter desired number of bits: 3

Generating an RSA key with a 1024-bit modulus.
```

Next, the program asks for a user ID, which is normally the users name and his/her password. This ID helps other users to find the required public key.

```
You need a user ID for your public key.  The desired form for this
user ID is your name, followed by your E-mail address enclosed in
<angle brackets>, if you have an E-mail address.
For example:  John Q. Smith <12345.6789@compuserve.com>
Enter a user ID for your public key:
Fred Bloggs <fred_b@myserver.com>
```

Next PGP asks for a pass phrase, which is used to protect the private key if another person gets hold of it. No person can use the secret key file, unless they know the pass phrase. Thus, the pass phase is like a password but is typically much longer. The phase is also required when the user is encrypting a message with his/her private key.

```
You need a pass phrase to protect your RSA secret key.
Your pass phrase can be any sentence or phrase and may have many
words, spaces, punctuation, or any other printable characters.
Enter pass phrase: fred bloggs
Enter same pass phrase again: fred bloggs
Note that key generation is a lengthy process.
```

The public and private keys are randomly derived by measuring the intervals between keystrokes. For this, the software asks for the user to type a number of keys.

```
We need to generate 384 random bits.  This is done by measuring the
time intervals between your keystrokes.  Please enter some random text
on your keyboard until you hear the beep:

We need to generate 384 random bits.  This is done by measuring the
time intervals between your keystrokes.  Please enter some random text
on your keyboard until you hear the beep:
<keyboard typing>

   0 * -Enough, thank you.
...................................****
...................................****
Pass phrase is good.  Just a moment....
Key signature certificate added.
Key generation completed.
```

This has successfully generated the public and private keys. The public key is placed on the public key ring (PUBRING.PGP) and the private key is place on the users secret key ring (SECRING.PGP).

```
C:\pgp> dir *.pgp
SECRING   PGP          518  12-29-98  11:20p secring.pgp
PUBRING   PGP          340  12-29-98  11:20p pubring.pgp
```

The –kx option can be used to extract the new public key from the public key ring and place it in a separate public key file, which can be sent to people who want to send an encrypted message to the user.

```
C:\pgp> pgp -kx fred_b
Extracting from key ring: 'pubring.pgp', userid "fred_b".
```

```
Key for user ID: Fred Bloggs <fred_b@myserver.com>
1024-bit key, key ID CD5AE745, created 1998/12/29
Extract the above key into which file? mykey

Key extracted to file 'mykey.pgp'.
```

The public key file (`mykey.pgp`) can be sent to other users, and can be added to their public key rings. Care must be taken never to send anyone a private key, but even if it is sent then it is still protected by the pass phase.

Often a user wants to publish their public key on their WWW page or transmit it by email. Thus, it requires to be converted into an ASCII format. For this the –kxa option can be used, such as:

```
C:\pgp> pgp -kxa fred_b

Extracting from key ring: 'pubring.pgp', userid "fred_b".
Key for user ID: Fred Bloggs <fred_b@myserver.com>
1024-bit key, key ID CD5AE745, created 1998/12/29

Extract the above key into which file? mykey
Transport armor file: mykey.asc
Key extracted to file 'mykey.asc'.

Extract the above key into which file? mykey

Transport armor file: mykey.asc

Key extracted to file 'mykey.asc'.
```

The file `mykey.asc` now contains an ASCII form of the key, such as:

```
Type Bits/KeyID      Date       User ID
pub  1024/CD5AE745 1998/12/29 Fred Bloggs <fred_b@myserver.com>

-----BEGIN PGP PUBLIC KEY BLOCK-----
Version: 2.6.3i

mQCNAzaJY84AAAEEAK0nvnuYcwGEaNdeqcDGXD6IrMFwX3iKtdGkZgyPyiENLb+C
bGX7P2zSG0z1d8c4f5OKYR/RgxzN4ILsAKthGaweGD0FJRgeIvn6FHJxEzmdBWIh
ME/8h2HZfegSXta8hFAMc8o9ASamolk5KBL0YWfsQlDNbR+dMJpPqQ7NWudFAAUT
tCFGcmVkIEJsb2dncyA8ZnJlZF9iQG15c2VydmVyLmNvbT6JAJUDBRA2iWPOmk+p
Ds1a50UBAfkoA/4gO5DllYko4DfjPnq4ItDtN55SgoE3upPWL52R5RQZF1BoJEF6
eLT/kejD5b7gli/yP1S456bh/k8ifi9RwSPUFN/zFUsVVYrSjZKD3kzClV1/QgTy
YmlDHHHgou6rYFXk7mGEtWc4g4D1rzds+ppc/UjN8uNp5KQUg1FsVatvPA==
=X5Xx
-----END PGP PUBLIC KEY BLOCK-----
```

Now, someone's public key can be added to the Fred's public key ring. In this case, Fred Bloggs wants to send a message to Bert Smith. Bert's public key, in an ASCII form, is:

```
Type Bits/KeyID      Date       User ID
pub  1024/770CA60D 1998/12/30 Bert Smith <Bert_s.otherserver.com>
```

```
-----BEGIN PGP PUBLIC KEY BLOCK-----
Version: 2.6.3i

mQCNAzaKE5AAAAEEAN+5td9acGlPcTKp5J42UpwbDqz6mHOaxcOllp6CoPE3+AXT
jfREEQ+TCOZxMP6cCcwtEMnjVqu2M7F6li3v/AVqQIRZZkFsEOZ+8hlseHBOFR8Y
f8FDpmgld6wNpp8ocOyVul/sBQl549u0C/KnVQ6LtXo7UlsBtnbua9J3DKYNAAUR
tCNCZXJOIFNtaXRoIDxCZXJ0X3Mub3RoZXJzZXJ2ZXIuY29tPokAlQMFEDaKE5B2
7mvSdwymDQEB2xkEANLMEDncVrFjR71abUIWHqquEFK+sqnOHPbHyIBni18x03UM
jeQJM1WA9/uIPqzeABJdD6anX4oK3yiByQjI5CT5+OdmU0y4e2+k1ab5mxxUWs7S
Tib3K5LLvPGxsOInOdunjFKaBLkrfU/L+zid3iW9FV6Zy8P07yDL2SmobRbh
=6rTj
-----END PGP PUBLIC KEY BLOCK-----
```

Fred can add Bert's key onto his public key ring with the –ka option:

```
C:\pgp> pgp -ka bert.pgp

Looking for new keys...
pub   1024/770CA60D 1998/12/30   Bert Smith <Bert_s.otherserver.com>

Checking signatures...
pub   1024/770CA60D 1998/12/30  Bert Smith <Bert_s.otherserver.com>
sig!        770CA60D 1998/12/30   Bert Smith <Bert_s.otherserver.com>


Keyfile contains:
   1 new key(s)

One or more of the new keys are not fully certified.
Do you want to certify any of these keys yourself (y/N)?
```

Bert's key has been added to Fred's public key ring. This ring can be listed with the –kv, as given next:

```
C:\pgp> pgp -kv

Key ring: 'pubring.pgp'
Type Bits/KeyID    Date        User ID
pub   1024/770CA60D 1998/12/30 Bert Smith <Bert_s.otherserver.com>
pub   1024/CD5AE745 1998/12/29 Fred Bloggs <fred_b@myserver.com>
2 matching keys found.
```

Next, a message can be sent to Bert, using his public key.

```
C:\pgp>edit message.txt
```
*Bert,*

*This is a secret message. Please*
*delete it after you have read it!*

*Fred.*

```
C:\pgp>pgp -e message.txt

Recipients' public key(s) will be used to encrypt.
A user ID is required to select the recipient's public key.
Enter the recipient's user ID: bert smith
```

```
Key for user ID: Bert Smith <Bert_s.otherserver.com>
1024-bit key, key ID 770CA60D, created 1998/12/30

WARNING: Because this public key is not certified with a trusted
signature, it is not known with high confidence that this public key
actually belongs to: "Bert Smith <Bert_s.otherserver.com>".

Are you sure you want to use this public key (y/N)? y
.
Ciphertext file: message.pgp
```

If the message needs to be transmitted by electronic mail or via a WWW page, it can be converted into text format with the –ea option, as given next:

```
C:\pgp>pgp -ea message.txt

Recipients' public key(s) will be used to encrypt.
A user ID is required to select the recipient's public key.
Enter the recipient's user ID: bert smith

Key for user ID: Bert Smith <Bert_s.otherserver.com>
1024-bit key, key ID 770CA60D, created 1998/12/30

WARNING: Because this public key is not certified with a trusted
signature, it is not known with high confidence that this public key
actually belongs to: "Bert Smith <Bert_s.otherserver.com>".
But you previously approved using this public key anyway.
.
Transport armor file: message.asc
```

The `message.asc` file is now in a form which can be transmitted in ASCII characters. In this case, it is:

```
-----BEGIN PGP MESSAGE-----
Version: 2.6.3i

hIwDdu5rOncMpg0BBAC7jOUx74vLb701lOCO0/5Fkc6pDJinqpA7isJH+JYbFkDj
wSv6vF/jAEonEPL8RVtqWncNDwjjwwV9OVPEZeaZ0qgZTWdbdSUilfqxZsaBo8Uz
dmmbzxd7CDTpnSYEyFWosPyzdxJqlsICig79Loh7l1BdJXEhKnMy+1VMieNYtKYA
AABrB8LTMj2lkk9t6JfS2yOc1t9EfpVMLX+rxtPZ+Tq1aCOwfid4E77FyiKN260N
APzF8J6elXhBgNM3zesA8fR8KdEnrI2BYC2XsBzTxOiKnpqoLMwWl0A7TTyhv24L
1PhwFi/YQ2SPhemdpqY=
=ooNT
-----END PGP MESSAGE-----
```

Bert can now simply decrypt the received message.

```
C:\pgp\bert> pgp message.pgp

File is encrypted.  Secret key is required to read it.
Key for user ID: Bert Smith <Bert_s.otherserver.com>
1024-bit key, key ID 770CA60D, created 1998/12/30

You need a pass phrase to unlock your RSA secret key.
Enter pass phrase: Bert Smith
Pass phrase is good.  Just a moment......
Plaintext filename: message
```

Or Bert can convert the ASCII form into a binary format with the –da option, and decrypt the message as before.

```
C:\pgp\bert> pgp -da message.asc
Stripped transport armor from 'message.asc', producing 'message.pgp'.
```

## 19.5 Exercises

**19.5.1** How many keys are used in the public-key system:

(a)  1                    (b)  3
(c)  2                    (d)  4

**19.5.2** A typical public-key system is:

(a)  IDE                  (b)  IDA
(c)  PGP                  (d)  IDEA

**19.5.3** In the PGP program, which option is used to create a public and a private key:

(a)  –key                 (b)  –ka
(c)  –kg                  (d)  –k

**19.5.4** Search for the PGP program on the Internet, and, if possible, download it. Next, do the following:

(a) Generate a public and a private key ring.
(b) Generate an ASCII form for your public key.
(c) Create the following message:

```
Help me! I'm on fire.

Martin.
```

(d) Create another user and a new public key, or determine another person's public key.
(e) Encrypt the message and give it to the other user.
(f) Decrypt the message.

**19.5.5** Explain why public-key methods tend to be more secure than private key methods. The discussion should include:

- Ease of changing the key.
- Ease of distribution.

- Additional extra bits to the key to make it more secure.
- Crackability (compared with the techniques discussed in Chapter 18).
- Compression techniques (especially in the PGP method).
- etc.

**19.5.6** The RSA encryption process involves factorising a prime number within a given range. Write an algorithm which determines whether a number is prime. If possible, implement it using a software language such as C, Pascal or BASIC. An outline of a C program is given next. With this program, identify how this program could be run faster, and benchmark the time it takes for the following ranges:

0 to 1,000,000 and     0 to 1,000,000,000

Note, for integers in these ranges the int data type must be changed to a long.

```
#include <stdio.h>
#define   TRUE   1
#define   FALSE  0

int main(void)
{
unsigned int i, j, prime;
    for (i=3;i<1000;i++)
    {
        prime=TRUE;
        for (j=2;j<=i/2;j++)
        {
            if ((i%j)==0)
            {
                prime=FALSE;
                break;
            }
        }
        if (prime) printf("%u ",i);
    }
    return(0);
}
```

A sample run is given next.

```
3 5 7 11 13 17 19 23 29 31 37 41 43 47 53 59 61 67 71 73 79 83
89 97 101 103 107 109 113 127 131 137 139 149 151 157 163 167
173 179 181 191 193 197 199 211 223 227 229 233 239 241 251 257
263 269 271 277 281 283 293 307 311 313 317 331 337 347 349 353
359 367 373 379 383 389 397 401 409 419 421 431 433 439 443 449
457 461 463 467 479 487 491 499 503 509 521 523 541 547 557 563
569 571 577 587 593 599 601 607 613 617 619 631 641 643 647 653
659 661 673 677 683 691 701 709 719 727 733 739 743 751 757 761
769 773 787 797 809 811 821 823 827 829 839 853 857 859 863 877
881 883 887 907 911 919 929 937 941 947 953 967 971 977 983 991
997
```

**19.5.7** Determine the number of iterations that a prime number factorising program would require for the following ranges:

1 to 10　　　1 to $10^2$　　　1 to $10^3$

1 to $10^6$　　　1 to $10^8$

**19.5.8** Modify the program in Section 19.2.3 so that it checks that the entered value is a prime number (rather than using a look-up table).

**19.5.9** The program in Section 19.2.3 causes a mathematical overflow when the prime number ($e$) is chosen to be large (such as 49). Investigate other methods of implementing this program so that there are no mathematical overflows. Also, check the range of integer values that can be implemented.

**19.5.10** How might a hacker spy on a sender who is using PGP, and determine the encryption code ($K_M$).

**19.5.11** Send me (*William Buchanan*) an email message that has been encrypted with my public key, which is available on my WWW page, a copy of which is:

```
Type Bits/KeyID     Date        User ID
pub  1024/AC7612DD 1998/12/30 William Buchanan
<w.buchanan@napier.ac.uk>
-----BEGIN PGP PUBLIC KEY BLOCK-----
Version: 2.6.3i

mQCNAzaKKSoAAAEEALQzETdRSHMO8QhyaEJe2bPP7suheyj3q2Wa3Xq8g34V6DS0
+APHRKLWmikt4SFqq8Y0q67Zq+NHhDGCjMEI3OlVXZiRjOiqKabkqheZTFf5eCJI
Ugq5hPcStb6bBjnXX0CTO9PW13XaSA0SJNALzRtOD2Ag+4i5tz7Wg2CsdhLdAAUT
tCpXaWxsaWFtIEJ1Y2hhbmFuIDx3LmJ1Y2hhbmFuQG5hcGllci5hYy51az6JAJUD
BRA2iikqPtaDYKx2Et0BAYM8A/wKbqPeNpRApfr+RaG0WxYVEGDUQIItzjFiR3+v
bjxJrUfK7vQ0STKVTPLaAQY7bBUaoaF9RtiT/pBbvLvMJMmUsmC3JJOZueFVsMf6
wY1BTYufTJ7OroFUxcNhiXRyvbVneR4xPsVlyoeqkPSnipyVpfjE48L/Plqs8PYu
PZzjLg==
=5bQj
-----END PGP PUBLIC KEY BLOCK-----
```

Note, if you want an encrypted message in reply, remember to send your public key.

## 19.6 Note from the author

*Public-key encryption methods are the key to the security of the Internet, and any information that is transmitted over the Internet. It so easy to change for a user to change public and private keys so that the transmitted data is more secure, and then to publicise the new public-key. Many governments are obviously against this move as it allows for the total security of many types of data. In fact, several governments have banned the usage of widely available public-key source code. So who is right? I think I know.*

*In the future, many forms of digital information will be encrypted. This could include telephone conversations, video conferencing, WWW accesses, remote login, file transfer, electronic commerce, running licensed applications, and so on.*

# 20 Authentication

## 20.1 Introduction

It is obviously important to encrypt a transmitted message, but how can it be proved that the user who originally encrypted the message sent the message. This is achieved with message authentication. The two users who are communicating are sometimes known as the principals. It should be assumed that an intruder (hacker) can intercept and listen to messages at any part of the communications, whether it be the initial communication between the two parties and their encryption keys or when the encrypted messages are sent. The intruder could thus playback any communications between the parties and pretend to be the other.

## 20.2 Shared secret-key authentication

With this approach a secret key, $K_{12}$ (between Fred and Bert) is used by both users. This would be transmitted through a secure channel, such as a telephone call, personal contact, mail message, and so on. The conversation will then be:

- The initiator (Fred) sends a challenge to the responder (Bert) which is a random number.
- The responder transmits it back using a special algorithm and the secret key. If the initiator receives back the correctly encrypted value then it knows that the responder is allowed to communicate with the user.

The random number should be large enough so that it is not possible for an intruder to listen to the communication and repeat it. There is little chance of the same 128-bit random number occurring within days, months or even years.

This method has validated Bert to Fred, but not Fred to Bert. Thus, Bert needs to know that the person receiving his communications is Fred. Thus, Bert initiates the same procedure as before, sending a random number to Fred, who then encrypts it and sends it back. After this has been successfully received by Bert, encrypted communications can begin.

## 20.3 Diffie-Hellman key exchange

In the previous section, a private key was passed over a secure line. The Diffie-Hellman method allows for keys to be passed electronically. For this, Fred and Bert pick two large prime numbers:

$a$=Prime Number 1
$b$=Prime Number 2

where:

$(a-1)/2$ is also prime. The values of $a$ and $b$ are public keys. Next, Fred picks a private key ($c$) and Bert picks a private key ($d$). Fred sends the values of:

$(a, b, b^c \bmod a)$

Bert then responds by sending:

$(b^d \bmod a)$

For example:

$a$=43 (first prime number), $b$=7 (second prime number), $c$=9 (Fred's private key), $d$=8 (Bert's private key). Note, that the value of $a$ (43) would not be used as $(a-1)/2$ is not prime (21).

Thus, the values sent by Fred will be:

(43, 7, 42)

The last value is 42 as $7^9$ is 40,353,607, and 40,353,607 mod 43, is 42. Bert will respond back with:

(6)

as $7^8$ is 5,764,801, and 5,764,801 mod 43 is 6.

Next Fred and Bert will calculate:

$b^{cd} \bmod a$

and both use this as their secret key. Figure 20.1 shows an example of the interchange. It is difficult for an intruder to determine the values of $c$ and $d$, when the values of $a$, $b$, $c$ and $d$ are large.

Unfortunately, this method suffers from the man-in-the-middle attack, where the intruder incepts the communications between Fred and Bert. Figure 20.2 shows an interceptor (Bob) who has chosen a private key of $e$. Thus, Fred thinks he is talking to Bert, and vice-versa, but Bob is acting as the man-in-the-middle. Bob then uses two different keys when talking with Fred and Bert.

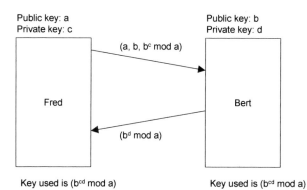

**Figure 20.1** Dillie-Hellman key exchange

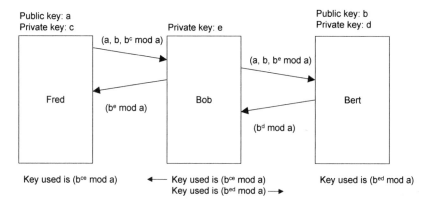

**Figure 20.2** Man-in-the-middle attack

## 20.4 Key distribution centre

The Dillie-Hellman method suffers from the man-in-the-middle attack, it also requires a separate key for each communication channel. A KDC (key distribution centre) overcomes these problems with a single key and a secure channel for authentication. In a KDC, the authentication and session keys are managed through the KDC. One method is the wide-mouth protocol, which does the following:

- Fred selects a session key ($K_{SESS}$).
- Fred sends an encrypted message which contains the session key. The message is encrypted with $K_{KDC1}$, which is the key that Fred uses to pass messages to and from the KDC.
- The KDC decrypts this encrypted message using the $K_{KDC1}$ key. It also extracts the session key ($K_{SESS}$). This session key is added to the encrypted message and then

encrypted with $K_{KDC2}$, which is the key that Bert uses to pass messages to and from the KDC.

This method is relatively secure as there is a separate key used between the transmission between Fred and the KDC, and between Bert and the KDC. These keys are secret to Fred and the KDC, and between Bert and the KDC. The drawback with the method is that if the intruder determines secret key used for Fred to communicate with the KDC then it is possible to trick the KDC that it is communicating with Fred. As the key is unchanging, the theft of a key may take some time to discover and the possible damage widespread. The intruder can simply choose a new session key each time there is a new session.

## 20.5 Digital signatures

Digital signatures provide a way of validating an electronic document, in the same way as a hand-written signature does on a document. It must provide:

- Authentication of the sender. This is important as the recipient can verify the sender of the message.
- Authentication of the contents of the message. This is important, as the recipient knows that a third party has not modified the original contents of the message. Normally, this is also time-stamped.
- Authentication that the contents have not been changed by the recipient. This is important in legal cases where the recipient can prove that the message was as the original.

### 20.5.1 Secret-key signatures

The secret-key signature involves a user selecting a secret-key which is passed to a central authority, who keeps the key private. When Fred wants to communicate with Bert, he passes the plaintext to the central authority and encrypts it with a secret-key and the time-stamp. The central authority then passes an encrypted message to Bert using the required secret-key. A time-stamp is added to the message that is sent to Bert. This provides for a legal verification of the time the message was sent, and also stops intruders from replaying a transmitted message. The main problem with this method is that the central authority (typically, banks, government departmental or legal professionals) must be trustworthy and reliable. They can also read all of the transmitted messages.

### 20.5.2 Message digests

Public and private-key signatures provide for both authentication and secrecy, but in many cases, all that is required is that a text message is sent with the required authentication. A method of producing authentication is message digest, which generates a unique message digest for every message. The most common form of message digest is MD5 (RFC1321, R.Rivest). It is designed to be relatively fast to compute and does not require any large substitution tables. In summary, its operation is:

- It takes as input a message of arbitrary length.
- Produces an 128-bit "fingerprint" (or message digest) of the input.
- It is not possible to produce two messages which have the same message digest, or to produce any message from a prespecified target message digest.

### 20.5.3 MD5 algorithm

Initially, the message with $b$ bits is arranged as follows:

$m_0\ m_1\ m_2\ m_3\ m_4\ m_5\ m_6\ ...\ m_{b-1}$

Next five steps are performed:

- Adding padding bits. The message is padded so that its length is 64 bits less than being a multiple of 512 bits. For example, if the message is 900 bits long, then an extra 60 bits will be added so that it is 64 bits short of 1024 bits. The padded bits are a single '1' bit followed by '0' bits. At least one bit must be added and, at the most, 512 bits are added.

- Append Length. A 64-bit representation of $b$ (the length of the message before the padding bits were added) is appended to the result of the previous step. The resulting message will thus be a multiple of 512 bits, or:

  $m_0\ m_1\ m_2\ m_3\ m_4\ m_5\ m_6\ ...\ m_{n-1}$

  where $n$ is a multiple of 512.

- MD Buffer initialised. A four-word buffer (A, B, C, D) is used to compute the message digest. These are initialised to the following hexadecimal values (low-order bytes first):

  A: 01 23 45 67h  (0000 0001 0010 ... 0111)   B: 89 ab cd efh
  C: fe dc ba 98h  (1111 1110 1101 ... 1000)   D: 76 54 32 10h

- Message processed in 16-word blocks. Next four auxiliary functions are defined which operate on three 32-bit words and produce a single 32-bit word. These are:

$$F(x, y, z) = X.Y + \overline{X}.Z$$
$$G(x, y, z) = X.Z + Y.\overline{Z}$$
$$H(x, y, z) = X \oplus Y \oplus Z$$
$$I(x, y, z) = Y \oplus \left(X + \overline{Z}\right)$$

This step also involves a 64-element table T[1 ... 64] which is made of a function , where T[i] is equal to the integer part of $4\,294\,967\,296$ times abs(sin(i)), where i is in radians.

The algorithm is as follows:

```
/* Process each 16-word block. */
For i = 0 to N/16-1 do
    /* Copy block i into X. */
    For j = 0 to 15 do
        Set X[j] to M[i*16+j].
    end /* of loop on j */

    /* Save A as AA, B as BB, C as CC, and D as DD. */
    AA = A    BB = B
    CC = C    DD = D

    /* Round 1. */
    /* Let [abcd k s i] denote the operation  a = b + ((a + F(b,c,d) + X[k] + T[i]) <<< s). */
    /* Do the following 16 operations. */
    [ABCD 0 7 1] [DABC 1 12 2] [CDAB 2 17 3] [BCDA 3 22 4]
    [ABCD 4 7 5] [DABC 5 12 6] [CDAB 6 17 7] [BCDA 7 22 8]
    [ABCD 8 7 9] [DABC 9 12 10] [CDAB 10 17 11] [BCDA 11 22 12]
    [ABCD 12 7 13] [DABC 13 12 14] [CDAB 14 17 15] [BCDA 15 22 16]

    /* Round 2. */
    /* Let [abcd k s i] denote the operation  a = b + ((a + G(b,c,d) + X[k] + T[i]) <<< s). */

    /* Do the following 16 operations. */
    [ABCD 1 5 17] [DABC 6 9 18] [CDAB 11 14 19] [BCDA 0 20 20]
    [ABCD 5 5 21] [DABC 10 9 22] [CDAB 15 14 23] [BCDA 4 20 24]
    [ABCD 9 5 25] [DABC 14 9 26] [CDAB 3 14 27] [BCDA 8 20 28]
    [ABCD 13 5 29] [DABC 2 9 30] [CDAB 7 14 31] [BCDA 12 20 32]

    /* Round 3. */
    /* Let [abcd k s t] denote the operation  a = b + ((a + H(b,c,d) + X[k] + T[i]) <<< s). */

    /* Do the following 16 operations. */
    [ABCD 5 4 33] [DABC 8 11 34] [CDAB 11 16 35] [BCDA 14 23 36]
    [ABCD 1 4 37] [DABC 4 11 38] [CDAB 7 16 39] [BCDA 10 23 40]
    [ABCD 13 4 41] [DABC 0 11 42] [CDAB 3 16 43] [BCDA 6 23 44]
    [ABCD 9 4 45] [DABC 12 11 46] [CDAB 15 16 47] [BCDA 2 23 48]

    /* Round 4. */
    /* Let [abcd k s t] denote the operation  a = b + ((a + I(b,c,d) + X[k] + T[i]) <<< s). */
    /* Do the following 16 operations. */
    [ABCD 0 6 49] [DABC 7 10 50] [CDAB 14 15 51] [BCDA 5 21 52]
    [ABCD 12 6 53] [DABC 3 10 54] [CDAB 10 15 55] [BCDA 1 21 56]
    [ABCD 8 6 57] [DABC 15 10 58] [CDAB 6 15 59] [BCDA 13 21 60]
    [ABCD 4 6 61] [DABC 11 10 62] [CDAB 2 15 63] [BCDA 9 21 64]

    /* Then perform the following additions */

    A = A + AA   B = B + BB   C = C + CC   D = D + DD
end
/* of loop on i */
```

Note that the $<<<$ symbol represent the rotate left operation, where the bits are rotated to the left.

- Output. The message digest is produced from A, B, C and D, where A is the low-order byte and D the high-order byte.

Standard test results give the following message digests:

| Message | Message digest |
| --- | --- |
| "" | d41d8cd98f00b204e9800998ecf8427e |
| "a" | 0cc175b9c0f1b6a831c399e269772661 |
| "abc" | 900150983cd24fb0d6963f7d28e17f72 |
| "abcdefghijklmnopqrstuvwxyz" | f96b697d7cb7938d525a2f31aaf161d0 |
| "ABCDEFGHIJKLMNOPQRSTUVWXYZabcdefghijklmnopqrstuvwxyz0123456789" | c3fcd3d76192e4007dfb496cca67e13b |
| "12345678901234567890123456789012345678901234567890123456789012345678901234567890" | 57edf4a22be3c955ac49da2e2107b67a |

## 20.6  PGP authentication

As well as encryption, PGP provides for a digital signature. This public-key method is an excellent way of authentication as it does not require the exchange of keys over a secure channel. In PGP, the sender's own private key is used to encrypt the message, thus signing it. This digital signature is then checked by the recipient by using the sender's public key to decrypt it. As previously mentioned, the advantages are:

- Authenticates the sender.
- Authentication of the contents of the message.
- Authentication that the message has not been modified by the recipient or any third party.
- Sender cannot undo a signature, once applied (there are no erasers with digital signatures).
- Message integrity.
- Allows signatures to be stored separately from messages, without actually revealing the contents of the message.

Thus, encryption is achieved by encrypting the message with the recipient's public key, and authentication by signing the message with the sender's private key. To make a digital signature, PGP encrypts using the secret key. It does not encrypt the whole message, only a message digest, which is a 128-bit extract of the message (a bit like a checksum). The MD5 algorithm is used for this, and provides a fingerprint that is extremely difficult to forge.

The MD5 algorithm is a standard algorithm and can be easily replicated, thus the senders private key is used to provide authentication, as the sender encrypts the message digest with his secret key. The steps are:

- Sender uses the message to determine the message digest.
- Sender's secret key encrypts the message digest and an electronic timestamp,

forming a digital signature, or signature certificate.

- Sender sends the digital signature along with the message.
- Recipient reads the message and the digital signature. The message is decrypted by the receiver using the recipients private key.
- Recipient recovers the original message digest from the digital signature by decrypting it with the sender's public key.
- Recipient calculates a new message digest from the message, and then check this against the recovered message digest from the received information. It they are the same then it authenticates the message and the sender.

A hacker, if they tried to modify the message in any way, would have to do the following:

- Recreate another identical message digest (which is not really possible)
- Produce an altered message which produces an identical message digest (which again is not really possible).
- Create a new message with a different message digest (which is not really possible without knowing the sender's private key).

With the PGP program, the –sa option can be used to generate the digital signature. For example:

```
C:\pgp\bert> pgp -sa message.txt
A secret key is required to make a signature.
You specified no user ID to select your secret key,
so the default user ID and key will be the most recently
added key on your secret keyring.

You need a pass phrase to unlock your RSA secret key. bert smith
Key for user ID: Bert Smith <Bert_s.otherserver.com>
1024-bit key, key ID 770CA60D, created 1998/12/30

Enter pass phrase: Pass phrase is good.  Just a moment....
Output file 'message.asc' already exists.  Overwrite (y/N)? y

Transport armor file: message.asc
```

The encrypted digital signature, in this case, is:

```
-----BEGIN PGP MESSAGE-----
Version: 2.6.3i

owHrZJjKzMpg1jVtTdm77EvlPMt4GRn/KDP/Yr7JWPN8/Zani1pkBBmWznvTsdl4
g1yN9+WoRz+WqFb9L3vC1jElv3xZ1v45jLdMCuTqdz5ZyKe5WFV06/yfTbu7ZZ78
nP93yhIb4XW8qSu2sdrHfbhjr9TNY+Om/6FzveeigymfyzZvcOT/l2PKky3iqCGi
WC2+4jnjbLUXKVNfWc7NfPbr4ZqMJO7c1OLixPRUvZKKEgYgcEotKtHh5eLlCsnI
LFYAokSF4tTkotQSBZhChYCc1MTiVF6ulNSc1JJUhcwShcS0ktQihcr8UoWMxLJU
haLUxBSgsCLIGLei1BQ9Xi4A
=iGfx
-----END PGP MESSAGE-----
```

The message and the digital signature can be produced using the –sea option. In this case, it produces the file:

```
-----BEGIN PGP MESSAGE-----
Version: 2.6.3i

hIwDdu5r0ncMpg0BBACF3bP4h0vt9ajaD3Vgf4aSUds03jfB9xXzZY9YjzjHyFBX
dO8IzMyDB6KdeX2cJk1pdPWhHi0cRQ2ddxoEBdS38XCJtjuTf0DYkwid+0dClt69
ntkwy0Lc4Y6QoDk9BHnVtDTkUu8J12KJrkoRx4DikumVbGB+CCAfCTOcr1U2vqYA
AAEMsURzRPLqwXDToFkzXA11EAfQ5ECJPFbsejBJhkbZAZ0aswVMYgX52wEnWxcI
MRmz0IdRLDtXtZ9SJvFzWMpPzVygOmOMDKhiDuEOI89D/HOomM1BaRH41Zx6xqf4
8LuhtJSwNdgHE07jiGAmvKkxRobUeOmZoEqs6BrU8hveJwGE4n0OVwWIzXbqH2BL
GTD8nAMFgqbh1LGfc3SV6bIst7z13HdFMSg1ZonbQj39i/ZTv8qzHY5rqN7uBPJb
eHU02wjCo3Dyc1atohPApcNEYmgkzaSQYkKeL9Zo3JRlk9xGbjZdtSk6+fxYU2WF
BQrW/AQheT51M68uDLe7OJ2+ny9m4nNEnwwDGqNaWg==
=f4f8
-----END PGP MESSAGE-----
```

The file can then be validated and decrypted as follows:

```
C:\pgp> pgp message
File has signature.  Public key is required to check signature.
.
Good signature from user "Bert Smith <Bert_s.otherserver.com>".
Signature made 1998/12/30 21:08 GMT using 1024-bit key, key ID 770CA60D

WARNING:  Because this public key is not certified with a trusted
signature, it is not known with high confidence that this public key
actually belongs to: "Bert Smith <Bert_s.otherserver.com>".
But you previously approved using this public key anyway.
Plaintext filename: message
```

## 20.7  Exercises

**20.7.1**  Which of the following is not an advantage of public-key authentication:

    (a)    Provides message integrity

    (b)    Signatures can be stored, independently of the message

    (c)    No party can change the contents of an encrypted message, even the sender

    (d)    It makes the encrypted message, even more secure

**20.7.2**  Which key does the recipient use to decrypt the main message:

    (a)    Recipients public key    (b)    Recipients private key

    (a)    Senders public key    (b)    Senders private key

**20.7.3**  Which key does the recipient use to authenticate the sender:

    (a)    Recipients public key    (b)    Recipients private key

    (a)    Senders public key    (b)    Senders private key

**20.7.4** How many bits does the message digest have in PGP:

    (a)   Depends on the message.   (b)   16
    (c)   128                        (d)   256

**20.7.5** Using the PGP program, pass a message with your digital and check the that recipient has validated your signature.

**20.7.6** Explain how PGP adds a digital signature to a message.

**20.7.7** Outline the advantages of authentication. Describe why a digital signature is a more secure method of authentication than a normal hand-written signature.

**20.7.8** What advantages does PGP authentication have over private-key methods.

**20.7.9** Show that in Diffie-Hellam that if $a=37$ (first prime number), $b=11$ (second prime number), $c=5$ (Fred's private key), $d=8$ (Bert's private key), the values sent be:

(37, 11, 27)

and

(10)

**20.7.10** Write a program (or use a spreadsheet or a calculator) to search for the solution to:

$11^x \bmod 7 = 2$

Prove that the value of $x$ is 5.

**20.7.11** Determine values of $a$ so that $a$ is prime and the following is also prime:

$(a-1)/2$

---

## 20.8 Note from the author

*Anyone who believes that a written signature is a good method of security is wrong. I have seen many occurrences of people forging another person's signature. Also, modern electronic scanning and near-perfect quality printing allows for easy forgeries. For example, it is extremely easy to scan-in a whole document, convert it to text (using optical character recognition) and then to reprint a changed version. Thus, digital authentication is the only real way to authenticate the sender and the contents of a message. But, unfortunately, the legal system tends to take a long time to catch up with technology, but it will happen someday.*

# 21 Internet Security

## 21.1 Introduction

As more information is stored on the Internet, and the amount of secure information, such as credit transfers and database transfers, increases, the need for a secure transmission mechanism also increases. The Internet has outgrown its founding protocol, HTTP. There thus has to be increased security in:

- Data encryption of WWW pages. This provides for secret information to be encrypted with a secret key.
- Message integrity. This provides a method of validating that the transmitted message is valid and has not been changed, either in transmission or in storage.
- Server authentication. This provides a method in which a server is authenticated to a client, to stop hackers pretending that they are the accessed server.
- Client authentication. This provides a method in which the client is authenticated to the server, to stop hackers from accessing a restricted server.

The main methods used are Secure Socket Layer (SSL) which was developed by Netscape, and Secure-HTTP (S-HTTP) which was developed by Enterprise Integration Technologies. Both are now being considered as International standards.

Two main problems are:

- Protection of transmitted information. For example, a person could access a book club over the Internet and then send information on the book and also credit-card information. The Book Club is likely to be a reputable company but criminals who can simply monitor the connection between the user and the Book Club could infiltrate the credit-card information.
- Protection of the client's computer. The Internet has little inherent security for the programs which can be downloaded from it. Thus, with no security, programs could be run or files can be download which could damage the local computer.

## 21.2 Secure Socket Layer (SSL)

Many WWW sites now state that they implement SSL. SSL was developed by Netscape and has now been submitted to the W3 Consortium for its acceptable as an International standard.

SSL allows the information stored and the server to be authenticated. Its advantages are:

- Open and non-propriety protocol.
- Data encryption, server authentication and message integrity.
- Firewall compatibility.
- Tunnelling connections.
- Supports S-MIME (Secure-MIME).

Figure 21.1 shows how SSL fits into the OSI model. It can be seen that it interfaces directly to TCP/IP. This thus has the advantage that it makes programs and high-level protocols secure, such as ftp, telnet, SMTP and HTTP. Most browsers now support SSL, and many servers also support it. Figure 21.2 shows that the current browser supports SSL Version 2 and also Version 3.

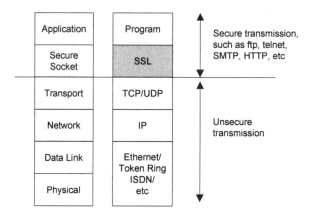

**Figure 21.1** SSL and the OSI model

### 21.2.1 Digital certificates

SSL supports independent certificate publishing authorities for server certificate authentication, as shown in Figure 21.3. These certificates have been validated by a reputable body and verify that the site is secure and genuine. These certificates can include Network server authentication, Network client authentication, Secure e-mail and Software Publishing, and can be viewed when connecting to the server. Typical certifying authorities are:

- ATT Certificate Services and ATT Directory Services.
- GTE Cyber Trust Root.
- internetMCI.
- Keywitness Canada.
- Microsoft Authenticode (TM) Root, Microsoft Root Authority, Microsoft Root SGC Authority and Microsoft Timestamp Root.
- Thawte Personal Basic CA, Thawte Personal Freemail CA, Thawte Personal Premium CA and Thawte Personal Server CA.

- VeriSign Class 1 Primary CA, VeriSign Class 2 Primary CA, VeriSign Class 2 Primary CA, VeriSign Class 2 Primary CA, VeriSign Commercial Software Publishers CA, VeriSign Individual Software Publishers CA, VeriSign Time Stamping CA, VeriSign/RSA Commercial CA and VeriSign/RSA Secure Server CA.

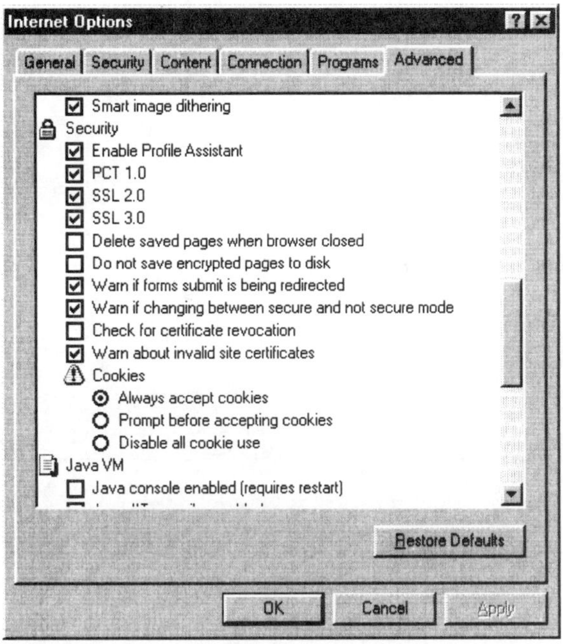

**Figure 21.2**  Security options

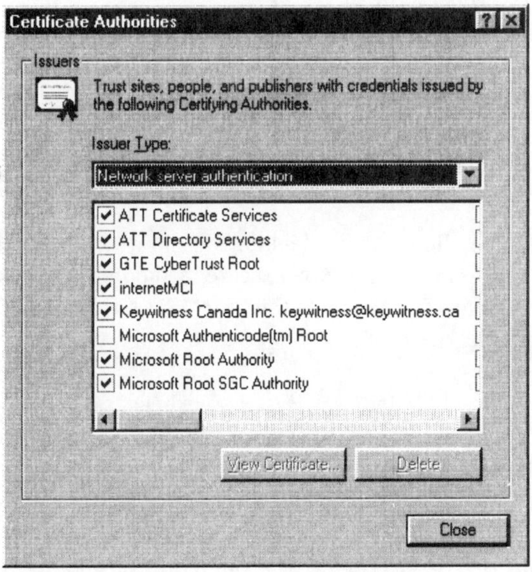

**Figure 21.3**  Certificate authorities

The WWW browser checks the certificate to see if it is valid. This includes checking the date that the certificate was issued, the site fingerprint (as show in Figure 21.4). The current date should be later than the issue date of the certificate. There is also an expiry date. If any of the information is not current and valid, the browser displays a warning.

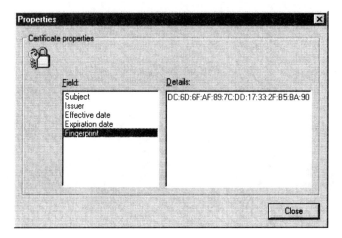

**Figure 21.4** Fingerprint

For example, for VeriSign/RSA Commercial:

Subject:         US, "RSA Data Security, Inc.", Commercial Certification Authority
Issuer:          US, "RSA Data Security, Inc.", Commercial Certification Authority
Effective date:  04/11/94 18:58:34
Expiration date: 03/11/99 18:58:34
Fingerprint:     5A:0B:DD:42:9E:B2:B4:62:97:32:7F:7F:0A:AA:9A:39

## 21.3  S-HTTP

HTTP supports the communication of multimedia information, such as audio, video, graphics and text. Unfortunately it is not a secure method of transmission and an external person can tap it into. To overcome this, S-HTTP has been developed to provide improved security. It features are:

- It is an extension to HTTP and uses HTTP-style headers.
- It incorporates encryption.
- It supports digital signatures for authentication.
- It supports certificates and key signing.

The Internet Engineering Task Force (IETF) are now considering S-HTTP for a standard method of transmitting secure HTTP over the Internet.

### 21.3.1 Message creation

An HTTP message contains both the message header and the message body. The header defines the type coding used in the body, its format, and so on. S-HTTP uses an encrypted message body and a message header, which includes the method that can be used to decrypt the message body. The process is as follows:

- The S-HTTP server (such as a WWW server) obtains the plain-text message of the information to send to the client (either locally or via a proxy). The message is either an HTTP message or some other data object (such as, a database entry or a graphical image).
- The server then encrypts the message body using the client's cryptographic preferences and the key provided by the client. The preference and key is passed in the initial handshake connection. This preference must also match the servers supported encryption techniques. The client normally sends a list of supported techniques and the server picks the most preferred one.
- The server sends the encrypted message to the client, in the same way as an HTTP transaction would occur, from which the client recovers the original message.

### 21.3.2 Message recovery

The encrypted file S-HTTP message is transmitted to the client, who then reads the message header to determine encryption technique. The client then decrypts it using the required private key, as shown in Figure 21.5. After this, the client displays the encapsulated HTTP or other data within the client's browser.

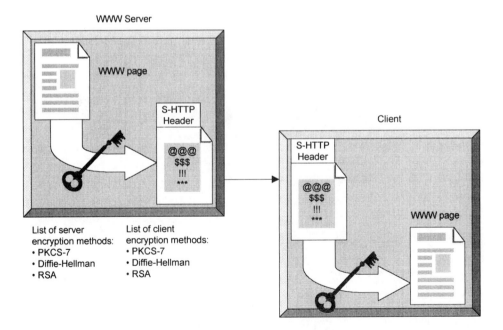

**Figure 21.5** Encryption of WWW page

Normally in an HTTP transaction, the server terminates the connection after the transmission of the HTTP data. In S-HTTP this does not occur, the server does not terminate the connection until the browser tells it so. This is because there is no need to perform a handshake, and thus the encryption key remains valid.

### 21.3.3 Browser and servers

SSL supports server authentication and also secure connections. This is achieved with:

- Secure transmission. Secure sites have URLs which begins with `https://`, where the `s` stands for secure. Other secure protocols are:

  - HTTPS (for HTTP).
  - FTPS (for FTP).
  - NNTPS (NNTP, news server).
  - UUCPS (UUCP).

Netscape Navigator and Microsoft Internet Explorer both show the connection to secure site. Navigator shows it with key at the bottom of the window (a broken key shows a non-secure site), and Netscape Communicator and Internet Explorer displays a padlock, as shown in Figure 21.6. Figure 21.7 shows how Communicator shows the security options when the user clicks on the padlock, and Figure 21.8 shows an example window for the security settings. Figure 21.9 shows the configuration for SSL Version 3.

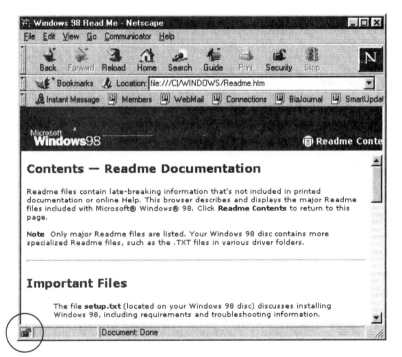

**Figure 21.6** Security lock

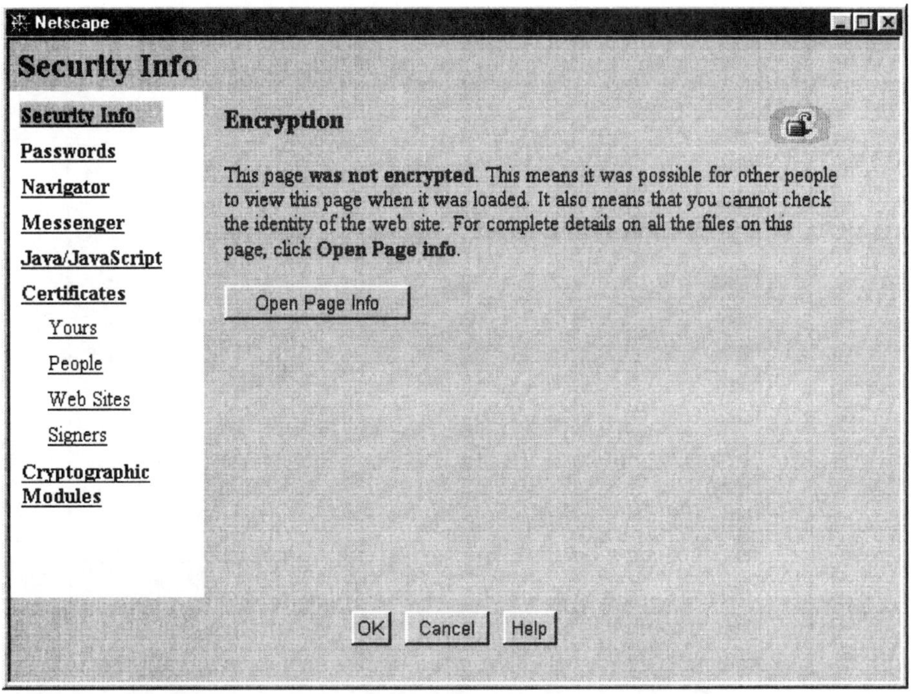

**Security Info**

Security Info
Passwords
Navigator
Messenger
Java/JavaScript
Certificates
   Yours
   People
   Web Sites
   Signers
Cryptographic
Modules

**Encryption**

This page **was not encrypted**. This means it was possible for other people to view this page when it was loaded. It also means that you cannot check the identity of the web site. For complete details on all the files on this page, click **Open Page info**.

Open Page Info

OK    Cancel    Help

**Figure 21.7**   Security information

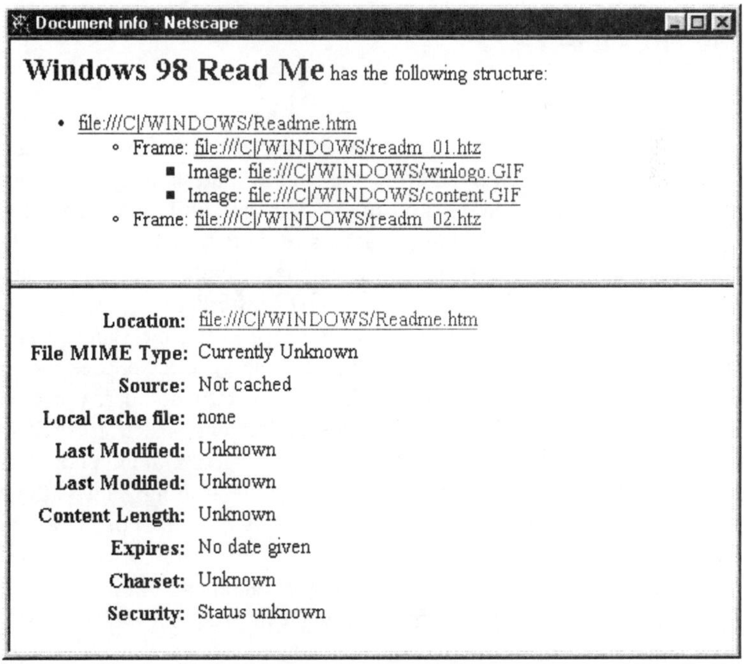

**Document info - Netscape**

**Windows 98 Read Me** has the following structure:

- file:///C|/WINDOWS/Readme.htm
   - Frame: file:///C|/WINDOWS/readm_01.htz
      - Image: file:///C|/WINDOWS/winlogo.GIF
      - Image: file:///C|/WINDOWS/content.GIF
   - Frame: file:///C|/WINDOWS/readm_02.htz

| | |
|---|---|
| **Location:** | file:///C|/WINDOWS/Readme.htm |
| **File MIME Type:** | Currently Unknown |
| **Source:** | Not cached |
| **Local cache file:** | none |
| **Last Modified:** | Unknown |
| **Last Modified:** | Unknown |
| **Content Length:** | Unknown |
| **Expires:** | No date given |
| **Charset:** | Unknown |
| **Security:** | Status unknown |

**Figure 21.8**   Page information

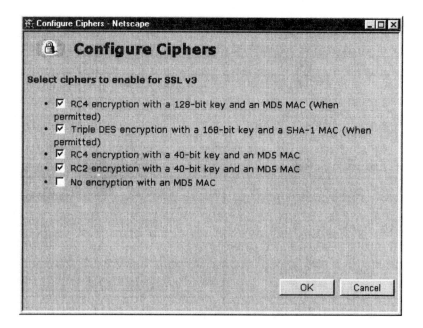

**Figure 21.9** SSL Version 3 configuration

## 21.4 Content advisor

A major problem with the Internet is the access to an almost unlimited amount of information, some of which may be unsuitable for certain users. An important consideration is the protection of children from unsuitable material, especially those of a violent or sexual content. Content advisors, which are built into browsers (Figure 21.10), allow a method of controlling the access to certain WWW pages. The ratings of WWW pages include four content types: language, nudity, sex and violence. The level of content can also be set and Table 21.1 gives different levels within each of the types. For example language is split into five levels: Inoffensive slang (least likely to offend), mild expletives, moderate expletives, obscene gestures and explicit or crude language (most likely to offend). These rating are industry-standards and have been defined independently by the Platform for Internet Content Selection (PICS) committee. It should be noted that note all Internet content is rated, although hopefully, in the future, that all the material from certified sites will have a rating. This is the only true way to protect users from objectionable content. Every parent whose child has access to the Internet, and site managers (especially in schools) should have knowledge of these ratings and set the system up so that it protects innocent minds. Children should not be left to their own devices on what, and what they cannot, be able to view. National laws cannot properly legislate against the content of material which is located in a foreign country.

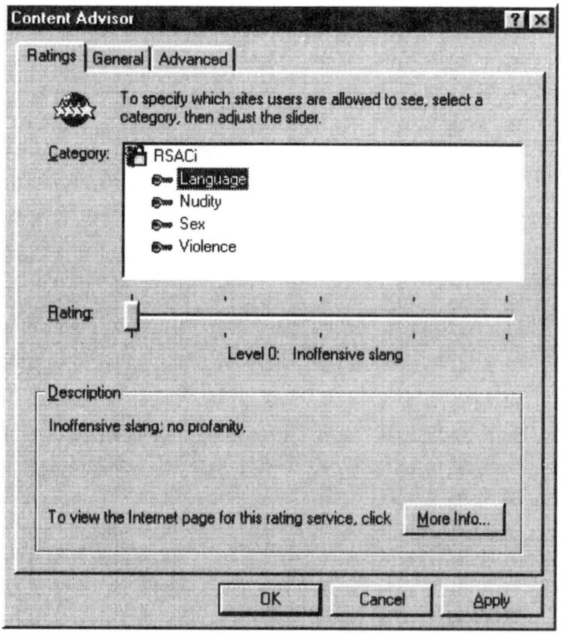

**Figure 21.10**  Content advisor

**Table 21.1**  Content advisor level settings

| Level | Language | Nudity | Sex | Violence |
|---|---|---|---|---|
| 0 | Inoffensive slang | None | No sexual activity portrayed / Romance. | No aggressive violence; No natural or accidental violence. |
| 1 | Mild expletives. Or mild terms for body functions. | Revealing attire | Passionate kissing | Creatures injured or killed; damage to realistic objects. |
| 2 | Expletives; non-sexual anatomical references. | Partial nudity | Clothed sexual touching | Humans or creatures injured or killed. Rewards injuring non-threatening creatures. |
| 3 | Strong, vulgar language; obscene gestures. Use of epithets. | Frontal nudity | Non-explicit sexual touching | Humans injured or killed. |
| 4 | Extreme hate, speech or crude language. Explicit sexual references. | Provocative nudity | Explicit sexual actual | Wanton and gratuitous violence |

Methods, which can be used to reduce the problem, are:

- Restrict access of WWW browsers to certified sites and set the content ratings for these sites.
- Log all DNS access. Many sites have a local DNS which tries to resolve IP addresses to domain names. Many of these programs allow a log to be kept to log DNS enquires and the IP address of the computer which accessed the site. The system manager can occasionally view the file to determine if certain users are abusing their privileges. A real-time trace can then be applied to catch these users (often a warning is the best medicine, followed by formal procedures if the accesses continue).
- Issue clear statements to all users, normally with large typed notices, which clearly state the sites and the type of content which should not be accessed. This is important from a legal point of view, and could be used as evidence that the organisation has a clear statement on Internet access. Organisations who fail to do this are in danger of being held responsible for objectionable accesses.

The best policing policy is one of trust and of educating users. Unfortunately, a minority of users are tempted by the ease of access to objectionable information.

## 21.5 Security zones

Security zones support different levels of security for different areas of the Web to protect your computer. Each zone has a suitable security level, this is shown on the right-hand side of the Internet Explorer status bar. The browser checks the WWW sites zone when a page is opened or downloaded. The four zones, as shown in Figure 21.11, are:

- **Local Intranet**. This is any address that doesn't require a proxy server. The default security level for this zone is Medium.
- **Trusted Sites**. This defines the sites that are most trusted, in which files can be run or downloaded without worrying about damaging the computer. The default security level for this zone is Low.
- **Restricted Sites**. This defines the sites that cannot be trusted. The default security level for this zone is High.
- **Internet**. This zone contains anything that is not on your computer or an intranet, or assigned to any other zone. The default security level for this zone is Medium.

Sites with a low security rate will generally be safe to run or download programs, whereas, they should be avoided in restricted sites. The security ratings are:

- High (most secure). Exclude content that could damage the local computer.
- Medium (more secure). Warn before running potentially damaging content.
- Low. Do not warn before running potentially damaging content.

- Custom. Allows users to set site security. An example of custom security settings is shown in Figure 21.12.

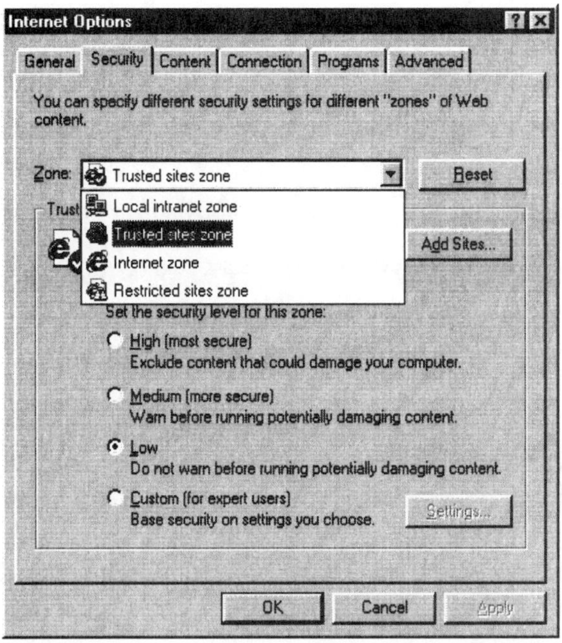

**Figure 21.11** Zones

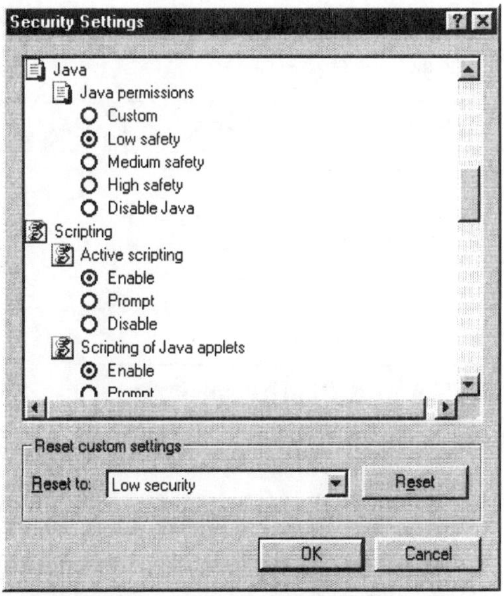

**Figure 21.12** Security settings

Security settings include:

- Active X controls and plugins.
- Java. Sets Java permissions. Figure 21.13 shows example permissions.
- Downloads. Enable file downloads (enable or disable) and font downloads (enable, disable or prompt).
- User authentication. Logon details, such as Automatic logon, Anonymous login, Prompt for user name and password and Automatic Logon with current user name and password.
- Miscellaneous. Such as drag-and-drop and installation of desktop files.

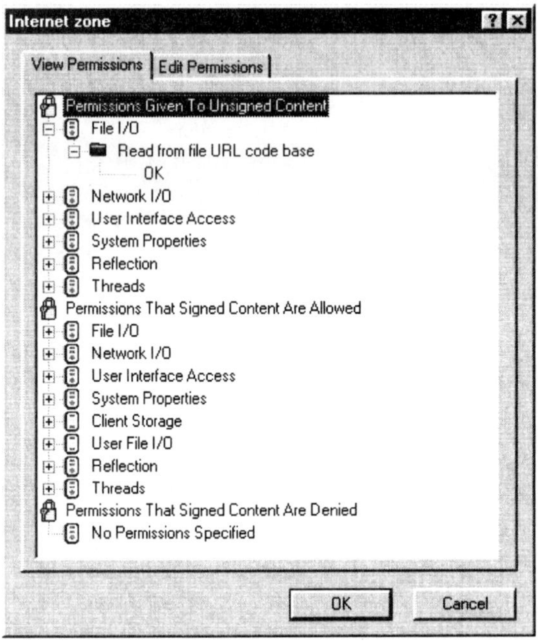

**Figure 21.13**   Java security

## 21.6  Microsoft Wallet and Profile Assistant

Microsoft Wallet is a new concept which was introduced in Internet Explorer Version 4. It stores address and payment method information on the local computer for on-line shopping. Figure 21.14 shows an example address book and Figure 21.15 shows a credit-card form. A wallet-enabled Internet site will automatically receive shipping address and credit card data. It is stored in a secure way and is password protected.

Internet Explorer also includes a Profile Assistant stores Internet-related information. Figure 21.16 shows an example profile, other information stored includes:

- Home information (such as home address, home telephone number and personal home pages).
- Business information (such as business address, business telephone number and business home pages).
- NetMeeting address and server.
- Digital ID.

Some WWW sites can request details of the Profile, the browser will not automatically send this information, and will display the following information.

- Site URL.
- The information that is being requested and how this information will be used.
- Whether this site has a secure connection (Secure Sockets Layer, or SSL). If it supports SSL the site's certificate can be viewed.

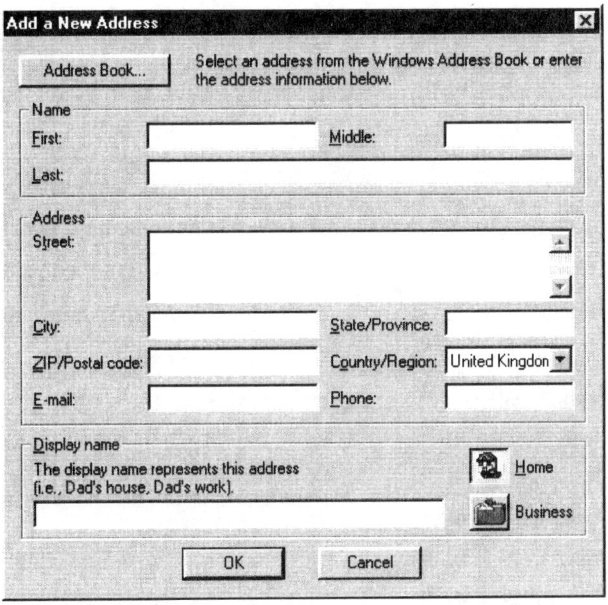

**Figure 21.14** Address for Microsoft Wallet

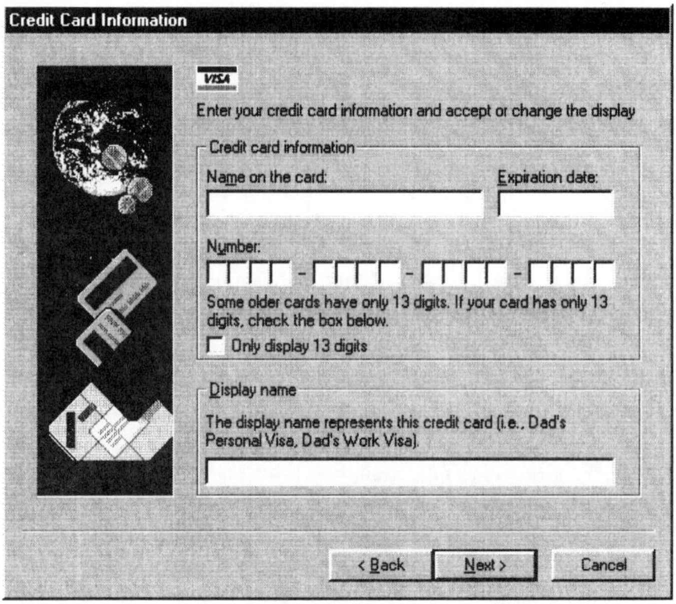

**Figure 21.15** Visa number for Microsoft Wallet

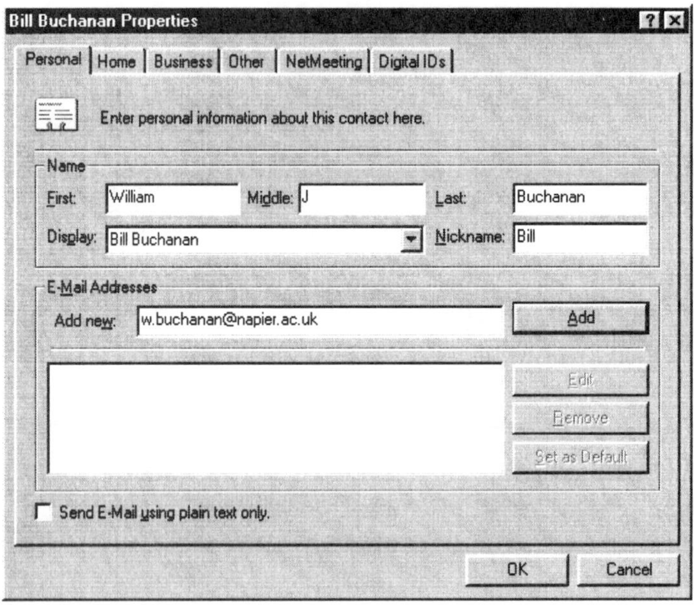

**Figure 21.16** User profile

**21.7.1** Locate a secure HTTP WWW site (typically sites which use electronic commerce on the Internet).

**21.7.2** Locate a site which has a Digital Certificate and view it.

**21.7.3** Locate a site which uses Internet-based Electronic Commerce and determine how goods are bought from it.

**21.7.4** If you have access to Microsoft Internet Explorer, investigate the Content Advisor. Also, access the Recreational Software Advisory Council WWW site (www.rsac.com) and investigate the content rating system. From who's work is the system based on?

## 21.8 Note from the author

*On a personal note, I have run a WWW site for many years and have seen how some users have abused their privileges, both by putting objectionable material on a WWW site and also in the material that they have accessed. One user, who held a responsible Post-Graduate position, put pages on the WWW which displayed animals and various world leaders being shot (mainly in the head). These pages had no links from the user's home page, but could be accessed directly with the correct URL. The only way that these pages were traced was that the WWW server ran a program which logged the number of accesses of all WWW pages, each day. Day after day the accesses to the hidden index page showed that it was being accessed at least ten times more than any other page, and these were from browsers all over the world. The URL of the page had obviously been lodged with some Internet database or a weird cult group, and searches for this type of offensive page brought users to it from all corners of the planet. Immediately when it was found the user was warned and he withdrew the pages. From this, the Departmental Management Team became very wary of users adding their own personal pages, and a ruling was made that all Post-Graduate students required permission from their Research Group Leader, or Course Coordinator, before they could add anything to the WWW server. A classic case of one person spoiling it for the rest. Often people with the most responsible for facilities (such as Managing Directors, Head of Divisions, and so on) are not technically able to access the formal risks in any system, and will typical bar accesses, rather than risk any legal problems.*

*Legal laws on Internet access will take some time to catch-up with the growth in technology, so in many cases it is the moral responsibility of site managers and division leaders to try and reduce the amount of objectionable material. If users want to download objection material or set-up their own WWW server with offensive material, they should do this at home and not at work or within an educational establishment. Often commercial organisations are strongly protected site, but in open-systems, such as Schools and Universities, it is often difficult to protect against these problems.*

# 22 Electronic Mail

## 22.1 Introduction

Electronic mail (email) is one use of the Internet which, according to most businesses, improves productivity. Traditional methods of sending mail within an office environment are inefficient, as it normally requires an individual requesting a secretary to type the letter. This must then be proof-read and sent through the internal mail system, which is relatively slow and can be open to security breaches.

A faster method, and more secure method of sending information is to use electronic mail, where messages are sent almost in an instant. For example, a memo with 100 words will be sent in a fraction of a second. It is also simple to send to specific groups, various individuals, company-wide, and so on. Other types of data can also be sent with the mail message such as images, sound, and so on. It may also be possible to determine if a user has read the mail. The main advantages are:

- It is normally much cheaper than using the telephone (although, as time equates to money for most companies, this relates any savings or costs to a user's typing speed).
- Many different types of data can be transmitted, such as images, documents, speech, and so on.
- It is much faster than the postal service.
- Users can filter incoming email easier than incoming telephone calls.
- It normally cuts out the need for work to be typed, edited and printed by a secretary.
- It reduces the burden on the mailroom.
- It is normally more secure than traditional methods.
- It is relatively easy to send to groups of people (traditionally, either a circulation list was required or a copy to everyone in the group was required).
- It is usually possible to determine whether the recipient has actually read the message (the electronic mail system sends back an acknowledgement).

The main disadvantages are:

- It stops people using the telephone.
- It cannot be used as a legal document.
- Electronic mail messages can be sent impulsively and may be later regretted (sending by traditional methods normally allows for a rethink). In extreme cases messages can be sent to the wrong person (typically when replying to an email message, where a message is sent to the mailing list rather than the originator).

- It may be difficult to send to some remote sites. Many organisations have either no electronic mail or merely an intranet. Large companies are particularly wary of Internet connections and limit the amount of external traffic.
- Not everyone reads their electronic mail on a regular basis (although this is changing as more organisations adopt email as the standard communications medium).

The main standards that relate to the protocols of email transmission and reception are:

- Simple Mail Transfer Protocol (SMTP) – which is used with the TCP/IP protocol suite. It has traditionally been limited to the text-based electronic messages.
- Multipurpose Internet Mail Extension (MIME) – which allows the transmission and reception of mail that contains various types of data, such as speech, images and motion video. It is a newer standard than SMTP and uses much of its basic protocol.
- S/MIME (Secure MIME). RSA Data Security created S/MIME which supports encrypted email transfers and digitally signed electronic mail.

## 22.2 Shared-file approach versus client/server approach

An email system can use either a shared-file approach or a client/server approach. In a shared-file system the source mail client sends the mail message to the local post office. This post office then transfers control to a message transfer agent which then stores the message for a short time before sending it to the destination post office. The destination mail client periodically checks its own post office to determine if it has mail for it. This arrangement is often known as store and forward, and the process is illustrated in Figure 22.1. Most PC-based email systems use this type of mechanism.

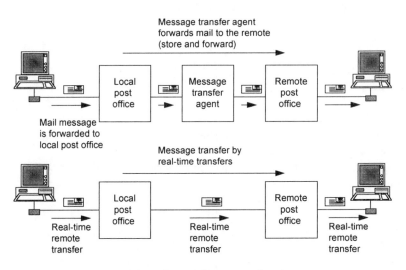

**Figure 22.1**  Shared-file versus client/server

A client/server approach involves the source client setting up a real-time remote connection with the local post office, which then sets up a real-time connection with the destination, which in turn sets up a remote connection with the destination client. The message will thus arrive at the destination when all the connections are complete.

## 22.3 Electronic mail overview

Figure 22.2 shows a typical email architecture. It contains four main elements:

1. Post offices – where outgoing messages are temporally buffered  (stored) before transmission and where incoming messages are stored. The post office runs the server software capable of routing messages (a message transfer agent) and maintaining the post office database.
2. Message transfer agents – for forwarding messages between post offices and to the destination clients. This software can either reside on the local post office or on a physically separate server.
3. Gateways – which provide part of the message transfer agent functionality. They translate between different email systems, different email addressing schemes and messaging protocols.
4. Email clients – normally the computer which connects to the post office. It contains three parts:

   - Email Application Program Interface (API), such as MAPI, VIM, MHS and CMC.
   - Messaging protocol. The main messaging protocols are SMTP or X.400. SMTP is defined in RFC 822 and RFC 821. X.400 is an OSI-defined email message delivery standard (Sections 22.5 and 22.6).
   - Network transport protocol, such as Ethernet, FDDI, and so on.

The main APIs are:

- MAP (messaging API) – Microsoft part of Windows Operation Services Architecture.
- VIM (vendor-independent messaging) – Lotus, Apple, Novell and Borland derived email API.
- MHS (message handling service) – Novell network interface which is often used as an email gateway protocol.
- CMC (common mail call) – Email API associated with the X.400 native messaging protocol.

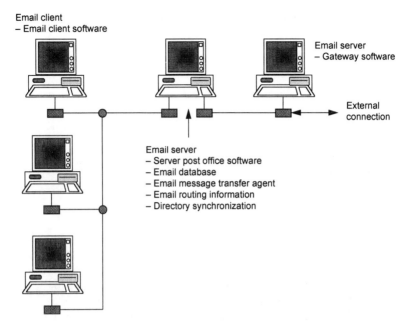

**Figure 22.2** Email architecture

Gateways translate the email message from one system to another, such as from Lotus cc:Mail to Microsoft Mail. Typical gateway protocols are:

- MHS  (used with Novell NetWare).
- SMTP.MIME (used with Internet environment).
- X.400 (used with X.400).
- MS Mail (used with Microsoft Mail).
- cc:Mail (used with Lotus cc:Mail).

## 22.4 Internet email address

The Internet email address is in the form of a name (such as `f.bloggs`), followed by an '@' and then the domain name (such as `anytown.ac.uk`). For example:

```
f.bloggs@anytown.ac.uk
```

No spaces are allowed in the address; periods are used instead. Figure 22.3 shows an example Internet address builder from Lotus cc:Mail.

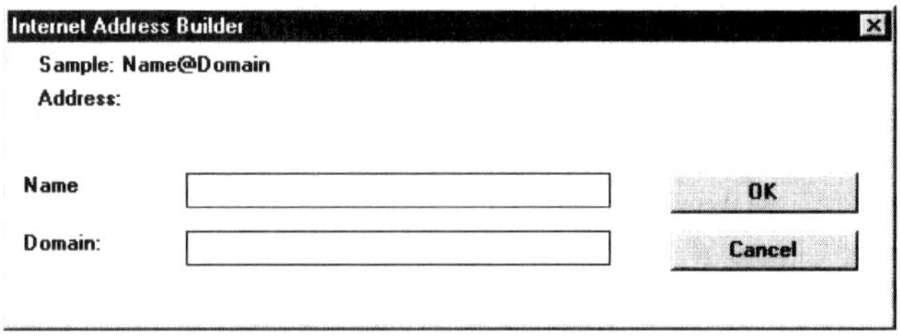

**Figure 22.3** Internet address format

# 22.5 SMTP

The IAB have defined the protocol SMTP in RFC 821 (Refer to Appendix E for a list of RFC standards). This section discusses the protocol for transferring mail between hosts using the TCP/IP protocol.

As SMTP is a transmission and reception protocol it does not actually define the format or contents of the transmitted message except that the data has 7-bit ASCII characters and that extra log information is added to the start of the delivered message to indicate the path the message took. The protocol itself is only concerned in reading the address header of the message.

### 22.5.1 SMTP operation

SMTP defines the conversation that takes place between an SMTP sender and an SMTP receiver. Its main functions are the transfer of messages and the provision of ancillary functions for mail destination verification and handling.

Initially the message is created by the user and a header is added which includes the recipient's email address and other information. This message is then queued by the mail server, and when it has time, the mail server attempts to transmit it.

Each mail may be have the following requirements:

- Each email can have a list of destinations; the email program makes copies of the messages and passes them onto the mail server.
- The user may maintain a mailing list, and the email program must remove duplicates and replace mnemonic names with actual email addresses.
- It allows for normal message provision, e.g. blind carbon copies (BCCs).

An SMTP mail server processes email messages from an outgoing mail queue and then transmits them using one or more TCP connections with the destination. If the mail message is transmitted to the required host then the SMTP sender deletes the destination from the message's destination list. After all the destinations have been sent to, the sender then deletes the message from the queue.

If there are several recipients for a message on the same host, the SMTP protocol allows a single message to be sent to the specified recipients. Also, if there are several messages to be sent to a single host, the server can simply open a single TCP connection and all the messages can be transmitted in a single transfer (there is thus no need to set up a connection for each message).

SMTP also allows for efficient transfer with error messages. Typical errors include:

- Destination host is unreachable. A likely cause is that the destination host address is incorrect. For example, `f.bloggs@toy.ac.uk` might actually be `f.bloggs@toytown.ac.uk`.
- Destination host is out of operation. A likely cause is that the destination host has developed a fault or has been shut down.
- Mail recipient is not available on the host. Perhaps the recipient does not exist on that host, the recipient name is incorrect or the recipient has moved. For example, `fred.bloggs@toytown.ac.uk` might actually be `f.bloggs@toytown.ac.uk`. To overcome the problem of user names which are similar to a user's name then some systems allow for certain aliases for recipients, such as `f.bloggs`, `fred.bloggs` and `freddy.bloggs`, but there is a limit to the number of aliases that a user can have. If a user has moved then some systems allow for a redirection of the email address. UNIX systems use the `.forward` file in the user's home directory for redirection. For example on a UNIX system, if the user has moved to `fred.bloggs@toytown.com` then this address is simply added to the `.forward` file.
- TCP connection failed on the transfer of the mail. A likely cause is that there was a time-out error on the connection (maybe due to the receiver or sender being busy or there was a fault in the connection).

SMTP senders have the responsibility for a message up to the point where the SMTP receiver indicates that the transfer is complete. This only indicates that the message has arrived at the SMTP receiver; does not indicate that:

- The message has been delivered to the recipient's mailbox.
- The recipient has read the message.

Thus, SMTP does not guarantee to recover from lost messages and gives no end-to-end acknowledgement on successful receipt (normally this is achieved by an acknowledgement message being returned). Nor are error indications guaranteed. However, TCP connections are normally fairly reliable.

If an error occurs in reception, a message will normally be sent back to the sender to explain the problem. The user can then attempt to determine the problem with the message.

SMTP receivers accept an arriving message and either place it in a user's mailbox or, if that user is located at another host, copies it to the local outgoing mail queue for forwarding.

Most transmitted messages go from the sender's machine to the host over a single TCP connection. But sometimes the connection will be made over multiple TCP connections over multiple hosts. The sender specifying a route to the destination in the form of a sequence of servers can achieve this.

### 22.5.2 SMTP overview

An SMTP sender initiates a TCP connection. When this is successful it sends a series of commands to the receiver, and the receiver returns a single reply for each command. All commands and responses are sent with ASCII characters and are terminated with the carriage return (CR) and line feed (LF) characters (often known as CRLF).

Each command consists of a single line of text, beginning with a four-letter command code followed by in some cases an argument field. Most replies are a single line, although multiple-line replies are possible. Table 22.1 gives some sample commands. SMTP replies with a three-digit code and possibly other information. Some of the responses are listed in Table 22.2. The first digit gives the category of the reply, such as $2xx$ (a positive completion reply), $3xx$ (a positive intermediate reply), $4xx$ (a transient negative completion reply) and $5xx$ (a permanent negative completion reply). A positive reply indicates that the requested action has been accepted, and a negative reply indicates that the action was not accepted.

Positive completion reply indicates that the action has been successful, and a positive intermediate reply indicates that the action has been accepted but the receiver is waiting for some other action before it can give a positive completion reply. A transient negative completion reply indicates that there is a temporary error condition which can be cleared by other actions and a permanent negative completion reply indicates that the action was not accepted and no action was taken.

**Table 22.1** SMTP commands

| Command | Description |
|---------|-------------|
| HELO *domain* | Sends an identification of the domain |
| MAIL FROM: *sender-address* | Sends identification of the originator (sender-address) |
| RCPT FROM: *receiver-address* | Sends identification of the recipient (receiver-address) |
| DATA | Transfer text message |
| RSEY | Abort current mail transfer |
| QUIT | Shut down TCP connection |
| EXPN *mailing-list* | Send back membership of mailing list |
| SEND FROM: *sender-address* | Send mail message to the terminal |
| SOML FROM: *sender-address* | If possible, send mail message to the terminal, otherwise send to mailbox |
| VRFY username | Verify user name (username) |

### 22.5.3 SMTP transfer

Figure 22.4 shows a successful email transmission. For example if:

```
f.bloggs@toytown.ac.uk
```

is sending a message to:

```
a.person@place.ac.de
```

Then a possible sequence of events is:

- Set up TCP connection with receiver host.
- If the connection is successful, the receiver replies back with a 220 code (server ready). If it is unsuccessful, it returns back with a 421 code.

- Sender sends a `HELO` command to the hostname (such as `HELO toytown.ac.uk`).
- If the sender accepts the incoming mail message then the receiver returns a `250 OK` code. If it is unsuccessful then it returns a 421, 451, 452, 500, 501 or 552 code.
- Sender sends a `MAIL FROM:` *sender* command (such as `MAIL FROM: f.bloggs@ toytown.ac.uk`).
- If the receiver accepts the incoming mail message from the sender then it returns a `250 OK` code. If it is unsuccessful then it returns codes such as 251, 450, 451, 452, 500, 501, 503, 550, 551, 552 or 553 code.
- Sender sends an `RCPT TO:` *receiver* command (such as `RCPT TO: a.person@place.ac.de`).
- If the receiver accepts the incoming mail message from the sender then it returns a `250 OK` code.
- Senders sends a `DATA` command.
- If the receiver accepts the incoming mail message from the sender then it returns a `354` code (start transmission of mail message).
- The sender then transmits the email message.
- The end of the email message is sent as two LF, CR characters.
- If the reception has been successful then the receiver sends back a `250 OK` code. If it is unsuccessful then it returns a 451, 452, 552 or 554 code.
- Sender starts the connection shutdown by sending a `QUIT` command.
- Finally the sender closes the TCP connection.

**Table 22.2** SMTP responses

| CMD | Description | CMD | Description |
|-----|-------------|-----|-------------|
| 211 | System status | 500 | Command unrecognised due to a syntax error |
| 214 | Help message | 501 | Invalid parameters or arguments |
| 220 | Service ready | 502 | Command not currently implemented |
| 221 | Service closing transmission channel | 503 | Bad sequence of commands |
| 250 | Request mail action completed successfully | 504 | Command parameter not currently implemented |
| 251 | Addressed user does not exist on system but will forward to receiver-address | 550 | Mail box unavailable, request action not taken |
| 354 | Indicate to the sender that the mail message can now be sent. The end of the message is identified by two CR, LF characters | 551 | The addressed user is not local, please try receiver-address |
| 421 | Service is not available | 552 | Exceeded storage allocation, requested mail action aborted |
| 450 | Mailbox unavailable and the requested mail action was not taken | 553 | Mailbox name not allowed, requested action not taken |

| 451 | Local processing error, requested action aborted | 554 | Transaction failed |
| 452 | Insufficient storage, requested action not taken | | |

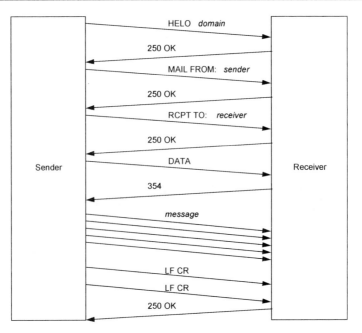

**Figure 22.4** Sample SMTP email transmission

The following text shows some of the handshaking that is used in transmitted an electronic mail message (the UNIX mail –v command is used to show the handshaking. The commands send to the mail server are highlighted in bold. It can be seen that the responses are 220 (Service ready), 221 (Request mail action completed successfully), 250 (Request mail action completed successfully) and 354 (Indicate to the sender that the mail message can now be sent.

```
> mail -v w.buchanan@napier.ac.uk
Subject: Test
This is a test message. Hello, how are you.
Fred.

EOT

w.buchanan@napier.ac.uk... Connecting to central.napier.ac.uk. (smtp)...
220 central.napier.ac.uk ESMTP Sendmail 8.9.1/8.9.1; Fri, 18 Dec 1998
15:55:45 GMT
>>> HELO www.eece.napier.ac.uk
250 central.napier.ac.uk Hello bill_b@www.eece.napier.ac.uk
[146.176.151.139], pleased to meet you
>>> MAIL From:<bill_b@www.eece.napier.ac.uk>
250 <bill_b@www.eece.napier.ac.uk>... Sender ok
>>> RCPT To:<w.buchanan@napier.ac.uk>
250 <w.buchanan@napier.ac.uk>... Recipient ok
```

```
>>> DATA
354 Enter mail, end with "." on a line by itself
>>> .
250 PAA24767 Message accepted for delivery
w.buchanan@napier.ac.uk... Sent (PAA24767 Message accepted for delivery)
Closing connection to central.napier.ac.uk.
>>> QUIT
221 central.napier.ac.uk closing connection
```

### 22.5.4 RFC 822

SMTP uses RFC 822, which defines the format of the transmitted message. RFC 822 contains two main parts:

- A header – which is basically the mail header and contains information for the successful transmission and delivery of a message. This typically contains the email addresses for sender and receiver, the time the message was sent and received. Any computer involved in the transmission can added to the header.
- The contents.

Normally the email-reading program will read the header and format the information to the screen to show the sender's email address; it splits off the content of the message and displays it separately from the header.

An RFC 822 message contains a number of lines of text in the form of a memo (such as To:, From:, Bcc:, and so on). A header line usually has a keyword followed by a colon and then followed by keyword arguments. The specification also allows for a long line to be broken up into several lines.

Here is an RFC 822 message with the header shown in italics and the message body in bold. Table 22.3 explains some of the RFC 822 items in the header.

*From FREDB@ACOMP.CO.UK Wed Jul  5 12:36:49 1995*
*Received: from ACOMP.CO.UK ([154.220.12.27]) by central.napier.ac.uk*
*(8.6.10/8.6.10) with SMTP id MAA16064 for*
*<w.buchanan@central.napier.ac.uk>;*

*Wed, 5 Jul 1995 12:36:43 +0100*

*Received: from WPOAWUK-Message_Server by ACOMP.CO.UK*
*  with Novell_GroupWise; Wed, 05 Jul 1995 12:35:51 +0000*

*Message-Id: <sffa8725.082@ACOMP.CO.UK >*

*X-Mailer: Novell GroupWise 4.1*

*Date: Wed, 05 Jul 1995 12:35:07 +0000*

*From: Fred Bloggs <FREDB@ACOMP.CO.UK>*

*To: w.buchanan@central.napier.ac.uk*
*Subject:  Technical Question*
*Status: REO*

**Dear Bill**
**  I have a big problem. Please help.**
**Fred**

**Table 22.3** Header line descriptions

| Header line | Description |
|---|---|
| From FREDB@ACOMP.CO.UK Wed Jul 5 12:36:49 1995 | Sender of the email is FREDB@ ACOM.CO.UK |
| Received: from ACOMP.CO.UK ([154.220.12.27]) by central.napier.ac.uk (8.6.10/8.6.10) with SMTP id MAA16064 for <w.buchanan@central.napier.ac.uk>; Wed, 5 Jul 1995 12:36:43 +0100 | It was received by CENTRAL.NAPIER.AC.UK at 12:36 on 5 July 1995 |
| Message-Id: <sffa8725.082@ACOMP.CO.UK > | Unique message ID |
| X-Mailer: Novell GroupWise 4.1 | Gateway system |
| Date: Wed, 05 Jul 1995 12:35:07 +0000 | Date of original message |
| From: Fred Bloggs <FREDB@ACOMP.CO.UK> | Sender's email address and full name |
| To: w.buchanan@central.napier.ac.uk | Recipient's email address |
| Subject:  Technical Question | Mail subject |

## 22.6  X.400

RFC 821 (the transmission protocol) and RFC 822 (the message format) have now become the de-facto standards for email systems. The CCITT, in 1984, defined new email recommendations called X.400. The RFC821/822 system is simple and works relatively well, whereas X.400 is complex and is poorly designed. These points have helped RFC 821/822 to become a de-facto standard, whereas X.400 is now almost extinct (see Figure 22.5 for the basic X.400 address builder and Figure 22.6 for the extended address builder).

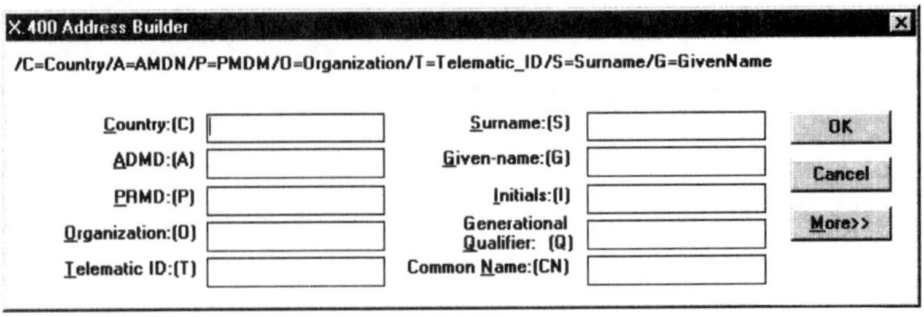

**Figure 22.5**  X.400 basic addressing

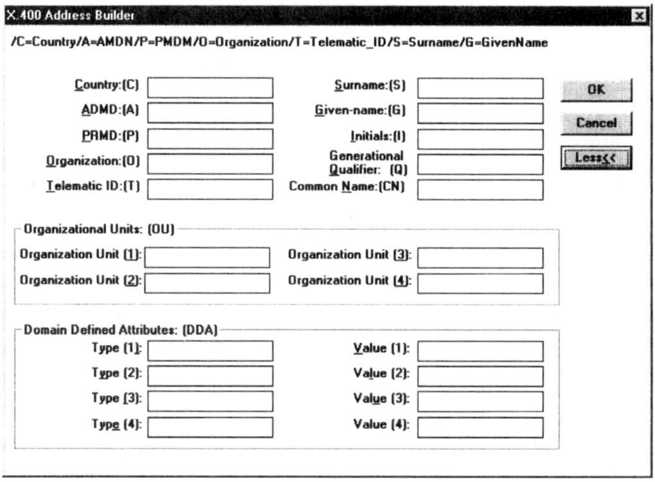

**Figure 22.6**  X.400 extended addressing

---

## 22.7 MIME

SMTP suffers from several drawback, such as:

- SMTP can only transmit ASCII characters and thus cannot transmit executable files or other binary objects.
- SMTP does not allow the attachment of files, such as images and audio.
- SMTP can only transmit 7-bit ASCII character thus it does support an extended ASCII character set.

A new standard, Multipurpose Internet Mail Extension (MIME), has been defined for this purpose, which is compatible with existing RFC 822 implementations. It is defined in the specifications RFC 1521 and 1522. Its enhancements include the following:

- Five new message header fields in the RFC 822 header, which provide extra information about the body of the message.
- Use of various content formats to support multimedia electronic mail.
- Defined transfer encodings for transforming attached files.

The five new header fields defined in MIME are:

- MIME-version – a message that conforms to RFC 1521 or 1522 is MIME-version 1.0.
- Content-type – this field defines the type of data attached.
- Content-transfer-encoding – this field indicates the type of transformation necessary to represent the body in a format which can be transmitted as a message.
- Content-id – this field is used to uniquely identify MIME multiple attachments in the email message.

- Content-description – this field is a plain-text description of the object with the body. It can be used by the user to determine the data type.

These fields can appear in a normal RFC 822 header. Figure 22.7 shows an example email message. It can be seen, in the right-hand corner, that the API has split the message into two parts: the message part and the RFC 822 part. The RFC 822 part is shown in Figure 22.8. It can be seen that, in this case, the extra MIME messages are:

```
MIME-Version: 1.0
Content-Type: text/plain; charset=us-ascii
Content-Transfer-Encoding: 7bit
```

This defines it as MIME Version 1.0; the content-type is text/plain (standard ASCII) and it uses the US ASCII character set; the content-transfer-encoding is 7-bit ASCII.

---

📖 **RFC 822 example file listing (refer to Figure 22.8)**
```
Received: from pc419.eece.napier.ac.uk by ccmailgate.napier.ac.uk
(SMTPLINK V2.11.01)
     ; Fri, 24 Jan 97 11:13:41 gmt
Return-Path: <w.buchanan@napier.ac.uk>
Message-ID: <32E90962.1574@napier.ac.uk>
Date: Fri, 24 Jan 1997 11:14:22 -0800
From: Dr William Buchanan <w.buchanan@napier.ac.uk>
Organization: Napier University
X-Mailer: Mozilla 3.01 (Win95; I; 16bit)
MIME-Version: 1.0
To: w.buchanan@napier.ac.uk
Subject: Book recommendation
Content-Type: text/plain; charset=us-ascii
Content-Transfer-Encoding: 7bit
```

---

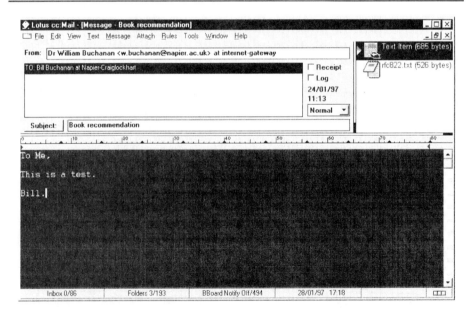

**Figure 22.7** Sample email message showing message and RFC822 part

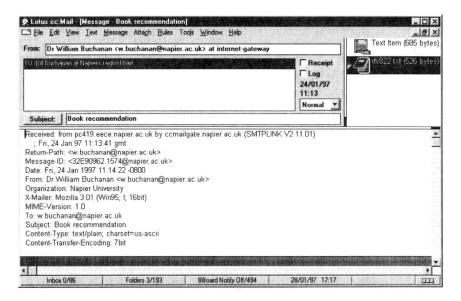

**Figure 22.8** RFC 822 part

### 22.7.1 MIME content types

Content types define the format of the attached files. There are a total of 16 different content types in seven major content groups. If the text body is pure text then no special transformation is required. RFC 1521 defines only one subtype, text/plain; this gives a standard ASCII character set.

A MIME-encoded email can contain multiple attachments. The content-type header field includes a boundary which defines the delimiter between multiple attachments. A boundary always starts on a new line and has the format:

```
-- boundary name
```

The final boundary is:

```
-- boundary name --
```

For example, the following message contains two parts:

---

📖 **Example MIME file with 2 parts**
```
From: Dr William Buchanan <w.buchanan@napier.ac.uk>
MIME-Version: 1.0
To: w.buchanan@napier.ac.uk
Subject: Any subject
Content-Type: multipart/mixed; boundary="boundary name"
This part of the message will be ignored.
-- boundary name
Content-Type: multipart/mixed; boundary="boundary name"
This is the first mail message part.
-- boundary name
And this is the second mail message part.
-- boundary name --
```

---

**Table 22.4** MIME content-types

| Content type | Description |
|---|---|
| text/plain | Unformated text, such as ASCII |
| text/richtext | Rich text format which is similar to HTML |
| multipart/mixed | Each attachment is independent from the rest and all should be presented to the user in their initial ordering |
| multipart/parallel | Each attachment is independent from the others but the order is unimportant |
| multipart/alternative | Each attachment is a different version of the original data |
| multipart/digest | This is similar to multipart/mixed but each part is message/rfc822 |
| message/rfc822 | Contains the RFC 822 text |
| message/partial | Used in fragmented mail messages |
| message/external-body | Used to define a pointer to an external object (such as an ftp link) |
| image/jpeg | Defines a JPEG image using JFIF file format |
| image/gif | Defines GIF image |
| video/mpeg | Defines MPEG format |
| audio/basic | Defines 8-bit μ-Law encoding at 8 kHz sampling rate |
| application/postscript | Defines postscript format |
| application/octet-stream | Defines binary format which consists of 8-bit bytes |

The part of the message after the initial header and before the first boundary can be used to add a comment. This is typically used to inform users that do not have a MIME-compatible program about the method used to encode the received file. A typical method for converting binary data into ASCII characters is to use the programs UUENCODE (to encode a binary file into text) or UUDECODE (to decode a uuencoded file).

The four subtypes of multipart type can be used to sequence the attachments; the main subtypes are:

- multipart/mixed subtype – which is used when attachments are independent but need to be arranged in a particular order.
- multipart/parallel subtype – which is used when the attachments should be present at the same; a typical example is to present an animated file along with an audio attachment.
- multipart/alternative subtype – which is used to represent an attachment in a number of different formats.

### 22.7.2 Example MIME

The following file listing shows the message part of a MIME-encoded email message (i.e. it excludes the RFC 822 header part). It can be seen that the sending email system has added the comment about the MIME encoding. In this case the MIME boundaries have been defined by:

```
-- IMA.Boundary.760275638
```

📖 **Example MIME file**

```
This is a Mime message, which your current mail reader
may not understand. Parts of the message will appear as
text. To process the remainder, you will need to use a Mime
```

```
compatible mail reader. Contact your vendor for details.
--IMA.Boundary.760275638

Content-Type: text/plain; charset=US-ASCII
Content-Transfer-Encoding: 7bit
Content-Description: cc:Mail note part

This is the original message .....

--IMA.Boundary.760275638--
```

### 22.7.3 Mail fragments

A mail message can be fragmented using the content-type field of message/partial and then reassembled back at the source. The standard format is:

```
Content-type: message/partial;
    id="idname"; number=x; total=y
```

where *idname* is the message identification (such as `xyz@hostname`, $x$ is the number of the fragment out of a total of $y$ fragments. For example, if a message had three fragments, they could be sent as:

📖 **Example MIME file with 3 fragments (first part)**
```
From: Fred Bloggs <f.bloggs@toytown.ac.uk>
MIME-Version: 1.0
To: a.body@anytown.ac.uk
Subject: Any subject
Content-Type: message/partial;
  id="xyz@toytown.ac.uk"; number=1; total=3
Content=type: video/mpeg
```
*First part of MPEG file*

📖 **Example MIME file with 3 fragments (second part)**
```
From: Fred Bloggs <f.bloggs@toytown.ac.uk>
MIME-Version: 1.0
To: a.body@anytown.ac.uk
Subject: Any subject
Content-Type: message/partial;
  id="xyz@toytown.ac.uk"; number=2; total=3
Content=type: video/mpeg
```
*Second part of MPEG file*

📖 **Example MIME file with 3 fragments (third part)**
```
From: Fred Bloggs <f.bloggs@toytown.ac.uk>
MIME-Version: 1.0
To: a.body@anytown.ac.uk
Subject: Any subject
Content-Type: message/partial;
  id="xyz@toytown.ac.uk"; number=3; total=3
Content=type: video/mpeg
```
*Third part of MPEG file*

## 22.7.4 Transfer encodings

MIME allows for different transfer encodings within the message body:

- 7bit – no encoding, and all of the characters are 7-bit ASCII characters.
- 8bit – no encoding, and extended 8-bit ASCII characters are used.
- quoted-printable – encodes the data so that non-printing ASCII characters (such as line feeds and carriage returns) are displayed in a readable form.
- base64 – encodes by mapping 6-bit blocks of input to 8-bit blocks of output, all of which are printable ASCII characters.
- x-token – another non-standard encoding method.

When the transfer encoding is:

```
Content-transfer-encoding: quoted-printable
```

then the message has been encoded so that all non-printing characters have been converted to printable characters. A typical transform is to insert =xx where xx is the hexadecimal equivalent for the ASCII character. A form feed (FF) would be encoded with '=0C',

A transfer encoding of base64 is used to map 6-bit characters to a printable character. It is a useful method in disguising text in an encrypted form and also for converting binary data into a text format. It takes the input bitstream and reads it 6 bits at a time, then maps this to an 8-bit printable character. Table 22.5 shows the mapping.

**Table 22.5**   MIME base64 encoding

| Bit value | Encoded character | Bit value | Encoded character | Bit value | Encoded character | Bit value | Encoded character |
|---|---|---|---|---|---|---|---|
| 0 | A | 16 | Q | 32 | g | 48 | w |
| 1 | B | 17 | R | 33 | h | 49 | x |
| 2 | C | 18 | S | 34 | i | 50 | y |
| 3 | D | 19 | T | 35 | j | 51 | z |
| 4 | E | 20 | U | 36 | k | 52 | 0 |
| 5 | F | 21 | V | 37 | l | 53 | 1 |
| 6 | G | 22 | W | 38 | m | 54 | 2 |
| 7 | H | 23 | X | 39 | n | 55 | 3 |
| 8 | I | 24 | Y | 40 | o | 56 | 4 |
| 9 | J | 25 | Z | 41 | p | 57 | 5 |
| 10 | K | 26 | a | 42 | q | 58 | 6 |
| 11 | L | 27 | b | 43 | r | 59 | 7 |
| 12 | M | 28 | c | 44 | s | 60 | 8 |
| 13 | N | 29 | d | 45 | t | 61 | 9 |
| 14 | O | 30 | e | 46 | u | 62 | + |
| 15 | P | 31 | f | 47 | v | 63 | / |

Thus if a binary file had the bit sequence:

```
101000101010100010101010101010
```

It would first be split into groups of 6 bits, as follows:

```
101000     101010   100010   101010   000000
```

This would be converted into the ASCII sequence:

```
YsSqA
```

which is in a transmittable form.

Thus the 7-bit ASCII sequence 'FRED' would use the bit pattern:

```
1000110 1010010 1000101 1000100
```

which would be split into groups of 6 bits as:

```
100011 010100 101000 101100 010000
```

which would be encoded as:

```
jUosQ
```

### 22.7.5 Example

The following parts of the RFC 822 messages.

(a)

```
Received: from publish.co.uk by ccmail1.publish.co.uk (SMTPLINK V2.11.01)
Return-Path: <FredB@local.exnet.com>
Received: from mailgate.exnet.com ([204.137.193.226]) by zeus.publish.co.uk
with SMTP id <17025>; Wed, 2 Jul 1997 08:33:29 +0100
Received: from exnet.com (assam.exnet.com) by mailgate.exnet.com with SMTP
id AA09732 (5.67a/IDA-1.4.4 for m.smith@publish.co.uk); Wed, 2 Jul 1997
08:34:22 +0100
Received: from maildrop.exnet.com (ceylon.exnet.com) by exnet.com with SMTP
id AA10740 (5.67a/IDA-1.4.4 for <m.smith@publish.co.uk>); Wed, 2 Jul 1997
08:34:10 +0100
Received: from local.exnet.com by maildrop.exnet.com (4.1/client-1.2DHD)
    id AA22007; Wed, 2 Jul 97 08:25:21 BST
From: FredB@local.exnet.com (Arthur Chapman)
Reply-To: FredB@local.exnet.com
To: b.smith@publish.co.uk
Subject: New proposal
Date: Wed, 2 Jul 1997 09:36:17 +0100
Message-Id: <66322430.1380704@local.exnet.com>
Organization: Local College
```

(b)

```
Received: from central.napier.ac.uk by ccmailgate.napier.ac.uk (SMTPLINK
V2.11.01) Return-Path: <fred@singnetw.com.sg>
Received: from server.singnetw.com.sg (server.singnetw.com.sg [165.21.1.15])
by central.napier.ac.uk (8.6.10/8.6.10) with ESMTP id DAA18783 for
<w.buchanan@napier.ac.uk>; Sun, 29 Jun 1997 03:15:27 GMT
Received: from si7410352.ntu.ac.sg (ts900-1908.singnet.com.sg [165.21.158.60])
    by melati.singnet.com.sg (8.8.5/8.8.5) with SMTP id KAA08773
    for <w.buchanan@napier.ac.uk.>; Sun, 29 Jun 1997 10:14:59 +0800 (SST)
Message-ID: <33B5C33B.6CCC@singnetw.com.sg>
Date: Sun, 29 Jun 1997 10:06:51 +0800
```

```
From: Fred Smith <fred@singnetw.com.sg>
X-Mailer: Mozilla 2.0 (Win95; I)
MIME-Version: 1.0
To: w.buchanan@napier.ac.uk
Subject: Chapter 15
Content-Type: text/plain; charset=us-ascii
Content-Transfer-Encoding: 7bit
```

(c)

```
Received: from central.napier.ac.uk by ccmailgate.napier.ac.uk (SMTPLINK
V2.11.01)
Return-Path: <bertb@scms.scotuni.ac.uk>
Received: from master.scms.scotuni.ac.uk ([193.62.32.5]) by cen-
tral.napier.ac.uk (8.6.10/8.6.10) with ESMTP id MAA20373 for
<w.buchanan@napier.ac.uk>; Tue, 1 Jul 1997 12:25:38 GMT
Received: from cerberus.scms.scotuni.ac.uk (cerberus.scms.scotuni.ac.uk
[193.62.32.46]) by master.scms.scotuni.ac.uk (8.6.9/8.6.9) with ESMTP id
MAA10056 for <w.buchanan@napier.ac.uk>; Tue, 1 Jul 1997 12:24:32 +0100
From: David Davidson <bertb@scms.scotuni.ac.uk>
Received: by cerberus.scms.scotuni.ac.uk (SMI-8.6/Dumb)
        id MAA03334; Tue, 1 Jul 1997 12:23:17 +0100
Date: Tue, 1 Jul 1997 12:23:17 +0100
Message-Id: <199707011123.MAA03334@cerberus.scms.scotuni.ac.uk>
To: w.buchanan@napier.ac.uk
Subject: Advert
Mime-Version: 1.0
Content-Type: text/plain; charset=us-ascii
Content-Transfer-Encoding: 7bit
Content-MD5: TzKyk+NON+vy6Cm6uqy9Cg==
```

## 22.8  Exercises

**22.8.1**    The main drawback of SMTP is:

     (a)     It is incompatible with most email systems
     (b)     It can only be used for text-based email
     (c)     It is slow when transferring an email
     (d)     It is only used on UNIX systems

**22.8.2**    The advantage that MIME has over SMTP is:

     (a)     That it allows the attachment of other data types (such as speech and images).
     (b)     It is faster when transferring
     (c)     It is compatible with more systems
     (d)     It is only used on UNIX systems

**22.8.3**    The share-file (store and forward) email approach involves:

     (a)     Sending the mail message to multiple sites
     (b)     Sending the mail message in fragments
     (c)     Using  real-time remote transfer
     (d)     Using a message transfer agent

**22.8.4** The client/server email approach involves:

    (a)    Sending the mail message to multiple sites
    (b)    Sending the mail message in fragments
    (c)    Using  real-time remote transfer
    (d)    Using a message transfer agent

**22.8.5** The main function of an email post office is to:

    (a)    Forward messages to clients
    (b)    Store incoming messages and temporarily store outgoing messages
    (c)    Translate messages between different systems
    (d)    Provide the user interface program

**22.8.6** The main function of an email gateway is to:

    (a)    Forward messages to clients
    (b)    Store incoming messages and temporarily store outgoing messages
    (c)    Translate messages between different systems
    (d)    Provide the user interface program

**22.8.7** The main function of an email message transfer agent is to:

    (a)    Forward messages to clients
    (b)    Store incoming messages and temporarily store outgoing messages
    (c)    Translate messages between different systems
    (d)    Provide the user interface program

**22.8.8** The standard text format used for email messages is:

    (a)    ISO characters
    (b)    ANSI characters
    (c)    EBCDIC characters
    (d)    7-bit ASCII characters

**22.8.9** The SMTP transmission protocol has been defined in which IAB standard:

    (a)    RFC 822
    (b)    RFC 821
    (c)    IEEE 802.2
    (d)    RFC 802

**22.8.10** The SMTP message format has been defined in which IAB standard:

(a)   RFC 821
(b)   RFC 822
(c)   IEEE 802.2
(d)   RFC 802

**22.8.11**   How is routing information added to an SMTP message

(a)   It is encoded with special codes
(b)   It is added to the end of the message
(c)   It is sent as a separate file
(d)   It is added to the header of the message

**22.8.12**   The likely reason that the X.400 standard has never been universally accepted is:

(a)   It is too complex
(b)   It is too simple
(c)   It is difficult to incorporate into email systems
(d)   It is not an international standard

**22.8.13**   The main disadvantage of SMTP is:

(a)   It is not suited to client/server applications
(b)   It does not support file attachments
(c)   It is too slow
(d)   It is incompatible with many systems

**22.8.14**   How are attachments delimited in MIME encoded messages:

(a)   `++ boundary name`
(b)   `-- boundary name`
(c)   `<< boundary name`
(d)   `>> boundary name`

**22.8.15**   A typical format used to convert binary files into ASCII text is:

(a)   LHA
(b)   PKZIP
(c)   UUENCODE
(d)   ZIP

**22.8.16**   How is the type of attachment defined:

(a)   It is defined in the address field
(b)   It is sent as separate message
(c)   Automatically with the type of encoding
(d)   With the content type

## 22.9 Tutorial

**22.9.1** Identify the main functional differences between SMTP and MIME.

**22.9.2** Contrast shared-file and client/server approach for electronic mail.

**22.9.3** Give an example set of messages between the sender and a recipient for a successful SMTP transfer.

**22.9.4** Give an example set of messages between the sender and a recipient for an unsuccessful SMTP transfer.

**22.9.5** If you have access to email read an email and identify each part of the header.

**22.9.6** Explain how base64 encoding can be used to attach binary information.

**22.9.7** Encode the following bit stream with base64 encoding:

(i)    0111000000000101011010100000001111110111110

(ii)   1111100011101101011100100111100110101111111

## 22.10 Smilies

| Smilie | Description | Smilie | Description |
|--------|-------------|--------|-------------|
| :-) | smile | :-> | sarcastic |
| ;-) | wink | :-))) | laughing or double chin |
| :.-) | laughing tears | ;-)=) | grin |
| :-D | laughing | :-} | wry smile |
| :-P | tongue | :-( | sad, angry |
| :-< | sad | :-I | indifferent/sad |
| :.-( | weeping | :-II | angry |
| :-@ | angry | }-) | evil |
| :-X | mute | :-() | talking |
| :-O | surprised/shocked | =:-) | shocked |
| O:-) | halo | :-3 | has eaten a lemon |
| :-/ | sceptical | :-Z | sleeping |
| :-x | kissing | :-* | sorry, I didn't want to say that |
| ?-( | sorry, I don't know what went wrong | :*) | drunk (red nose) |
| %-) | stared too long at monitor | #-) | dead |
| X-) | unconscious | :-Q | smoking |
| (:-) | bald | .-) | one-eyed |
| -:-) | punk | <:-) | stupid question (donkey's hat) |
| <|-) | chinese | @:-) | arab |
| 8:-) | little girl | :-)-8 | big girl |
| [:-] | robot | ::-) | wearing glasses |
| 8-) | wearing glasses / wide-eyed grin | B-) | horn-rimmed glasses |

| | | | |
|---|---|---|---|
| B:-) | sunglasses on head | .^) | side view |
| :<) | moustache | _O-) | aquanaut |
| {:-) | wig | :-E | vampire |
| :-[ | vampire | (-: | left-handed |
| :o) | boxer's nose | :) | happy |
| [:] | robot | :] | gleep, friendly |
| =) | variations on a theme | :} | (what should we call these?) |
| :> | (what?) | :@ | (what?) |
| :D | laughter | :I | hmmm... |
| :( | sad | | |

<br>

## 22.11 Acronyms

| Acronym | Description | Acronym | Description |
|---|---|---|---|
| 2U2 | to you, too | AAMOF | as a matter of fact |
| AFAIK | as far as I know | AFK | away from keyboard |
| ASAP | as soon as possible | BBL | be back later |
| BOT | back on topic | BRB | be right back |
| BTW | by the way | BYORL | bring your own rocket launcher |
| C4N | ciao for now | CFD | call for discussion |
| CFV | call for vote | CU | see you |
| CUL | see you later | CYA | see ya |
| DIY | do it yourself | EOD | end of discussion |
| EOT | end of transmission | F2F | face to face |
| FAI | frequently argued issue | FAQ | frequently asked questions |
| FOAF | friend of a friend | FWIW | for what it's worth |
| FYI | for your information | GAL | get a life |
| GFC | going for coffee | GRMBL | grumble |
| GTG | got to go | HAND | have a nice day |
| HTH | hope this helps | IAC | in any case |
| IC | I see | IDGI | I don't get it |
| IMHO | in my humble opinion | IMNSHO | in my not so humble opinion |
| IMO | in my opinion | IMPE | in my previous/personal experience |
| IMVHO | in my very humble opinion | IOW | in other words |
| IRL | in real life | KISS | keep it simple stupid |
| LOL | laughing out loud | NC | no comment |
| ONNA | oh no, not again! | OOTC | obligatory on-topic content |
| OTOH | on the other hand | REHI | hello again (re-Hi!) |
| ROFL | rolling on the floor laughing | RTDox | read the documentation |
| SHTSI | somebody had to say it | SO | significant other |
| THX | thanks | TIA | thanks in advance |
| TLA | three letter acronym | TOS | terms of service |
| TTFN | ta-ta for now | TTYL | talk to you later |
| WIIWD | what it is we do | WWDWIIWD | when we do what it is we do |
| YGWYPF | you get is what you pay for | | |

# 23 Viruses

## 23.1 Introduction

Computer systems, especially PC, are susceptible to computer viruses. A computer virus is a program which infects other programs by modifying them and making a direct, or a modified, copy of itself. Most viruses are annoying and do little damage to the computer system, apart from replicating itself.

The PC has always been plagued with viruses for many reasons, including:

- Ease of access to system files. These include boot files (IO.SYS and MSDOS. SYS) and start-up files.
- Ease of access to hardware drivers and interrupts. This danger has been reduced with Windows 95/98 and NT/2000, which do not allow user program to access the hardware directly and the operating system.
- The lack of file attributes. Most PC systems have simple file attributes for read, write and execute. These attributes can also be easily changed, as the files are not owned by anyone. UNIX makes this difficult as users have limited access to files in other user directories and also to system file.
- The challenge. There are more PCs on the planet than all the other types of computer systems put together. Thus for some people there is a thrill in the thought of infecting computers around the world.
- Ease to transfer. Most users use floppy disk drives to transfer files. These are a perfect mechanism for transporting virus. Many companies have even banned the use of floppy disk drives to try and reduce the spread of virus.
- Boot disks. Until recently, many floppy disks were formatted so that they could be used as a boot disk. Unfortunately, a boot disk allows viruses to be transferred through the boot sector.
- Accidental release. Many viruses started life as a prototype program or an experimental program, which were accidentally released into the 'wild'. These are typically developed by undergraduate students had just learned machine code and also PC system architecture. Most virus do not mean to damage computer system, but they typically have bugs in them which causes them to do some damage, such as slow the computer down, or halt the computer.
- Thrill of event-driven programming. Many programmers love to write program which are triggered by an event. Typical virus events are date (such as Friday the 13th and April 1st), time, and hardware or software interrupts.
- Criminal activity. This is actually not very common, as there are very few criminals who are computer programmers. Virus programmers typically write virus programs for the thrill of it.

- Jokes. These are harmless programs that do 'amusing' things (although many users think they have been infected by a serious virus).

The damage caused by viruses is normally graded into five main definitions:

- Trivial. No physical damage and all the user has to do is to run an anti-virus program to get rid of the virus. Typically, the virus will occasionally display a message.
- Minor. Some files require to be re-installed from a backup or from a disk.
- Moderate. Virus trashes the hard disk, scrambles the FAT, or low-level formats the drive. This is typically recovered from a recent backup.
- Major. Virus gradually corrupts data files, of which the user is unaware. This is more severe than moderate damage as earlier backups are likely to contain the virus. Many weeks or months worth or data may be lost.
- Severe. Virus gradually corrupts data files, but the user continues to use the computer. There is thus no simple way of knowing whether the data files, or the backup files, are good or bad).
- Unlimited. Virus gives a hacker access to your network, by stealing the supervisor password. The damage is then done by the hacker, who controls the network.

## 23.2 Virus types

### 23.2.1 Partition viruses

When starting PCs, the system automatically reads the partition sector and executes the code it finds there. The partition sector (or Master Boot Record) is the first sector on a hard disk and it contains system start-up information, such as:

- Number of sectors in each partition.
- The start of the DOS partition starts.
- Small programs.

Viruses, which attach themselves to the partition sector, modify the code associated with the partition section. The system must be booted from a clean boot virus to eradicate this type of virus. Partition viruses only attack hard disks, as floppy disks do not have partition sectors. A partition is created with the FDISK program. Hard disks cannot be accessed unless they have a valid partition. Typical partitions are FAT-16, FAT-32 and NTFS.

### 23.2.2 Boot sector viruses

The boot sector resides on the first sector of a partition on a hard disk, or the first sector on a floppy disk. On starting, the PC reads from the active partition on the hard disk (identified by C:) or tries to read from the boot sector of the floppy disk. Boot sector viruses replace the boot sector with new code and moves, or deletes the original code.

Non-bootable floppy disks have executable code in their boot sector, which displays the message "Not bootable disk" when the computer is booted from it. Thus any floppy disk, whether it is bootable or non-bootable, can contain a virus, and can thus infect the PC.

### 23.2.3 File viruses

File viruses append or insert themselves into/onto executable files, such as .COM and .EXE programs. An indirect-action file virus installs itself into memory when the infected file is run, and infects other files when they are subsequently accessed.

### 23.2.4 Overwriting viruses

Overwriting viruses overwrite all, or part, of the original program. They are easy to detect as missing files are easily detected.

## 23.3 Anti-virus programs

Viruses use two main methods to introduce themselves to a computer system. These are through:

- Boot records on floppy and hard disks.
- Files. These are contained in either binary executable files or are macro viruses, which require another program to run them. A typical virus is the Word Macro virus, which effects the macros in Word 6.0. It cannot run itself and needs to hide within a Word document.

Virus scanning programs use a number of techniques to detect viruses. These include:

- Scanning. Most viruses have a digital signature within a file or boot sector which identifies the virus. For example, the Murphy virus has the ASCII characters of Murphy added to the end of a file. The virus-scanning program thus has a table of known digital signatures, which it compares with a byte-by-byte, read of the disk drive. Care must be taken, though, that the file does not normally contain a genuine sequence of bytes which are mistaken for the virus. The scanner will thus report a virus when there is none.
- Change detection. This allows the virus checker to keep a list of the date and time that files were last changed. Any changes to the files can then be checked for viruses. Typically, the change detector keeps a track of changes to the main boot files. Unfortunately, virus programmers can change the date of a file so that it has the date of the original 'uninfected' file.
- Heuristic analysis. This technique attempts to detect viruses by watching for appearance or behaviour that is characteristic of some class of known viruses. This allows for anti-virus program to detect new viruses which are not defined in the scanning technique.

- Verification. Scanning, change detection and heuristics can only identify a possible virus, only a verification program can prove that it really exists. Verifying program operates on the identified virus file and proves if it has been infected.

### 23.3.1 Disinfection

Disinfection involves removing a virus from the system, if possible it should be used with the minimum of damage. The two main methods are:

- Specific knowledge disinfection. With this method the disinfection program reverses the actions of the virus infection. This requires some knowledge of how the virus infects the system in the first place.
- Generic disinfection. This method has information about what the original file or boot record. This typically involves methods, such as storing system files, reinstalling system files, and rebuilding the boot record.

It is sometimes difficult to disinfect system which has a memory-resident virus, as the disinfection program could be tampered with as it is being run. Thus, it is often advisable to boot the anti-virus program from a clean boot disk.

An disinfector is intelligent in that it will not damage an infected file, and will generally prompt the user to delete the infected file rather than damage it (which could cause more problems).

## 23.4 Trojan horses

A Trojan horse virus hides itself as a tempting-looking executable file or in a compressed file. Until recently virus checkers did not test compressed files for viruses, but most currently available virus checkers checker test the uncompressed files within a compressed file. Many also test files as they are executed, and the virus would thus be detected as the compressed file was uncompressed. A Trojan horse virus attached to an executable file will typically have an interesting name, such as:

```
hello.exe
nice.exe
mail.exe
```

One Trojan horse virus, available from a WWW page, contains a single executable which is said to contain over 100 viruses. This, the owner of the WWW page, states that it can be used against someone's worst enemy. The WWW page quotes that it can be spread by sending the user an email with the attached executable file or to leave it on a targeted user's computer. Writing a Trojan horse virus is extremely simple and can simply involve a batch file which has:

```
cd \                    ; or 'cd /' on a UNIX system
rm -r *.*
```

which, on a UNIX system or a PC system with the rm utility installed, will change the directory to the top-level and then try to delete all subdirectories below the top-level directory. It is also extremely easy for a user to write a program which scans all the subdirectories below the current directory, and delete their contents.

## 23.5 Polymorphic viruses

A polymorphic virus encrypts itself so that its signature is invisible to a virus scanner. It propagates itself by first decrypting itself using a decryption routine. This decrypted program can then do damage, such as spreading itself or deleting files on the computer. A non-polymorphic encrypted virus uses a decryption routine that does not change. Thus is it easy to detect as the signature is unchanging. A polymorphic virus uses a changeable decryption routine (known as a mutation engine), in which the signature is different each time. The mutation engine normally uses a random number and a simple mathematical algorithm to change the virus's signature.

Typical COM/EXE virus infectors are:

- Yankee Doodle. It infects EXE and COM files (and adds 2772 bytes). When an infected file is run, the virus automatically loads into memory and infects any program which is run. At 5:00 pm the virus causes the system to sometimes play "Yankee Doodle".
- SatanBug. It infects EXE and COM files (and adds between 3500 to 5000 bytes). When an infected file is executed, the virus installs itself in memory and infects any program which is executed. A SatanBug infected system generally runs slow and some programs may fail, but does no long term damage to the computer.
- Frodo. It infects EXE and COM files (and adds between 4096 bytes). As above it infects all programs which are executed. When the date is between September 22 and December 31, the virus typically hangs the computer. This is because there are bugs in the virus code) which intends to overwrite the boot record with a program to display the message "Frodo Lives" when the machine boots.

## 23.6 Stealth viruses

Stealth viruses hide themselves in system files, or in boot records. They are then called when a certain action occurs on the computer. Typically, the system files which are used to start the computer are infected, such as IO.SYS and MSDOS.SYS (which are called when the computer starts). Once the virus is in memory, it can hook itself onto a given action, such as interrupt routine. For example, by hooking on interrupt 21h the virus can interrupt all accesses to DOS services, such as reading and writing to the hard disk.

A stealth size virus attaches itself to a file, when the file is accessed the virus copies itself, which increases the size of the file. A read stealth virus intercepts a request to an infected file and presents uninfected contents. Thus to the user, files seem to be operating as normal. Unfortunately, this stealth rapidly spreads through the system.

A stealth virus is relatively easy to detect and erase, as they do not change their digital signature. It is important, though, when eradicating a stealth virus that the system is booted with a clean boot disk. Typical stealth viruses include:

- Stoned. The Stoned virus infects floppy and hard disk boot sectors. When the computer starts from an infected diskette, the virus infects the master boot record of the first physical hard disk. It installs itself in memory and occasionally displays the message "Your PC is now Stoned!". It then infects the boot sectors of any inserted disk. Luckily, it does not cause damage to computer files and there is no loss of data.
- Ping Pong. This virus infects diskettes and the hard disk partition (non-master) boot record. It sometimes produces a bouncing dot on the screen after booting and adds approximately 975 bytes to the size of files.

## 23.7 Slow viruses

A slow virus operates by targeting the copying or modify of a file, and leave the original file untouched. Thus, a virus scanner may not pick-up that the file has been modified by the virus as it looks as if it was modified by some other normal operation. An example slow virus is:

- Dark Avenger. This is a resident COM and EXE file virus and adds 1800 bytes onto infected COM files. When an infected program is run, the virus installs itself in memory. It then only infects EXE or COM files which are run, opened, renamed, or operated on. Roughly every 16 times an infected program is run, it overwrites a random sector of the disk and displays the message: "Eddie lives...somewhere in time!".

These viruses can be defeated by memory-resident virus checkers who test the creation of new files (an integrity shell).

## 23.8 Retro viruses

Retro viruses (or anti-anti viruses) try to disrupt the operation of an anti-virus program. They are designed by analysing publicly available anti-virus programs (such as Dr Solomon's or Mcafee's) and identifying potential weaknesses. Typical methods include:

- Modifying operation. In this method the virus program changes the operation of the virus scanner, such as stopping it from scanning certain files, or blocking any system messages, or even, mimicking the output of the anti-virus program.

- Modify database. In this method the virus program modifies the virus signature database file so that the retro virus has the wrong digital signature (or even modify it when it is loaded into the computer's memory).
- Detect and run. This method involves the virus program detecting when the anti-virus program is run, and then hiding from it, either by deleting itself from memory or hiding in a file for a short time.

## 23.9 Worms

Before the advent of LANs and the Internet, the most common mechanism for spreading virus was through floppy disks and CD-ROM disks. Anti-virus programs can easily keep up-to-date with the latest virus, and modify their databases. This is a relatively slow method of spreading a virus and will take many months, if not years, to spread a virus over a large geographical area. Figure 23.1 illustrates the spread of viruses.

LANs and the Internet have changed all this. A virus can now be transmitted over a LAN in a fraction of a second, and around the world in less than a second. Thus a virus can be created and transmitted around the world before an anti-virus program can even detect that it is available.

A worm is a program which runs on a computer and creates two threads. A thread in a program is a unit of code that can get a time slice from the operating system to run concurrently with other code units. Each process consists of one or more execution threads that identify the code path flow as it is run on the operating system. This enhances the running of an application by improving throughput and responsiveness. With the worm, the first thread searches for a network connection and when it finds a connection it copies itself to that computer. Next, the worm makes a copy of itself, and runs it on the system. Thus, a single copy will become two, then four, eight, and so on. This continues until the system, and the other connected systems, will be shutdown. The only way to stop the worm is to shutdown all the effected computers at the same time and then restart them. Figure 23.2 illustrates a worm virus.

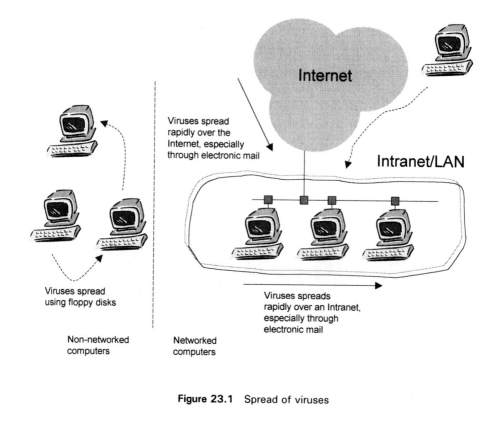

Viruses spread rapidly over the Internet, especially through electronic mail

Internet

Intranet/LAN

Viruses spread using floppy disks

Viruses spreads rapidly over an Intranet, especially through electronic mail

Non-networked computers

Networked computers

**Figure 23.1**   Spread of viruses

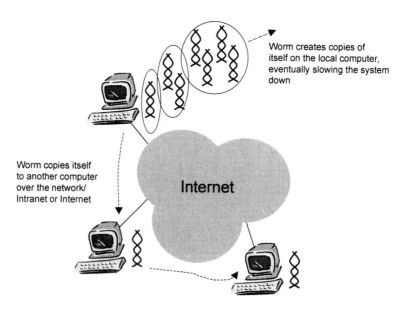

Worm creates copies of itself on the local computer, eventually slowing the system down

Worm copies itself to another computer over the network/ Intranet or Internet

Internet

**Figure 23.2**   Worm viruses

## 23.10 Macro viruses

One of the most common viruses is the macro virus, which attacks macro or scripting facilities which are available in word processors (such as Microsoft Word), spreadsheets (such as Microsoft Excel), and remote transfer programs. A typical virus is the WM/CAP virus which modifies macros within Microsoft Word Version 6.0. When a macro is executed it can cause considerable damage, such as: deleting files, corrupting files, and so on.

The greatest increase in macro viruses is the number of viruses which use Microsoft Visual Basic for Applications (VBA) as this integrates with Microsoft Office (although recent releases have guarded against macro viruses). A macro virus in Word 6.0 is spread by:

- The file is either transmitted over email, over a LAN or from floppy disk.
- The infected file is opened and the `normal.dot` main template file is modified so that it contains the modified macros. Any files that are opened or created will now have the modified macros. The WM/CAP macro virus does not do much damage and simply overwrites existing macros.
- VBA is made to be event-driven, so operations, such as File Open or File Close, can have an attached macro. This makes it easy for virus programmers to write new macros.

Figure 23.3 shows an example of a macro created by Visual Basic programming. The developed macro (`Macro1()`) simply loads a file called AUTHOR.doc, selects all the text, converts the text to bold, and then saves the file as AUTHOR.rtf. It can be seen that this macro is associated with `normal.dot`.

## 23.11 Other viruses

Other viruses include:

- Armoured. This type of virus uses special code which makes them difficult to detect, or even understand.
- Companion. This type of virus creates an executable program which contains the virus, which then calls the mimicked program. For example, a virus could create a program called EXCEL.EXE which would contain the virus, and this could call the standard Microsoft Excel program.
- Phage. This type of virus modifies the code of a program, and unlike the previously discussed viruses they do not attach themselves onto a file. This type of virus is extremely dangerous as it is very difficult to recovery the original program code, without having some knowledge of the changes that the phage virus is likely to do.

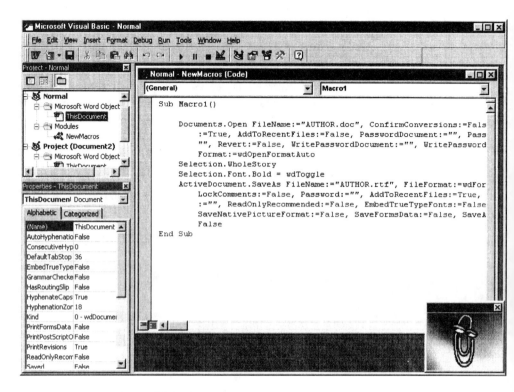

**Figure 23.3**  Sample macro using VB programming

---

## 23.12  Exercises

**23.12.1**  Before the usage of networks and the Internet, what was the main source of transferring viruses:

    (a)    CD-ROMs
    (b)    Tape drives
    (c)    Floppy disks
    (d)    Serial and parallel port connections

**23.12.2**  The major source of modern-day viruses is:

    (a)    Electronic mail
    (b)    CD-ROMs
    (c)    Remote login
    (d)    Remote file transfer

**23.12.3** How does a macro virus operate:

    (a)    They move themselves around the system
    (b)    The make viruses smaller
    (c)    It makes viruses larger
    (d)    It uses the macro or scripting language within the package to do damage to the computer

**23.12.4** What is the most likely cause of a computer crashing when a virus is run.

    (a)    It changes system configurations
    (b)    It changes file locations
    (c)    The virus is badly written and performs an illegal operation
    (d)    It reboots the computer, but fails

**23.12.5** Locate the Microsoft macro virus protection update for Microsoft Word Version 6.0 on the Microsoft WWW site. If you use Microsoft Word Version 6.0, download the update and install it.

**23.12.6** If you use Microsoft Word Version 7.0, or greater, locate the macro virus protection option (for Tools→Options→General) and check its state.

**23.12.7** Discuss the methods that viruses use to hide themselves from anti-virus programs.

**23.12.8** Explain how a worm virus is eradicated from a network. How might it be eradicated from networks spread over a large geographical network?

**23.12.9** Discuss the methods that an anti-virus program uses to locate viruses.

**23.12.10** Locate an anti-virus program and list some of the viruses it has in its database. If possible determine the number of bytes it adds, its different aliases it has and a description of the damage it causes.

## 23.13 Note from the author

*These days, viruses tend to be more annoying than dangerous. In fact, they tend to be more embarrassing than annoying, because a macro virus sent to a business colleague can often lead to a great deal of embarrassment (and a great deal of loss of business confidence).*

*A particularity-worrying source of viruses is the Internet, either through the running of programs over Internet, the spread of worms or the spreading of macro viruses in electronic mail attachments. The best way to avoid getting these viruses is to purchase an up-to-date virus scanner which checks all Internet programs and documents when they are loaded.*

*So, with viruses and worms, it is better to be safe than sorry. Let the flu be the only virus you catch, and the only worms you have to deal with are the ones in your garden.*

# 24 HTTP/Socket Programming

## 24.1 Introduction

Java 1.0 was first released in 1995 and was quickly adopted as it fitted well with Internet-based programming. It was followed by Java 1.1 which gave faster interpretation of Java applets and included many new features. This book documents the basic features of Java 1.0 and the enhancements that have been made in Java 1.1. Java 1.2 (which will be known as Java 2.0) includes further enhancements, especially related to security.

It is a general-purpose, concurrent, class-based, object-oriented language and has been designed to make it relatively simple to build complex applications. Java is developed from C and C++, but some parts of C++ have been dropped and others added.

Java has the great advantage over conventional software languages that it produces code which is computer hardware independent. This is because the compiled code (called bytecodes) is interpreted by the WWW browser. Unfortunately this leads to slower execution, but, as much of the time in a graphical user interface program is spent updating the graphics display, then the overhead is, as far as the user is concerned, not a great one.

The other advantages that Java has over conventional software languages include:

- It is a more dynamic language than C/C++ and Pascal, and was designed to adapt to an evolving environment. It is extremely easy to add new methods and extra libraries without affecting existing applets and programs. It is also useful in Internet applications as it supports most of the standard compressed image, audio and video formats.
- It has networking facilities built into it. This provides support for TCP/IP sockets, URLs, IP addresses and datagrams.
- While Java is based on C and C++ it avoids some of the difficult areas of C/C++ code (such as pointers and parameter passing).
- It supports client/server applications. In the most extreme case the client can simply be a graphics terminal which runs Java applets over a network. The small 'black-box' networked computer is one of the founding principles of Java, and it is hoped in the future that small Java-based computers could replace the complex PC/workstation for general-purpose applications, like accessing the Internet or playing network games. This 'black-box' computer concept is illustrated in Figure 24.1.

Most existing Web browsers are enabled for Java applets (such as Internet Explorer 3.0 and Netscape 2.0 and later versions). Figure 24.2 shows how Java applets are created. First the source code is produced with an editor, next a Java compiler compiles the Java source code into bytecode (normally appending the file name with .class). An HTML page is then constructed which has the reference to the applet. After this a Java-enabled browser or applet viewer can then be used to run the applet.

The Java Development Kit (JDK) is available, free, from Sun Microsystems from the WWW site http://www.javasoft.com. This can be used to compile Java applets and standalone programs. There are versions for Windows NT/95/98/2000, Apple Mac and UNIX-based systems with many sample applets.

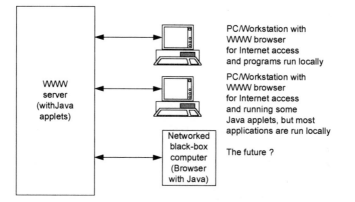

**Figure 24.1** Internet accessing

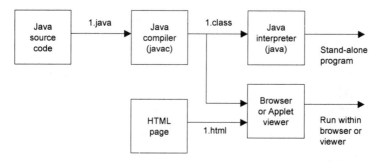

**Figure 24.2** Constructing Java applets and standalone programs

## 24.2 Java sockets

Figure 24.1 shows the operation of a connection of a client to a server. The server is defined as the computer which waits for a connection, the client is the computer which initially makes contact with the server.

On the server the computer initially creates a socket with ServerSocket() method, and then listens for a connection. The client creates a socket with the Socket() method. When the server receives this connection it accepts it with the accept()

method. Streams can then be set up on these sockets with the `getInputStream()` and `getOutputStream()` methods, and the `readUTF()` and `writeUTF()` methods can be used to read and write data to/from the stream. When the data transfer is complete the `close()` method is used to close any open sockets.

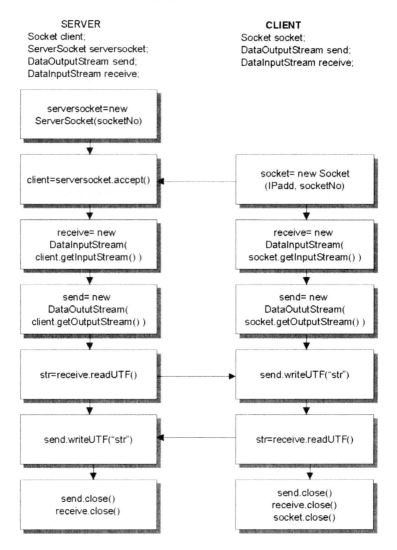

**Figure 24.3** Socket connection

Data is received using:

```
try
 {
  DataOutputStream send=new DataOutputStream(client.getOutputStream());
  send.writeUTF(str);
 }
 catch (IOException e)
 {
```

```
   //something
 }
```

and transmitted with:

```
try
 {
   DataInputStream receive=new DataInputStream(client.getInputStream());
   str=receive.readUTF();
 }
 catch (IOException e)
 {      //something  }
```

### 24.2.1 class java.net.Socket

The TCP protocol links two computers using sockets and ports. The constructors for
`java.net.Socket` are:

| | |
|---|---|
| `public Socket(InetAddress address,`<br>`            int port)` | Creates a stream socket and connects it to the specified address (`address`) on the specified port (`port`). |
| `public Socket(String host,`<br>`            int port)` | Creates a stream socket and connects it to the specified port (`port`) on the specified host (`host`). |

The methods are:

| | |
|---|---|
| `public synchronized void close()` | Closes the socket. |
| `public InetAddress getInetAddress()` | Returns the address to which the socket is connected. |
| `public InputStream getInputStream()` | Returns the `InputStream` for this socket. |
| `public int getLocalPort()` | Returns the local port to which the socket is connected. |
| `public OutputStream`<br>`            getOutputStream()` | Returns an `OutputStream` for this socket. |
| `public int getPort()` | Returns the remote port to which the socket is connected. |
| `public String toString()` | Converts the Socket to a String. |

### 24.2.2 Creating a socket

Java applet 24.1 constructs a socket for `www.eece.napier.ac.uk` using port 19
(`Socket remote = new Socket("www.eece.napier.ac.uk",19)`). After this the data
stream is created and assigned to `DataIn`. The `readUTF()` method is then used to get
the text from the stream.

### 📖 Java applet 24.1

```
import java.io.*;
import java.net.*;
import java.awt.*;
import java.applet.*;

public class client1 extends Applet
```

```
{
  TextArea tarea = new TextArea(5,50);

  public void init()
  {
  String        Instr;
  InputStream   Instream;
  TextArea      tarea;

        add(tarea);
        try
        {
            Socket remote = new Socket("www.eece.napier.ac.uk",19);

            Instream = remote.getInputStream();
            DataInputStream DataIn = new DataInputStream(Instream);
            do
            {
                Instr = DataIn.readUTF();
                if (Instr!=null)  tarea.setText(Instr);
            } while (Instr!=null);
        }
        catch (UnknownHostException err)
        {
            tarea.setText("UNKNOWN HOST: "+err);
        }
        catch (IOException err)
        {
            tarea.setText("Error" + err); }
        }
}
```

Java program 2 contacts a server on a given port and returns the local and remote port. It uses command line arguments, and the program is run in the form:

```
java client2 host port
```

where java is the Java interpreter, client2 is the name of the class file, *host* is the name of the host to contact and *port* is the port to use. The args.length parameter is used to determine the number of command line options. Anything other than two will display the following message:

```
Usage : client2 host port
```

### 📖 Java program 24.2
```
import java.net.*;
import java.io.*;

public class client2
{
  public static void main (String args[])
  {
      if (args.length !=2)
            System.out.println(" Usage : client2 host port");
      else
      {
          String inp;
          try
          {
              Socket sock = new Socket(args[0],
```

```
                    Integer.valueOf(args[1]).intValue());
        DataInputStream is =
                    new DataInputStream(sock.getInputStream());

        System.out.println("address : " +  sock.getInetAddress());
        System.out.println("port : " +   sock.getPort());
        System.out.println("Local address : " +
                                    sock.getLocalAddress());
        System.out.println("Localport : " + sock.getLocalPort());

        while((inp = is.readUTF()) != null)
        { System.out.println(inp);}
    }
    catch (UnknownHostException e)
    {
        System.out.println(" Known Host : " + e.getMessage());
    }
    catch (IOException e)
    {
        System.out.println("error I/O : " + e.getMessage());
    }
    finally
    {
        System.out.println("End of program");
    }
  }
 }
}
```

Sample run 24.1 shows a sample run which connects to port 13 on
www.eece.napier.ac.uk. It can be seen that the connection to this port causes the
server to return back the current date and time. Sample run 24.2 connects into the same
server, in this case on port 19. It can be seen that a connection to this port returns a
sequence of characters. Typical port values are: echo (7), null (9), daytime (13), character test (19), ftp (21), telnet (23), SMTP (25), TIME (37), DNS (53), HTTP (80) and
POP3 (110).

---

📟 Sample run 24.1
```
>> java client2 www.eece.napier.ac.uk 13
Host and IP address : www.eece.napier.ac.uk/146.176.151.139
port : 13
Local address :pc419.eece.napier.ac.uk
Localport : 1393
Fri May  8 13:19:59 1998
End of program
```

---

📟 Sample run 24.2
```
>> java client2 www.eece.napier.ac.uk 19
Host and IP address : www.eece.napier.ac.uk/146.176.151.139
port : 19
Local IP address :pc419.eece.napier.ac.uk
Localport : 1403
 !"#$%&'()*+,-./0123456789:;<=>?@ABCDEFGHIJKLMNOPQRSTUVWXYZ[\]^_`abcdefg
!"#$%&'()*+,-./0123456789:;<=>?@ABCDEFGHIJKLMNOPQRSTUVWXYZ[\]^_`abcdefgh
"#$%&'()*+,-./0123456789:;<=>?@ABCDEFGHIJKLMNOPQRSTUVWXYZ[\]^_`abcdefghi
#$%&'()*+,-./0123456789:;<=>?@ABCDEFGHIJKLMNOPQRSTUVWXYZ[\]^_`abcdefghij
$%&'()*+,-./0123456789:;<=>?@ABCDEFGHIJKLMNOPQRSTUVWXYZ[\]^_`abcdefghijk
%&'()*+,-./0123456789:;<=>?@ABCDEFGHIJKLMNOPQRSTUVWXYZ[\]^_`abcdefghijkl
&'()*+,-./0123456789:;<=>?@ABCDEFGHIJKLMNOPQRSTUVWXYZ[\]^_`abcdefghijklm
```

```
'()*+,-./0123456789:;<=>?@ABCDEFGHIJKLMNOPQRSTUVWXYZ[\]^_`abcdefghijklmn
()*+,-./0123456789:;<=>?@ABCDEFGHIJKLMNOPQRSTUVWXYZ[\]^_`abcdefghijklmno
)*+,-./0123456789:;<=>?@ABCDEFGHIJKLMNOPQRSTUVWXYZ[\]^_`abcdefghijklmnop
*+,-./0123456789:;<=>?@ABCDEFGHIJKLMNOPQRSTUVWXYZ[\]^_`abcdefghijklmnopq
+,-./0123456789:;<=>?@ABCDEFGHIJKLMNOPQRSTUVWXYZ[\]^_`abcdefghijklmnopqr
```

### 24.2.3 Client/server program

A server is a computer which runs a special program which passively waits for another computer (a client) to connect to it. This server normally performs some sort of special operation, such as FTP, Telnet or WWW service.

Java program 24.3 acts as a server program and waits for a connection on port 1111. When a connection is received on this port it sends its current date and time back to the client. This program can be run with Java program 24.2 (which is running on a remote computer) with a connection to the server's IP address (or domain name) and using port 1111. When the client connects to the server, the server responds back to the client with its current date and time. Figure 24.2 shows a sample run from the server. It can be seen that it has received connection from the client with the IP address of 62.136.29.76.

📖　Java program 24.3

```java
import java.net.*;
import java.io.*;
import java.util.*;

class server
{
  public static void main( String arg[])
  {
      try
      {
        ServerSocket sock = new ServerSocket(1111);
        Socket sock1 = sock.accept();

        System.out.println(sock1.toString());
        System.out.println("address : " +     sock1.getInetAddress());
        System.out.println("port    : " +     sock1.getPort());

        DataOutputStream out =
             new DataOutputStream(sock1.getOutputStream());

        out.writeUTF("Welcome "+ sock1.getInetAddress().getHostName()+
             ". We are "+ new Date()+ "\n");

        sock1.close();
        sock.close();
      }
      catch(IOException err)
      {
        System.out.println(err.getMessage());
      }
      finally
      {
        System.out.println("End of the program");
      }
  }
}
```

**Figure 24.4** Sample run of client/server programs

## 24.3 Java networking methods

Java directly supports TCP/IP communications and has the following classes:

| | |
|---|---|
| `java.net.ContentHandler` | Class which reads data from a URLConnection and also supports MIME (Multipurpose Internet Mail Extension). |
| `java.net.DatagramPacket` | Class representing a datagram packet which contains packet data, packet length, Internet addresses and the port number. |
| `java.net.DatagramSocket` | Class representing a datagram socket class. |
| `java.net.InetAddress` | Class representing Internet addresses. |
| `java.net.ServerSocket` | Class representing Socket server class. |
| `java.net.Socket` | Class representing Socket client classes. |
| `java.net.SocketImpl` | Socket implementation class. |
| `java.net.URL` | Class URL representing a Uniform Reference Locator (URL) which is a reference to an object on the WWW. |

| | |
|---|---|
| `java.net.URLConnection` | Class representing an active connection to an object represented by a URL. |
| `java.net.URLEncoder` | Converts strings of text into URLEncoded format. |
| `java.net.URLStreamHandler` | Class for opening URL streams. |

When an error occurs in the connection or in the transmission and reception of data it causes an exception. The classes which handle these are:

| | |
|---|---|
| `java.io.IOException` | To handle general errors. |
| `java.net.MalformedURLException` | Malformed URL. |
| `java.net.ProtocolException` | Protocol error. |
| `java.net.SocketException` | Socket error. |
| `java.net.UnknownHostException` | Unknown host error. |
| `java.net.UnknownServiceException` | Unknown service error. |

### 24.3.1 class java.net.InetAddress

This class represents Internet addresses. The methods are:

| | |
|---|---|
| `public static synchronized InetAddress[] getAllByName(String host)` | This returns an array with all the corresponding InetAddresses for a given host name (`host`). |
| `public static synchronized InetAddress getByName(String host)` | This returns the network address of an indicated host. A hostname of null return the default address for the local machine. |
| `public String getHostAddress()` | This returns the IP address string (WW.XX.YY.ZZ) in a string format. |
| `public byte[] getAddress()` | This returns the raw IP address in network byte order. The array position 0 (addr[0]) contains the highest order byte. |
| `public String getHostName()` | Gets the hostname for this address. If the host is equal to null, then this address refers to any of the local machine's available network addresses. |
| `public static InetAddress getLocalHost()` | Returns the local host. |
| `public String toString()` | Converts the InetAddress to a String. |

Java applet 24.4 uses the `getAllByName` method to determine all the IP addresses associated with an Internet host. In this case the host is named `www.microsoft.com`. It can be seen from the test run that there are 18 IP addresses associated with this domain name. It can be seen that the applet causes an exception error as the loop tries to display 30 such IP addresses. When the program reaches the 19th InetAddress, the exception error is displayed (`ArrayIndexOutOfBoundsException`).

📖 Java applet 24.4
```
import java.net.*;
import java.awt.*;
import java.applet.*;
```

```
public class http1 extends Applet
{
InetAddress[] address;
int i
  public void start()
  {
      System.out.println("Started");
      try
      {
          address=InetAddress.getAllByName("www.microsoft.com");
          for (i=0;i<30;i++)
          {
              System.out.println("Address " + address[i]);
          }
      }
      catch (Exception e)
      {
          System.out.println("Error :" + e);
      }
  }
}
```

🖳 Sample run 24.3

```
Started
Address www.microsoft.com/207.68.137.59
Address www.microsoft.com/207.68.143.192
Address www.microsoft.com/207.68.143.193
Address www.microsoft.com/207.68.143.194
Address www.microsoft.com/207.68.143.195
Address www.microsoft.com/207.68.156.49
Address www.microsoft.com/207.68.137.56
Address www.microsoft.com/207.68.156.51
Address www.microsoft.com/207.68.156.52
Address www.microsoft.com/207.68.137.62
Address www.microsoft.com/207.68.156.53
Address www.microsoft.com/207.68.156.54
Address www.microsoft.com/207.68.137.65
Address www.microsoft.com/207.68.156.73
Address www.microsoft.com/207.68.156.61
Address www.microsoft.com/207.68.156.16
Address www.microsoft.com/207.68.156.58
Address www.microsoft.com/207.68.137.53
Error :java.lang.ArrayIndexOutOfBoundsException: 18
```

Java applet 24.5 overcomes the problem of the displaying of the exception. In this case the exception is caught by inserting the address display within a try {} statement then having a catch statement which does nothing. Sample run 24.4 shows a sample run.

📖 Java applet 24.5

```
import java.net.*;
import java.awt.*;
import java.applet.*;

public class http2 extends Applet
{
InetAddress[] address;
int i;

  public void start()
  {
```

```
       System.out.println("Started");
       try
       {
           address=InetAddress.getAllByName("www.microsoft.com");
           try
           {
               for (i=0;i<30;i++)
               {
                   System.out.println("Address " + address[i]);
               }
           }
           catch(Exception e)
           { / * Do nothing about the exception, as it
               is not really an error */
           }
       }
       catch (Exception e)
       {
           System.out.println("Error :" + e);
       }
   }
}
```

---

📟 Sample run 24.4

```
Started
Address www.microsoft.com/207.68.137.59
Address www.microsoft.com/207.68.143.192
Address www.microsoft.com/207.68.143.193
Address www.microsoft.com/207.68.143.194
Address www.microsoft.com/207.68.143.195
Address www.microsoft.com/207.68.156.49
Address www.microsoft.com/207.68.137.56
Address www.microsoft.com/207.68.156.51
Address www.microsoft.com/207.68.156.52
Address www.microsoft.com/207.68.137.62
Address www.microsoft.com/207.68.156.53
Address www.microsoft.com/207.68.156.54
Address www.microsoft.com/207.68.137.65
Address www.microsoft.com/207.68.156.73
Address www.microsoft.com/207.68.156.61
Address www.microsoft.com/207.68.156.16
Address www.microsoft.com/207.68.156.58
Address www.microsoft.com/207.68.137.53
```

---

Java applet 24.6 shows an example of displaying the local host name (getLocalHost), the host name (getHostName) and the host's IP address (getHostAddress). Test run 24.5 shows a sample run.

📖 Java applet 24.6

```
import java.net.*;
import java.awt.*;
import java.applet.*;

public class http3 extends Applet
{
InetAddress host;
String str;
int i;
  public void start()
  {
       System.out.println("Started");
```

```
    try
    {
        host=InetAddress.getLocalHost();
        System.out.println("Local host " + host);

        str=host.getHostName();
        System.out.println("Host name: " + str);

        str=host.getHostAddress();
        System.out.println("Host address: " + str);
    }
    catch (Exception e)
    {
        System.out.println("Error :" + e);
    }
  }
}
```

---

🖳 Sample run 24.5
```
Started
Local host toshiba/195.232.26.125
Host name: toshiba
Host address: 195.232.26.125
```

---

The previous Java applets have all displayed their output to the output terminal (with `System.out.println`). Java applet 24.7 uses the `drawString` method to display the output text to the Applet window. Figure 24.5 shows a sample run.

📖 Java applet 24.7

```
import java.net.*;
import java.awt.*;
import java.applet.*;

public class http4 extends Applet
{
InetAddress[] address;
int i;

  public void paint(Graphics g)
  {
      g.drawString("Addresses for WWW.MICROSOFT.COM",5,10);
      try
      {
          address=InetAddress.getAllByName("www.microsoft.com");

          for (i=0;i<30;i++)
          {
              g.drawString(" "+ address[i].toString(),5,20+10*i);
          }
      }
      catch (Exception e)
      {
          System.out.println("Error :" + e);
      }
  }
}
```

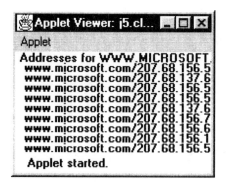

**Figure 24.5** Sample run

### 24.3.2 class java.net.URL

The URL (Uniform Reference Locator) class is used to reference to an object on the World Wide Web. The main constructors are:

| | |
|---|---|
| `public URL(String protocol, String host, int port, String file)` | Creates an absolute URL from the specified protocol (`protocol`), host (`host`), port (`port`) and file (`file`). |
| `public URL(String protocol, String host, String file)` | Creates an absolute URL from the specified protocol (`protocol`), host (`host`) and file (`file`). |
| `public URL(String spec)` | Creates a URL from an unparsed absolute URL (`spec`) |
| `public URL(URL context, String spec)` | Creates a URL from an unparsed absolute URL (`spec`) in the specified context. |

The methods are:

| | |
|---|---|
| `public int getPort()` | Returns a port number. A return value of −1 indicates that the port is not set. |
| `public String getProtocol()` | Returns the protocol name. |
| `public String getHost()` | Returns the host name. |
| `public String getFile()` | Returns the file name. |
| `public boolean equals(Object obj)` | Compares two URLs, where `obj` is the URL to compare against. |
| `public String toString()` | Converts to a string format. |
| `public String toExternalForm()` | Reverses the URL parsing. |
| `public URLConnection openConnection()` | Creates a URLConnection object that contains a connection to the remote object referred to by the URL. |
| `public final InputStream openStream()` | Opens an input stream. |

| | |
|---|---|
| `public final Object getContent()` | Gets the contents from this opened connection. |

### 24.3.3 class java.net.URLConnection

Represents an active connection to an object represented by a URL. The main methods are:

| | |
|---|---|
| `public abstract void connect()` | URLConnection objects are initially created and then they are connected. |
| `public URL getURL()` | Returns the URL for this connection. |
| `public int getContentLength()` | Returns the content length, a −1 if not known. |
| `public String getContentType()` | Returns the content type, a null if not known. |
| `public String getContentEncoding()` | Returns the content encoding, a null if not known. |
| `public long getExpiration()` | Returns the expiration date of the object, a 0 if not known. |
| `public long getDate()` | Returns the sending date of the object, a 0 if not known. |
| `public long getLastModified()` | Returns the last modified date of the object, a 0 if not known. |
| `public String getHeaderField` `(String name)` | Returns a header field by name (name), a null if not known. |
| `public Object getContent()` | Returns the object referred to by this URL. |
| `public InputStream getInputStream()` | Used to read from objects. |
| `public OutputStream getOutputStream()` | Used to write to objects. |
| `public String toString()` | Returns the String URL representation. |

### 24.3.4 class java.net.URLStreamHandler

Abstract class for URL stream openers. Subclasses of this class know how to create streams for particular protocol types.

| | |
|---|---|
| `protected abstract URLConnection` `openConnection(URL u)` | Opens an input stream to the object referenced by the URL (u). |
| `protected void parseURL(URL u, String spec, int start, int limit)` | Parses the string (spec) into URL (u), where start and limit refer to the range of characters in spec that should be parsed. |
| `protected String toExternalForm(URL u)` | Reverses the parsing of the URL. |
| `protected void setURL(URL u, String protocol, String host, int port, String file, String ref)` | Calls the (protected) set method out of the URL given. |

### 24.3.5 java.applet.AppletContext

The AppletContext can be used by an applet to obtain information from the applet's environment, which is usually the browser or the applet viewer. Related methods are:

```
public abstract void showDocument(URL url)
public abstract void showDocument(URL url,
    String target)
```

Shows a new document.
Show a new document in a target window or frame.

### 24.3.6 Connecting to a WWW site

Java applet 24.8 shows an example of an applet that connects to a WWW site. It allows the user to enter a URL and it also shows a status window (status). Figure 24.4 show a sample run. The upper window of Figure 24.4 shows that the user has added an incorrect URL (www.sun.com). The status windows shows that this is an error. The lower window of the Figure 24.6 shows a correct URL (http://www.sun.com).

### 📖 Java applet 24.8

```java
import java.net.*;
import java.awt.*;
import java.applet.*;

public class j1 extends Applet
{
URL       urlWWW;
Button    btn;
Label     label = new Label("Enter a URL:");
TextField inURL = new TextField(30);
TextArea status = new TextArea(3,30);

    public void init()
    {
        add(label);
        add(inURL);
        btn = (new Button("Connect"));
        add(btn);
        add(status);
    }

    public void getURL()//Check for valid URL
    {
        try
        {
            String str;
            str=inURL.getText();
            status.setText("Site: " + str);
            urlWWW  = new URL(str);
        }
        catch (MalformedURLException e)
        {
            status.setText("URL Error: " + e);
        }
    }

    public boolean action(Event evt, Object obj)
    {
        if (evt.target.equals(btn))
        {
            status.setText("Connecting...\n");
            getURL();
            getAppletContext().showDocument(urlWWW);
```

```
            return true;
        }
        return false;
    }
}
```

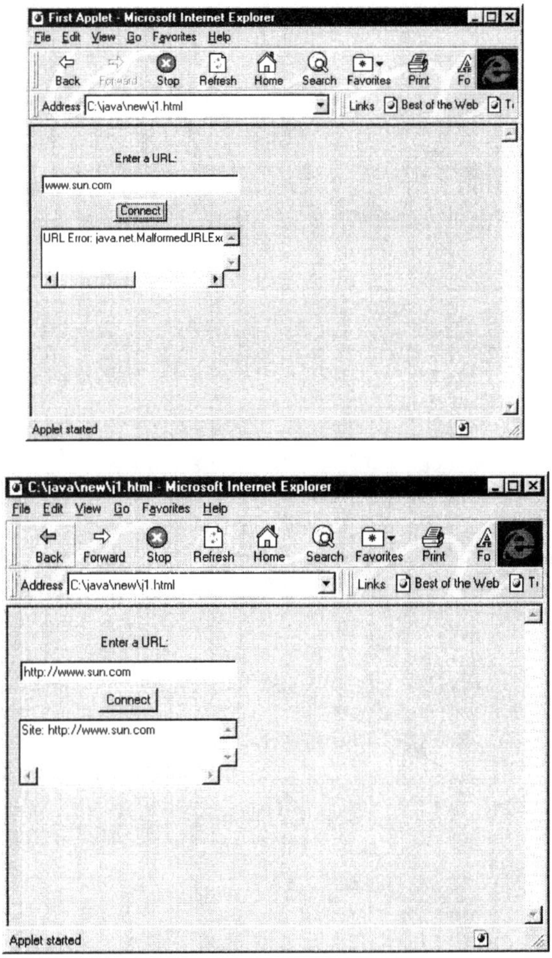

**Figure 24.6** WWW connection

## 24.4 Note

Many WWW browsers do not allow Java applets to access ports over the network, as this could lead to viruses being downloaded onto the computer which is running the applet. They could also allow a remote hacker to gain access to the computer running the applet, as the applet could contact the hacker's server socket and make a connection. Information on the local computer could be sent to the hacker. Thus, many Java applet programs will not work fully, and give security exceptions. If this happens the Java applet should be changed to a Java stand-alone program, and run with the Java interpreter (or use Visual Basic/Borland Delphi or C++).

## 24.5 Exercises

**24.5.1** Write a Java applet in which the user selects from one of the following pop-up menu URLs. Theses are:

www.microsoft.com     www.ibm.com
www.intel.com         www.sun.com

**24.5.2** Use Java program 24.2 connect to some WWW servers. Try different port values.

**24.5.3** Find two computers which can be connected over TCP/IP. Determine their IP addresses (or DNS) and connect them over a network.

**24.5.4** Connect two computers over a network and set up a chat connection. One of the computers should be the chat server and the other the chat client. Modify it so that the server accepts calls from one or many clients.

**24.5.5** Develop a Java program which has send and receive text windows. The program should allow the user to specify the IP address (or DNS) of the server. The send and receive windows will then show the text sent and received.

**Common Abbreviations**

| | |
|---|---|
| AA | auto-answer |
| AAL | ATM adaptation layer |
| AAN | autonomously attached network |
| ABM | asynchronous balanced mode |
| AbMAN | Aberdeen MAN |
| ABNF | augmented BNF |
| AC | access control |
| ACAP | application configuration access protocol |
| ACK | acknowledge |
| ACL | access control list |
| ADC | analogue-to-digital converter |
| ADPCM | adaptive delta pulse code modulation |
| AES | audio engineering society |
| AFI | authority and format identifier |
| AGENTX | agent extensibility protocol |
| AGP | accelerated graphics port |
| AM | amplitude modulation |
| AMI | alternative mark inversion |
| ANSI | American National Standard Institute |
| APCM | adaptive pulse code modulation |
| API | application program interface |
| ARM | asynchronous response mode |
| ARP | address resolution protocol |
| ASCII | American standard code for information exchange |
| ASK | amplitude-shift keying |
| AT | attention |
| ATM | asynchronous transfer mode |
| AUI | attachment unit interface |
| BCC | blind carbon copy |
| BCD | binary coded decimal |
| BGP | border gateway protocol |
| BIOS | basic input/output system |
| B-ISDN | broadband ISDN |
| BMP | bitmapped |
| BNC | British Naval Connector |
| BOM | beginning of message |
| BOOTP | bootstrap protocol |
| BPDU | bridge protocol data units |
| bps | bits per second |
| BVCP | Banyan Vines control protocol |
| CAD | computer-aided design |

| | |
|---|---|
| CAN | concentrated area network |
| CASE | common applications service elements |
| CATNIP | common architecture for the Internet |
| CC | carbon copy |
| CCITT | International Telegraph and Telephone Consultative |
| CD | carrier detect |
| CD | compact disk |
| CDE | common desktop environment |
| CDFS | CD file system |
| CD-R | CD-recordable |
| CD-ROM | compact disk - read-only memory |
| CF | control field |
| CGI | common gateway interface |
| CGM | computer graphics metafile |
| CHAP | challenge handshake authentication protocol |
| CHARGEN | character generator protocol |
| CIF | common interface format |
| CMC | common mail call |
| CMOS | complementary MOS |
| CN | common name |
| COM | continuation of message |
| CON-MD5 | content-MD5 header field |
| CPCS | convergence protocol communications sublayer |
| CPI | common part indicator |
| CPSR | computer professionals for social responsibility |
| CPU | central processing unit |
| CRC | cyclic redundancy check |
| CRLF | carriage return, line feed |
| CRT | cathode ray tube |
| CSDN | circuit-switched data network |
| CSMA | carrier sense multiple access |
| CSMA/CA | CSMA with collision avoidance |
| CSMA/CD | CSMA with collision detection |
| CS-MUX | circuit-switched multiplexer |
| CSPDN | circuit-switched public data network |
| CTS | clear to send |
| DA | destination address |
| DAA | digest access authentication |
| DAC | digital-to-analogue converter |
| DAC | dual attachment concentrator |
| DARPA | Defense Advanced Research Projects Agency |
| DAS | dual attachment station |
| DASS | distributed authentication security |
| DAT | digital audio tape |
| DAYTIME | daytime protocol |
| dB | decibel |
| DBF | NetBEUI frame |

| | |
|---|---|
| DC | direct current |
| DCC | digital compact cassette |
| DCD | data carrier detect |
| DCE | data circuit-terminating equipment |
| DC-MIB | dial control MIB |
| DCT | discrete cosine transform |
| DD | double density |
| DDE | dynamic data exchange |
| DENI | Department of Education for Northern Ireland |
| DES | data encryption standard |
| DHCP | dynamic host configuration program |
| DIB | device-independent bitmaps |
| DIB | directory information base |
| DISC | disconnect |
| DISCARD | discard protocol |
| DLC | data link control |
| DLL | dynamic link library |
| DM | disconnect mode |
| DMA | direct memory access |
| DNS | domain name server |
| DNS-SEC | domain name system security extensions |
| DOS | disk operating system |
| DPCM | differential PCM |
| DPSK | differential phase-shift keying |
| DQDB | distributed queue dual bus |
| DR | dynamic range |
| DRAM | dynamic RAM |
| DSN | delivery status notifications |
| DSP | domain specific part |
| DSS | digital signature standard |
| DTE | data terminal equipment |
| DTR | data terminal ready |
| EASE | embedded advanced sampling environment |
| EaStMAN | Edinburgh/Stirling MAN |
| EBCDIC | extended binary coded decimal interchange code |
| EBU | European broadcast union |
| ECHO | echo protocol |
| ECP | extended communications port |
| EEPROM | electrically erasable PROM |
| EF | empty flag |
| EFF | electronic frontier foundation |
| EFM | eight-to-fourteen modulation |
| EGP | exterior gateway protocol |
| EIA | Electrical Industries Association |
| EISA | extended international standard interface |
| EMF | enhanced metafile |
| ENQ | inquiry |

| | |
|---|---|
| EOM | end of message |
| EOT | end of transmission |
| EPP | enhanced parallel port |
| EPROM | erasable PROM |
| EPS | encapsulated postscript |
| ESP | IP encapsulating security payload |
| ETB | end of transmitted block |
| ETHER-MIB | ethernet MIB |
| ETX | end of text |
| FAT | file allocation table |
| FATMAN | Fife and Tayside MAN |
| FAX | facsimile |
| FC | frame control |
| FCS | frame check sequence |
| FDDI | fiber distributed data interface |
| FDDI-MIB | FDDI management information base |
| FDM | frequency division multiplexing |
| FDX | full duplex |
| FEC | forward error correction |
| FF | full flag |
| FFIF | file format for internet fax |
| FIFO | first in, first out |
| FINGER | finger protocol |
| FM | frequency modulation |
| FRMR | frame reject |
| FS | frame status |
| FSK | frequency-shift keying |
| FTP | file transfer protocol |
| FTP | file transfer protocol |
| FYI | for your information |
| GFI | group format identifier |
| GGP | gateway-gateway protocol |
| GIF | graphics interface format |
| GQOS | guaranteed quality of service |
| GSSAP | generic security service application |
| GUI | graphical user interface |
| HAL | hardware abstraction layer |
| HD | high density |
| HDB3 | high-density bipolar code no. 3 |
| HDLC | high-level data link control |
| HDTV | high-definition television |
| HDX | half duplex |
| HEFCE | Higher Education Funding Councils of England |
| HEFCW | Higher Education Funding Councils of Wales |
| HF | high frequency |
| HMUX | hybrid multiplexer |
| HPFS | high performance file system |

| | |
|---|---|
| HTML | hypertext mark-up language |
| HTTP | hypertext transfer protocol |
| Hz | Hertz |
| I/O | input/output |
| IA5 | international alphabet no. 5 |
| IAB | internet advisory board |
| IAP | internet access provider |
| IARP | inverse ARP |
| IBM | International Business Machines |
| ICMP | internet control message protocol |
| ICP | internet connectivity provider |
| IDEA | international data encryption algorithm |
| IDENT | identification Protocol |
| IDI | initial domain identifier |
| IDP | initial domain part |
| IDPR | inter-domain policy routing |
| IEEE | Institute of Electrical and Electronic Engineers |
| IEFF | internet engineering task force |
| IFS | installable file system |
| IGMP | internet group management protocol |
| IGMP | internet group multicast protocol |
| IGP | interior gateway protocol |
| ILD | injector laser diode |
| IMAC | isochronous MAC |
| IMAP | internet message access protocol |
| IOS | input/output supervisor |
| IP | internet protocol |
| IP-ARC | IP over ARCNET networks |
| IP-ARPA | IP over ARPANET |
| IP-ATM | IP over ATM |
| IP-CMPRS | IP with compressed headers |
| IP-DC | IP over DC Networks |
| IP-E | IP over ethernet networks |
| IP-EE | IP over experimental ethernet networks |
| IP-FDDI | IP over FDDI networks |
| IP-FR | IP over frame relay |
| IP-HC | IP over hyperchannel |
| IP-HIPPI | IP over HIPPI |
| IP-IEEE | IP over IEEE 802 |
| IP-IPX | IP over IPX networks |
| IP-MTU | path MTU discovery |
| IP-NETBIOS | IP over NETBIOS |
| IPNG | IP next generation |
| IPP | internet presence provider |
| IP-SLIP | IP over serial lines |
| IP-SMDS | IP datagrams over SMDS |
| IP-TR-MC | IP Multicast over token-ring LANs |

| | |
|---|---|
| IPV6-FDDI | IPv6 over FDDI |
| IPv6-Jumbo | IPv6 Jumbograms |
| IPV6-PPP | IPv6 over PPP |
| IP-WB | IP over wideband network |
| IPX | internet packet exchange |
| IP-X.25 | IP over ISDN |
| IPX-IP | IPX over IP |
| IRQ | interrupt request |
| ISA | international standard interface |
| ISDN | integrated services digital network |
| IS-IS | immediate system to intermediate system |
| ISO | International Standards Organization |
| ISP | internet service provider |
| ITOT | ISO transport service on top of TCP |
| ITU | International Telecommunications Union |
| JANET | joint academic network |
| JFIF | jpeg file interchange format |
| JISC | Joint Information Systems Committee |
| JPEG | Joint Photographic Expert Group |
| KDC | key distribution centre |
| KERBEROS | Kerberos network authentication service |
| LAN | local area network |
| LAPB | link access procedure balanced |
| LAPD | link access procedure |
| LCN | logical channel number |
| LDAP-URL | LDAP URL Format |
| LD-CELP | low-delay code excited linear prediction |
| LED | light emitting diode |
| LGN | logical group number |
| LIP | large IPX packets |
| LLC | logical link control |
| LRC | longitudinal redundancy check |
| LSL | link support level |
| LSP | link state protocol |
| LSRR | loose source and record route |
| LZ | Lempel-Ziv |
| LZW | LZ-Welsh |
| MAC | media access control |
| MAIL-MIB | mail monitoring MIB |
| MAN | metropolitan area network |
| MAP | messaging API |
| MAU | multi-station access unit |
| MD | message digest |
| MDCT | modified discrete cosine transform |
| MDI | media dependent interface |
| MHS | message handling service |
| MIB-II | management information base-II |

| | |
|---|---|
| MIC | media interface connector |
| MIME | multi-purpose internet mail extension |
| MLID | multi-link interface driver |
| MODEM | modulation/demodulator |
| MOS | metal oxide semiconductor |
| MPEG | motion picture experts group |
| MPI | multi-precision integer |
| MSL | maximum segment lifetime |
| MTP | multicast transport protocol |
| NAK | negative acknowledge |
| NCP | netware control protocols |
| NCSA | National Center for Supercomputer Applications |
| NDIS | network device interface standard |
| NDS | Novell Directory Services |
| NETBEUI | NetBIOS extended user interface |
| NETFAX | network file format for the exchange of images |
| NHRP | next hop resolution protocol |
| NIC | network interface card |
| NICNAME | whois protocol |
| NIS | network information system |
| NLSP | netware link-state routing protocol |
| NNTP | network news transfer protocol |
| NRZI | non-return to zero with inversion |
| NSAP | network service access point |
| NSCA | National Center for Supercomputing Applications |
| NSM-MIB | network services monitoring MIB |
| NSS | named service server |
| NTE | network terminal equipment |
| NTFS | NT file system |
| NTP | network time protocol |
| NTSC | National Television Standards Committee |
| ODI | open data-link interface |
| OH | off-hook |
| ONE-PASS | one-time password system |
| OSI | open systems interconnection |
| OSI-UDP | OSI TS on UDP |
| OSPF | open shortest path first |
| OUI | originators unique identifier |
| PA | point of attachment |
| PAL | phase alternation line |
| PAP | password authentication protocol |
| PC | personal computer |
| PCM | pulse code modulation |
| PCT | personal communications technology |
| PDN | public data network |
| PGP | pretty good privacy |
| PHY | physical layer protocol |

| | |
|---|---|
| PING | packet internet gopher |
| PISO | parallel-in-serial-out |
| PKP | public key partners |
| PLL | phase-locked loop |
| PLS | physical signalling |
| PMA | physical medium attachment |
| PMD | physical medium dependent |
| POP3 | post office protocol, Version 3 |
| POP-URL | POP URL Scheme |
| PPP | point-to-point protocol |
| PPP-AAL | PPP over AAL |
| PPP-CCP | PPP compression control protocol |
| PPP-CHAP | PPP challenge handshake authentication |
| PPP-EAP | PPP extensible authentication protocol |
| PPP-HDLC | PPP in HDLC framing |
| PPP-IPCP | PPP control protocol |
| PPP-ISDN | PPP over ISDN |
| PPP-LINK | PPP link quality monitoring |
| PPP-MP | PPP multilink protocol |
| PPP-NBFCP | PPP NetBIOS frames control protocol |
| PPP-SNACP | PPP SNA control protocol |
| PPP-SONET | PPP over SONET/SDH |
| PPP-X25 | PPP in X.25 |
| PPSDN | public packet-switched data network |
| PS | postscript |
| PSDN | packet-switched data network |
| PSE | packet switched exchange |
| PSK | phase-shift keying |
| PSTN | public-switched telephone network |
| QAM | quadrature amplitude modulation |
| QCIF | quarter common interface format |
| QIC | quarter inch cartridge |
| QoS | quality of service |
| QT | quicktime |
| QUOTE | quote of the day protocol |
| RADIUS | remote authentication dial-in service |
| RAID | redundant array of inexpensive disks |
| RAM | random-access memory |
| RD | receive data |
| REJ | reject |
| RFC | request for comment |
| RGB | red, green and blue |
| RI | ring in |
| RIF | routing information field |
| RIP | routing information protocol |
| RIP2-MD5 | RIP-2 MD5 Authentication |
| RIP2-MIB | RIP Version 2 MIB Extension |

| | |
|---|---|
| RIPNG-IPV6 | RIPng for IPv6 |
| RIP-TRIG | Trigger RIP |
| RLE | run-length encoding |
| RMON | remote monitoring |
| RMON-MIB | remote network monitoring MIB |
| RNR | receiver not ready |
| RO | ring out |
| ROM | read-only memory |
| RPC | remote procedure call |
| RPSL | routing policy specification language |
| RR | receiver ready |
| RSA | Rivest, Shamir and Adleman |
| RSVP | resource reservation protocol |
| RTF | rich text format |
| RTMP | routing table maintenance protocol |
| RTP | real-time transport protocol |
| RTSP | real-time streaming protocol |
| S/PDIF | Sony/Philips digital interface format |
| SA | source address |
| SABME | set asynchronous balanced mode extended |
| SAC | single attachment concentrator |
| SAP | service advertising protocol |
| SAPI | service access point identifier |
| SAR | segment and reassemble |
| SARPDU | segmentation and reassembly protocol data unit |
| SAS | single attachment station |
| SASL | simple authentication and security layer |
| SASL-ANON | anonymous SASL mechanism |
| SB-ADCMP | sub-band ADPCM |
| SCMS | serial copy management system |
| SCSI | small computer systems interface |
| SCSP | server cache synchronisation protocol |
| SD | sending data |
| SD | start delimiter |
| SDH | synchronous digital hierarchy |
| SDIF | Sony digital interface |
| SDLC | synchronous data link control |
| SDNSDU | secure domain name system dynamic update |
| SDP | session description protocol |
| SECAM | séquential couleur à mémoire |
| SEL | selector/extension local address |
| SHEFC | Scottish Higher Education Funding Council |
| SIPO | serial-in parallel-out |
| SIPP | simple internet protocol plus |
| SLM-APP | system-level managed objects for applications |
| SLP | service location protocol |
| SMDS | switched multi-bit data stream |

| | |
|---|---|
| SMI | structure of management information |
| SMP | symmetrical multiprocessing |
| SMT | station management |
| SMTP | simple mail transfer protocol |
| SNA | serial number arithmetic |
| SNA | systems network architecture (IBM) |
| SND | send |
| SNMP | simple network management protocol |
| SNMP-AT | SNMP over AppleTalk |
| SNMP-IPX | SNMP over IPX |
| SNMP-OSI | SNMP over OSI |
| SNR | signal-to-noise ratio |
| SONET | synchronous optical network |
| SPKM | simple public-key GSS-API mechanism |
| SPX | sequenced packet exchange |
| SQTV | studio-quality television |
| SRAM | static RAM |
| SSL | secure socket layer |
| SSM | single sequence message |
| SSRR | strict source and record route |
| STA | spanning-tree architecture |
| STM | synchronous transfer mode |
| STP | shielded twisted-pair |
| SVGA | super VGA |
| TCB | transmission control block |
| TCC | transmission control code |
| TCP | transmission control protocol |
| TDAC | time-division aliasing cancellation |
| TDM | time-division multiplexing |
| TEI | terminal equipment identifier |
| TELNET | Telnet Protocol |
| TFTP | trivial file transfer Protocol |
| TIFF | tag image file format |
| TIFF | tagged input file format |
| TIME | time server protocol |
| TIP | transaction internet protocol |
| TMUX | transport multiplexing protocol |
| TOS | type of service |
| TP-TCP | ISO transport service on top of the TCP |
| TR | transmit data |
| TSR | terminate and stay resident |
| TTL | time-to-live |
| TUBA | TCP and UDP with bigger addresses |
| UDP | user datagram protocol |
| UI | unnumbered information |
| UNI | universal network interface |
| UNI | user network interface |

| | |
|---|---|
| UPS | uninterruptable power supplies |
| URI | universal resource identifier |
| URL | uniform resource locator |
| USB | universal serial bus |
| USERS | active users protocol |
| UTF-8 | UTF-8 transformation format of ISO 10646 |
| UTP | unshielded twisted pair |
| UV | ultra violet |
| VCI | virtual circuit identifier |
| VCO | voltage controller oscillator |
| VCR | video cassette recorder |
| VDD | virtual device driver |
| VGA | variable graphics adapter |
| VIM | vendor-independent messaging |
| VLC-LZW | variable-length-code LZW |
| VLM | virtual loadable modules |
| VMM | virtual machine manager |
| VRC | vertical redundancy check |
| VRRP | virtual router redundancy protocol |
| WAIS | wide area information servers |
| WAN | wide area network |
| WIMPs | windows, icons, menus and pointers |
| WINS | windows internet name service |
| WINSOCK | windows sockets |
| WORM | write-once read many |
| WWW | World Wide Web |
| XDR | external data representation |
| XOR | exclusive-OR |

# B Glossary of Common Terms

**100Base-FX** IEEE-defined standard for 100 Mbps Ethernet using multimode fibre-optic cable.

**100Base-TX (802.3u)**
IEEE-defined standard for 100Mbps Ethernet using two pairs of Cat-5 twisted-pair cable.

**100VG-AnyLAN**
HP-derived network architecture based on the IEEE 802.12 standard that uses 100Mbps transmission rates. It uses a centrally controlled access method referred to as the Demand Priority Protocol (DPP), where the end node requests permission to transmit and the hub determines which node may do so, depending on the priority of the traffic.

**10Base-T** IEEE-defined standard for 10Mbps Ethernet using twisted-pair cables.

**802.10** IEEE-defined standard for LAN security. It is sometimes used by network switches as a VLAN protocol and uses a technique where frames on any LAN carry a virtual LAN identification. For large networks this can be modified to provided security over the Internet.

**802.12 Demand Priority Protocol**
IEEE-defined standard of transmitting 100Mbps over voice grade (telephone) twisted-pair cabling. *See* 100VG-AnyLAN.

**802.1d** IEEE-defined bridging standard for Spanning Tree protocol that is used to determine factors on how bridges (or switches) forward packets and avoid networking loops. Networks which use redundant loops (for alternative routes) need to implement the IEEE 802.1d standard to stop packets from looping forever.

**802.2** A set of IEEE-defined specifications for Logical Link Control (LLC) layer. It provides some network functions and interfaces the IEEE 802.5, or IEEE 802.3, standards to the transport layer.

**802.3** IEEE-defined standard for CSMA/CD networks. IEEE 802.3 is the most popular implement of Ethernet.

**802.3u** IEEE-defined standard for 100Mbps Fast Ethernet. It also covers a technique called autosensing which allows 100 Mbps devices to connecting to 10 Mbps devices.

**802.4** IEEE-defined token bus specifications.

**802.5** IEEE-defined standard for token ring networks.

**Adapter** Device which usually connects a node onto a network, normally called a network interface adapter (NIC).

**Adaptive cut-through switching**
A forwarding technique on a switch which determines when the error count on frames received has exceeded the pre-configured limits. When this count is exceed, it modifies its own operating state so that it no

longer performs cut-through switching and goes into a store-and-forward mode. The cut-through method is extremely fast but suffers from the inability to check the CRC field. Thus if incorrect frames are transmitted they could have severe effects on the network segment. This is overcome with an adaptive cut-through switch by checking the CRC as the frame moves through the switch. When errors become too great the switch implements a store-and-forward method.

**Adaptive delta modulation PCM**

Similar to delta modulation PCM, but uses a number of bits to code the slope of the signal.

**Adaptive Huffman coding**

Uses a variable Huffman coding technique which responds to local changes in probabilities.

**Address**     A unique label for the location of data or the identity of a communications device. This address can either be numeric or alphanumeric.

**Address aging**

The time that a dynamic address stays in the address routing table of a bridge or switch.

**Address Resolution Protocol (ARP)**

A TCP/IP process which dynamically binds an IP address to a hardware address (such as an Ethernet MAC address). It can only operate across a single network segment.

**Address tables**

These are used routers, switches and hubs to store either physical (such as MAC addresses) or higher-level addresses (such as IP addresses). The tables map node addresses to network addresses or physical domains. These address tables are dynamic and change due to nodes moving around the network.

**Agent**      A program which allows users to configure or fault-find nodes on a network.

**Aging**      The removing of an address in the address table of a router or switch that is no longer referenced to forward a packet.

**American National Standards Institute (ANSI)**

ANSI is a non-profit organisation which is made up of expert committees that publish standards for national industries.

**American Standard Code for Information Interchange (ASCII)**

An ANSI-defined character alphabet which has since been adopted as a standard international alphabet for the interchange of characters.

**Amplitude modulation (AM)**

Information is contained in the amplitude of a carrier.

**Amplitude-Shift Keying (ASK)**

Uses two, or more, amplitudes to represent binary digits. Typically used to transmit binary over speech-limited channels.

**Application layer**

The highest layer of the OSI model.

**Asynchronous**

Communication which does not depend on a clock.

**Asynchronous transmission**

Transmission where individual characters are sent one-by-one. Normally each character is delimited by a start and a stop bit. With asynchronous communications the transmitter and receiver only have to be roughly synchronised.

**ATM (Asynchronous Transfer Mode)**

Networking technology which involves sending 53-byte fast packets (ATM cell), as specified by the ANSI T1S1 subcommittee. The first 5 bytes are the header and the remaining bytes are the information field which can hold 48 bytes of data. Optionally the data can contain a 4-byte ATM adaptation layer and 44 bytes of actual data. The ATM adaptation layer field allows for fragmentation and reassembly of cells into larger packets at the source and destination respectively. The control field also contains bits which specify whether this is a flow control cell or an ordinary data cell, a bit to indicate whether this packet can be deleted in a congested network, and so on.

**AUI** Connection between the network adapter and an external transceiver.

**Automatic broadcast control**

Technique which minimises broadcast and multicast traffic flooding through a switch. A switch acts as a proxy server and screens previously resolved ARP. This eliminates broadcasts associated with them.

**Autonegotiation**

Technique used by a IEEE 802.3u node which determines whether a device that it is receiving or transmitting data in one of a number of Ethernet modes (100Base-TX, 100Base-TX Full Duplex, 10Base-T, 10Base-T Full Duplex or 100Base-T4). When the mode is learned, the device then adjusts to either transmission mode.

**Autosensing** Used by a 100Base-TX device to determine if the incoming data is transmitted at 10Mbps or 100Mbps.

**Back pressure**

Technique which slows the incoming data rate into the buffer of a 802.3 port preventing it from receiving too much data. Switches which implement back pressure will transmit a jam signal to stop data input.

**Backbone network**

The portion of a communications facility that connects primary nodes. A primary shared communications path that serves multiple users at designated jumping-off points.

**Bandwidth** In an analogue system it is defined as the range of frequencies contained in a signal. As an approximation it is the difference between the highest and lowest frequency in the signal. In a digital transmission system it is normally quoted as bits per second.

**Bandwidth allocation control protocol (BACP)**

Protocol which monitors network traffic and allows or disallows access to users, depending on their needs. It is awaiting approval by the IETF.

**Baseband** Data transmission using unmodulated signals.

**Basic rate interface (BRI)**

Connection between ISDN and the user. It has three separate channels, one D-channel (which carries control information) and two B channels (which carry data).

**Baud rate** The number of signalling elements sent per second with RS-232, or modem, communications. In RS-232 the baud rate is equal to the bit-rate. With modems, two or more bits can be encoded as a single signalling element, such as 2 bits being represented by four different phase shifts (or one signalling element). The signalling element could change its amplitude, frequency or phase-shift to increase the bit-rate. Thus the bit-rate is a better measure of information transfer.

**Bit stuffing** The insertion of extra bits to prevent the appearance of a defined sequence. In HDLC the bit sequence 01111110 delimits the start and end of a frame. Bit stuffing stops this bit sequence from occurring anywhere in the frame by the receiver inserting a 0 whenever there are five consecutive 1's transmitted. At the receiver if five consecutive 1's are followed by a 0 then the 0 is deleted.

**BNC** A commonly used connector for coaxial cable.

**BOOTP** A standard TCP/IP protocol which allows nodes to be dynamically allocated an IP address.

**Bridge** A device which physically links two or more networks using the same communications protocols, such as Ethernet/ Ethernet or token ring/ token ring. It allows for the filtering of data between network segments.

**Broadband** Data transmission using multiplexed data using an analogue signal or high-frequency electromagnetic waves.

**Broadcast** Message sent to all users on the network.

**Broadcast domain**
Network where broadcasts can be reported to all nodes on the network bounded by routers. Broadcast packets cannot traverse a router.

**Broadcast storm**
Flood of broadcast packets generated by a broadcast transmission where high numbers of receivers are targeted for a long period of time.

**Buffer** A temporary-storage space in memory.

**Bus** A network topology where all nodes share a common transmission medium.

**Byte** A group of eight bits, *see* octet.

**Capacity** The maximum data rate in Mbps.

**Carrier Sense Multiple Access/ Carrier Detect (CSMA/CD)**
A network where all nodes share a common bus. Nodes must contend for the bus and if a collision occurs then all colliding nodes back off for a random time period.

**Cat-3 cable** An EIA/TIA-568 wiring standard for unshielded or shielded twisted pair cables.

**Cat-5 cable** An EIA/TIA-568 wiring standard for unshielded or shielded twisted pair cables for the transmission of over 100 Mbps.

**CHAP (challenge-handshake authentication protocol)**
Identification method used by PPP to determine the originator of a connection.

**checksum** An error-detection scheme in which bits are grouped to form integer values and then each of the values are summated. Normally, the negative of this value is then added as a checksum. At the receiver, all the grouped values and the checksum are summated and, in the absence of errors, the result should be zero.

**Client**          Node or program that connects to a server node or program.

**Coaxial cable**

A transmission medium consisting of one or more central wire conductors surrounded by an insulating layer and encased in either a wire mesh or extruded metal sheathing. It supports RF frequencies from 50 to about 500 MHz. It comes in either a 10-mm diameter (thick coax) or a 5-mm diameter (thin coax).

**Collision**       Occurs when one or more devices try to transmit over an Ethernet network simultaneously.

**Copper distributed data interface (CDDI)**

FDDI over copper.

**Cost**            An arbitrary value used by routers to compare different routes. Typically it is measured by hop counts, typical time delays or bandwidth.

**CRC**             Cyclic Redundancy Check. An error-detection scheme. Used in most HDLC-related data link applications.

**Cross-talk**      Interference noise caused by conductors radiating electromagnetic radiation to couple into other conductors.

**Cut-through switching**

Technique where a switching device directs a packet to the destination port(s) as soon as it receives the destination and source address scanned from the packet header.

**Data Communications Equipment (DCE)**

Devices which establish, maintain and terminate a data communications conversation.

**Data link layer**

Second layer of the OSI model which is responsible for link, error and flow control. It normally covers the framing of data packets, error control and physical addressing. Typical data link layers include Ethernet and FDDI.

**Data Terminal Equipment (DTE)**

Device at the end of the data communications connection.

**Delta modulation PCM**

Uses a single-bit code to represent the analogue signal. A 1 is transmission when the current sample increases its level, else a 0 is transmitted. Delta modulation PCM requires a higher sampling rate that the Nyquist rate, but the actual bit rate is normally lower.

**Destination MAC address**

A 6-byte data unique of the destination MAC address. It is normally quoted as a 12-digit hexadecimal number (such as A5:B2:10:64:01:44).

**Destination network address**

A unique Internet Protocol (IP) or Internet Packet Exchange (IPX) address of the destination node.

**Differential encoding**

Source coding method which is used to code the difference between two samples. Typically used in real-time signals where there is limited change between one sample and the next, such as in audio and speech.

**Dynamic host control protocol (DHCP)**

It manages a pool of IP addresses for computers without a known IP address. This allows a finite number of IP addresses to be reused quickly and efficiently by many clients.

**Entropy coding**

Coding scheme which does not take into account the characteristics of the data and treats all the bits in the same way. It produces lossless coding. Typical methods used are statistical encoding and suppressing repetitive sequences.

**Ethernet** A local area network which uses coaxial, twisted-pair or fibre optic cable as a communication medium. It transmits at a rate of 10 Mbps and was developed by DEC, Intel and Xerox Corporation. The IEEE 802.3 network standard is based upon Ethernet.

**Ethernet address**

A 48-bit number that identifies a node on an Ethernet network. Ethernet addresses are assigned by the Xerox Corporation.

**Even parity** An error-detection scheme where defined bit-groupings have an even number of 1's.

**Extended Binary Coded Decimal Interchange Code (EBCDIC)**

An 8-bit code alphabet developed by IBM allowing 256 different bit patterns for character definitions.

**Fast Ethernet**

See IEEE 802.3u standard.

**Fat pipe** Term used to indicate a high level of bandwidth the defined port.

**Fibre Distributed Data Interface (FDDI)**

A standard network technology that uses a dual counter-rotating token-passing fibre ring. It operates at 100 Mbps and provides for reliable backbone connections.

**File server** Computer that allows the sharing of files over a network.

**File transfer protocol (FTP)**

A protocol for transmitting files between host computers using the TCP/IP protocol.

**Firewall** Device which filters incoming and outgoing traffic.

**Flow control** Procedure to regulate the flow of data between two nodes.

**Forward adaptive bit allocation**

This technique is used in audio compression and makes bit allocation decisions adaptively, depending on signal content.

**Fragment free cut-through switching**

A modified cut-through switching technique where a switch or switch module waits until it has received a large enough packet to determine if it is error free.

**Frame** Normally associated with a packet which has layer 2 information added to it. Packets are thus contained within frames. Frames and packets have variable lengths as opposed to cells which have fixed lengths.

**Frame check sequence (FCS)**

Standard error detection scheme.

**Frequency-shift Keying (FSK)**
Uses two, or more, frequencies to represent binary digits. Typically used to transmit binary data over speech-limited channels.

**Full duplex**  Simultaneous, two-way communications.

**Gateway**  A device that connects networks using different communications protocols, such as between Ethernet and FDDI. It provides protocol translation, in contrast to a bridge which connects two networks that are of the same protocol.

**GIF**  Standard image compression technique which is copyrighted by CompuServe Incorporated. It uses LZW compression and supports a palette of 256 24-bit colours (16.7M colours). GIF support local and global colour tables and animated images.

**Half-duplex (HDX)**
Two-way communications, one at a time.

**Handshaking**
A reliable method for two devices to pass data.

**HDLC**  ISO standard for the data link layer.

**Hello packet**  Message transmitted from a root bridge to all other bridges in the network to constantly verify the Spanning Tree setup.

**Hop**  The number of gateways and routers in a transmission path.

**Hop count**  Used by the RIP routing protocol to measure the distance between a source and a destination.

**Host**  A computer that communicates over a network. A host can both initiate communications and respond to communications that are addressed to it.

**Huffman coding**
Uses a variable length code for each of the elements within the data. It normally analyses the probability of the element in the data and codes the most probable with fewer bits than the least probable.

**Hub**  A hub is a concentration point for data and repeats data from one node to all other connected nodes.

**Hypertext markup language (HTML)**
Standard language that allows the integration of text and images over a distributed network.

**Integrated systems digital network (ISDN)**
Communication technology that contains two data channels (2B) and a control channel (H). It supports two 64 kbps data channels and sets up a circuit-switched connection.

**International Telegraph Union Telecommunications Standards Sector (ITU-TSS)**
Organization which has replaced the CCITT.

**Internet**  Connection of nodes on a global network which use a DARPA-defined Internet address.

**internet**  Two or more connected networks that may, or may not, use the same communication protocol.

**Internet address**
An address that conforms to the DARPA-defined Internet protocol. A unique, four byte number identifies a host or gateway on the Internet.

This consists of a network number followed by a host number. The host number can be further divided into a subnet number.

**Internet Engineering Task Force (IETF)**
> A committee that reviews and supports Internet protocol proposals.

**IP (Internet Protocol)**
> Part of the TCP/IP which provides for node addressing.

**IP address** An address which is used to identify a node on the Internet.

**IP multicast** Addressing technique that allows IP traffic to be propagated from one source to a group of destinations.

**IPX (Internet Packet Exchange)**
> Novell NetWare communications protocol which is similar to the IP protocol. The packets include network addresses and can be routed from one network to another.

**IPX address** Station address on a Novell NetWare network. It consists of two fields: a network number field and a node number field. The node number is the station address of the device and the network number is assigned to the network when the network is started up. It is written in the form: NNNNNNNN:XXXXXX-XXXXXX, where N's represent the network number and X's represent the station address. An example of an IPX address is: DC105333:542C10-FF1432.

**ISO** International Standards Organisation.

**ITU-T** The Consultative Committee for International Telephone and Telegraph (now known at the ITU-TSS) is an advisory committee established by the United Nations. They attempt to establish standards for inter-country data transmission on a worldwide basis.

**Jabber** Occurs when the transmission of network signals exceeds the maximum allowable transmission time (20 ms to 150 ms). The medium becomes overrun with data packets. This is caused by a faulty node or wiring connection.

**Jitter** Movement of the edges of pulse over time, that may introduce error and loss of synchronisation.

**JPEG** Image compression technique defined by the Joint Photographic Expert Group (JPEG), a subcommittee of the ISO/IEC. It uses a DCT, quantisation, run-length and Huffman coding.

**Latency** Defines the amount of time between a device receiving data and it being forwarded on. Hubs have the lowest latency (less than 10µs), switches the next lowest (between 40µs and 60µs), then bridges (200µs to 300µs) and routers have the highest latency (around 1000 µs).

**Learning bridge**
> Bridge which learns the connected nodes to it. It uses this information to forward or drop frames.

**Leased line** A permanent telephone line connection reserved exclusively by the leased customer. There is no need for any connection and disconnection procedures.

**Lempel-Ziv coding**
> Coding method which takes into account repetition in phases, words or parts of words. It uses pointers to refer to previously defined sequences.

**Lempel-Ziv Welsh (LZW) coding**
Coding method which takes into account repetition in phases, words or parts of words. It builds up a dictionary of previously sent (or stored) sequences.

**Line driver** A device which converts an electrical signal to a form that is transmittable over a transmission line. Typically, it provides the required power, current and timing characteristics.

**Link layer** Layer 2 of the OSI model.

**Link segment**
A point-to-point link terminated on either side by a repeater. Nodes cannot be attached to a link segment.

**Lossless compression**
Where information, once uncompressed, is identical to the original uncompressed data.

**Lossy compression**
Where information, once uncompressed, cannot be fully recovered.

**MAC address**
A 6-byte data unique data-link layer address. It is normally quoted as a 12-digit hexadecimal number (such as A5:B2:10:64:01:44).

**Masking effect**
Where noise is only heard by a person when there are no other sounds to mask it.

**MDI (Medium Dependent Interface)**
The IEEE standard for the twisted-pair interface to 10Base-T (or 100Base-TX).

**Media Access Control (MAC)**
Media-specific access-control for Token Ring and Ethernet.

**Media Interface Controller (MIC)**
Media-specific access-control for Token Ring and Ethernet.

**Medium Attachment Unit (MAU)**
Method of converting digital data into a form which can be transmitted over a band-limited channel. Methods use either ASK, FSK, PSK or a mixture of ASK, FSK and PSK.

**Modem (Modulator-Demodulator)**
A device which converts binary digits into a form which can be transmitted over a speech-limited transmission channel.

**MTU (Maximum Transmission Unit)**
The largest packet that the IP protocol will send through the selected interface or segment.

**Multicast** Packets which are sent to all nodes on a subnet of a group within a network. This differs from a broadcast which forwards packet to all users on the network.

**Multimode fibre**
Fibre-optic cable that has the ability to carry more than one frequency (mode) of light at a time.

**N-series connectors**
Connector used with thick coaxial cable.

**Network driver interface specification (NDIS)**

Software specification for network adapter drivers. It support multiple protocols and multiple adapters, and is used in many operating systems, such as Windows 95/88/NT/2000.

**Network layer**

Third layer of the OSI model, which defines is responsible for ensuring that data passed to it from the transport layer is routed and delivered through the network. It provides end-to-end addressing and routing. It provides support for a number of protocols, including IP, IPX, CLNP, X.25, or DDP.

**Network termination (NT1)**

Network termination for ISDN.

**Node**            Any point in a network which provides communications services or where devices interconnect.

**Intranet**        A company specific network which has additional security against external users.

**Octet**           Same as a byte, a group of eight bits (typically used in communications terminology).

**Odd parity**      An error-detection scheme where a defined bit-grouping has an odd number of 1's.

**Open Data-Link Interface (ODLI)**

Software specification for network adapter drivers used in NetWare and Apple networks. It supports multiple protocols and multiple adapters.

**Optical Repeater**

A device that receives, restores, and re-times signals from one optical fibre segment to another.

**Packet**          A sequence of binary digits that is transmitted as a unit in a computer network. A packet usually contains control information and data. They normally are contained with data link frames.

**Packet switching**

Network switching in which data is processed in units of whole packets rather than attempting to process data by dividing packets into fixed-length cells.

**Password authentication protocol (PAP)**

Protocol which checks a user's password.

**Phase-Locked Loop (PLL)**

Tunes into a small range of frequencies in a signal and follows any variations in them.

**Phase-Shift Keying (PSK)**

Uses two, or more, phase-shifts to represent binary digits. Typically used to transmit binary data over speech-limited channels.

**Physical layer**

Lowest layer of the OSI model which is responsible for the electrical, mechanical, and handshaking procedures over the interface that connects a device to a transmission medium

**Ping**            Standard protocol used to determine if TCP/IP nodes are alive. Initially a node sends an ICMP (Internet Control Message Protocol) echo request packet to the remote node with the specified IP address and waits for echo response packets to return.

**Point of presence (POP)**
:    Physical access point to a long distance carrier interchange.

**Point-to-point protocol (PPP)**
:    Standard protocol to transfer data over the Internet asynchronously or synchronously.

**Port**
:    Physical connection on a bridge or hub that connects to a network, node or other device.

**Protocol**
:    A specification for coding of messages exchanged between two communications processes.

**Quadrature modulation**
:    Technique used in PAL and NSTC where the U and V information are added to the carrier with a 90° phase difference between them.

**Quantisation**
:    Involves converting an analogue level into a discrete quantised level. The number of bits used in the quantization process determines the number of quantisation levels.

**Quartet signalling**
:    Signalling technique used in 100VG-AnyLAN networks that allows data transmission at 100 Mbps over frame pairs of UTP cabling.

**Repeater**
:    A device that receives, restores, and re-times signals from one segment of a network and passes them on to another. Both segments must have the same type of transmission medium and share the same set of protocols. A repeater cannot translate protocols.

**Reverse address resolution protocol (RARP)**
:    The opposite of ARP which maps an IP address to a MAC address.

**RJ-45**
:    Connector used with US telephones and with twisted-pair cables. It is also used in ISDN networks, hubs and switches.

**RMON**
:    An SNMP MIB that specifies the types of information listed in a number of special MIB groups that are commonly used for traffic management. Some of the popular groups used are Statistics, History, Alarms, Hosts, Hosts Top N, Matrix, Filters, Events, and Packet Capture.

**Routing node**
:    A node that transmits packets between similar networks. A node that transmits packets between dissimilar networks is called a gateway.

**RS-232C**
:    EIA-defined standard for serial communications.

**RS-422, 423**
:    EIA-defined standard which uses higher transmission rates and cable lengths than RS-232.

**RS-449**
:    EIA-defined standard for the interface between a DTE and DCE for 9- and 37-way D-type connectors.

**RS-485**
:    EIA-defined standard which is similar to RS-422 but uses a balanced connection.

**Run-length encoding (RLE)**
:    Coding technique which represents long runs of a certain bit sequence with a special character.

**SAP**
:    Service Access Point. Field defined by the IEEE 802.2 specification that is part of the address specification.

**SAP**  Service Advertisement Protocol. Used by the IPX protocol to provide a means of informing network clients, via routers and servers of available network resources and services.

**Segment**  A segment is any length of LAN cable terminated at both ends. In a bus network, segments are electrically continuous pieces of the bus, connected at by repeaters. It can also be bounded by bridges and routers.

**Serial line internet protocol (SLIP)**
A standard used for the point-to-point serial connections running TCP/IP.

**Simplex**  One-way communication.

**SNMP (Simple Network Management Protocol)**
Standard protocol for managing network devices, such as hubs, bridges, and switches.

**Source encoding**
Coding method which takes into account the characteristics of the information. Typically used in motion video and still image compression.

**Statistical encoding**
Where the coding analyses the statistical pattern of the data. Commonly occurring data is coded with a few bits and uncommon data by a large number of bits.

**Suppressing repetitive sequences**
Compression technique where long sequences of the same data is compressed with a short code.

**Switch**  A very fast, low-latency, multiport bridge that is used to segment local area networks.

**Synchronous**
Data which is synchronised by a clock.

**TCP**  Part of the TCP/IP protocol which provides an error-free connection between two cooperating programs.

**TCP/IP Internet**
An Internet is made up of networks of nodes that can communicate with each other using TCP/IP protocols.

**Telnet**  Standard program which allows remote users to log into a station using the TCP/IP protocol.

**TIFF**  Graphics format that supports many different types of images in a number of modes. It is supported by most packages and, in one mode, provides for enhanced high-resolution images with 48-bit colour.

**Time to live**  A field in the IP header which defines the number of routers that a packet is allowed to traverse before being discarded.

**Token**  A token transmits data around a token ring network.

**Topology**  The physical and logical geometry governing placement of nodes on a network.

**Transceiver**  A device that transmits and receives signals.

**Transform encoding**
Source-encoding scheme where the data is transformed by a mathematical transform in order to reduce the transmitted (or stored) data. A typical technique is the discrete cosine transform (DCT) and the fast Fourier

transform (FFT).

**Transport layer**
> Fourth layer of the OSI model. It allows end-to-end control of transmitted data and the optimised use of network resources.

**Universal asynchronous receiver transmitter (UART)**
> Device which converts parallel data into a serial form, which can be transmitted over a serial line, and vice-versa.

**V.24**    ITU-T-defined specification, similar to RS-232C.

**V.25bis**    ITU-T specification describing procedures for call set-up and disconnection over the DTE-DCE interface in a PSDN.

**V.32**    ITU-T standard serial communication for bi-directional data transmissions at speeds of 4.8 or 9.6 Kbps.

**V.34**    Improved v.32 specification with higher transmission rates (28.8 Kbps) and enhanced data compression.

**Variable-length-code LZW (VLC-LZW) code**
> Uses a variation of LZW coding where variable-length codes are used to replace patterns detected in the original data.

**Virtual circuit**
> Logical circuit which connects two networked devices together.

**X-ON/ X-OFF**
> The Transmitter On/ Transmitter Off characters are used to control the flow of information between two nodes.

**X.21**    ITU-T-defined specification for the interconnection of DTEs and DCEs for synchronous communications.

**X.25**    ITU-T-defined specification for packet-switched network connections.

# C | HDLC

## C.1 Introduction

The data link layer is the second layer in the OSI seven-layer model and its protocols define rules for the orderly exchange of data information between 2 adjacent nodes connected by a data link. Final framing, flow control between nodes, and error detection and correction are added at this layer. In previous chapters the data link layer was discussed in a practical manner. In this chapter its functions will be discussed with reference to HDLC.

The two types of protocol are:

- Asynchronous protocol.
- Synchronous protocol.

Asynchronous communications uses start-stop method of communication where characters are sent between nodes, as illustrated in Figure C.1. Special characters are used to control the data flow. Typical flow control characters are End of Transmission (EOT), Acknowledgement (ACK), Start of Transmission (STX) and Negative Acknowledgement (NACK).

Synchronous communications involves the transmission of frames of bits with start and end bit characters to delimit the frame. The most popular are IBM's synchronous data link communication (SDLC) and high-level data link control (HDLC). Many network data link layers are based upon these standards, examples include the LLC layer in IEE 802.x LAN standards and LAPB in the X.25 packet switching standard.

Synchronous communications normally uses a bit-oriented protocol (BOP), where data is sent one bit at a time. The data link control information is interpreted on a bit-by-bit basis rather than with unique data link control characters.

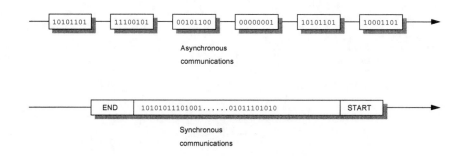

**Figure C.1** Asynchronous and synchronous communications

HDLC is a standard developed by the ISO to provide a basis for the data link layer for point-to-point and multi-drop connections. It can transfer data either in a simplex, half-duplex, or full-duplex mode. Frames are generally limited to 256 bytes in length and a single control field performs most data link control functions.

## C.2   HDLC protocol

In HDLC, a node is either defined as a primary station or a secondary station. A primary station controls the flow of information and issues commands to secondary stations. The secondary station then sends back responses to the primary. A primary station with one or more secondary stations is known as unbalanced configuration.

HDLC allows for point-to-point and multi-drop. In point-to-point communications a primary station communicates with a single secondary station. For multi-drop, one primary station communications with many secondary stations.

In point-to-point communications it is possible for a station be operate as a primary and a secondary station. At any time, one of the stations can be a primary and the other the secondary. Thus, commands and responses flow back and forth over the transmission link. This is known as a balanced configuration, or combined stations.

### C.2.1   HDLC modes of operation

HDLC has three modes of operation. Unbalanced configurations can use the normal response mode (NRM). Secondary stations can only transmit when specifically instructed by the primary station. When used as a point-to-point or multi-drop configuration only one primary station is used. Figure C.2 shows a multi-drop NRM configuration.

Unbalanced configurations can also use the asynchronous response mode (ARM). It differs from NRM in that the secondary is allowed to communicate with the primary without receiving permission from the primary.

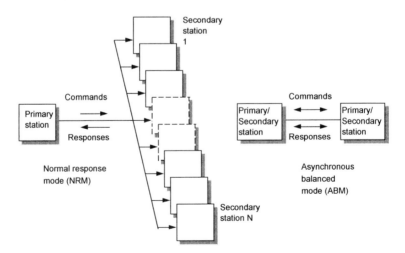

**Figure C.2**   NRM and ABM mode

In asynchronous balanced mode (ABM) all stations have the same priority and can perform the functions of a primary and secondary station.

### C.2.2 HDLC frame format

HDLC frames are delimited by the bit sequence `01111110`. Figure C.3 shows the standard format of the HDLC frame, the 5 fields are the:

- Flag field.
- Address field.
- Control field.
- Information field.
- Frame check sequence (FCS) field.

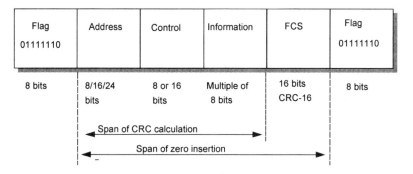

**Figure C.3** HDLC frame structure

### C.2.3 Information field

The information fields contain data, such as OSI level 3, and above, information. It contains an integer number of bytes and thus the number of bits contained is always a multiple of eight. The receiver determines the number of bytes in the data because it can detect the start and end flag. By this method, it also finds the FCS field. Note that the number of characters in the information can be zero as not all frames contain data.

### C.2.4 Flag field

A unique flag sequence, `01111110` (or `7Eh`), delimits the start and end of the frame. As this sequence could occur anywhere within the frame a technique called bit-insertion is used to stop this happening except at the start and end of the frame.

### C.2.5 Address field

The address field is used to address connected stations an, in basic addressing, it contains an 8-bit address. It can also be extended, using extended addressing, to give any multiple of 8 bits.

When it is 8 bits wide it can address up to 254 different nodes, as illustrated in Figure C.4. Two special addresses are `00000000` and `11111111`. The `00000000` address defines the null or void address and the `11111111` broadcasts a message to all secondaries. The other 254 addresses are used to address secondary nodes individually.

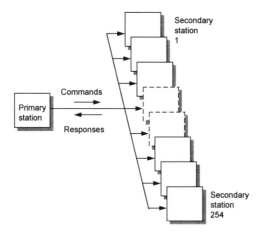

**Figure C.4** HDLC addressing range

If there are a large number of secondary stations then extended address can be used to extend the address field indefinitely. A 0 in the first bit of the address field allows a continuation of the address, or a 1 ends it. For example:

```
XXXXXXX1 XXXXXXX0 XXXXXXX0 XXXXXXX0
```

### C.2.6 *Control field*

The control field can either be 8 or 16 bits wide. It is used to identify the frame type and can also contain flow control information. The first two bits of the control field define the frame type, as shown in Figure C.5. There are three types of frames, these are:

- Information frames.
- Supervisory frames.
- Unnumbered frames.

When sent from the primary the P/F bit indicates that it is polling the secondary station. In an unbalanced mode a secondary station cannot transmit frames unless the primary sets the poll bit.

When sending frames from the secondary, the P/F bit indicates whether the frame is the last of the message, or not. Thus if the P/F bit is set by the primary it is a poll bit (P), if it is set by the secondary it is a final bit (F).

The following sections describe 8-bit control fields. Sixteen-bit control fields are similar but reserve a 7-bit field for the frame counter variables N(R) and N(S).

**Information frame**

An information frame contains sequenced data and is identified by a 0 in the first bit position of the control field. The 3-bit variable N(R) is used to confirm the number of transmitted frames received correctly and N(S) is used to number an information frame. The first frame transmitted is numbered 0 as (000), the next as 1 (001), until the eighth which is numbered 111. The sequence then starts back at 0 again and this gives a sliding window of eight frames.

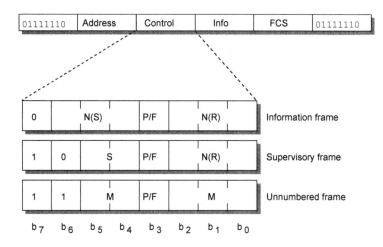

**Figure C.5**  Format of an 8-bit control field

## Supervisory frame

Supervisory frames contain flow control data. They confirm or reject previously received information frames and also can indicate whether a station is ready to receive frames.

The N(S) field is used with the S bits to acknowledge, or reject, previously transmitted frames. Responses from the receiver are set in the S field, these are receiver ready (RR), ready not to receive (RNR), reject (REJ) and selectively reject (SREJ). Table C.1 gives the format of these bits.

RR informs the receiver that it acknowledges the frames sent up to N(R). RNR tells the transmitter that the receiver cannot receive any more frames at the present time (RR will cancel this). It also acknowledges frames up to N(R). The REJ control rejects all frames after N(R). The transmitter must then send frames starting at N(R).

**Table C.1**  Supervisory bits

| $b_5$ | $b_4$ | Receiver status |
|---|---|---|
| 0 | 0 | Receiver ready (RR) |
| 1 | 0 | Receiver not ready (RNR) |
| 0 | 1 | Reject (REJ) |
| 1 | 1 | Selectively reject (SREJ) |

## Unnumbered frame

If the first two bits of the control field are 1's then it is an unnumbered frame. Apart from the P/F flag the other bits are used to send unnumbered commands. When sending commands, the P/F flag is a poll bit (asking for a response), and for responses it is a flag bit (end of response).

The available commands are SARM (set asynchronous response mode), SNRM (set normal response mode), SABM (set asynchronous balance mode), RSET (reset), FRMR (frame reject) and Disconnect (DISC). The available responses are UA (unnumbered acknowledge), CMDR (command reject), FRMR (frame reject) and DM (disconnect mode). Bit definitions for some of these are:

| | | | | | |
|------|----------|------|----------|------|----------|
| SABM | 1111P110 | DM   | 1111F000 | DISC | 1100P010 |
| UA   | 1100F110 | FRMR | 1110F001 |      |          |

### C.2.7 *Frame check sequence field*

The frame check sequence (FCS) field contains an error detection code based on cyclic redundancy check (CRC) polynomials. It is used to check the address, control and information fields, as previously illustrated in Figure C.2. HDLC uses a polynomial specified by CCITT V.41, which is $G(x) = x^{16} + x^{12} + x^5 + x^1$. This is also known as CRC-16 or CRC-CCITT.

## C.3 Transparency

The flag sequence 01111110 can occur anywhere in the frame. To prevent this a transparency mechanism called zero-bit insertion or zero stuffing is used. There are two main rules that are applied, these are:

- In the transmitter, a 0 is automatically inserted after five consecutive 1's, except when the flag occurs.
- At the receiver, when five consecutive 1's are received and the next bit is a 0 then the 0 is deleted and removed. If it is a 1 then it must be a valid flag.

In the following example a flag sequence appears in the data stream where it is not supposed to (spaces have been inserted around it). Notice that the transmitter detects five 1's in a row and inserts a 0 to break them up.

Message:  00111000101000 01111110  01011111 1111010101
Sent:     00111000101000 011111**0**10 0101111**0**1111010101

## C.4 Flow control

Supervisory frames (S[]) send flow control information to acknowledge the reception of data frames or to reject frames. Unnumbered frames (U[]) set up the link between a primary and a secondary, by the primary sending commands and the secondary replying with responses. Information frames (I[]) contain data.

### C.4.1 *Link connection*

Figure C.6 shows how a primary station (node A) sets up a connection with a secondary station (node B) in NRM (normal response mode). In this mode one or many secondary stations can exist. First the primary station requests a link by sending an unnumbered frame with: node B's address (ADDR_B), the set normal response mode

(SNRM) command and with poll flag set (P=1), that is, U[SNRM,ABBR_B,P=1]. If the addressed secondary wishes to make a connection then it replies back with an unnumbered frame containing: its own address (ADDR_B), the unnumbered acknowledge (UA) response and the final bit set (F=1), i.e. U[UA,ABBR_B,F=1]. The secondary sends back its own address because many secondaries can exist and it thus identifies which station has responded. There is no need to send the primary station address as only one primary exists.

Once the link is set up data can flow between the nodes. To disconnect the link, the primary station sends an unnumbered frame with: node B's address (ADDR_B), the disconnect (DISC) command and the poll flag set (P=1), that is, U[DISC,ABBR_B,P=1]. If the addressed secondary accepts the disconnection then it replies back with an unnumbered frame containing: its own address (ADDR_B), the unnumbered acknowledge (UA) response and the final bit set (F=1), i.e. U[UA,ABBR_B,F=1].

When two stations act as both primaries and secondaries then they use the asynchronous balanced mode (ABM). Each station has the same priority and can perform the functions of a primary and secondary station. Figure C.7 shows a typical connection. The ABM mode is set up initially using the SABM command (U[SABM,ABBR_B,P=1]). The connection between node A and node B is then similar to the NRM but, as node B operates as a primary station, it can send a disconnect command to node A (U[DISC,ABBR_B,P=1]).

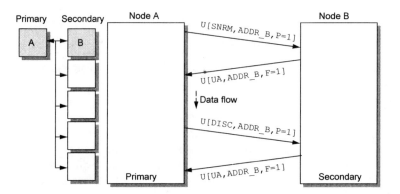

**Figure C.6**  Connection between a primary and secondary in NRM

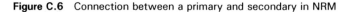

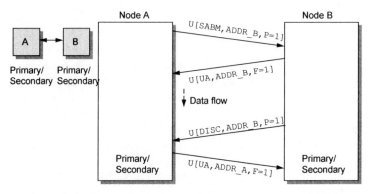

**Figure C.7**  Connection between a primary/secondary in SABM

The SABM, SARM and SNRM modes set up communications using an 8-bit control field. Three other commands exist which set up a 16-bit control field, these are SABME (set asynchronous balanced mode extended), SARME and SNRME. The format of the 16-bit control field is given in Figure C.8.

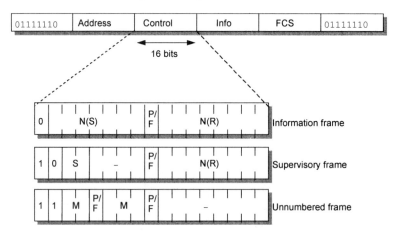

**Figure C.8** Extended control field.

Figure C.9 shows an example conversation between a sending station (node A) and a receiving station (node B). Initially three information frames are sent numbered 2, 3 and 4 (I[N(S)=2], I[N(S)=3] and I[N(S)=4, P=1]). The last of these frames has the poll bit set, which indicates to node B that node A wishes it to respond, either to acknowledge or reject previously unacknowledged frames. Node B does this by sending back a supervisory frame (S[RR, N(R)=5]) with the receiver ready (RR) acknowledgement. This informs node A that node B expects to receive frame number 5 next. Thus it has acknowledged all frames up to and including frame 4.

In the example in Figure C.9 an error has occurred in the reception of frame 5. The recipient informs the sender by sending a supervisory frame with a reject flow command (S[REJ, N(R)=5]). After the sender receives this it resends each frame after and including frame 5.

If the receiver does not want to communicate, at the present, it sends a receiver not ready flow command. For example S[RNR, N(R)=5] tells the transmitter to stop sending data, at the present. It also informs the sender that all frames up to frame 5 have been accepted. The sender will transmit frames once it has received a receiver ready frame from the receiver.

Figure C.9 shows an example of data flow in only the one direction. With ABM both stations can transmit and receive data. Thus each frame sent contains receive and send counter values. When stations send information frames the previously received frames can be acknowledged, or rejected, by piggy-backing the receive counter value. In Figure C.10, node A sends three information frames with I[N(S)=0,N(R)=0], I[N(S)=1, N(R)=0], and I[N(S)=2,N(R)=0]. The last frame informs node B that node A expects to receive frame 0 next. Node B then sends frame 0 and acknowledges the reception of all frames up to, and including frame 2 with I[N(S)=0,N(R)=3], and so on.

## C.5 Derivatives of HDLC

There are many derivatives of HDLC, including:

- LAPB (link access procedure balanced) is used in X.25 packet switched networks;
- LAPM (link access procedure for modems) is used in error correction modems;
- LLC (logical link control) is used in Ethernet and Token Ring networks;
- LAPD (link access procedure D-channel) is used in Integrated Services Digital Networks (ISDNs).

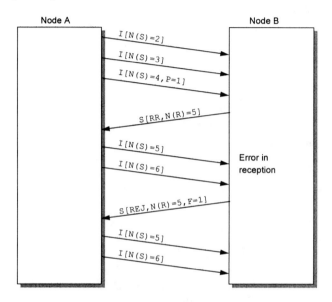

**Figure C.9**  Example flow

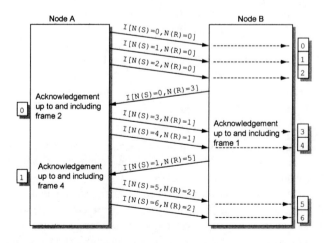

**Figure C.10**  Example flow with piggy-backed acknowledgement

## D.1  Introduction

The cable type used to transmit a signal depends on several parameters, including:

- The signal bandwidth.
- The reliability of the cable.
- The maximum length between nodes.
- The possibility of electrical hazards.
- Power loss in the cables.
- Tolerance to harsh conditions.
- Expense and general availability of the cable.
- Ease of connection and maintenance.
- Ease of running cables, and so on.

The main types of networking cables are twisted-pair, coaxial and fibre-optic. Twisted-pair and coaxial cables transmit electric signals, whereas fibre-optic cables transmit light pulses. Twisted-pair cables are not shielded and thus interfere with nearby cables. Public telephone lines generally use twisted-pair cables. In LANs they are generally used up to bit rates of 10 Mbps and with maximum lengths of 100 m.

Coaxial cable has a grounded metal sheath around the signal conductor. This limits the amount of interference between cables and thus allows higher data rates. Typically, they are used at bit rates of 100 Mbps for maximum lengths of 1 km.

The highest specification of the three cables is fibre-optic. This type of cable allows extremely high bit rates over long distances. Fibre-optic cables do not interfere with nearby cables and give greater security, give more protection from electrical damage by external equipment and greater resistance to harsh environments; they are also safer in hazardous environments.

### D.1.1  Cable characteristics

The main characteristics of cables used in video communication are attenuation, crosstalk and characteristic impedance. Attenuation defines the reduction in the signal strength at a given frequency for a defined distance. It is normally defined in dB/100 m, which is the attenuation (in dB) for 100 m. An attenuation of 3 dB/100 m gives a signal voltage reduction of 0.5 for every 100 m. Table D.1 lists some attenuation rates and equivalent voltage ratios; they are illustrated in Figure D.1.

The characteristic impedance of a cable and its connectors are important, as all parts of the transmission system need to be matched to the same impedance. This impedance is normally classified as the characteristic impedance of the cable. Any differences in the matching result in a reduction of signal power and also produce signal reflections (or ghosting).

**Table D.1**  Attenuation rates as a ratio

| dB | Ratio | dB | Ratio | dB | Ratio |
|----|-------|----|-------|----|-------|
| 0  | 1.000 | 10 | 0.316 | 60 | 0.001 |
| 1  | 0.891 | 15 | 0.178 | 65 | 0.0006 |
| 2  | 0.794 | 20 | 0.100 | 70 | 0.0003 |
| 3  | 0.708 | 25 | 0.056 | 75 | 0.0002 |
| 4  | 0.631 | 30 | 0.032 | 80 | 0.0001 |
| 5  | 0.562 | 35 | 0.018 | 85 | 0.00006 |
| 6  | 0.501 | 40 | 0.010 | 90 | 0.00003 |
| 7  | 0.447 | 45 | 0.0056 | 95 | 0.00002 |
| 8  | 0.398 | 50 | 0.0032 | 100 | 0.00001 |
| 9  | 0.355 | 55 | 0.0018 |   |       |

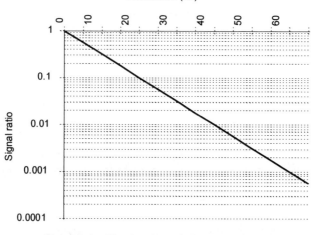

**Figure D.1**  Signal ratio related to attenuation

Crosstalk is important as it defines the amount of signal that crosses from one signal path to another. This causes some of the transmitted signal to be received back where it was transmitted.

Capacitance (pF/100 m) defines the amount of distortion in the signal caused by each signal pair. The lower the capacitance value, the lower the distortion.

The main types of cable used in networking and data communications are:

- Coaxial cable – cables with an inner core and a conducting shield having a characteristic impedance of either $75\,\Omega$ for TV signal or $50\,\Omega$ for other types.
- Cat-3 UTP cable – level 3 cables have non-twisted-pair cores with a characteristic impedance of $100\,\Omega$ ($\pm15\,\Omega$) and a capacitance of 59 pF/m. Conductor resistance is around $9.2\,\Omega/100$ m.

- Cat-4 UTP cable – level 4 cables have twisted-pair cores with a characteristic impedance of $100\,\Omega$ ($\pm15\,\Omega$) and a capacitance of 49.2 pF/m. Conductor resistance is around $9\,\Omega/100$ m.
- Cat-5 UTP cable – level 5 cables have twisted-pair cores with a characteristic impedance of $100\,\Omega$ ($\pm15\,\Omega$) and a capacitance of 45.9 pF/m. Conductor resistance is around $9\,\Omega/100$ m.

The Electrical Industries Association (EIA) has defined five main types of cables. Levels 1 and 2 are used for voice and low-speed communications (up to 4 Mbps). Level 3 is designed for LAN data transmission up to 16 Mbps and level 4 is designed for speeds up to 20 Mbps. Level 5 cables, have the highest specification of the UTP cables and allow data speeds of up to 100 Mbps. The main EIA specification on these types of cables is EIA/TIA568 and the ISO standard is ISO/IEC11801.

Coaxial cables have an inner core separated from an outer shield by a dielectric. They have an accurate characteristic impedance (which reduces reflections), and because they are shielded they have very low crosstalk levels.

UTPs (unshielded twisted-pair cables) have either solid cores (for long cable runs) or are stranded patch cables (for shorts run, such as connecting to workstations, patch panels, and so on). Solid cables should not be flexed, bent or twisted repeatedly, whereas stranded cable can be flexed without damaging the cable. Coaxial cables use BNC connectors while UTP cables use either the RJ-11 (small connector which is used to connect the handset to the telephone) or the RJ-45 (larger connector which is used to connect LAN networks to a hub).

Table D.2 and Figure D.2 show typical attenuation rates (dB/100 m) for the Cat-3, Cat-4 and Cat-5 cables. Notice that the attenuation rates for Cat-4 and Cat-5 are approximately the same. These two types of cable have lower attenuation rates than equivalent Cat-3 cables. Notice that the attenuation of the cable increases as the frequency increases. This is due to several factors, such as the skin effect, where the electrical current in the conductors becomes concentrated around the outside of the conductor, and the fact that the insulation (or dielectric) between the conductors actual starts to conduct as the frequency increases.

The Cat-3 cable produces considerable attenuation over a distance of 100 m. The table shows that the signal ratio of the output to the input at 1 MHz, will be 0.76 (2.39 dB), then, at 4 MHz it is 0.55 (5.24 dB), until at 16 MHz it is 0.26. This differing attenuation at different frequencies produces not just a reduction in the signal strength but also distorts the signal (because each frequency is affected differently by the cable. Cat-4 and Cat-5 cables also produce distortion but their effects will be lessened because attenuation characteristics have flatter shapes.

Coaxial cables tend to have very low attenuation, such as 1.2 dB at 4 MHz. They also have a relatively flat response and virtually no crosstalk (due to the physical structure of the cables and the presence of a grounded outer sheath).

Table D.3 and Figure D.3 show typical near end crosstalk rates (dB/100 m) for Cat-3, Cat-4 and Cat-5 cables. The higher the figure, the smaller the crosstalk. Notice that Cat-3 cables have the most crosstalk and Cat-5 have the least, for any given frequency. Notice also that the crosstalk increases as the frequency of the signal increases. Thus, high-frequency signals have more crosstalk than lower-frequency signals.

**Table D.2** Attenuation rates (dB/100 m) for Cat-3, Cat-4 and Cat-5 cable

| Frequency (MHz) | Attenuation rate (dB/100m) | | |
|---|---|---|---|
| | Cat-3 | Cat-4 | Cat-5 |
| 1 | 2.39 | 1.96 | 2.63 |
| 4 | 5.24 | 3.93 | 4.26 |
| 10 | 8.85 | 6.56 | 6.56 |
| 16 | 11.8 | 8.2 | 8.2 |

**Table D.3** Near-end crosstalk (dB/100 m) for Cat-3, Cat-4 and Cat-5 cable

| Frequency (MHz) | Near end crosstalk (dB/100m) | | |
|---|---|---|---|
| | Cat-3 | Cat-4 | Cat-5 |
| 1 | 13.45 | 18.36 | 21.65 |
| 4 | 10.49 | 15.41 | 18.04 |
| 10 | 8.52 | 13.45 | 15.41 |
| 16 | 7.54 | 12.46 | 14.17 |

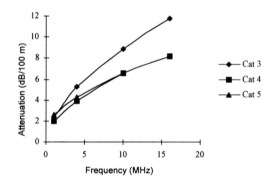

**Figure D.2** Attenuation characteristics for Cat-3, Cat-4 and Cat-5 cables

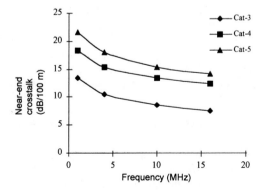

**Figure D.3** Near-end crosstalk characteristics for Cat-3, Cat-4 and Cat-5 cables

# E RFCs

The IAB (Internet Advisor Board) has published many documents on the TCP/IP protocol family. They are known as RFC (request for comment) and can be obtained using FTP from the following:

- Internet Network Information Center (NIC) at `nic ddn mil`, or one of several other FTP sites, such as from the InterNIC Directory and Database Services server at `ds.internic.net`
- Through electronic mail from the automated InterNIC Directory and Database Services mail server at `mailserv@ds.internic.net` The main body of the message should contain the command:

    `document-by-name rfcNNNN`

    where NNNN is the number of the RFC  Multiple requests can be made by sending a single message with each specified document separated by comma-separated list.

The main RFC documents are:

| | |
|---|---|
| **RFC768** | **User Datagram Protocol** |
| RFC775 | Directory-Oriented FTP Commands |
| RFC781 | Specification of the Internet Protocol Timestamp Option |
| RFC783 | TFTP Protocol |
| RFC786 | User Datagram Protocol (UDP) |
| **RFC791** | **Internet Protocol (IP)** |
| **RFC792** | **Internet Control Message Protocol (ICMP)** |
| **RFC793** | **Transmission Control Protocol (TCP)** |
| RFC799 | Internet Name Domains |
| RFC813 | Window and Acknowledgment in TCP |
| RFC815 | IP Datagram Reassembly Algorithms |
| **RFC821** | **Simple Mail-Transfer Protocol (SMTP)** |
| **RFC822** | **Standard for the Format of ARPA Internet Text Messages** |
| RFC823 | DARPA Internet Gateway |
| RFC827 | Exterior Gateway Protocol (EGP) |
| **RFC877** | **Standard for the Transmission of IP Datagrams over Public Data Networks** |
| RFC879 | TCP Maximum Segment Size and Related Topics |
| RFC886 | Proposed Standard for Message Header Munging |
| RFC893 | Trailer Encapsulations |
| **RFC894** | **Standard for the Transmission of IP Datagrams over Ethernet Networks** |
| **RFC895** | **Standard for the Transmission of IP Datagrams over Experimental Ethernet Networks** |
| RFC896 | Congestion Control in TCP/IP Internetworks |
| RFC903 | Reverse Address Resolution Protocol |
| RFC904 | Exterior Gateway Protocol Formal Specifications |
| RFC906 | Bootstrap Loading Using TFTP |

440

| | |
|---|---|
| **RFC919** | **Broadcast Internet Datagram** |
| RFC920 | Domain Requirements |
| RFC932 | Subnetwork Addressing Schema |
| RFC949 | FTP Unique-Named Store Command |
| RFC950 | Internet Standard Subnetting Procedure |
| RFC951 | Bootstrap Protocol |
| **RFC959** | **File Transfer Protocol** |
| **RFC974** | **Mail Routing and the Domain System** |
| RFC980 | Protocol Document Order Information |
| RFC1009 | Requirements for Internet Gateways |
| **RFC1011** | **Official Internet Protocol** |
| RFC1013 | X Windows System Protocol |
| RFC1014 | XDR: External Data Representation Standard |
| RFC1027 | Using ARP to Implement Transparent Subnet Gateways |
| RFC1032 | Domain Administrators Guide |
| RFC1033 | Domain Administrators Operation Guide |
| **RFC1034** | **Domain Names - Concepts and Facilities** |
| RFC1035 | Domain Names - Implementation and Specifications |
| RFC1041 | Telnet 3270 Regime Option |
| **RFC1042** | **Standard for the Transmission of IP Datagrams over IEEE 802 Networks** |
| RFC1043 | Telnet Data Entry Terminal Option |
| **RFC1044** | **Internet Protocol on Network System's HYPERchannel** |
| **RFC1053** | **Telnet X 3 PAD Option** |
| **RFC1055** | **Nonstandard for Transmission of IP Datagrams over Serial Lines** |
| RFC1056 | PCMAIL: A Distributed Mail System for Personal Computers |
| **RFC1058** | **Routing Information Protocol** |
| RFC1068 | Background File Transfer Program (BFTP) |
| RFC1072 | TCP Extensions of Long-Delay Paths |
| RFC1073 | Telnet Window Size Option |
| RFC1074 | NSFNET Backbone SPF-based Interior Gateway Protocol |
| RFC1079 | Telnet Terminal Speed Option |
| RFC1080 | Telnet Remote Flow Control Option |
| RFC1084 | BOOTP Vendor Information Extensions |
| **RFC1088** | **Standard for the Transmission of IP Datagrams over NetBIOS Network** |
| RFC1089 | SNMP over Ethernet |
| RFC1091 | Telnet Terminal-Type Option |
| RFC1094 | NFS: Network File System Protocol Specification |
| RFC1101 | DNS Encoding of Network Names and Other Types |
| RFC1102 | Policy Routing in Internet Protocols |
| RFC1104 | Models of Policy-Based Routing |
| **RFC1112** | **Host Extension for IP Multicasting** |
| **RFC1122** | **Requirement for Internet Hosts - Communication Layers** |
| **RFC1123** | **Requirement for Internet Hosts - Application and Support** |
| RFC1124 | Policy Issues in Interconnecting Networks |
| RFC1125 | Policy Requirements for Inter-Administrative Domain Routing |
| RFC1127 | Perspective on the Host Requirements RFC |
| RFC1129 | Internet Time Protocol |
| RFC1143 | Q Method of Implementing Telnet Option Negotiation |
| RFC1147 | FYI on a Network Management Tool Catalog |
| RFC1149 | Standard for the Transmission of IP Datagrams over Avian Carriers |
| **RFC1155** | **Structure and Identification of Management Information for TCP/IP-Based Internets** |
| **RFC1156** | **Management Information Base for Network Management of TCP/IP-Based** |

**Internets**

| RFC1521 | MIME (Multipurpose Internet Mail Extensions) Part One : Mechanisms for Specifying and Describing the Format of Internet Mail Message Bodies) |
|---|---|
| RFC1583 | OSPF Version2 |
| RFC1630 | Universal Resource Identifiers in WWW |
| RFC1738 | Uniform Resource Identifiers (URL) |
| RFC1752 | The Recommendation for the IP Next-Generation Protocol |
| RFC1771 | A Border Gateway Protocol 4 (BGP-4) |
| RFC1808 | Relative Uniform Resource Identifiers |
| RFC1809 | Using the Flow Label in IPv6 |
| RFC1825 | Security Architecture for the Internet Protocol |
| RFC1826 | IP Authentication Header |
| RFC1827 | IP Encapsulating Security Payload (ESP) |
| RFC1828 | IP Authentication Using Keyed MD5 |
| RFC1829 | The ESP DES-CBC Transform |
| RFC1883 | Internet Protocol, Version 6 Specification |
| RFC1884 | IP Version 6 Addressing Architecture |
| RFC1885 | Internet Control Message Protocol (ICMPv6) for the Internet Protocol Version-6 (IPv6) Specification |
| RFC1886 | DNS Extensions to Support IP Version 6 |
| RFC1887 | An Architecture for IPv6 Unicast Address Allocation |
| RFC1901 | Introduction to Community-Based SNMPv2 |
| RFC1902 | Structure of Management Information for SNMPv2 |
| RFC1903 | Textual Conventions for SNMPv2 |
| RFC1904 | Conformance Statements for SNMPv2 |
| RFC1905 | Protocol Operations for SNMPv2 |
| RFC1906 | Transport Mappings for SNMPv2 |
| RFC1907 | Management Information Base for SNMPv2 |
| RFC1908 | Coexistence Between Version 1 and Version2 of the Internet-Standard Network Management Framework |
| RFC1909 | An Administrative Infrastructure for SNMPv2 |
| RFC1910 | User-based Security Model for SNMPv2 |
| RFC1911 | Voice Profile for Internet Mail |
| RFC1912 | Common DNS Operational and Configuration Errors |
| RFC1913 | Architecture of the Whois++ Index Service |
| RFC1914 | How to Interact with a Whois++ Mesh |
| RFC1915 | Variance for The PPP Connection Control Protocol and The PPP Encryption Control Protocol |
| RFC1916 | Enterprise Renumbering: Experience and Information Solicitation |
| RFC1917 | An Appeal to the Internet Community to Return Unused IP Networks (Prefixes) to the IANA |
| RFC1918 | Address Allocation for Private Internets |
| RFC1919 | Classical versus Transparent IP Proxies |
| **RFC1920** | **INTERNET OFFICIAL PROTOCOL STANDARDS** |
| RFC1922 | Chinese Character Encoding for Internet Messages |
| RFC1923 | RIPv1 Applicability Statement for Historic Status |
| RFC1924 | A Compact Representation of IPv6 Addresses |
| RFC1925 | The Twelve Networking Truths |
| RFC1926 | An Experimental Encapsulation of IP Datagrams on Top of ATM |
| RFC1927 | Suggested Additional MIME Types for Associating Documents |
| RFC1928 | SOCKS Protocol Version 5 |
| RFC1929 | Username/Password Authentication for SOCKS V5 |
| RFC1930 | Guidelines for creation, selection, and registration of an Autonomous System (AS) |
| RFC1931 | Dynamic RARP Extensions for Automatic Network Address Acquisition |

| RFC1932 | IP over ATM: A Framework Document |
| RFC1933 | Transition Mechanisms for IPv6 Hosts and Routers |
| RFC1934 | Ascend's Multilink Protocol Plus (MP+) |
| RFC1935 | What is the Internet, Anyway? |
| RFC1936 | Implementing the Internet Checksum in Hardware |
| RFC1937 | "Local/Remote" Forwarding Decision in Switched Data Link Subnetworks |
| RFC1938 | A One-Time Password System |
| **RFC1939** | **Post Office Protocol - Version 3** |
| RFC1940 | Source Demand Routing: Packet Format and Forwarding Specification (Version 1) |
| RFC1941 | Frequently Asked Questions for Schools |
| RFC1942 | HTML Tables |
| RFC1943 | Building an X 500 Directory Service in the US |
| RFC1944 | Benchmarking Methodology for Network Interconnect Devices |
| RFC1945 | Hypertext Transfer Protocol -- HTTP/1 0 |
| RFC1946 | Native ATM Support for ST2+ |
| RFC1947 | Greek Character Encoding for Electronic Mail Messages |
| RFC1948 | Defending Against Sequence Number Attacks |
| RFC1949 | Scalable Multicast Key Distribution |
| RFC1950 | ZLIB Compressed Data Format Specification version 3 3 |
| RFC1951 | DEFLATE Compressed Data Format Specification version 1 3 |
| RFC1952 | GZIP file format specification version 4 3 |
| RFC1953 | Ipsilon Flow Management Protocol Specification for IPv4 Version 1 0 |
| RFC1954 | Transmission of Flow Labelled IPv4 on ATM Data Links Ipsilon Version 1 0 |
| RFC1955 | New Scheme for Internet Routing and Addressing (ENCAPS) for IPNG |
| RFC1956 | Registration in the MIL Domain |
| RFC1957 | Some Observations on Implementations of the Post Office Protocol (POP3) |
| RFC1958 | Architectural Principles of the Internet |
| RFC1959 | An LDAP URL Format |
| RFC1960 | A String Representation of LDAP Search Filters |
| RFC1961 | GSS-API Authentication Method for SOCKS Version 5 |
| RFC1962 | The PPP Compression Control Protocol (CCP) |
| RFC1963 | PPP Serial Data Transport Protocol (SDTP) |
| RFC1964 | The Kerberos Version 5 GSS-API Mechanism |
| RFC1965 | Autonomous System Confederations for BGP |
| RFC1966 | BGP Route Reflection An alternative to full mesh IBGP |
| RFC1967 | PPP LZS-DCP Compression Protocol (LZS-DCP) |
| RFC1968 | The PPP Encryption Control Protocol (ECP) |
| RFC1969 | The PPP DES Encryption Protocol (DESE) |
| RFC1970 | Neighbor Discovery for IP Version 6 (IPv6) |
| RFC1971 | IPv6 Stateless Address Autoconfiguration |
| RFC1972 | A Method for the Transmission of IPv6 Packets over Ethernet Networks |
| RFC1973 | PPP in Frame Relay |
| RFC1974 | PPP Stac LZS Compression Protocol |
| RFC1975 | PPP Magnalink Variable Resource Compression |
| RFC1976 | PPP for Data Compression in Data Circuit-Terminating Equipment (DCE) |
| RFC1977 | PPP BSD Compression Protocol |
| RFC1978 | PPP Predictor Compression Protocol |
| RFC1979 | PPP Deflate Protocol |
| RFC1980 | A Proposed Extension to HTML : Client-Side Image Maps |
| RFC1981 | Path MTU Discovery for IP version 6 |
| RFC1982 | Serial Number Arithmetic |
| RFC1983 | Internet Users' Glossary |
| RFC1984 | IAB and IESG Statement on Cryptographic Technology and the Internet |

| RFC1985 | SMTP Service Extension for Remote Message Queue Starting |
| RFC1986 | Experiments with a Simple File Transfer Protocol for Radio Links using Enhanced Trivial File Transfer Protocol (ETFTP) |
| RFC1987 | Ipsilon's General Switch Management Protocol Specification Version 1 1 |
| RFC1988 | Conditional Grant of Rights to Specific Hewlett-Packard Patents In Conjunction With the Internet Engineering Task Force's Internet-Standard Network Management Framework |
| RFC1989 | PPP Link Quality Monitoring |
| RFC1990 | The PPP Multilink Protocol |
| RFC1991 | PGP Message Exchange Formats |
| RFC1992 | The Nimrod Routing Architecture |
| RFC1993 | PPP Gandalf FZA Compression Protocol |
| RFC1994 | PPP Challenge Handshake Authentication Protocol (CHAP) |
| RFC1995 | Incremental Zone Transfer in DNS |
| RFC1996 | A Mechanism for Prompt Notification of Zone Changes |
| RFC1997 | BGP Communities Attribute |
| RFC1998 | An Application of the BGP Community Attribute in Multi-home Routing |
| RFC1999 | Request for Comments Summary RFC Numbers 1900-1999 |
| **RFC2000** | **INTERNET OFFICIAL PROTOCOL STANDARDS** |
| RFC2001 | TCP Slow Start, Congestion Avoidance, Fast Retransmit, and Fast |
| RFC2002 | IP Mobility Support |
| RFC2003 | IP Encapsulation within IP |
| RFC2004 | Minimal Encapsulation within IP |
| RFC2005 | Applicability Statement for IP Mobility Support |
| RFC2006 | The Definitions of Managed Objects for IP Mobility Support using SMIv2 |
| RFC2007 | Catalogue of Network Training Materials |
| RFC2008 | Implications of Various Address Allocation Policies for Internet Routing |
| RFC2009 | GPS-Based Addressing and Routing |
| RFC2010 | Operational Criteria for Root Name Servers |
| RFC2011 | SNMPv2 Management Information Base for the Internet Protocol using SMIv2 |
| RFC2012 | SNMPv2 Management Information Base for the Transmission Control Protocol using SMIv2 |
| RFC2013 | SNMPv2 Management Information Base for the User Datagram Protocol using SMIv2 |
| RFC2014 | IRTF Research Group Guidelines and Procedures |
| RFC2015 | MIME Security with Pretty Good Privacy (PGP) |
| RFC2016 | Uniform Resource Agents (URAs) |
| RFC2017 | Definition of the URL MIME External-Body Access-Type |
| RFC2018 | TCP Selective Acknowledgement Options |
| RFC2019 | Transmission of IPv6 Packets Over FDDI |
| RFC2020 | IEEE 802 12 Interface MIB |
| RFC2021 | Remote Network Monitoring Management Information Base Version2 using SMIv2 |
| RFC2022 | Support for Multicast over UNI 3 0/3 1 based ATM Networks |
| RFC2023 | IP Version 6 over PPP |
| RFC2024 | Definitions of Managed Objects for Data Link Switching using SMIv2 |
| RFC2025 | The Simple Public-Key GSS-API Mechanism (SPKM) |
| RFC2026 | The Internet Standards Process -- Revision 3 |
| RFC2027 | IAB and IESG Selection, Confirmation, and Recall Process: Operation of the Nominating and Recall Committees |
| RFC2028 | The Organizations Involved in the IETF Standards Process |
| RFC2029 | RTP Payload Format of Sun's CellB Video Encoding |
| RFC2030 | Simple Network Time Protocol (SNTP) |

| RFC2031 | IETF-ISOC relationship |
| RFC2032 | RTP Payload Format for H 261 Video Streams |
| RFC2033 | Local Mail Transfer Protocol |
| RFC2034 | SMTP Service Extension for Returning Enhanced Error Codes |
| RFC2035 | RTP Payload Format for JPEG-compressed Video |
| RFC2036 | Observations on the use of Components of the Class A Address Space within the Internet |
| RFC2037 | Entity MIB using SMIv2 |
| RFC2038 | RTP Payload Format for MPEG1/MPEG2 Video |
| RFC2039 | Applicability of Standards Track MIBs to Management of World Wide Web Servers |
| RFC2040 | The RC5, RC5-CBC, RC5-CBC-Pad, and RC5-CTS Algorithms |
| RFC2041 | Mobile Network Tracing |
| RFC2042 | Registering New BGP Attribute Types |
| RFC2043 | The PPP SNA Control Protocol (SNACP) |
| RFC2044 | UTF-8, a transformation format of Unicode and ISO 10646 |
| RFC2045 | Multipurpose Internet Mail Extensions (MIME) Part One: Format of Internet Message Bodies |
| RFC2046 | Multipurpose Internet Mail Extensions (MIME) Part Two: Media Types |
| RFC2047 | MIME (Multipurpose Internet Mail Extensions) Part Three: Message Header Extensions for Non-ASCII Text |
| RFC2048 | Multipurpose Internet Mail Extension (MIME) Part Four: Registration Procedures |
| RFC2049 | Multipurpose Internet Mail Extensions (MIME) Part Five: Conformance Criteria and Examples |
| RFC2050 | INTERNET REGISTRY IP ALLOCATION GUIDELINES |
| RFC2051 | Definitions of Managed Objects for APPC using SMIv2 |
| RFC2052 | A DNS RR for specifying the location of services (DNS SRV) |
| RFC2053 | The AM (Armenia) Domain |
| RFC2054 | WebNFS Client Specification |
| RFC2055 | WebNFS Server Specification |
| RFC2056 | Uniform Resource Locators for Z39 50 |
| RFC2057 | Source Directed Access Control on the Internet |
| RFC2058 | Remote Authentication Dial In User Service (RADIUS) |
| RFC2059 | RADIUS Accounting |
| RFC2060 | INTERNET MESSAGE ACCESS PROTOCOL - VERSION 4rev1 |
| RFC2061 | IMAP4 COMPATIBILITY WITH IMAP2BIS |
| RFC2062 | Internet Message Access Protocol - Obsolete Syntax |
| RFC2063 | Traffic Flow Measurement: Architecture |
| RFC2064 | Traffic Flow Measurement: Meter MIB |
| RFC2065 | Domain Name System Security Extensions |
| RFC2066 | TELNET CHARSET Option |
| RFC2067 | IP over HIPPI |
| RFC2068 | Hypertext Transfer Protocol -- HTTP/1 1 |
| RFC2069 | An Extension to HTTP: Digest Access Authentication |
| RFC2070 | Internationalization of the Hypertext Markup Language |
| RFC2071 | Network Renumbering Overview: Why would I want it and what is it anyway? |
| RFC2072 | Router Renumbering Guide |
| RFC2073 | An IPv6 Provider-Based Unicast Address Format |
| RFC2074 | Remote Network Monitoring MIB Protocol Identifiers |
| RFC2075 | IP Echo Host Service |
| RFC2076 | Common Internet Message Headers |
| RFC2077 | The Model Primary Content Type for Multipurpose Internet Mail Extensions |
| RFC2078 | Generic Security Service Application Program Interface, Version2 |

| RFC2079 | Definition of an X 500 Attribute Type and an Object Class to Hold Uniform Resource Identifiers (URIs) |
|---|---|
| RFC2080 | RIPng for IPv6 |
| RFC2081 | RIPng Protocol Applicability Statement |
| RFC2082 | RIP-2 MD5 Authentication |
| RFC2083 | PNG (Portable Network Graphics) Specification |
| RFC2084 | Considerations for Web Transaction Security |
| RFC2085 | HMAC-MD5 IP Authentication with Replay Prevention |
| RFC2086 | IMAP4 ACL extension |
| RFC2087 | IMAP4 QUOTA extension |
| RFC2088 | IMAP4 non-synchronizing literals |
| RFC2089 | V2ToV1 Mapping SNMPv2 onto SNMPv1 within a bi-lingual SNMP agent |
| RFC2090 | TFTP Multicast Option |
| RFC2091 | Triggered Extensions to RIP to Support Demand Circuits |
| RFC2092 | Protocol Analysis for Triggered RIP |
| RFC2093 | Group Key Management Protocol (GKMP) Specification |
| RFC2094 | Group Key Management Protocol (GKMP) Architecture |
| RFC2095 | IMAP/POP AUTHorize Extension for Simple Challenge/Response |
| RFC2096 | IP Forwarding Table MIB |
| RFC2097 | The PPP NetBIOS Frames Control Protocol (NBFCP) |
| RFC2098 | Toshiba's Router Architecture Extensions for ATM : Overview |
| RFC2099 | Request for Comments Summary RFC Numbers2000-2099 |
| RFC2100 | The Naming of Hosts |
| RFC2101 | IPv4 Address Behavior Today |
| RFC2102 | Multicast Support for Nimrod : Requirements and Solution Approaches |
| RFC2103 | Mobility Support for Nimrod : Challenges and Solution Approaches |
| RFC2104 | HMAC: Keyed-Hashing for Message Authentication |
| RFC2105 | Cisco Systems' Tag Switching Architecture Overview |
| RFC2106 | Data Link Switching Remote Access Protocol |
| RFC2107 | Ascend Tunnel Management Protocol - ATMP |
| RFC2108 | Definitions of Managed Objects for IEEE 802 3 Repeater Devices using SMIv2 |
| RFC2109 | HTTP State Management Mechanism |
| RFC2110 | MIME E-mail Encapsulation of Aggregate Documents, such as HTML (MHTML) |
| RFC2111 | Content-ID and Message-ID Uniform Resource Locators |
| RFC2112 | The MIME Multipart/Related Content-type |
| RFC2113 | IP Router Alert Option |
| RFC2114 | Data Link Switching Client Access Protocol |
| RFC2115 | Management Information Base for Frame Relay DTEs Using SMIv2 |
| RFC2116 | X 500 Implementations Catalog-96 |
| RFC2117 | Protocol Independent Multicast-Sparse Mode (PIM-SM): Protocol |
| RFC2118 | Microsoft Point-To-Point Compression (MPPC) Protocol |
| RFC2119 | Key words for use in RFCs to Indicate Requirement Level |
| RFC2120 | Managing the X 500 Root Naming Context |
| RFC2121 | Issues affecting MARS Cluster Size |
| RFC2122 | VEMMI URL Specification |
| RFC2123 | Traffic Flow Measurement: Experiences with NeTraMet |
| RFC2124 | Cabletron's Light-weight Flow Admission Protocol Specification |
| RFC2125 | The PPP Bandwidth Allocation Protocol (BAP) / The PPP Bandwidth Allocation Control Protocol (BACP) |
| RFC2126 | ISO Transport Service on top of TCP (ITOT) |
| RFC2127 | ISDN Management Information Base using SMIv2 |
| RFC2128 | Dial Control Management Information Base using SMIv2 |
| RFC2129 | Toshiba's Flow Attribute Notification Protocol (FANP) |

| | |
|---|---|
| RFC2189 | Core Based Trees (CBT version2) Multicast Routing |
| RFC2190 | RTP Payload Format for H 263 Video Streams |
| RFC2191 | VENUS - Very Extensive Non-Unicast Service |
| RFC2192 | IMAP URL Scheme |
| RFC2193 | IMAP4 Mailbox Referrals |
| RFC2194 | Review of Roaming Implementations |
| RFC2195 | IMAP/POP AUTHorize Extension for Simple Challenge/Response |
| RFC2196 | Site Security Handbook |
| RFC2197 | SMTP Service Extension for Command Pipelining |
| RFC2198 | RTP Payload for Redundant Audio Data |
| RFC2200 | INTERNET OFFICIAL PROTOCOL STANDARDS |
| RFC2201 | Core Based Trees (CBT) Multicast Routing Architecture |
| RFC2202 | Test Cases for HMAC-MD5 and HMAC-SHA-1 |
| RFC2203 | RPCSEC_GSS Protocol Specification |
| RFC2204 | ODETTE File Transfer Protocol |
| RFC2205 | Resource ReSerVation Protocol (RSVP) -- Version 1 Functional Specification |
| RFC2206 | RSVP Management Information Base using SMIv2 |
| RFC2207 | RSVP Extensions for IPSEC Data Flows |
| RFC2208 | Resource ReSerVation Protocol (RSVP) -- Version 1 Applicability Statement Some Guidelines on Deployment |
| RFC2209 | Resource ReSerVation Protocol (RSVP) -- Version 1 Message Processing Rules |
| RFC2210 | The Use of RSVP with IETF Integrated Services |
| RFC2211 | Specification of the Controlled-Load Network Element Service |
| RFC2212 | Specification of Guaranteed Quality of Service |
| RFC2213 | Integrated Services Management Information Base using SMIv2 |
| RFC2214 | Integrated Services Management Information Base Guaranteed Service Extensions using SMIv2 |
| RFC2215 | General Characterization Parameters for Integrated Service Network Elements |
| RFC2216 | Network Element Service Specification Template |
| RFC2217 | Telnet Com Port Control Option |
| RFC2218 | A Common Schema for the Internet White Pages Service |
| RFC2219 | Use of DNS Aliases for Network Services |
| RFC2220 | The Application/MARC Content-type |
| RFC2221 | IMAP4 Login Referrals |
| RFC2222 | Simple Authentication and Security Layer (SASL) |
| RFC2223 | Instructions to RFC Authors |
| RFC2224 | NFS URL Scheme |
| RFC2226 | IP Broadcast over ATM Networks |
| RFC2227 | Simple Hit-Metering and Usage-Limiting for HTTP |
| RFC2228 | FTP Security Extensions |
| RFC2229 | A Dictionary Server Protocol |
| RFC2230 | Key Exchange Delegation Record for the DNS |
| RFC2231 | MIME Parameter Value and Encoded Word Extensions: Character Sets, Languages, and Continuations |
| RFC2232 | Definitions of Managed Objects for DLUR using SMIv2 |
| RFC2233 | The Interfaces Group MIB using SMIv2 |
| RFC2234 | Augmented BNF for Syntax Specifications: ABNF |
| RFC2235 | Hobbes' Internet Timeline |
| RFC2236 | Internet Group Management Protocol, Version2 |
| RFC2237 | Japanese Character Encoding for Internet Messages |
| RFC2238 | Definitions of Managed Objects for HPR using SMIv2 |
| RFC2239 | Definitions of Managed Objects for IEEE 802 3 Medium Attachment Units (MAUs) using SMIv2 |

| RFC2240 | A Legal Basis for Domain Name Allocation |
| RFC2241 | DHCP Options for Novell Directory Services |
| RFC2242 | NetWare/IP Domain Name and Information |
| RFC2243 | OTP Extended Responses |
| RFC2244 | ACAP -- Application Configuration Access Protocol |
| RFC2245 | Anonymous SASL Mechanism |
| RFC2247 | Using Domains in LDAP/X 500 Distinguished Names |
| RFC2248 | Network Services Monitoring MIB |
| RFC2249 | Mail Monitoring MIB |
| RFC2250 | RTP Payload Format for MPEG1/MPEG2 Video |
| RFC2251 | Lightweight Directory Access Protocol (v3) |
| RFC2252 | Lightweight Directory Access Protocol (v3): Attribute Syntax Definitions |
| RFC2253 | Lightweight Directory Access Protocol (v3): UTF-8 String Representation of Distinguished Names |
| RFC2254 | The String Representation of LDAP Search Filters |
| RFC2255 | The LDAP URL Format |
| RFC2256 | A Summary of the X 500(96) User Schema for use with LDAPv3 |
| RFC2257 | Agent Extensibility (AgentX) Protocol Version 1 |
| RFC2258 | Internet Nomenclator Project |
| RFC2259 | Simple Nomenclator Query Protocol (SNQP) |
| RFC2260 | Scalable Support for Multi-homed Multi-provider Connectivity |
| RFC2261 | An Architecture for Describing SNMP Management Frameworks |
| RFC2262 | Message Processing and Dispatching for the Simple Network Management Protocol (SNMP) |
| RFC2263 | SNMPv3 Applications |
| RFC2264 | User-based Security Model (USM) for version 3 of the Simple Network Management Protocol (SNMPv3) |
| RFC2265 | View-based Access Control Model (VACM) for the Simple Network Management Protocol (SNMP) |
| RFC2266 | Definitions of Managed Objects for IEEE 802 12 Repeater Devices |
| RFC2267 | Network Ingress Filtering: Defeating Denial of Service Attacks which employ IP Source Address Spoofing |
| RFC2268 | A Description of the RC2(r) Encryption Algorithm |
| RFC2269 | Using the MARS model in non-ATM NBMA networks |
| RFC2270 | Using a Dedicated AS for Sites Homed to a Single Provider |
| RFC2271 | An Architecture for Describing SNMP Management Frameworks |
| RFC2272 | Message Processing and Dispatching for the Simple Network Management Protocol (SNMP) |
| RFC2273 | SNMPv3 Applications |
| RFC2274 | User-based Security Model (USM) for version 3 of the Simple Network Management Protocol (SNMPv3) |
| RFC2275 | View-based Access Control Model (VACM) for the Simple Network Management Protocol (SNMP) |
| RFC2276 | Architectural Principles of Uniform Resource Name Resolution |
| RFC2277 | IETF Policy on Character Sets and Languages |
| RFC2278 | IANA Charset Registration Procedures |
| RFC2279 | UTF-8, a transformation format of ISO 10646 |
| RFC2280 | Routing Policy Specification Language (RPSL) |
| RFC2281 | Cisco Hot Standby Router Protocol (HSRP) |
| RFC2282 | IAB and IESG Selection, Confirmation, and Recall Process: Operation of the Nominating and Recall Committees |
| RFC2283 | Multiprotocol Extensions for BGP-4 |
| RFC2284 | PPP Extensible Authentication Protocol (EAP) |

| RFC2285 | Benchmarking Terminology for LAN Switching Devices |
| RFC2286 | Test Cases for HMAC-RIPEMD160 and HMAC-RIPEMD128 |
| RFC2287 | Definitions of System-Level Managed Objects for Applications |
| RFC2288 | Using Existing Bibliographic Identifiers as Uniform Resource Names |
| RFC2289 | A One-Time Password System |
| RFC2290 | Mobile-IPv4 Configuration Option for PPP IPCP |
| RFC2291 | Requirements for a Distributed Authoring and Versioning Protocol for the World Wide Web |
| RFC2292 | Advanced Sockets API for IPv6 |
| RFC2293 | Representing Tables and Subtrees in the X 500 Directory |
| RFC2294 | Representing the O/R Address hierarchy in the X 500 Directory Information Tree |
| RFC2295 | Transparent Content Negotiation in HTTP |
| RFC2296 | HTTP Remote Variant Selection Algorithm -- RVSA/1 |
| RFC2297 | Ipsilon's General Switch Management Protocol Specification Version2 0 |
| RFC2298 | An Extensible Message Format for Message Disposition Notifications |
| **RFC2300** | **INTERNET OFFICIAL PROTOCOL STANDARDS** |
| RFC2301 | File Format for Internet Fax |
| RFC2302 | Tag Image File Format (TIFF) - image/tiff MIME Sub-type Registration |
| RFC2303 | Minimal PSTN address format in Internet Mail |
| RFC2304 | Minimal FAX address format in Internet Mail |
| RFC2305 | A Simple Mode of Facsimile Using Internet Mail |
| RFC2306 | Tag Image File Format (TIFF) - F Profile for Facsimile |
| RFC2307 | An Approach for Using LDAP as a Network Information Service |
| RFC2308 | Negative Caching of DNS Queries (DNS NCACHE) |
| RFC2309 | Recommendations on Queue Management and Congestion Avoidance in the Internet |
| RFC2310 | The Safe Response Header Field |
| RFC2311 | S/MIME Version2 Message Specification |
| RFC2312 | S/MIME Version2 Certificate Handling |
| RFC2313 | PKCS #1: RSA Encryption Version 1 5 |
| RFC2314 | PKCS #10: Certification Request Syntax Version 1 5 |
| RFC2315 | PKCS #7: Cryptographic Message Syntax Version 1 5 |
| RFC2316 | Report of the IAB Security Architecture Workshop |
| RFC2317 | Classless IN-ADDR ARPA delegation |
| RFC2318 | The text/css Media Type |
| RFC2319 | Ukrainian Character Set KOI8-U |
| RFC2320 | Definitions of Managed  Objects for Classical IP and ARP Over ATM Using SMIv2 (IPOA-MIB) |
| RFC2321 | RITA -- The Reliable Internetwork Troubleshooting Agent |
| RFC2322 | Management of IP numbers by peg-dhcp |
| RFC2323 | IETF Identification and Security Guidelines |
| RFC2324 | Hyper Text Coffee Pot Control Protocol (HTCPCP/1 0) |
| RFC2325 | Definitions of Managed Objects for Drip-Type Heated Beverage Hardware Devices using SMIv2 |
| RFC2326 | Real Time Streaming Protocol (RTSP) |
| RFC2327 | SDP: Session Description Protocol |
| **RFC2328** | **OSPF Version2** |
| RFC2329 | OSPF Standardization Report |
| RFC2330 | Framework for IP Performance Metrics |
| RFC2331 | ATM Signalling Support for IP over ATM - UNI Signalling  4 0 Update |
| RFC2332 | NBMA Next Hop Resolution Protocol (NHRP) |
| RFC2333 | NHRP Protocol Applicability Statement |
| RFC2334 | Server Cache Synchronization Protocol (SCSP) |

| RFC2335 | A Distributed NHRP Service Using SCSP |
|---------|----------------------------------------|
| RFC2336 | Classical IP to NHRP Transition |
| RFC2337 | Intra-LIS IP multicast among routers over ATM using Sparse Mode PIM |
| RFC2338 | Virtual Router Redundancy Protocol |
| RFC2339 | An agreement between the Internet Society, the IETF and Sun Microsystems, Inc in the matter of NFS V 4 protocols |
| RFC2340 | Nortel's Virtual Network Switching (VNS) Overview |
| RFC2341 | Cisco Layer Two Forwarding (Protocol) 'L2F' |
| RFC2342 | IMAP4 Namespace |
| RFC2343 | RTP Payload Format for Bundled MPEG |
| RFC2344 | Reverse Tunneling for Mobile IP |
| RFC2345 | Domain Names and Company Name Retrieval |
| RFC2346 | Making Postscript and PDF International |
| RFC2347 | TFTP Option Extension |
| RFC2348 | TFTP Blocksize Option |
| RFC2349 | TFTP Timeout Interval and Transfer Size Options |
| RFC2350 | Expectations for Computer Security Incident Response |
| RFC2351 | Mapping of Airline Reservation, Ticketing, and Messaging Traffic over IP |
| RFC2352 | A Convention For Using Legal Names as Domain Names |
| RFC2353 | APPN/HPR in IP Networks APPN Implementers' Workshop Closed Pages Document |
| RFC2354 | Options for Repair of Streaming Media |
| RFC2355 | TN3270 Enhancements |
| RFC2356 | Sun's SKIP Firewall Traversal for Mobile IP |
| RFC2357 | IETF Criteria For Evaluating Reliable Multicast Transport and Application Protocols |
| RFC2358 | Definitions of Managed Objects for the Ethernet-like Interface Types |
| RFC2359 | IMAP4 UIDPLUS extension |
| RFC2360 | Guide for Internet Standards Writers |
| RFC2361 | WAVE and AVI Codec Registries |
| RFC2362 | Protocol Independent Multicast-Sparse Mode (PIM-SM): Protocol Specification |
| RFC2363 | PPP Over FUNI |
| RFC2364 | PPP over AAL5 |
| RFC2365 | Administratively Scoped IP Multicast |
| RFC2366 | Definitions of Managed Objects for Multicast over UNI 3 0/3 1 based ATM Networks |
| RFC2367 | PF_KEY Key Management API, Version2 |
| RFC2368 | The mailto URL scheme |
| RFC2369 | The Use of URLs as Meta-Syntax for Core Mail List Commands and their Transport through Message Header Fields |
| RFC2370 | The OSPF Opaque LSA Option |
| RFC2371 | Transaction Internet Protocol Version 3 0 |
| RFC2372 | Transaction Internet Protocol - Requirements and Supplemental Information |
| RFC2373 | IP Version 6 Addressing Architecture |
| RFC2374 | An IPv6 Aggregatable Global Unicast Address Format |
| RFC2375 | IPv6 Multicast Address Assignments |
| RFC2376 | XML Media Types |
| RFC2377 | Naming Plan for Internet Directory-Enabled Applications |
| RFC2378 | The CCSO Nameserver (Ph) Architecture |
| RFC2379 | RSVP over ATM Implementation Guidelines |
| RFC2380 | RSVP over ATM Implementation Requirements |
| RFC2381 | Interoperation of Controlled-Load Service and Guaranteed Service with ATM |
| RFC2382 | A Framework for Integrated Services and RSVP over ATM |

| RFC2383 | ST2+ over ATM Protocol Specification - UNI 3 1 Version |
|---|---|
| RFC2384 | POP URL Scheme |
| RFC2385 | Protection of BGP Sessions via the TCP MD5 Signature Option |
| RFC2386 | A Framework for QoS-based Routing in the Internet |
| RFC2387 | The MIME Multipart/Related Content-type |
| RFC2388 | Returning Values from Forms: multipart/form-data |
| RFC2389 | Feature negotiation mechanism for the File Transfer Protocol |
| RFC2390 | Inverse Address Resolution Protocol |
| RFC2391 | Load Sharing using IP Network Address Translation (LSNAT) |
| RFC2392 | Content-ID and Message-ID Uniform Resource Locators |
| RFC2396 | Uniform Resource Identifiers (URI): Generic Syntax |
| RFC2397 | The 'data' URL scheme |
| RFC2398 | Some Testing Tools for TCP Implementors |
| **RFC2400** | **INTERNET OFFICIAL PROTOCOL STANDARDS** |
| RFC2401 | Security Architecture for the Internet Protocol |
| RFC2402 | IP Authentication Header |
| RFC2410 | The NULL Encryption Algorithm and Its Use With IPsec |
| RFC2411 | IP Security Document Roadmap |
| RFC2413 | Dublin Core Metadata for Resource Discovery |
| RFC2414 | Increasing TCP's Initial Window |
| RFC2415 | Simulation Studies of Increased Initial TCP Window Size |
| RFC2416 | When TCP Starts Up With Four Packets Into Only Three Buffers |
| RFC2417 | Definitions of Managed Objects for Multicast over UNI 3 0/3 1 based ATM Networks |
| RFC2418 | IETF Working Group Guidelines and Procedures |
| RFC2419 | The PPP DES Encryption Protocol, Version2 (DESE-bis) |
| RFC2420 | The PPP Triple-DES Encryption Protocol (3DESE) |
| RFC2421 | Voice Profile for Internet Mail - version2 |
| RFC2422 | Toll Quality Voice - 32 kbit/s ADPCM MIME Sub-type Registration |
| RFC2423 | VPIM Voice Message MIME Sub-type Registration |
| RFC2424 | Content Duration MIME Header Definition |
| RFC2425 | A MIME Content-Type for Directory Information |
| RFC2426 | vCard MIME Directory Profile |
| **RFC2427** | **Multiprotocol Interconnect over Frame Relay** |
| RFC2428 | FTP Extensions for IPv6 and NATs |
| RFC2429 | RTP Payload Format for the 1998 Version of ITU-T Rec H 263 Video (H 263+) |
| RFC2430 | A Provider Architecture for Differentiated Services and Traffic Engineering (PASTE) |
| RFC2431 | RTP Payload Format for BT 656 Video Encoding |
| RFC2432 | Terminology for IP Multicast Benchmarking |
| RFC2433 | Microsoft PPP CHAP Extensions |
| RFC2434 | Guidelines for Writing an IANA Considerations Section in RFCs |
| RFC2435 | RTP Payload Format for JPEG-compressed Video |
| RFC2436 | Collaboration between ISOC/IETF and ITU-T |
| RFC2437 | PKCS #1: RSA Cryptography Specifications Version2 0 |
| RFC2438 | Advancement of MIB specifications on the IETF Standards Track |
| RFC2439 | BGP Route Flap Damping |
| RFC2440 | OpenPGP Message Format |
| RFC2441 | Working with Jon Tribute delivered at UCLA |
| RFC2442 | The Batch SMTP Media Type |
| RFC2443 | A Distributed MARS Service Using SCSP |
| RFC2444 | The One-Time-Password SASL Mechanism |
| RFC2445 | Internet Calendaring and Scheduling Core Object Specification (iCalendar) |

| RFC2446 | iCalendar Transport-Independent Interoperability Protocol (iTIP) Scheduling Events, BusyTime, To-dos and Journal Entries |
| RFC2447 | iCalendar Message-based Interoperability Protocol (iMIP) |
| RFC2448 | AT&T's Error Resilient Video Transmission Technique |
| RFC2449 | POP3 Extension Mechanism", |
| **RFC2453** | **RIP Version2 Carrying Additional Information",** |
| RFC2455 | Definitions of Managed Objects for APPN", |
| RFC2456 | Definitions of Managed Objects for APPN TRAPS |
| RFC2457 | Definitions of Managed Objects for Extended Border Node |
| RFC2458 | Toward the PSTN/Internet Inter-Networking --Pre-PINT Implementations |
| RFC2468 | I REMEMBER IANA |

**Quick Guide**

| | |
|---|---|
| 802.12-MIB | RFC2020 |
| 802.3-MIB | RFC2108 |
| 802.5-MIB | RFC1748 |
| ABNF | RFC2234 |
| ACAP | RFC2244 |
| AGENTX | RFC2257 |
| APPN-MIB | RFC2155 |
| ARCH-SNMP | RFC2271 |
| ARP | RFC26 |
| ATM-ENCAP | RFC83/1695/1755 |
| BGP | RFC1771/1745/1772/1657/1997/1269/1403 |
| BOOTP | RFC951/2132 |
| CLDAP | RFC1798 |
| CON-MD5 | RFC1864 |
| CONTENT | RFC1049 |
| DAA | RFC2069 |
| DASS | RFC1507 |
| DAYTIME | RFC867 |
| DC-MIB | RFC2128 |
| DECNET-MIB | RFC1559 |
| DHCP | RFC2131/1534/2132/2241 |
| DISCARD | RFC863 |
| DNS | RFC2181/1886/1995/2163/974/2308/1996/1612/2065/1611/2136 |
| DOMAIN | RFC1034/1035 |
| DSN | RFC1894 |
| ECHO | RFC862 |
| ENTITY-MIB | RFC2037 |
| ESP | RFC1827 |
| ETHER-MIB | RFC1643 |
| FDDI-MIB | RFC1285/1512 |
| FFIF | RFC2301 |
| FINGER | RFC1288 |
| FRAME-MIB | RFC2115 |
| FTP | RFC959/2389/1415/2228 |
| GQOS | RFC2212 |

| | |
|---|---|
| GSSAP | RFC2078/1509/1964/1961 |
| HOST-MIB | RFC1514 |
| HTML | RFC1866/2070 |
| HTTP-1.1 | RFC2068/2109 |
| IARP | RFC2390 |
| ICMP | RFC792/1256/1885 |
| IDENT | RFC1413/1414 |
| IGMP | RFC2236/1112 |
| IMAP | RFC2086/1731/2177/2088/2221/2193/2342/2087 |
| | 2359/2195/2192/2060 |
| IP-ARC | RFC1 |
| IP-ARPA | RFC22 |
| IP-ATM | RFC25 |
| IP-FDDI | RFC90 |
| IP-FR | RFC2427 |
| IP-IEEE | RFC42 |
| IP-IPX | RFC32 |
| IP-NETBIOS | RFC88 |
| IPNG | RFC1752 |
| IP-SLIP | RFC55 |
| IP-SMDS | RFC1209 |
| IPV6 | RFC1883/1826/1971/1972/2019/2147/1970/2023 |
| IP | RFC7/56/1552/1234 |
| ISDN-MIB | RFC2127 |
| IS-IS | RFC1195 |
| KERBEROS | RFC1510 |
| LDAP | RFC2252/2253/1960/1959/2255/2251 |
| MAIL | RFC822/2249/2142 |
| MHTML | RFC2110 |
| MIB | RFC1212/1213/2011/2012/2013/1239 |
| MIME | RFC2045/2422/2049/1767/1847/2231/2046/2077 |
| | 2047/2015/2387/1892/1848/2426/2421/2423 |
| MOBILEIP | RFC2005/2006/2002/2344 |
| MODEM-MIB | RFC1696 |
| NETBIOS | RFC1001/1002 |
| NETFAX | RFC1314 |
| NETWAREIP | RFC2242 |
| NHRP | RFC2332/2333/2335 |
| NICNAME | RFC954 |
| NNTP | RFC977 |
| NTP | RFC1119/1305 |
| ONE-PASS | RFC2289 |
| OSI-NSAP | RFC1629 |
| OSI-UDP | RFC1240 |
| OSPF | RFC2328/1793/2370/1850/1584/1587 |
| PEM | RFC1423/1422/1421/1424 |
| POP3 | RFC1939/1734/2384 |

| | |
|---|---|
| PPP | RFC1661/1662/1474/1473/1471/1472/ 2364 |
| | 1378/1638/1962/1994/1762/2284/1968/1973 |
| | 2363/1332/1618/1570/1989/1990/2097/1377 |
| | 2043/1619/1663/1598 |
| QUOTE | RFC865 |
| RADIUS | RFC2138 |
| RARP | RFC3 |
| RIP | RFC1723/1722/2082/1724/1582 |
| RIPNG | RFC2080/2091 |
| RMON-MIB | RFC2021/2074/1757 |
| RPC | RFC1831/ 2203 |
| RPSL | RFC2280 |
| RREQ | RFC1812 |
| RSVP | RFC2205/2208/2207/2210/2206/2209 |
| RTP | RFC1889/1890/2029/2032/2035/2250/2198 |
| RTSP | RFC2326/2222 |
| SDP | RFC2327 |
| SIP-MIB | RFC1694 |
| SLM-APP | RFC2287 |
| SLP | RFC2165 |
| SMFAX-IM | RFC2305 |
| SMI | RFC1155/1902 |
| SMTP | RFC821/1870/1869/2197/1652/1891/2034/1985 |
| SNA | RFC1982/2051/1666 |
| SNMP | RFC1157/1351/1419/1420/1381/1418/1353 |
| | 1352/1441/1907/2273/1382/2274 |
| SOCKSV5 | RFC1928 |
| SONET-MIB | RFC1595 |
| STR-LDAP | RFC2254 |
| TABLE-MIB | RFC2096 |
| TCP | RFC793/2018/1323/2001 |
| TELNET | RFC854/855 |
| TFTP | RFC1350/2347/2348/2349 |
| TIFF | RFC2302 |
| TIME | RFC868 |
| TIP | RFC2371 |
| TMUX | RFC1692 |
| TOS | RFC1349 |
| TP-TCP | RFC1006 |
| TRANS-IPV6 | RFC1933 |
| TRANS-MIB | RFC1906 |
| TXT-DIR | RFC2425 |
| UDP | RFC768 |
| UPS-MIB | RFC1628 |
| URI | RFC2079/2396 |
| URL | RFC1738/1808/2017/2368/ 2056 |
| USERS | RFC866 |

| | |
|---|---|
| UTF-8 | RFC2279 |
| VRRP | RFC2338 |
| WHOIS++ | RFC1835/1913/1914 |
| X.500 | RFC1777/1778/1567 |
| X25-MIB | RFC1461 |
| XDR | RFC1832 |

# ASCII

## F.1 International alphabet No. 5

ANSI defined a standard alphabet known as ASCII. This has since been adopted by the CCITT as a standard, known as IA5 (International Alphabet No. 5). The following tables define this alphabet in binary, as a decimal value, as a hexadecimal value and as a character.

| Binary | Decimal | Hex | Character | Binary | Decimal | Hex | Character |
|--------|---------|-----|-----------|--------|---------|-----|-----------|
| 00000000 | 0 | 00 | NUL | 00010000 | 16 | 10 | DLE |
| 00000001 | 1 | 01 | SOH | 00010001 | 17 | 11 | DC1 |
| 00000010 | 2 | 02 | STX | 00010010 | 18 | 12 | DC2 |
| 00000011 | 3 | 03 | ETX | 00010011 | 19 | 13 | DC3 |
| 00000100 | 4 | 04 | EOT | 00010100 | 20 | 14 | DC4 |
| 00000101 | 5 | 05 | ENQ | 00010101 | 21 | 15 | NAK |
| 00000110 | 6 | 06 | ACK | 00010110 | 22 | 16 | SYN |
| 00000111 | 7 | 07 | BEL | 00010111 | 23 | 17 | ETB |
| 00001000 | 8 | 08 | BS | 00011000 | 24 | 18 | CAN |
| 00001001 | 9 | 09 | HT | 00011001 | 25 | 19 | EM |
| 00001010 | 10 | 0A | LF | 00011010 | 26 | 1A | SUB |
| 00001011 | 11 | 0B | VT | 00011011 | 27 | 1B | ESC |
| 00001100 | 12 | 0C | FF | 00011100 | 28 | 1C | FS |
| 00001101 | 13 | 0D | CR | 00011101 | 29 | 1D | GS |
| 00001110 | 14 | 0E | SO | 00011110 | 30 | 1E | RS |
| 00001111 | 15 | 0F | SI | 00011111 | 31 | 1F | US |

| Binary | Decimal | Hex | Character | Binary | Decimal | Hex | Character |
|--------|---------|-----|-----------|--------|---------|-----|-----------|
| 00100000 | 32 | 20 | SPACE | 00110000 | 48 | 30 | 0 |
| 00100001 | 33 | 21 | ! | 00110001 | 49 | 31 | 1 |
| 00100010 | 34 | 22 | \\ | 00110010 | 50 | 32 | 2 |
| 00100011 | 35 | 23 | # | 00110011 | 51 | 33 | 3 |
| 00100100 | 36 | 24 | $ | 00110100 | 52 | 34 | 4 |
| 00100101 | 37 | 25 | % | 00110101 | 53 | 35 | 5 |
| 00100110 | 38 | 26 | & | 00110110 | 54 | 36 | 6 |
| 00100111 | 39 | 27 | / | 00110111 | 55 | 37 | 7 |
| 00101000 | 40 | 28 | ( | 00111000 | 56 | 38 | 8 |
| 00101001 | 41 | 29 | ) | 00111001 | 57 | 39 | 9 |
| 00101010 | 42 | 2A | * | 00111010 | 58 | 3A | : |
| 00101011 | 43 | 2B | + | 00111011 | 59 | 3B | ; |
| 00101100 | 44 | 2C | , | 00111100 | 60 | 3C | < |
| 00101101 | 45 | 2D | – | 00111101 | 61 | 3D | = |
| 00101110 | 46 | 2E | . | 00111110 | 62 | 3E | > |
| 00101111 | 47 | 2F | / | 00111111 | 63 | 3F | ? |

| Binary | Decimal | Hex | Character | Binary | Decimal | Hex | Character |
|--------|---------|-----|-----------|--------|---------|-----|-----------|
| 01000000 | 64 | 40 | @ | 01010000 | 80 | 50 | P |
| 01000001 | 65 | 41 | A | 01010001 | 81 | 51 | Q |
| 01000010 | 66 | 42 | B | 01010010 | 82 | 52 | R |
| 01000011 | 67 | 43 | C | 01010011 | 83 | 53 | S |
| 01000100 | 68 | 44 | D | 01010100 | 84 | 54 | T |
| 01000101 | 69 | 45 | E | 01010101 | 85 | 55 | U |
| 01000110 | 70 | 46 | F | 01010110 | 86 | 56 | V |
| 01000111 | 71 | 47 | G | 01010111 | 87 | 57 | W |
| 01001000 | 72 | 48 | H | 01011000 | 88 | 58 | X |
| 01001001 | 73 | 49 | I | 01011001 | 89 | 59 | Y |
| 01001010 | 74 | 4A | J | 01011010 | 90 | 5A | Z |
| 01001011 | 75 | 4B | K | 01011011 | 91 | 5B | [ |
| 01001100 | 76 | 4C | L | 01011100 | 92 | 5C | \ |
| 01001101 | 77 | 4D | M | 01011101 | 93 | 5D | ] |
| 01001110 | 78 | 4E | N | 01011110 | 94 | 5E | ` |
| 01001111 | 79 | 4F | O | 01011111 | 95 | 5F |  |

| Binary | Decimal | Hex | Character | Binary | Decimal | Hex | Character |
|--------|---------|-----|-----------|--------|---------|-----|-----------|
| 01100000 | 96 | 60 |  | 01110000 | 112 | 70 | p |
| 01100001 | 97 | 61 | a | 01110001 | 113 | 71 | q |
| 01100010 | 98 | 62 | b | 01110010 | 114 | 72 | r |
| 01100011 | 99 | 63 | c | 01110011 | 115 | 73 | s |
| 01100100 | 100 | 64 | d | 01110100 | 116 | 74 | t |
| 01100101 | 101 | 65 | e | 01110101 | 117 | 75 | u |
| 01100110 | 102 | 66 | f | 01110110 | 118 | 76 | v |
| 01100111 | 103 | 67 | g | 01110111 | 119 | 77 | w |
| 01101000 | 104 | 68 | h | 01111000 | 120 | 78 | x |
| 01101001 | 105 | 69 | i | 01111001 | 121 | 79 | y |
| 01101010 | 106 | 6A | j | 01111010 | 122 | 7A | z |
| 01101011 | 107 | 6B | k | 01111011 | 123 | 7B | { |
| 01101100 | 108 | 6C | l | 01111100 | 124 | 7C | : |
| 01101101 | 109 | 6D | m | 01111101 | 125 | 7D | } |
| 01101110 | 110 | 6E | n | 01111110 | 126 | 7E | ~ |
| 01101111 | 111 | 6F | o | 01111111 | 127 | 7F | DEL |

## F.2    Extended ASCII code

The standard ASCII character has 7 bits and the basic set ranges from 0 to 127. This code is rather limited as it does not contains symbols such as Greek letters, lines, and so on. For this purpose the extended ASCII code has been defined. This fits into character numbers 128 to 255. The following four tables define a typical extended ASCII character set.

| Binary | Decimal | Hex | Character | Binary | Decimal | Hex | Character |
|--------|---------|-----|-----------|--------|---------|-----|-----------|
| 10000000 | 128 | 80 | Ç | 10010000 | 144 | 90 | É |
| 10000001 | 129 | 81 | ü | 10010001 | 145 | 91 | æ |
| 10000010 | 130 | 82 | é | 10010010 | 146 | 92 | Æ |
| 10000011 | 131 | 83 | â | 10010011 | 147 | 93 | ô |
| 10000100 | 132 | 84 | ä | 10010100 | 148 | 94 | ö |
| 10000101 | 133 | 85 | à | 10010101 | 149 | 95 | ò |
| 10000110 | 134 | 86 | å | 10010110 | 150 | 96 | û |
| 10000111 | 135 | 87 | ç | 10010111 | 151 | 97 | ù |
| 10001000 | 136 | 88 | ê | 10011000 | 152 | 98 | ÿ |
| 10001001 | 137 | 89 | ë | 10011001 | 153 | 99 | Ö |
| 10001010 | 138 | 8A | è | 10011010 | 154 | 9A | Ü |
| 10001011 | 139 | 8B | ï | 10011011 | 155 | 9B | ¢ |
| 10001100 | 140 | 8C | î | 10011100 | 156 | 9C | £ |
| 10001101 | 141 | 8D | ì | 10011101 | 157 | 9D | ¥ |
| 10001110 | 142 | 8E | Ä | 10011110 | 158 | 9E | ☐ |
| 10001111 | 143 | 8F | Å | 10011111 | 159 | 9F | ƒ |

| Binary | Decimal | Hex | Character | Binary | Decimal | Hex | Character |
|--------|---------|-----|-----------|--------|---------|-----|-----------|
| 10100000 | 160 | A0 | á | 10110000 | 176 | B0 | |
| 10100001 | 161 | A1 | í | 10110001 | 177 | B1 | |
| 10100010 | 162 | A2 | ó | 10110010 | 178 | B2 | |
| 10100011 | 163 | A3 | ú | 10110011 | 179 | B3 | |
| 10100100 | 164 | A4 | ñ | 10110100 | 180 | B4 | |
| 10100101 | 165 | A5 | Ñ | 10110101 | 181 | B5 | |
| 10100110 | 166 | A6 | a | 10110110 | 182 | B6 | |
| 10100111 | 167 | A7 | o | 10110111 | 183 | B7 | |
| 10101000 | 168 | A8 | ¿ | 10111000 | 184 | B8 | |
| 10101001 | 169 | A9 | ☐ | 10111001 | 185 | B9 | |
| 10101010 | 170 | AA | ¬ | 10111010 | 186 | BA | |
| 10101011 | 171 | AB | ½ | 10111011 | 187 | BB | |
| 10101100 | 172 | AC | ¼ | 10111100 | 188 | BC | |
| 10101101 | 173 | AD | ¡ | 10111101 | 189 | BD | |
| 10101110 | 174 | AE | « | 10111110 | 190 | BE | |
| 10101111 | 175 | AF | » | 10111111 | 191 | BF | |

| Binary | Decimal | Hex | Character | Binary | Decimal | Hex | Character |
|--------|---------|-----|-----------|--------|---------|-----|-----------|
| 11000000 | 192 | C0 | | 11010000 | 208 | D0 | |
| 11000001 | 193 | C1 | | 11010001 | 209 | D1 | |
| 11000010 | 194 | C2 | | 11010010 | 210 | D2 | |
| 11000011 | 195 | C3 | | 11010011 | 211 | D3 | |
| 11000100 | 196 | C4 | | 11010100 | 212 | D4 | |
| 11000101 | 197 | C5 | | 11010101 | 213 | D5 | |
| 11000110 | 198 | C6 | | 11010110 | 214 | D6 | |
| 11000111 | 199 | C7 | | 11010111 | 215 | D7 | |
| 11001000 | 200 | C8 | | 11011000 | 216 | D8 | |
| 11001001 | 201 | C9 | | 11011001 | 217 | D9 | |
| 11001010 | 202 | CA | | 11011010 | 218 | DA | |
| 11001011 | 203 | CB | | 11011011 | 219 | DB | |
| 11001100 | 204 | CC | | 11011100 | 220 | DC | |
| 11001101 | 205 | CD | | 11011101 | 221 | DD | |
| 11001110 | 206 | CE | | 11011110 | 222 | DE | |
| 11001111 | 207 | CF | | 11011111 | 223 | DF | |

| Binary | Decimal | Hex | Character | Binary | Decimal | Hex | Character |
|--------|---------|-----|-----------|--------|---------|-----|-----------|
| 11100000 | 224 | E0 | | 11110000 | 240 | F0 | |
| 11100001 | 225 | E1 | | 11110001 | 241 | F1 | |
| 11100010 | 226 | E2 | | 11110010 | 242 | F2 | |
| 11100011 | 227 | E3 | | 11110011 | 243 | F3 | |
| 11100100 | 228 | E4 | | 11110100 | 244 | F4 | |
| 11100101 | 229 | E5 | | 11110101 | 245 | F5 | |
| 11100110 | 230 | E6 | | 11110110 | 246 | F6 | |
| 11100111 | 231 | E7 | | 11110111 | 247 | F7 | |
| 11101000 | 232 | E8 | | 11111000 | 248 | F8 | |
| 11101001 | 233 | E9 | | 11111001 | 249 | F9 | |
| 11101010 | 234 | EA | | 11111010 | 250 | FA | |
| 11101011 | 235 | EB | | 11111011 | 251 | FB | |
| 11101100 | 236 | EC | | 11111100 | 252 | FC | |
| 11101101 | 237 | ED | | 11111101 | 253 | FD | |
| 11101110 | 238 | EE | | 11111110 | 254 | FE | |
| 11101111 | 239 | EF | | 11111111 | 255 | FF | |

# Index

QWERTY, 254

radiation, 418
RAID, 410
RAM, 51, 405, 410, 412
random number generators, 285
RC4/RC5, 301
RD, 60, 410
real-time, 43, 55, 72, 82, 88, 89, 90, 91,
    104, 107, 110, 123, 124, 206, 207, 209,
    346, 354, 370, 371, 411, 418
real-time sampling, 89
receiver not ready, 35, 130
receiver ready, 35, 130
recreational software advisory council, 351
redundancy, 30, 31, 64, 72, 132, 285, 408,
    413, 432
reflections, 437, 438
REJ, 35, 130, 410, 431, 434
remote login, 384
remote Procedure Call, 202
repeater, 21, 45, 55, 59, 68, 422, 424
repeaters, 22, 68
repetitive sequences, 419
reservation bits, 65
resistance, 26, 49, 436–438
resolution, 91, 99, 104, 105, 106, 403,
    409, 424
restricted sites, 346
revision, 445
RFC, 106, 269, 288, 301, 354, 356, 361,
    362, 363, 364, 365, 366, 369, 371, 372,
    410, 440, 441, 444, 445, 447, 449
RFC821, 354, 356, 362, 371, 372
RFC822, 269, 354, 361–366, 369, 371,
    372
RG-50, 38, 39
RG-6, 39
RGB, 410
RI, 66, 410
rich text format, 411
ring fails, 71
ring in, 66, 76, 410
ring network, 19, 20, 21, 27, 43, 62, 66,
    67, 70, 79, 139, 147, 435
ring out, 66, 411
ring topology, 72
RIP, 214, 216, 217, 222
RJ-45, 23, 38, 39, 43, 49, 59, 67, 68, 126,
    424, 438
RLE, 411
RNR, 35, 130, 411, 431, 434
RO, 66, 374, 411

ROM, 404, 411
routers, 21, 24, 104, 159, 216, 251, 252,
    256, 444
routing protocol
    NLSP, 409
    OSPF, 24, 409, 442, 443, 448, 451,
        452, 455
routing protocols
    BGP, 24, 403
    EGP, 24, 405
    RIP, 24, 98, 200, 214, 216, 217, 222,
        410, 420, 447, 454, 456
RPC, 202
RR, 35, 130, 411, 431, 434, 446
RS-232, 417, 424
    frame format, 77, 126
RS-422, 58, 424
RS-449, 424
RS-485, 424
RSA, 282, 284, 300, 301, 311–320, 323,
    325, 334, 339, 340, 353, 411, 451, 453
    key generation, 319
RTF, 411
Run-length encoding, 411, 424

S/PDIF, 411
SABME, 130, 131, 411, 434
SAC, 411
SAFER, 301, 302
sampled data, 123
sampling, 88, 89, 90, 91, 110, 134, 135,
    366, 405, 418, 425
sampling rate, 89, 91, 110, 135, 366, 418
sampling theory, 89
SAP packet format, 218
SAPI, 128, 129, 133, 411
SB-ADCMP, 411
s-box, 305, 306, 307
scaleability, 41
SCMS, 411
Scotland, 84, 113, 114, 118, 121
scrambled, 280
SCSI, 411
SD, 63, 77, 411
SDH, 103, 113, 120, 410, 411, 448
search, 139, 167, 224, 226, 232, 234, 235,
    236, 250, 284, 306, 309, 310, 336
SECAM, 411
secret key, 282, 300, 318–320, 323, 327,
    328, 330, 333, 334, 337
sectors, 376, 380
security settings, 347, 348
security zones, 346